THE BROTHERHOOD OF THE RED NILE

America Rebuilds

BY DAN PERKINS

D1005509

Produced by:

FriesenPress
Suite 300 – 852 Fort Street
Victoria, BC, Canada V8W 1H8

www.friesenpress.com

Distributed to the trade by The Ingram Book Company

"Just when you thought the story couldn't get any scarier, the author releases the next installment. You think you couldn't put his first book down? Try book 2. No reader is 'safe' as long as Dan Perkins' imagination is on the loose."

— Mark Jerome Walters, D.V.M.

Associate Professor
Director, M.A. in Digital Journalism and Design
Department of Journalism and Media Studies
University of South Florida St. Petersburg

ACKNOWLEDGEMENTS

"Thank you" to my editor Mary Metcalfe who loved the story and brought her years of working in the intelligence arena to the book. She is a true professional guiding me with thoughts and suggestions that complemented the story.

Nancy Daversa, the teacher at Big Arts Center on Sanibel Island, unleashed whatever was inside me and has continued to encourage me to tell stories by painting pictures with words.

To all my friends and family who read this manuscript and the first book and encouraged me to go forward, and wanted to know when this book was going to be published.

One of my two principal readers throughout this writing adventure has been my sister Kathy Baughn. Our older brother Tim charged Kathy with the responsibility of keeping my feet firmly on the ground. I thank her for doing just that, especially when I stray away from my roots.

MEMORIAL

Two men had a profound influence on my life and sadly, neither is here to see what happened to me. To Mike Farrell and Keith Brodkin, if you are still watching, both of you helped shape me into who I am today. Here's hoping that Jobs is sharing his IPAD and you can read this book.

DEDICATION

To My wife Gerri who has been an author's widow for three books, now, and the other primary reader that helped me to write a compelling story. She has been my wife for 45 years and has always supported me in whatever I wanted to do. We all need someone we can count on, our anchor; Gerri is my anchor. I love you.

FOREWORD

This is the second book in the Trilogy. I get this question about book 2, "Do I have to have read book one in order to understand what is happening in book two?" The answer is no, but in all candor book two is even more compelling if you have read book one! My instructor told me, "If you are going to write a Trilogy or more, each book must stand alone." I believe that this book does stand alone, but you will have a more exciting ride having read book one first.

As you will quickly see, book two starts 12 hours before the end of book one. Early readers of book two tell me that they feel like they take a breath on page one and then take their next breath on page 100. Speaking of page 100, book two will be considerably longer than book one. I was initially concerned about that, but a writing professor told me, "Tell the story and let a full robust story tell you how many pages it takes."

I call book one the psychological thriller whereas book two is the physical thriller, meaning there are many physical images and lots of action happening at the same time. It's like the feeling you get riding the biggest and baddest rollercoaster in the world. I hope you enjoy the second installment of the Trilogy, **Brotherhood of the Red Nile, America Rebuilds**.

Writers need people to tell them what they think of their books. As a writer, I want people to tell me what they think about what I created. If you read the book, I need your feedback. Go to the web site where you bought the book, write an honest review and then post it for all to see: the good, the bad, and the ugly of my work. When finished, I hope you will have enjoyed it as much as I enjoyed writing it for you.

Dan Perkins

PROLOGUE

Terrorists from the Brotherhood of the Red Nile have attacked America. A nuclear device has exploded in Texas City, Texas--an explosion designed to shut down the free flow of crude oil and natural gas, along with refined petroleum products from Texas refineries. Power plants in the north, east and western United States that depend on gas and oil from Texas have had to shut down.

The Texas explosion has put the oil, gas and electrical grids in crisis as public demand is high during the peak summer months. The excess demand causes blackouts all over the country. Gasoline, diesel, and aircraft fuels are going to be in short supply and the price of energy will likely go up every day on the commodity exchanges. West Texas sweet crude oil futures will probably more than double in price in a matter of days.

The president will be speaking to the American people to warn them that life will be very difficult for some time, but he tells them that he and his government will bring to bear all of the resources of the United States to return stability and prosperity to all Americans. The only problem for President Nathan Jordan is that polling data shows that he has the lowest creditability rating of any U.S. president in history.

CHAPTER 1

12 PM

John Bowman turned around and headed back home the second he learned that a bomb exploded in Texas City, Texas. He was on his way there to inspect the welds on a new pipeline that was being laid in south Texas. The pipeline was to carry gasoline from the BP refinery in Texas City, Texas, northwards in the pipeline grid. Driving north with Chandler, his Jack Russell Terrier, he saw bright orange lights flashing with great intensity, very similar to the ones he saw from his house in Springfield, Texas just a few weeks ago.

Traffic had picked up and moved very slowly. He had no idea how long it would take him to get home, so he stopped to fill up his gas tank and get some food for him and Chandler. Bowman saw more and more trucks speeding by on Interstate 45 with the familiar crest of the Department of Homeland Security.

On the outskirts of Texas City, people were on their phones talking about the explosion without realizing a nuclear bomb caused it, destroying all the refineries in Texas City, including the largest refinery in the United States, the BP facility.

The town of Texas City had a population of fifty-four thousand people and probably more on a workday. They were all dead. This single nuclear device killed more Americans on American soil at one time than any battle of the American Civil War. There were fires everywhere. Flames were shooting out of what remained of the refinery stacks, some of the gas and oil pipelines were ruptured, and flames and smoke were billowing hundreds of feet in the air. Most of the metal was red hot, glowing like a steel smelting furnace.

Washington DC was fifteen hundred miles away. It was 12:08 PM Eastern Time.

Nathan Jordan, the president of the United States, had been briefed that the Texas explosion was not an industrial accident, but a terrorist attack committed by the Brotherhood of the Red Nile. The Intelligence Community had been expecting such an attempt and law enforcement had been trying to intercept it. Jordan told his executive assistant, Mary Washington, "Initiate Protocol Four. We have experienced a nuclear event that is affecting our critical infrastructure. Call the cabinet secretaries, along with the Chief of Staff, the National Security Advisor, the Joint Chiefs of Staff, and the vice president for an urgent National Security meeting.

"I want them in the War Room in one hour; if a Secretary is unable to attend in person then we will link him or her by videophone or conference call. If for some reason, the Secretary cannot be found, bring in the most senior Under Secretary. Contact the White House Communications Office to arrange any links necessary to connect everyone to this meeting. And please get Martin Simons on the phone."

Nathan had served two terms in the Senate and then decided not to run for a third term. He instead chose to run for the presidency. The campaign took a toll on him physically. At the start of the campaign, he was six foot three, with broad shoulders and looked as fit as a much younger man. His hair was blond with just a touch of silver, his eyes a steely blue that could look right into your soul. His posture was perfect; it was as if he had a steel rod up his back.

Now after just twenty-four months in office, his hair was more silver than blond and he had picked up a few pounds. However, his eyes were just as strong as ever and, when he put on a dark blue suit with a white shirt and striped tie, he looked presidential.

The news from Texas made him slouch over just a little, as if he was carrying more weight on his back. The reality was that Jordan would find the weight getting increasingly heavier as the hours and days passed and the magnitude of what had happened affected the Office of the President.

As Mary punched in the secure number code for the Secretary of Homeland Security, she could see by the president's body language that he was somber but extremely focused. *In all the years I've worked for him, since he was a freshman congressional representative all the way to the White House, he's always had an ability to focus despite any distractions.* Secretary Simons' office answered.

"Please hold for the president," she said.

Simons picked up the phone and waited. He knew about the Texas explosion and expected the president to be very angry.

In a very sober voice Jordan spoke. "Mark, we lost fifty-four thousand people today. An entire town, How in God's name did this happen?"

"Sir, we believe this is the work of the Brotherhood of the Red Nile we were following in Syria. Somehow, my people lost them and couldn't follow their movements the past few weeks. They went quiet in the chat rooms and stopped emailing each other.

"Sir, our intel is that they had two nuclear devices and every indication is that the bombing in Texas City was the work of one. So, if in fact they have a second device, then we should expect a second explosion soon, perhaps within twelve to twenty-four hours."

"Mark, what will be the impact of this bomb?"

"Sir, I would have to defer to our nuclear bomb blast specialists, but the best I can figure is that this section of Texas will most likely be uninhabitable for at least fifty years. It appears from the first satellite images that most of the structural damage occurred at the refineries. The four refineries accounted for at least twenty-five percent of the finished petroleum product in the United States.

"In that area, a large proportion of the pipelines is above ground and is now covered by radioactive steel and debris. Although the pipelines are made of steel, the radiation goes right through to the crude oil, finished product and natural gas. All this contaminated energy is slowly working its way north, east and west. Most pipelines move oil and other products at the speed of about six miles per hour. At that speed, assuming that the pressure stays up, it will take about three weeks to reach New York. A decision must be made today on shutting down all pipelines coming out of and through the Texas City region. Shutting down the pipelines will not be an easy task, but much of it can be done remotely through the SCADA systems."

"What is SCADA? I've heard the acronym but what is it, exactly?" Jordan nodded his thanks as Mary set a steaming mug of coffee before him.

"It stands for 'Supervisory Control and Data Acquisition', the technology which allows thousands of miles of pipeline throughout North America to be controlled electronically from command centers throughout the grid. Almost all the grid is networked now, which will make the job of shutting down the contaminated pipelines much easier.

"We've run simulations and exercises for just this kind of contingency. My office is organizing a conference call with key pipeline company executives right after our cabinet meeting to get a handle on how long it will take to shut them down.

"We've also dispatched two hundred people from FEMA to work on-site with the local companies to look for termination points. Once you give us the go ahead I shall send teams by car and helicopter to start shutting down the compressors and closing valves when the pressure drops to a safe point. I'm hopeful that the cabinet will reach consensus on what to do next."

"Mark, I have the same wish and prayer. See you shortly."

"Mr. President, Nathan, by the time we meet, the radiation will have moved six to eight miles north."

As Nathan hung up the phone he thought, *I hope to God that we make the right decisions. God help America, and me, if we don't.*

The oil has moved four miles closer to League City, Texas

CHAPTER 2

Air Force One

President Jordan buzzed Ms. Washington on the intercom and asked her to come into his office. "Mary, please set up a conference call with the head of the Secret Service and the chief pilot of Air Force One for about ten minutes from now."

"Right away, sir. Should I tell them what it's about?"

Jordan smiled wanly. "No. I'll discuss it directly with them. And please cancel all my non-essential meetings for the next week."

"What should I say is the reason for the cancellations, sir?"

"Tell them it's a matter of national security."

Mary returned to her desk to organize the conference call. An assistant had put out the Protocol Four calls to all the cabinet members to notify them of the meeting at 2:15 and was getting updates on its status.

Mary called the president to advise him his secure conference call was operational.

"Gentlemen, I need to tell you something and I want your confidence and your support."

"Yes, Mr. President, how can I help?" Two deep voices chimed in unison.

"I received confirmation that at noon today a nuclear device detonated in the town of Texas City. To the best of our knowledge, over fifty thousand people were killed. We have no idea how many more are injured and dying. I have a full cabinet meeting shortly to begin the process of trying to stop a wave of radioactive crude oil, natural gas and finished product that is moving into the North American pipeline grid.

"After the cabinet meeting, I want to fly to see the devastation in Texas City. Before either of you open your mouths, you are being given a direct order from the commander-in-chief. There is no room for discussion. I do not intend us to land. Airport operations are already being shut down as a safety measure. But I have to go there, is that understood?"

William Rummels, head of the Secret Service coughed, "But sir, I think …"

The president interrupted, "No, we are going."

The chief pilot, General George Thomas responded, "Sir, I don't know how close we can get you to the City. You just said a nuclear bomb went off. I have no idea the range of the radiation. We may not be able to get within miles of the Town."

"I don't care how close we can get, I need to go. I will be speaking to the country tonight. I need to see the devastation in Texas City firsthand. What is the flying time from Andrews to Texas City?"

"Give me a moment, sir. I'll check."

"What is the fewest number of agents we need?"

"Well, sir, that depends on what aircraft we take."

Thomas came back on the line, "it looks like two and a half hours each way if we take Air Force One."

"What other options do we have to get us there quicker?"

"A smaller jet will be faster but less secure. We could us the Gulfstream G650, which flies six hundred and ten miles per hour with eleven people on board. We can make the trip in less than two hours, look around for say thirty minutes and head back."

"All right, file your flight plan for a 4 PM takeoff. We'll aim to be back by 8:30. I could then speak to the Nation by 11:30. Excellent, gentlemen! Make it happen. See you at four."

Twenty minutes before the cabinet meeting, Jordan walked out the Oval Office door and asked Mary to call his wife. "Tell her I'm on my way. I need to spend a few minutes alone with her."

"Right away, sir." Mary punched in the number for the private apartment. An aide answered.

"The president is on his way up. He wants to see the first lady alone."

THE BROTHERHOOD OF THE RED NILE

"Thank you, Mary. I will make it happen." As he hung up the phone, he saw the first lady's chief of staff coming down the hall. "Maggie, the president is on his way up and wants to see the first lady in private."

"I'll let her know." Maggie had been with Karen Jordan for over ten years. She came to work for then Senator Jordan, and was well thought of as bright and efficient. As the Senator moved into a greater leadership position, Maggie received more and more responsibility, handling her work flawlessly. When the Senator decided to run for president, she was invaluable in his campaign.

Maggie lived on Capitol Hill in a modestly sized, but not modestly priced condominium that put her within walking distance to the White House. She usually put in very long days and sometimes spent the night in the White House instead of going home. A graduate of Harvard and Columbia Law School, Maggie passed the New York bar exam the first time but never practiced law. Instead, she got involved in politics and loved the life. She was slender, about five foot ten, and had striking red hair that was naturally curly above her bright green eyes. Her clothes were tailored and muted so not to detract from the first lady.

She walked quickly down the hall to the sun porch and told the first lady, "Your husband is on his way to see you, Ma'am. I'm to make sure you're not disturbed."

They were on the Truman Balcony. The white wrought iron furniture was covered with over-stuffed bright yellow linen cushions. The four chairs were set in pairs with a small coffee table between them. The glass-topped tables had small baskets of white flowers suspended underneath. Hanging in baskets all around the railing were vibrant red geraniums of different sizes and shades. Karen and Nathan loved to sit out here at the end of the day and watch the sunset.

Married to Nathan for thirty years, Karen Jordan was now in her mid-fifties. They had married shortly after graduation and just before Nathan went off to law school. As Karen sat waiting for him, she thought about their life together and of the struggles they had while Nathan was in law school. She thought those days were some of the best times in their lives. She enjoyed being first lady, but she loved Sunday mornings making love and just holding each other, a much simpler life than today.

She had always been supportive of Nathan's ambitions, including running for president. On the table next to the chair where she was sitting was a family picture of her and Nathan and their children. Nathan Jr. was the oldest, then Margret, and finally William. All three were grown now. Nathan Jr. was married, with two children. Margret and William were still in college; Margret was a senior at William and Mary, while William was a sophomore at NYU.

Karen was a regal First lady. Almost as tall as Nathan, she kept in shape by working out at least three times a week in the White House gym. Nathan was a golfer and when he had time, he and Karen would play. Karen had recently taken up racket ball with Maggie and found it was a great workout. She loved the water and swam on a regular basis. Some said she was perhaps the most athletic first lady in the history of the White House.

She always looked elegant whether she was wearing slacks for gardening or an evening gown for a state dinner. She devoted her life to her husband, their children and then her country in that order, and was proud of what she believed in. She was sipping a glass of iced tea with Maggie when the president came through the door.

Maggie stood up and greeted the president. "Ma'am, I will see you later," she said and walked back inside.

"Karen, I had to see you. I don't have a great deal of time but I wanted to tell you something before you saw it on the news."

"If you mean the explosion in Texas, I already know about it. Such a tragedy."

"What you don't know is that it was a nuclear bomb."

The oil has moved six miles closer to League City, Texas

CHAPTER 3

Frank Williams

The Secretary of Homeland Security called Frank Williams to come to his office immediately and to come alone. As Williams arrived, he was quickly shuttled into Simons' office and the door closed.

"Frank, that explosion in Texas City? It was some kind of a nuclear bomb. Initial reports are that thousands are dead and untold more are injured. Because of the high levels of radiation and the fires, we can't get within five miles of the four refineries that were affected.

"We have every reason to believe that this bombing is the work of the group your people have been following: the Brotherhood of the Red Nile."

"Would you like my resignation, Mr. Secretary?"

"Hell no, and nobody else wants it either, nor has anyone requested it. I have a meeting with the president and cabinet in about fifteen minutes. We have radioactive oil, natural gas and refined product moving out of the area into a network of pipelines that is more complex than any of us can imagine.

"While I'm at the meeting, I want you to start working on a pipeline shutdown for all the pipelines running through the area in and around Texas City. Protocol Four has been initiated. We need to implement quickly a system-wide shut-down as per the Protocol. I want a conference call with the CEOs of the affected companies by four o'clock for a status update. They already know that their pipelines are spreading radioactive material.

"I want them all on the call. They need to hear from me that the president wants their full cooperation throughout this national security crisis. The future of the United States is at stake, and this time it is not a simulation.

"The president will talk to the American people about the crisis within the next few hours. He has a plan but he has to be able to say he has all the oil companies on his side. We have to be proactive about the radioactive oil flow and our plan to contain it. We'll be shutting down the pipelines and closing the valves so the contaminated oil can go no further."

Williams was listening and thinking at the same time. He understood the need to shut down the pipelines. *They'll also have to stop pumping the crude oil. It's just adding to the flow, pushing contaminated oil north, east and west.*

"Sir, before you go into the meeting, please keep in mind that we may well have to shut down the wells, pumps and the other refineries in Texas in order to help stop the flow. This is a huge undertaking and I don't think we have the personnel to do this alone. We can clearly start, but I think we're going to need help from the Department of Defense to muster the people and the equipment to attack this challenge."

"We've already done simulations. It's all doable with the SCADA systems currently in place. There are over fifty-five thousand miles of oil pipelines and 2.3 million miles of gas pipelines in America. Many of the major pipeline networks in the nation flow through this area and there could be ten to fifteen thousand and perhaps more compressors, pumping stations and valves in the area around and north of Texas City.

"Frank, I have just a few minutes before I have to leave for the cabinet meeting. We have to keep this situation under tight wraps until the president has a chance to tell the American people about the plans in place under Protocol Four. Inform those staff who have been security-cleared under Protocol Four and implement immediately the Protocol plan to shut down the oil and natural gas in Texas as quickly as possible.

"You also need to think about how we can put out the fires in Texas City from long distance. I'm sorry that I can't stay, but this is one meeting I can't be late for." Simons stood up and pulled on his suit jacket. "And just as a reminder, I want no further talk about resignation, understood?"

"Understood, sir."

As Simons left his office, Frank stayed back, stunned. His first thought was, *How can I tell Ellen that the threat I feared the most about the Brotherhood of the Red Nile has come to pass? They have attacked America! We know they had two bombs. What the hell has happened to the second one?*

The oil has moved seven miles closer to League City, Texas

CHAPTER 4

White House Balcony

Karen pulled her hands away from her husband's hands and clasped one over her heart. "My God, all those people, what happened?"

"We believe that a terrorist group we've been tracking is responsible for the bombing. It's called the Brotherhood of the Red Nile."

"Is this an al-Qaeda group?"

"No, it's a new group that wants to destroy America and everything we stand for and believe in. We have some information about the group, but not enough, obviously."

Nathan spoke softly. "I have to go to a cabinet meeting. The pipelines are carrying radioactive oil and natural gas towards the rest of the country. We have a Protocol to stop the flow of this contaminated oil and gas, but also have to figure out how we can put out the fires to reduce the contamination spreading through the air.

"Karen, I have one other thing to tell you that you must keep secret; you can't tell anyone, including Maggie."

"Agreed." She looked at him with a puzzled look on her face.

"After the cabinet meeting I'm flying to Texas City or as close as I can to assess the damage."

"Can I go with you?" She sent him a worried look.

"I don't think that's a good idea. One of us needs to be here. Besides, if both of us are gone, the press may speculate that we've left in fear. It could cause chaos: They saved themselves but not us.

"No, the only people that will know that I'm gone are the vice president, my chief of staff, the pilots, the head of the secret service, the team assigned and you.

"It's already getting very crazy and very scary. Survivors are sending out videos and texts by the minute. We can't control them or the press. The news services are all over this and are demanding answers. We can keep them away from the blast site but that will not keep the story from spreading. I should be gone about four hours or so. I'll call you from the plane when I'm on my way back. I'll need you by my side tonight. We have to present a caring and united front.

"After the cabinet meeting, a speech will have to be drafted for me to deliver to the nation sometime this evening. I want you to head the team. Over the years, you've always helped me when I had a difficult speech to write and give. This is the most important speech I shall ever give and perhaps one of the most important speeches any president has ever given. I trust you. I think your sense of the people is why they like you better than me; it's so obvious that you really care about people. I need that perspective in my Address to the Nation." He stood and massaged the back of his neck.

"I have to go to the cabinet meeting. I shall be leaving around four o'clock. If everything works out, I should be back here by 8:30 tonight. The vice president will remain in the War Room while I'm away. Should something happen to me he will be in charge."

"What could happen?" Karen stood and put a hand up to rub his neck.

"We believe that the terrorists have a second bomb. We have no idea where, when, or if they plan to use it. I actually think that being close to Texas City might just be one of the most dangerous but also one of the safest places to be for a while."

Nathan took Karen in his arms and held her tight. As he started to pull away, Karen pulled him back and kissed him warmly. *I wonder if this is the last time we will see and hold each other.*

The oil has moved eight miles closer to League City, Texas

CHAPTER 5

The War Room

All the invited cabinet members and special advisors assembled in the War Room and awaited the arrival of the president. Promptly at 2:15 PM, President Nathan Jordan walked in and went to the head of a very long table that was not quite long enough for everyone invited.

The computer screens and TV monitors on the walls were blank. Marine guards in battle gear were assigned to secure the doors into the room. All the attendees stood, waiting for the president to sit.

Once things quieted down Jordan looked around the table before speaking. He knew it was vital that he display his confidence, leadership, and resolve.

"Ladies and gentlemen, thank you for coming. At approximately noon Central Standard Time today a nuclear device detonated in Texas City." He nodded his head and the TV monitors come to life with images from a satellite appearing on all the screens.

"You've seen these images flying across the press − both news and social media − over the past couple of hours. Therefore, you already know that at least fifty-four thousand people are known to be dead and there is a good chance many more have perished, and thousands injured and exposed to high levels of radiation.

"The four refineries in the town − including the largest refinery in the United States − are in shambles and on fire. New pictures of the four refineries are now on the screens. As you can see, they are glowing red-hot and the destruction is concentrated around them. The entire area

14

is contaminated with radioactive material, so all the debris, in addition to being hot from the fire, is also hot from radiation.

"I've been advised that an area within a radius of at least five miles is contaminated and unapproachable. I'm told that we don't know how long it will remain contaminated.

"Now, please focus your attention to the TV monitors on the walls. All through this part of Texas are tens of thousands of pipelines carrying crude oil, gasoline, jet fuel, diesel fuel and natural gas. I've been briefed – as most of you have been already – that all the debris is lying on the pipelines above ground. This debris is radioactive. The radiation is seeping through the pipes and into whatever material is being carried by those pipelines. The contaminated energy is moving north, east and west at the rate of six to eight miles an hour."

The president turned to Secretary Simons as a new image was displayed.

"We've all seen this image before. It's the tsunami after the earthquake in Japan," he said. "What we have in Texas is a tsunami of radioactive energy moving towards all points of the United States."

The president added, "We all know that this is an important part of the United States, for over twenty-five percent of our domestic energy comes from this region alone. With that said, let's move on to the two questions we are here to discuss. First, how do we stop the radioactive tsunami and second, what are the implications of losing twenty-five percent of our energy and perhaps never getting it back?"

The room was quiet as a tomb. Nobody knew what to say in response to the president's questions. They were still reeling over the information and the photos on the screens.

Finally, one Secretary said in a somewhat subdued tone. "Mr. President, off the top of my head I would guess that between crude oil, finished products and natural gas there could be tens of thousands of miles of pipeline running through this part of the country. If I may, Mr. President, I think I can illustrate the magnitude. Secretary Michael Findley opened the laptop in front of him and asked the tech in the room, "Can the image on my screen be seen on the wall monitors?"

"Sir, pull up the image and I'll project it for you."

Findley finds what he is looking for and the tech puts it on the screen for everybody to see.

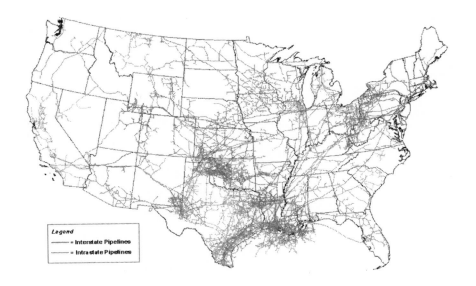

Legend
—— = Interstate Pipelines
—— = Intrastate Pipelines

"Gentlemen, this is a map of the pipelines throughout the United States. As you can see, they are all interconnected. The bulk of them are in Texas, Louisiana, and Oklahoma, and from these high concentration areas they spread east, west, north, and south. The flow rate of product through these pipelines is about six to eight miles per hour. Therefore, if the device exploded at noon and it's now about 1:30 there, the contamination has already reached League City. At the current flow rate, it will be in Oklahoma City in about seventy hours. If it makes it to Oklahoma City, the contaminated oil will be propelled at a faster rate. This section is called the slingshot because from this point oil, natural gas, and all the refined products move west, east, north and south at a rapid pace.

"The entire pipeline network in the United States could be contaminated in about three weeks. So, the bottom line is that we have to shut down the pipelines running through Texas in about twenty-four hours at most, keeping in mind every hour, the radioactive tsunami is moving at the rate of seven miles per hour." He nodded to Secretary Simons, "I believe you have people already implementing the Protocol Four shutdown process?"

Simons affirmed the president's question with a thumbs-up signal.

THE BROTHERHOOD OF THE RED NILE

President Jordan spoke. "Thank you Secretary Findley, for scaring the hell out of us.

"The question on the table is how do we effectively and efficiently implement Protocol Four without causing mass panic to the public and the markets? I realize that there will be some significant problems in the markets and perhaps a significant recession in the offing, but we can't spend our time now on those issues. We must focus on the resources necessary to stop the oil flow."

Mark Simons spoke up. "Sir, as you know, we'll be in touch with all the pipeline owners and operators after this meeting to implement Protocol Four. I am not an energy expert, but I think of pipelines as tubes that need pressure to push something through them. If you put a straw in a glass of water and suck the water into the straw there are only two ways to get the water out of the straw. Either you tip the straw down vertically to let it drain or you blow it out. Although a great proportion of the pipeline system is above ground in that region, we obviously can't lift the underground pipelines out and let them drain. Therefore, we have to figure out how to stop the blowing that moves the stuff in the underground pipelines.

"Secretary of the Interior William Summons worked in the oil business and suggested that perhaps his department should be the one to work with the pipelines in the call that has been planned.

"I think if we work with Energy the two of us can help locate the compressors that, as you said, blow the product in the pipelines."

Findley jumped back into the conversation, "The compressors are in the pipelines and can be as close as a few miles to as many as twenty-five miles apart. Even if we could identify them with the help of Interior, I just don't think we can shut them all down in seventy hours or seventy days. I think it's an impossible task, even with SCADA."

The oil has moved ten miles closer to League City, Texas

CHAPTER 6

Texas City, Texas

It's was an hour and a half since the explosion. Emergency responder radios were fried and nobody knew why. The intensity of the fires kept everybody at bay, away from the fire but also the intense radiation. Police helicopters flew as close as they could to assess the damage. However, the intensity of the heat kept them a significant distance away.

One co-pilot took photos with his digital camera. When he checked the screen, there was no picture. He didn't know that he and the camera had been exposed to radiation at such a high level that no image could be held on the flash card.

After several more tries, he finally said to the pilot, "We need to get the hell out of here. Something's not right." The chopper pilot immediately banked the aircraft away from Texas City and headed to the airport.

Upon landing, they were met by a sheriff's deputy. "You need to come into the hangar. The sheriff wants to talk with you."

Heading towards the hangar, they walked past the side of the helicopter and noticed that the paint had melted off the side that faced the fires. They knew it was hot, but to melt the paint off the helicopter? Something *is* seriously wrong.

They walked inside the hangar where the sheriff directed them to a tall canvas cubicle. He ordered the two pilots into the showers immediately. The pilot stammered, "You want us to take a shower in our flight suits?"

"Get in the shower now and I'll explain later."

"How long do we need to stay in the shower?"

"I'll tell you when you can come out; now get your butts in those showers."

"Yes, sir."

They got into the showers, flight suits and turned on the handle. Instead of water, a light blue liquid shot rapidly out of the showerhead. Ordered to stand under the showerheads starting with the top of their heads they next move to the shoulders and gradually rinse their flight suits all the way down to their feet.

"Okay, we're done," the pilot informed the sheriff.

"Now take them off and hand them out to us," the sheriff ordered.

"Why?" Both men looked at each other and shook their heads. *What the ...?*

"Never mind, just do it."

The pilots took off their flight suits and handed them out through a slit in the booth.

"Now what?"

"Start over again with your head and work your way down to your feet."

"Why?"

"Just do it."

So, they started over again. When they were done, the chief pilot asked, "Can we come out now?"

A voice says, "No, take off your clothes and hand them out to us."

"Are you crazy?"

"This is an order. Either you do it or you will die."

"Yes, sir."

The two pilots, now naked in the showers, handed their clothes out through the curtain. "Can we come out now?"

"No. Start over again with your head and wash off and when you're done we'll give you a robe and tell you what's going on, understood?"

"Yes, sir." Now they were very concerned about what they would hear when they finished their shower.

They rinsed off with clear water and were given a towel to dry off and then passed the towels out through the curtain and received a robe in exchange. Finally, they could come out of the shower. Both men looked to the sheriff, "What the hell is going on?"

"We got a call from St. Francis Hospital in La Marque that the radiation detector in their CAT scan room went off the dial. They checked the level in several other suites in the hospital and all had radiation levels way above normal. The hospital president became concerned when he heard about the explosion in Texas City and called me to see if any other hospitals in the area near Texas City reported increased levels of radiation.

"I called a guy in Homeland Security who told me they weren't aware of any radiation in the Texas City explosion. However, he said he would make a few calls. I called the regional office and they said that they had no notification of any nuclear material involved in the Texas City explosion, but they would launch a helicopter with a radiation detector right away.

"About a half an hour later I got a call that there were high levels of radiation in the air and that we should advise people to stay away from Texas City. Anybody that had exposure to high levels of radiation or was within five miles of the blast site needed to be decontaminated and immediately taken to a trauma center for treatment for possible radiation poisoning.

Both men stared at the sheriff in stunned silence. "Are we going to die?"

The radioactive tsunami has moved ten miles closer to League City, Texas

CHAPTER 7

Homeland Security

While the cabinet meeting was going on, Frank Williams, the Under Secretary for Terrorist Activity of the Department of Homeland Security, was on his way back to his office. Upon arriving, he stopped at his assistant's desk. "Marie, would you see if you could get my wife on the phone, please?"

Marie called his wife Ellen, who was working at the Social Security office in downtown DC, but got her voicemail. Marie buzzed her boss, "She wasn't there. I left a message to call you."

"Thank you Marie, please put her through the minute she calls back."

Marie Ryan had been with Frank for fifteen years. She started with him at the CIA where Williams was in charge of covert operations. Single and never married, she cut a striking figure of a professional woman. At five feet nine inches tall, well-proportioned and dressed in very fine business clothes, her only quirk is that she didn't like to wear slacks to work. She felt that proper attire was a dress or a suit, not slacks, but when she was at her home in Georgetown, she would occasionally wear form fitting jeans and a form-fitting top. This outfit really showed off her curves and most of the time she felt uncomfortable wearing these kinds of clothes because she felt like she was showing off. For some reason today, she wanted to show her stuff to whomever wanted to look. And they did.

Marie knew that Frank and Ellen were very much in love. In the entire time she had worked for Frank, she never did anything that would cause problems between them. Because of her respect for both of them, they invited her to parties at their house hoping they could find a special someone for her.

Frank called Ted Baker and asked him to come to his office immediately. Ted was the lead intelligence analyst first monitoring and then subsequently investigating the Brotherhood of the Red Nile. In a matter of moments, Baker was in Williams' office.

"Close the door, Ted. I just came from a meeting with the Secretary and he informed me that a nuclear device was detonated in Texas City."

"Oh my God. I heard about the explosion." Ted put his head in his hands. "There's press speculation that it was nuclear. The Brotherhood is the only group we even suspected had a nuclear capability. Do you want my resignation?"

Frank smiled slightly. "It looks like we're both offering our resignations to our bosses. I'll tell you the same thing the secretary said to me, 'hell no, we need you.'

"Ted, I don't blame you for this bombing, I think we did everything possible to find the bomb before it got into the United States. My concern is that, when you were monitoring them, you thought they might have two devices. Everything we know about the explosion in Texas City is that it was the work of one."

"So you think they got both bombs into the States?"

"Yes, unless you have other intelligence. I think there is another bomb, but the question is where and when will it go off? I need you to go over your notes on all the contacts and intercepted communications we had with the Brotherhood and see if you can get any clue as to the target for the second bomb."

Ted stood. "Yessir! I'm on it."

Ted Baker was an assistant to Williams and senior assistant G-3 for the last year. An alumnus of West Point who graduated second in his class, he came to Homeland Security in Langley, Virginia, where he had worked in Special Ops planning for almost ten years. He had a good mind for thinking like a terrorist and had helped break up several terrorist cells based on strong situational awareness, his instincts, and good old-fashioned research and analysis. He was well regarded in Langley for all these reasons. In fact, the Director of the CIA was upset when DHS Secretary Simons asked specifically for Baker to work in DHS intelligence.

Ted lived in the Washington DC suburb of Arlington, Virginia and most days took the Metro to his office. At his Metro stop was a gym, so several times a week he would stop on his way home to work out. Ted had been married, but realized, after about three years, that he was more married to his job than to his wife. With no children, they had quietly separated and their divorce was finalized just over a year ago. The funny thing was that they still regularly went out on dates. Ted guessed that dating and the job put had less pressure on a relationship than marriage and a job.

At six feet two and about a hundred and sixty pounds of pure muscle, he had a classic West Point body: broad shoulders, narrow waist. All his clothes, regardless of whether they for were work or casual, were tailored to that 'West Point look.' Ted joined an Army reserve unit after he finished his stint in the Army and attended meetings once a month.

As he started back to his office he began thinking about the four targets the Brotherhood had reviewed. The first thing he thought about was the cities they had discussed targeting. For the Internet, it was Chicago and San Antonio; for the power grid, it was New York and Hoover Dam; the energy infrastructure focused on Texas and Louisiana, while fallout was Jersey City, New Jersey. The first bomb went off in Texas City, Texas and, while Texas was mentioned, no specific city had ever been discussed. The same was true for Louisiana. The other places were specific; the sites in Texas were undetermined.

Baker wondered if, since they seem to have used one bomb against energy infrastructure, they would therefore use the other bomb in one of the other cities. In his notes, he noted that fallout only needed one bomb. *The two other targets required two bombs, so are we looking at New York or another energy target?* He decided to eliminate the Internet and go with fallout in Jersey City or some place in Louisiana. *What is their thinking? Which is correct? Jersey City is very specific and Louisiana is very general. Jersey City is relatively easier to defend. I'll ask Williams to contact the governor of New Jersey and tell, him we need two companies of National Guard MPs to guard the power station 24/7 until this is resolved.*

He thought, *The second bomb — if they're going to use it — will be detonated somewhere in Louisiana. But where? What if I'm wrong and the target is one of the two places I've dismissed? If I'm wrong, those two could have casualties many times greater than in Texas City. Can I live with the thought of the millions of lives this miscalculation could cost?*

The radioactive tsunami has moved ten miles closer to League City, Texas

CHAPTER 8

The War Room

The Chairman of the Joint Chiefs of Staff, four-star General Blanchard Powell looked around at the concerned faces in the War Room. "Under Protocol Four, I have the authority to set the DEFCON status. It has been set at DEFCON 2 due to the detonation of a nuclear device and the potential of a second device being detonated on American soil."

A wave of whispers gathered voice. "But sir, that's above the level set for 9-11!" one of the undersecretaries blurted out.

"I'm well aware of that. But, we are facing a national security situation that goes beyond 9-11." The general held up his hand for silence.

"We will need a great deal of personnel and equipment to move out and shut down the compressors. My understanding is that every time we shut down a pipeline compressor, in a small way we slow down the flow. If we shut down enough compressors, we can stop the flow. Once we have stopped the flow or slowed it enough, we can begin to close the pipeline valves.

"Under Protocol Four, I have the authority to call out all needed military personnel, including the National Guard and Reserves. Among all branches of the military, we have over one hundred thousand personnel in Texas. We will use Army, Marine and Air Force helicopters to transport teams to start shutting down compressors and pumps, working from the furthest points to points just beyond the radioactive tsunami.

"It was mentioned earlier that the Departments of the Interior and Energy would hold a conference call after our meeting with the pipeline owners and operators. In that call we need them to brief us on the best way to shut down the pipelines, based on their current SCADA network capabilities.

"The Pentagon will be on the call. Once we know the current road map, we will deploy personnel and equipment to start shutting down the pipelines within two hours. The pipelines have right-of-way and, while they don't run in straight lines, they do need compressor stations in the line to keep all the stuff moving. We will put teams in helicopters to fly the pipelines looking for compressor stations. The choppers land and a team gets out, shuts down the compressor, and then they quickly get back in and fly to the next one and so on.

"We'll have additional teams to shut down any pumping stations that are pushing product in the pipelines outside of the SCADA networks. Again, with the help of the pipeline companies we can locate the pumping stations and we should deal with them the same way."

The room filled with applause and shouts of encouragement from the president and all the officials in the room. The president looked around and saw nothing but confirming nods and smiles.

The general concluded, "It may take a little longer than two hours but at the current flow rate it could cross the Texas border in about fifty-five hours. I'll need confirmation from the owners and operators, but my hunch is this just might work."

The president looked visibly relieved. "Before I conclude this meeting we have to talk about two other factors. I need to talk to America tonight. We owe it to the. Karen and her Chief of Staff are heading up a speech-writing team to give me some thoughts and ideas. If you have any suggestions, please feel free to call Maggie.

"Now to the more serious problem. Texas City, Texas is destroyed. Over fifty-four thousand people have been vaporized and will never be found. There are fires in the town and the four refineries are polluting the air with radioactive fallout. The heat from the fires and the radiation will not let us to get within five miles of the outskirts of the town. If we can stop the flow of oil and natural gas, we can stop the fuel that is feeding the fires. General Powell's plan will address that.

"However, the Nuclear Regulatory Commission tells me that, after the fires are out, it may be decades before we can go back to whatever is left of

Texas City. We have to find a way to isolate it to protect our citizens. Any suggestions would be greatly appreciated."

Air Force Chief of Staff General Winfield Hancock spoke up, "Sir, might I suggest we establish a no fly zone manned by the Air Force? And, at a safe distance away from the city the Army, set up a perimeter of concrete and razor wire with mounted patrols 24/7."

"Excellent suggestions, General. Please action that and brief me on progress tomorrow.

"I realize we have covered a great deal but we have one more very serious issue, and that is the world markets tomorrow morning. It's very possible that the markets will be in chaos, particularly if word leaks that there may be a second device on U.S. soil. I have not called any other world leaders yet for fear of leaks that would add to the instability. I will call the key authorities just before I speak to the American people tonight."

The president turned to secretary of the Treasury, Porter Smyth, "Porter, do we close the capital markets and banks until further notice?"

"Sir, it would be for the best, yes. The markets in Beijing and Tokyo are closed for a few more hours. We need to temporarily shut down the exchanges as soon as possible to prevent a collapse once the full details get out."

The president shook his head slowly. "I agree. Make it so."

The radioactive tsunami has moved ten miles closer to League City, Texas

CHAPTER 9

Ellen Calls Back

Williams had just finished his meeting with Ted Baker when Marie buzzed him that Ellen was on line one. Frank's soul mate for over three decades, they dated in high school and, although they went to different colleges, they went together until graduation. They graduated in May and got married in June, almost twenty-five years ago.

They'd been talking about where to go on their Silver Anniversary next year. *Frommer's Travel Guide* had recently picked Sanibel Island, Florida as the best resort vacation spot in the world. Frank sent away for vacation brochures and they both saw why it was such a magical place.

Looking at a recent picture of Ellen, he was amazed at her looks and figure. *She watches what she eats and exercises regularly, more than I do. She's as gorgeous today as she was when we married.*

It had always been his nature to protect her. The only time that she got pregnant, she miscarried in the first trimester and he worried about her for a long time afterward. Ultimately, they couldn't have children so they spent the last twenty-five years simply being in love with each other.

How can I tell her? You can't tell your wife something this horrible over the phone and just hang up. She's going to need to be held for a long time. She's going to need to have my arms around her. She'll want to bury her head under my chin so she can feel I'm her security blanket.

How could he leave the office to see her and then leave her to return to the office? He'd almost forgotten, with all of his daydreaming, that Ellen was on hold. He had an idea just as he picked up the phone.

"Ellen, sweetheart, I'm so sorry I made you wait. I was working on something that needed to be taken care of right away. Would it be possible for you to leave work early, come over here and spend some time with me before we head home?"

"Frank, is there something wrong?"

"Well, I'm up to my knees in alligators and I need a break. I thought that, if you could leave early, we could spend some time together. You know you're a gorgeous distraction. We could close my door and fool around a little bit."

Something must be seriously wrong for Frank to ask me to come to his office and fool around. He has never asked this in twenty-five years. Oh my God, something is seriously wrong and he wants me with him.

"Everyone is talking about the explosion in Texas. I can be there by three o'clock. Would that be okay?"

"Perfect darling, I'll alert security that you're on your way and to expect you. By the way, as a way to compliment you, are you wearing a bra today?"

"Frank, it's a work day, but no I'm not." She grinned at her phone. "I'll see you at three."

How the hell do I tell her about the bomb? When I told her about even the pos-sibility of a nuclear bomb, she came apart. I've never seen her so afraid and shaken. He wondered how she would react to the reality of the bomb in Texas City. He had to tell her, because it was only a matter of hours before the whole world would find out, and he didn't want her to be alone when she heard it on the TV or the car radio. However, because he knew he was not leaving his post, he wouldn't be able to tell her until three o'clock.

He called Ted Baker to come to his office for an update. It was 2:45. However, while he knew Ellen would be prompt, it would nevertheless take a few moments for her to clear security and be escorted to his office.

"Ted what did you find in your notes that might be of help on the loca-tion of the second bomb?"

"Sir, I feel confident that two of the options are off the table: the destruction of the Internet and the sabotage of the power grid are elimi-nated because both of these attacks would take two bombs. That leaves us with two possibilities: the coal-fired electric plant in Jersey City, New Jersey, and an energy facility in Louisiana.

"We can ask the Governor of New Jersey to call up two companies of National Guardsmen to guard the power plant so that it would be eliminated as a target. That leaves us with some place in Louisiana. There are eighteen operating refineries in the state. If we look at Texas City as a template, then we need to look for a city in Louisiana that has multiple refineries. Based on the listing on the Internet I can only find one city in Louisiana that has more than one refinery and that city is ..."

The radioactive tsunami has moved ten miles closer to League City, Texas

THE BROTHERHOOD OF THE RED NILE

CHAPTER 10

War Room

"If we close the markets and the banks, we can't do that without advising our NATO partners plus Russia, Japan, China and Saudi Arabia. We close our markets and the other markets collapse." Secretary of State Michelle Borders looked around the crowded but quiet room. "Ours will eventually be impacted. However, the longer we're 'closed till further notice', the bigger the impact will be on our relationships with our friends. If I may, Mr. President, how long do you think the markets will be closed?"

"Michelle, I have no way of telling for sure, but let me try and put this in perspective as I see it. When they took out the Twin Towers, the markets were closed for six days. Given that we have already lost twenty-five percent of our energy and refining capacity, that may take decades to ever come back on line, my best guess is some time greater than six days and probably less than six years. I am not being facetious when I say that."

When the president said six years, the expressions on the faces of the cabinet officers were of unabashed shock. "Yes ladies and gentlemen. I don't know how long it will take to rebuild America, but we will not be back online in six days. We had better get used to dealing with an extended timeframe. We can clearly say that if we can't get this radioactive tsunami stopped soon, six years could turn into sixty.

"I would like to go back to Porter. What will happen when we close the banks?"

"Sir, without American institutions operating fully in all facets of the capital markets, liquidity will dry up. Who would want to buy anything if there is a chance you may not be able to sell it for some extended period? The bigger issue is that all the IRAs, 401(k)s and public employee pension funds are invested in the stock and bond markets. If there is no liquidity, then how do these funds get the money to pay benefits? If the U.S. Government cannot sell its bills, notes and bonds, how does it pay people and pay its own bills when they are due? We have to consider whether a wildly volatile market is better than no market at all.

"Mr. President, I will need a bit more time to think before we make a decision. My people are running the scenarios now. For tonight, it's probably best that you stress the word 'consider' when referring to closing the markets and banks for a short time, and this only when we have more impact information.

"We are focused on stopping the tsunami, and if we get it stopped we can celebrate for ten seconds and then analyze the long-term consequences to our economy and the world. I will revisit this issue with you again before your speech to the nation this evening."

"Thank you, Porter. Your thoughts will help us focus on some of the other important issues that may well take years to fix. I would like to move back to Secretary of State Borders.

"Michelle, what are the ten most important countries you need to contact and by when?"

"Sir, the second part is much easier than the first. I think the contact must be made shortly before your speech to the nation."

"When you name your ten, which should I call and which should you call?"

"Sir, if you would call all the odd numbers, I will contact the even numbers. That way, you spread yourself among all ten and make them think you called all of them.

"My staff is drafting a diplomatic release to all the ambassadors to the U.S. to instruct them to call on their head of state to notify them of the challenges America is experiencing. I recommend this release be sent out just before your speech."

"Excellent, Madam Secretary."

"Thank you, sir."

"Attorney General Clinton, what is the status on notification to state and local law enforcement?"

Drew Clinton's brief was crisp and short. "Initial notification to law enforcement about the explosion has gone out, with a Top Secret Law Enforcement Eyes Only classification. I've been in touch with my counterpart in Texas, and the authorities are on full alert. The Governor has declared a state of emergency for the entire State in order to free up resources for support, rescue and recovery operations in and surrounding Texas City.

"Initially, the bad guys will stay at home in shock, but very quickly they'll be looking for ways to make money out of this disaster, both physically and online. The problem is that there will be no money if the banks can't open, so the bad guys will turn to other opportunities, including bogus charities. It happened after Katrina and again after the tsunami in Japan.

"My concern is that desperate people will do desperate things. They will do things that in other situations they would not normally do. I think, as difficult as it may be, you will have no choice but to …"

The radioactive tsunami has moved ten miles closer to League City, Texas

CHAPTER 11

Texas City Aircraft Hangar

Shortly after the ambulance pulled out of the hangar, the EMTs placed badges on the two pilots and themselves to monitor their radiation levels. All the badges initially read at a level below the safe level of 300 millrems. The transport to the hospital was not an emergency, so it would take about twenty minutes to make the five-and-a-half mile trip.

A person exposed to a sustained high level of radiation could have an elevated millrems level even after a thorough decontamination process. It is unlikely that the millrems level of the EMTs would be affected by transporting an exposed person.

The ambulance was well away from hangar and Texas City when one of the EMTs noticed that everyone's badges were above 300 millrems. An EMT called the hospital to report that the millrems were increasing on all the badges of the passengers in the ambulance.

The doctor at the other end replied, "I don't understand. You're getting further and further away from Texas City, yet the millrems level is increasing when if anything it should be going down.

"When you get to the hospital please park the ambulance in the remote parking lot till I can get some direction. Hopefully, I'll have an answer for you by the time you get here."

How is it possible for the millrems to increase the further you get away from the bombsite? On a hunch, the doctor called the radiology department and asked for the resident. "Are you wearing your radiation badge?"

The resident replied, "Yes, why?'

"What is the millrems count?"

The resident looked and responded, "Four hundred. That can't be. It should be under 300 millrems."

The doctor replied, "It's starting to look like the explosion in Texas City has some sort of nuclear connection and somehow the radiation is coming to us, but I don't know how. Thanks. I'll keep you posted on what I find out."

The doctor didn't know who he should call to report his concerns and to ask ideas about the source of the radiation. Nevertheless, he finally concluded that the Fire Chief's office would be the best option.

Dr. William Smith picked up his phone and dialed a secure number reserved for major public safety incidents. The line rang twice.

"What is the emergency?

"It's Dr. Smith from St. James Hospital. I must talk to Chief Bradley. We have five people – four of whom are in an ambulance in the parking lot – with elevated levels on their radiation badges.

"I'll page him immediately, sir. May I have a number where I can reach you should we get disconnected?"

He gave her a secure number. The line went quiet and stayed that way for what seemed like forever. *C'mon, John, we have an issue. Pick up!*

Finally, a gruff voice says, "Hi, Bill. I take it this is not a simulation?"

"It most definitely is not. We have two DHS pilots on their way to us with radiation contamination. They have been through the full decontamination process out at the airport, but one of our EMTs noticed that the badges of all the people in the ambulance registered 400 millrems. That is about 100 millrems above normal.

"Have you heard anything about there being a nuclear explosion in Texas City?"

There was a pause. "No, I haven't heard anything like that. We're all watching the news reports. I have my people on standby in case we're called out to assist."

"I spoke to our radiology department and all of their badges are registering around 400 millrems. I don't know what the source of the radiation is. The only unusual event was at Texas City."

"Well, Bill. This is not my area of expertise, but the deputy chief is our person in charge of hazardous material response. Let me see if I can get him in a conference call in with us."

The line went quiet. Smith tried to think about how the radiation levels could have gone up. Was there was indeed a nuclear detonation in Texas City? He saw in his mind the mushroom cloud in classic nuclear explosions. The TV monitors in the ER waiting room showed footage of the blast, but there was no mushroom cloud, just billowing clouds of black smoke.

Just then, a new voice interrupted his musings. "This is deputy chief Randall Jones. How can I help?"

"Hello, Deputy Jones. I'm Dr. William Smith of the St. James Hospital ER. Has John filled you in on my concerns?"

"Yes sir, he has. My first reaction was that it might be fallout from the explosion. However, as John told you, we've had no official notification that there was a nuclear element to the explosion."

"That was my thought also, but I did a quick check and I can't see any significant amount of dust on the cars in our parking lot. Therefore, I've pretty much eliminated fallout as the source of the radiation. Nevertheless, if it's not coming from fallout then what could be the source of the radiation?"

"That's a good question. My concern is that your staff and all of your patients are being exposed to 400 millrems of radiation at a minimum."

Smith nodded. "My concern, exactly. We may have a major health issue. If my people are exposed, then it is very possible that the entire population of La Marque is being exposed. We have to find the source of the radiation."

"I agree doctor, but I think that, if it is not from fallout, it has to be from ..."

The radioactive tsunami is six miles west of Texas City

THE BROTHERHOOD OF THE RED NILE

CHAPTER 12

Frank Williams' Office

Ted Baker was reporting to Frank Williams about his review of his notes and was trying to identify a likely target for the second bomb.

"Sir, as I was saying, the only potential target similar to Texas City is Lake Charles, Louisiana. The three refineries there process about 700,000 barrels of oil a day. Texas City had four refineries that were processing about a million barrels a day. You add the two together you take a lot of crude oil out of the system.

"Now, add to this that you have two waves heading north. There is a good possibility the crude from these refineries is headed to other refineries in Texas and Louisiana. I think the Secretary needs to contact the Governor of Louisiana to dispatch a Hazmat Team, three bomb squads and a battalion of National Guards to search all their refineries and look for the bomb and disarm it as quickly as possible."

"Ted, I agree. I will convey your thoughts to the Secretary as soon as he returns from the War Room meeting with the president. Thanks for the great piece of intelligence work."

As Ted was leaving the office, Marie held the door for Ellen. Frank got up, went over to the door, and closed it behind them. As he closed the door, he turned Ellen around and gently pushed her up against the door. As he leaned in to give her a kiss, he felt her breasts flatten against his chest.

He kissed her with gentle passion as he reached up to cup one of her full breasts. She squirmed a little, not from pain, but due to sexual stimulation. She kissed him back as passionately as he kissed her and rubbed a hand down the inseam of his trousers. They held each other for what seemed like a long time and then gently separated.

Ellen looked up into Frank's eyes and smiled. "I should have been coming to your office more frequently."

"You know how much I love you, how much I love holding you, and making love to you. I'm the luckiest guy in the world. I know that sounds old-fashioned, but that's how I feel."

"I feel the same way Frank and I don't think it's old-fashioned."

"I wanted you to come here because I needed to see you, hold you and tell you something that I wanted you to hear from me first and not on the radio or TV."

"What is it?"

"Do you remember the conversations we had about the terrorist group the Brotherhood of the Red Nile?"

"Yes, they are the group you thought had a couple of old Soviet Union dirty bombs, which they were trying to get upgraded. You lost track of them, however."

"Yes, that is the group."

"So, has something happened?"

Frank led her to a worn leather couch, sat next to her and took her hands in his. "We believe that a nuclear device was detonated at one of the refineries in Texas City. The town had a population of over fifty thousand. They're all dead."

Ellen began to cry. "All those poor people."

Frank continued softly. "The president will speak to the nation some-time tonight to inform America about this unbelievable disaster. We also believe that the nuclear fallout has contaminated the oil and natural gas in the pipelines and that this contaminated energy is heading north."

"Is it coming our way?" Ellen looked up. Worry lines were etched in her husband's furrowed brow.

"We don't know. We'll be working with the owners and operators to shut down their pipelines to keep it from going too far north."

With her tears stopping and with more control, she asked, "What if you can't stop it?"

"While I can't be sure, it is possible that the contaminated oil, gas, and fuels will spread throughout the entire United States, effectively making our current energy systems useless. I do have one more thing to tell you but I have to ask you not to say anything about any of this until after the president speaks tonight, agreed?"

"Yes."

"We believe that the Brotherhood has another bomb that has not yet exploded. We have every reason to believe that they will strike with the second bomb in Louisiana at Lake Charles. Texas City and Lake Charles are similar in that both cities have multiple refineries. Lake Charles has a population of about seventy-two thousand. We're taking steps to dispatch personnel to Lake Charles to see if we can find the bomb and disarm it."

Ellen reached out and put her arms around Frank, "Please hold me and hold me tight."

While he had her in his arms, he knew he had to talk about what she was going to do until after the president spoke, and then what about tomorrow and the days after until the crisis passed.

"Ellen, you know that I shall have to stay here for the time being. I can't tell you when I'm coming home. I want you to stay with me until at least after the president speaks to the nation. I'm having Marie get me a couple of cots. I want you to spend the night. I may have to be leaving throughout the night, but I want you close.

"In the morning, I will want you to go home only if we're sure that it's safe. Each day, I want you to go to work and bring with you a small suitcase with a change of shirt and underwear and then bring it to me after work. On your way here, I want you to stop and get us something to eat. Then, later in the evening, you will go home and get some rest.

"I don't know how long we'll have to work this way, but I hope that someday soon we'll both be able to cuddle in our own bed again. I realize that it will be difficult with me not being there, but I have to do this. I have to protect you and America but, until the Secretary needs me, let me just hold you."

The radioactive tsunami has moved ten miles closer to League City, Texas

CHAPTER 13

War Room

The president looked at his watch and saw that it was 3:15 PM. He wanted to make it to Andrews by four o'clock but needed to hear what the attorney general had to say. The screens around the room were blank, so all attention was focused on AG Clinton.

Clinton was a physically impressive man, in addition to having an impressive legal career in both private practice and in government work at all levels. He looked like a very successful businessman and he was dominating in what he knew and how he delivered.

He was six feet five inches tall and had a muscular medium physique. His striking features were his hair, his hands, and his eyes. His eyes were cobalt blue; his hair was long and well-kept, but all silver grey. While for most people these features would be striking enough, his hands were massive. He had been an All-American in basketball for Georgetown and had been good enough to play professional ball but had wanted to be a lawyer and hadn't wanted to wait until after a pro career. He was a tall man but his hands were much larger than you would expect for a man of his size. He had used these hands to command attention from people all of his life. He was clearly the tallest man in the cabinet and in the room.

He knew he was going to say something important and so he stood up. Because of his size when he stood, he dominated the room and most of the people in the room, except for the president.

"Mr. President, the chaos that could be caused by the closing of the banks and the capital markets, if you should decide to do such a thing, leaves you with only one option. If you are going to close the banks and the markets, then at the same time you will have to declare martial law across the entire nation."

The reaction for the room was outrage.

"You can't declare martial law; it would suspend the Constitution!"

"People will riot in the streets; Congress will call for your impeachment."

Many other comments came from all over the room, some with anger in their voices, some with fear and, in some cases, with pure rage.

The president raised his hand, the room quieted down, and then he turned to Clinton, "Mr. Attorney General, it seems that you have stirred up a hornet's nest. Would you care to enlighten us as to why you think this way?"

"Mr. President, I don't see that you have any choice."

"Why not, don't we always have choices?"

"Sir, I have been listening to all the discussion this afternoon and, in my career, I have always tried to put myself in the opposition's shoes. If I may, let me tell you what I have already heard. A nuclear bomb has wiped out a town in Texas of fifty-four thousand people. They have been melted down; there will be no trace of these people. On top of that, we have a river as wide as Texas that is full of radiation heading north at six to eight miles an hour.

"I didn't know how deep these pipelines are buried but while all of the discussions were going on I did a Google search on the average depth of pipelines in America and found that, depending on terrain and factors such as river and railroads, the average depth is three to five feet. So if we have, as was stated earlier, a tsunami of contaminated oil, gas and refined product running in these pipelines at three to five feet deep, could the radiation be leaking into the soil and out from the soil? We know that the tsunami underground is now past League City, but is the radiation coming up from the ground into League City? Has this radioactive tsunami already infected every man, woman, and child in the city and all the people between Texas City and League City?

"Sir, I suggest that it's only a matter of time before some news outlet finds out what happened to Texas City and the story will go viral over the Internet across the entire United States and the world in minutes. The news will cause runs on the ATM at every bank and every convenience store across the nation. People will break into storefronts looking for food, water, and whatever else they may want.

"When the stores are depleted then neighbors will turn against neighbors. This chaos will not be limited to just a few towns in Texas. It will happen all over, for people will not know if the gas in their kitchen stove or their furnace is burning clean gas or radioactive gas that will kill them."

The room is ghastly silent at the remarks of the attorney general, not only because of what he said but also because everybody in the room realized the dire truth of his remarks.

"Sir, to answer your question, I recommend we advise state and local police that the president is declaring martial law, with curfews, until further notice, and that the military will be in charge along with the assistance of the local police in protecting all of us."

The attorney general slowly sat down.

The president stood. "Ladies and gentlemen, we've talked about what we need to do immediately to stop the flow of the contaminated oil and gas. As of this moment, we have Protocol Four in full effect. We have worked through this in simulations. Those simulations have helped us prepare for Operation Save America. Under my executive order, Operation Save America is now initiated.

"Break out your teams immediately and start working with the industry experts on how to shut down these pipelines. Contact scientists from the Nuclear Regulatory Commission and the best minds in the field: the 2011 Nobel laureates in physics – Nathan Perlmutter of UC Berkley and Adam Rice Burrows of Johns Hopkins. Madam Secretary, have State handle getting these people to the White House. Get Perlmutter on a plane in less than an hour. Contact Burrows and get him to the White House by 8 PM tonight. I don't think this will be an issue, but do not accept 'no' for an answer, under my authority.

"I know we have a lot more issues to deal with, and we will discuss these, but it is possible to become so overwhelmed that, with so many things to do, nothing gets done, and we become frozen like deer in the headlights of a car. Let's make the phone calls to the pipeline companies, get the experts on their way to the White House and, most importantly, stop that damn oil. Make yourself available to meet again on short notice, cancel all planned trips and quietly arrange to stay in your offices until further notice.

"Oh and one more thing: STOP THE DAMN OIL. Clear?"

All respond in unison: "STOP THE DAMN OIL."

It is now 3:30 PM and the radioactive tsunami has moved
12 miles closer to League City Texas

CHAPTER 14

Let's Go Fly

The cabinet meeting was very intense, but, overall, very productive, the president thought. *I'm pleased at how the cabinet and other key players came together. We're facing perhaps the greatest threat to America in its history — and potentially its very survival.* He looked at his watch. *It's 3:30 PM; I have thirty minutes to get to Andrews if we want to leave on schedule.*

His plan was to leave the White House and drive to Georgetown University football field where he would take the car onto the field. Marine One would land and pick him up and take him to Andrews Air Force base where he would board the Gulfstream and take off immediately for Texas City.

He left the War Room and went back to the Oval Office, and exited through a side door with one Secret Service agent. The president had changed in the Oval Office and was now dressed in casual clothes. As he usually did in the apartment upstairs in the White House, he had left his clothes on the floor. He was wearing a baseball cap that said 'Washington Nationals' on it and had it pulled down low on his forehead.

As the president approached the black SUV, he opened and held the door for the Secret Service agent. The agent was wearing a dark suit and the president thought that anybody looking towards the car would focus on the agent and not on the president.

The two of them got in the black SUV, which then glided almost silently out of a side gate from the White House. They were on their way to the Georgetown football field. The agent in the car with the president

44

used his secure phone to call for the release of Marine One at the rendez-vous point at the center of the field. With heavy afternoon DC traffic, they expected to be on the field in twenty minutes. It would be close. The agent informed that twenty seconds on the ground were necessary for Marine One, and then out.

"Everybody roger that?" All teams reported in and were ready to go.

The Secret Service had arranged with campus security at Georgetown to have the football field at Georgetown cleared so they could use it for a VIP transport. They had used this field several times before, but never for the president. It would take about ten minutes to get to the ramp leading onto the field. The agent held the SUV until he got the message that Marine One was ten seconds out. When the agent had a visual, he pulled the SUV onto the ramp and, in a matter of seconds, as Marine One approached from the other end of the field, he headed for the circle at the fifty-yard line. As Marine One made its approach, the door of the SUV opened and, within ten seconds of the landing gear's contact with the artificial turf, the president was in the helicopter and on his way. The agent slowly drove the SUV back down the ramp and back to the White House motor pool. Meanwhile, Marine One headed straight for Andrews at full power.

The president was secure and sitting in his seat looking out the window, wondering how many gas pipelines run through the nation's capital. If they can't turn of the flow, he wondered if Washington, DC would become a ghost town like Pripyat, the Ukrainian city next to the Chernobyl nuclear power plant. As he played back this morning's meeting in his mind, the one thought that had haunted him, since the moment it was spoken, was the idea that the U.S. could be a nation under martial law. He opened his laptop and found that martial law has been used only twice in America, the more recent being when Pearl Harbor was bombed by the Japanese; the first time was during the Civil War. He thought it ironic that Abraham Lincoln, the president who thought of as the great emancipator, was the first to take away so many freedoms.

The flight to Andrews was about ten minutes. The plan was to land Marine One near a service hangar - not at the normal presidential heliport - and take a car to the hangar where the Gulfstream was kept. The plane would be towed out of the hangar to the flight line, where it would await its turn to take off. Whenever the president flew, the plane was called Air

Force One. Any other time the plane used its registration or its call letters. In this case, however, for discretion, they would employ the call letters, not Air Force One. Marine One landed and, in a matter of moments, the president was on board the Gulfstream along with two pilots and eight Secret Service bodyguards. At 4:02 PM, the plane lifted off.

President Jordan was a kind man and always treated the White House staff and the Secret Service with great respect. The team that was on the plane with him was new to him, with the exception of William Rummels, the head of the Service, who volunteered to guard the president on this trip.

Williams Rummels had been a member of the Secret Service for over thirty years. He had just joined the service when President Reagan was shot, and had always taken his responsibility very seriously. Over the years, he had guarded several presidents and in every case he knew, regardless of politics, he would take a bullet for the president if, in doing so, he was saving the life of the leader of the free world.

Billy, as his friends called him, was small but very strong and quite compact. He just made the height requirement to join the Service, and over the years, he never had much of a personal life. He never married, but he dated around. Billy knew that many of the agents were married and had families, but they were just as committed as he was to doing their duty. If he had to choose between a wife and family and the president he knew he would always choose the president.

In his off time, he loved to play golf and was an avid bowler. He was six years from retirement and at times, he wondered if he might want to be more cautious than in the past. He was thinking more about the chances he had taken, and if he did take a risk for the president, his retirement could be affected. Billy wasn't afraid; he was just more cautious than he had been in the past.

Billy asked himself, *So, why are you flying with the president to the site of a nuclear detonation that occurred just three hours ago? You don't know how much radiation is in the air and how the plane will deal with the massive heat.* Billy sat back in his chair. *If President Jordan has the courage to go and see the devastation of an entire town of fifty-four thousand people, how can I not go with him? This is a risk I'm willing to take.*

At that moment, President Jordan came over to thank him for coming on the flight.

"Sir, I would have it no other way."

It is now 4:20 PM and the radioactive tsunami has moved
18 miles closer to League City, Texas

CHAPTER 15

The Pipeline Companies

Staff of the Secretaries of Interior and Energy had been trying to get as many of the pipeline companies as possible on a 4:15 PM call. There are major trunk lines that run through Texas and then hundreds of smaller interstate and intrastate pipeline companies. Many had not returned the calls.

It was now 4:15. Both Secretaries welcomed the leaders of the companies who could make the call. Energy Secretary Michael Findley opened the call. "Thank you for joining us today in what may well be the most extraordinary actions taken by your companies to protect the safety of the American public and economy. What you are about to do may save the United States for your children and grandchildren.

"Protocol Four has been implemented by executive order of the president. Operation Save America has been launched. This is not a desk exercise. We have a national security crisis on our hands. I remind you that you are required under Protocol Four to shut down all communication devices. You are to communicate to no one during the call unless he or she has been previously cleared on a 'need to know' basis. Anyone who leaks information about this call is subject to severe criminal penalties.

"You have agreed in writing that you will not contact family, friends or colleagues. You must adhere to this requirement if we are to avoid a public panic."

At the beginning of Findley's statement, there was a great deal of background chatter, shuffling of papers on desks and even some beeping cell phones. By the time he finished his opening statement, one could hear a pin drop through the speakers.

"Ladies and gentlemen, America needs your help. We need it in two ways. First, we have been unable, on such short notice to make contact with many pipeline companies that operate in the State of Texas, so any help you can give us after this call about how we can reach them would be invaluable.

"What I am about to tell you must not be disclosed until the president makes the problem known to the American people. As you know, Texas City was wiped out at noon today local time by a massive explosion. It has destroyed all the refineries in the area. That explosion was caused by a nuclear device."

Findley continued, "Radiation levels are high and fires are burning out of control. All the pipelines above ground appear to be intact, but are covered with radioactive debris. We have every reason to believe that radiation is leaching into the soil via natural gas and refined products carried by pipelines through the region. The radiation is moving north at about six to eight miles an hour, and if it continues at this rate in about sixty-five hours it will hit the Oklahoma hub and slingshot further north, west, east, south and southwest.

"With that said, we need your help to hopefully stop this tsunami of radioactive energy as quickly as possible; we must stop it from getting to the slingshot if we are going to save America."

"Are we allowed to speak now?" a voice comes over the speaker.

"By all means."

"Sir, I'm Red Collins, chairman of a major trunk line running through Texas. First of all, I want to say 'holy shit'. I had hoped never to see this day.

"Based on our last desk exercise, we should be able to begin shutting down our trunk line within about two hours. Others on this call can do the same thing, from what I know. I will reach out to them right away.

"Mr. Secretary, we have multiple command centers with networked SCADA systems that control the compressors, pumps and valves on our pipeline. We can do it from the center all at one time. Our system is linked with the other operators but there are thousands of miles of pipelines in Texas that don't have a central system to shut down the flow."

"Thanks, Mr. Collins." Findley wiped a hand across his forehead. "Is there anybody on the call that runs a pipeline that doesn't have a central operations station?"

Over the speaker, Findley heard a lot of 'yes's. "Just a moment. Could I speak to one of you at a time?"

"Sir, my name is Bud Kessler. I am CEO of the Kessler Pipeline Company. We run a transfer pipeline. Oil and gas wells pump into our feeder lines and then we pump into one of our main lines. Therefore, we don't have central control like the big guys; we have pumps and compressors in the lines. If you want us to shut them down, we would have to go to each pumping station or compressor station and turn them off manually. Sir, that is a lot of miles of pipeline, and I don't have the personnel to go the whole length to shut down the equipment. We can do our best, but I just don't know."

"Mr. Kessler, my name is General Blanchard Powell. I am the Chairman of the Joint Chiefs of Staff. I want to ask you a question about your pipeline. You others, please feel free to respond if what I am about to suggest is helpful. You have a pipeline that picks up oil and gas from the wells and then transports it to a main line, and this line at various points might require a compressor to move the energy along. Is that correct?"

"Yes, sir."

"If the pipeline is moving product at, let's say, seven miles an hour, what happens if you shut down one compressor; will it slow the flow?"

"Well, General, if we shut down one compressor it probably won't make a change because the other compressors will sense a drop in pressure and pump harder."

"So we have to shut down several compressors to begin to make a difference?"

"Yes sir. I can't tell you how many it would take but the more we shut down the slower it will flow, that's for sure."

"My guess is that none of us have the personnel to shut down enough pipelines to make a difference. We can try, but there are just too many miles of pipeline. General, I can assure you that the trunk lines will be closed within two hours but, as much as we would like to help, I just don't know of any way to stop all the oil."

It is now 4:45 PM and the radioactive tsunami has arrived at League City, Texas

CHAPTER 16

St. James Hospital

Dr. William Smith looked out into the parking lot at the ambulance idling at the outer reaches of the property. *First, two pilots with above normal readings for radiation exposure and then the two EMTs with elevated readings. I can't let them in the hospital until I get some answers. What the hell is going on?* He thought, as he pondered his phone conversation with deputy chief Jones.

"Dr. Smith, if what I suspect is true, that explosion in Texas City was no accident and it was nuclear. No one has said anything officially, yet, but that is my suspicion, particularly with all the Homeland Security vehicles reported coming into the area.

"As best I can tell there are only two possibilities and I'm not sure how valid either one is at the moment. If it was a nuclear explosion, the first possibility is water runoff from fighting the fires may have sent contaminated water into the storm sewer system. I would have to check and see if there's any connection between the Texas City storm system and ours; it's possible, but I don't really think so."

"You're saying that the water used to fight the fires in Texas City has somehow infiltrated into our storm sewers giving off radiation up through the ground? My radiology department is on the seventh floor. Contaminated sewer water can't go from the sewers to the seventh floor."

"Then my first option is not the source of the radiation. My second option is frightening."

"Please explain." The doctor stepped out through the doors and paced back and forth along the sidewalk, as people stepped around him.

"There are oil and natural gas pipelines running in, around and under La Marque, and the radiation in Texas City is contaminating the energy in the pipelines. Many of the pipes are on the surface as the oil and gas cross through the radiation field around Texas City, and the full force of the radiation is going through the pipes into the oil. As that contaminated oil keeps flowing, it's spreading the radiation."

"Any other options?" Smith stopped pacing.

"None that I can think of at the moment."

"Is there a way to find out if what you're saying is true?"

"I'll call Homeland Security. There's a reason for all their vehicles being here."

"Call them and tell them we have two of their pilots that have been contaminated, plus two EMTs with them, and that we need help."

"I'll call my contact in the Houston office and see if I can get him. If not, I'll call DHS in DC."

"Please let me know what you find out so I can figure out how to treat these two pilots and possibly many more people in La Marque."

"Will do." John hung up and called up the speed dial number for Carl Booker, the DHS agent in Houston. He hit enter and soon heard a voice message: 'We can't take your call right now. If this is an emergency, please call Homeland Security in Washington at 1-202-282-8000. Tell the operator your problem and you will be directed to the proper party.'

John hung up and dialed the number. After several rings, he got a recorded voice with a list of options. He listened to all the options, chose 'terrorist activity' and found himself connected with Ted Baker.

"Mr. Baker, Deputy Fire Chief Randal Jones for the city of La Marque just down the road from Texas City, Texas. I'm in charge of hazardous material."

Baker perked up at the name of Texas City, "How can I help you, Chief Jones?"

"Well Mr. Baker, our local hospital has two of your pilots, who flew close – well as close as they could get – to the destruction in Texas City. When they landed, they were told proceed to a hangar and were decontaminated due to radiation exposure. After they were cleaned up and transported to St. James Hospital, en route all the people in the ambulance had higher than normal millrems readings.

"The hospital reported that they were seeing elevated levels of radiation. So, two questions, Mr. Baker. Did a nuclear device cause the explosion in Texas City? And is it possible that the radiation is now contaminating all the oil, gas and refined product running through the pipelines and that this contaminated product is running through La Marque?"

Baker sighed. "As you know, the Governor of Texas has declared a statewide state of emergency because of the Texas City explosion. Law enforcement has been notified. And yes, it was nuclear."

"Oh God help us." Jones' voice was a whisper.

"I don't know the direction of the flow of oil through Texas City, Chief Jones. What I do know is that teams are en route to make every effort to mitigate this disaster." What Baker did not say was that the government was focusing on the flow north towards the slingshot, and that nobody had discussed flows going west and or south out of Texas City.

Jones suggested, "If contaminated oil is flowing west and south in addition to north then all of Texas could be contaminated from the leaching effect of the radiation in the pipelines. I have an idea that may help us quantify the magnitude of the spread."

"I'm all ears. The sound you hear will be me taking notes on my laptop for a briefing in a few hours."

"Okay, I don't know how much you know about the oil business, but the cost of bringing in a well is very expensive. One of the ways oil drillers have increased their chances in finding oil is through satellite technology. The satellite can see the formations of oil deep in the earth using infrared beams. If we could get one of those mapping satellites to photograph the area, say about fifty miles north and west of Texas City, we should be able to see the flowing oil and how far it has spread."

"Chief, what a great idea! I'll get right on it. Let me have a number where I can reach you and let you know what we find out."

Baker called Williams to tell him about the idea from the fire chief. "I'm going to call the USGS – the U.S. Geological Survey – and see if they can give me any information on how we could track the flow of the radiation. As soon as I hear anything, I'll let you know."

"Sounds promising. Let's hope it works."

Baker looked up a USGS telephone number on the government intranet directory. Dialing the main number, he told the person who answered what he wanted to find out and the operator replied, "I'll connect you to the Executive Director's office; perhaps he can help."

"This is Mr. Benjamin Craddick's office. May I help you?"

"This is Ted Baker, senior assistant to the Under Secretary for Homeland Security. I need to talk to Mr. Craddick right away."

"He's in a meeting."

"This is a matter of National Security. I am under the orders of the president under the Authority of Protocol Four."

"Please hold."

Is there nothing that flaps these assistants? His wife could be in labor and she'd say, 'Please hold.' He pinched in his nose as he said the words. And stopped abruptly.

"This is Ben Craddick. How can I help you, Mr. Baker?"

"We need your advice and counsel concerning a very grave national security and public safety issue. Are you aware of Protocol Four?"

"Yes, I am."

"Then you understand that under no circumstances may you share this information in any form with any person unless there is an urgent operational need to know."

"Understood, Mr. Baker. Please continue."

Baker quickly told Craddick of the events in Texas City, adding the fact that the explosion was caused by a nuclear device.

"Oh my God. How horrible."

"Yes, sir, it is. We believe that there are thousands of miles of pipelines running through this contaminated area and that the fallout from the explosion is covering the exposed pipes for at least five miles around. In turn, the radiation is seeping into the pipes, and the contaminated oil and gas is heading north towards the slingshot in Oklahoma. We have just received word from La Marque, Texas, which is at least ten miles from the center of the blast site, that the radiation level is rising."

"Mr. Baker, how can we help?"

"Sir, it has been suggested that the infrared mapping that is used to find the best sites to drill might be helpful to track the flow of contaminated oil, gas and other product. We have been informed that your agency controls that satellite."

"We do. You want to know if our mapping satellite could track the flow of contaminated energy, is that correct?"

"Exactly."

"Can you give me just a moment to ask one of my colleagues in the room with me? I will not disclose the details, but if anybody will know he will."

Baker waited what seemed like hours and then heard a click. "Mr. Baker, are you still there."

"Yes, sir. What have you determined?"

"Well, Mr. Baker, given that pipelines run on a comparatively shallow basis in the ground, we think we could easily track your energy."

"Excellent! The big question is: how long before the satellite's orbit takes it over the area, and then how long to read the data?"

"Mr. Baker, as it happens, the satellite is currently east of Texas and should begin to pass over within the next two hours. We'll have to recalibrate it to pick up the radiation but I would think we can do this and get you a reading today."

"That's unbelievable!" Baker took in a deep breath. Finally, a window was opening. "What will you need to get started?"

"Under Protocol Four, I will need to speak with at least the Under Secretary of Homeland Security."

"I'll have him on the line to you within five minutes. Thank you, sir. You may have just saved millions of lives."

It is now 5:15 PM and the radioactive tsunami has passed through League City, Texas

CHAPTER 17

Flying to Texas City

The president's plane had been in the air for over an hour. Chief pilot General Maxwell Thomas turned over the controls to his co-pilot, Major Bob Whittaker. The general went back to sit next to the president to talk about the trip and his expectations. Walking towards the president, he got his first real look at the newest plane in the fleet. He'd trained on the Gulfstream but had never flown this executive jet. It was definitely more real than the flight simulator.

The plane was quite roomy for an aircraft that can fly at almost the speed of sound. There was a grouping of two seats with a fold-down table in the rear of the plane where the president was sitting. Forward were a series of seats in pairs across from each other, and between the presidential section and the other seats was a small couch that faced the president. The president's seat was upholstered in rich light brown leather while the other seats and the couch were covered with tan colored leather. There was a bathroom in the rear and one in the front. Also in the front was a small galley, all bright and shiny.

"May I sit, Mr. President?"

"Absolutely."

"Sir, we need to talk about Texas City and what you want to accomplish. We have never taken a plane so close to a radioactive area. At this moment, I have no idea what the conditions will be. All of us on board have one and only one obligation, and that is to keep you safe. So, if you would Mr. President, please tell me what you want to try to do when we get there."

"General, I'm the president of all the people including the thousands that died today in Texas City. I need to see where they died. I will tell the American people that I came to pay my respects and to be a witness to the massive loss of innocent American lives. At the moment, the best I can tell you is that I want to get as close as possible without endangering anyone.

"We need to get photographs that can help us assess the damage, not only to the town, but also to the pipeline infrastructure. I have a nice big window on my side of the plane, which is also your side, so you are my tour guide. If you think something is worth noting, I'll trust your judgment."

"Sir, there two things I need to consider so that I can make flight changes."

"And they are?"

"The radiation level and the outside temperature. If the radiation level gets above 500 millrems, we have to move away, and if the outside temperature gets above freezing, we will have to climb to bring the outside air below freezing. Other than these two matters, we also have to watch for additional explosions, which could create wind shear and cause the plane to plummet. I suggest we slowly work our way in and if we experience one of the two parameters, I have to take us out of danger. Agreed, Mr. President?"

"Yes. I would like to stay as long as possible, but I have to be back at the White House for a meeting with the cabinet at 8:30 this evening. Anything else you want to ask, General?"

"No sir, I have my orders and I'll do my best."

"I have no doubt, General Maxwell."

"Mr. President, I have a headset for you so that we can talk back and forth. See the button on the clip-on portion? If you want to talk with me just push the button and I'll hear you."

The plane was now thirty minutes out from Texas City and through his window the president could see bright yellow and red lights on the horizon.

"Mr. President, that is Texas City on your left. For now, I will try to keep it in view on your side of the plane. We will circle the city and each time around, we will get a little closer until we reach the limits for millrems or temperature. I plan to keep us at thirty-five thousand feet till I get a better feel for the atmosphere."

"General, how far away are we from Texas City?"

"Sir, we are three hundred miles out over the Gulf of Mexico."

The illumination from the fires was unbelievable as the plane approached Texas City.

"How we doing with the temperature?"

"Fine, sir. It's about minus sixty-five degrees and the millrems are about one hundred, which is within normal levels. At about fifty miles out, I will slowly drop the aircraft about a thousand feet and check the readings before descending further."

At fifty miles out, the glowing intensity of the fires suggested what hell must be like. At forty miles, "Sir, we are seeing an increase in temperature but it's still within limits. The millrems are now up to three hundred, which is also acceptable."

The sturdy jet, however, was being buffeted by the wind turbulence caused by the intense fires.

"General, what level of millrems would be fatal?"

"Sir, I'm not a radiation specialist, but I've been told it would have to be a very high level to be fatal quickly."

"How much, would you guess?"

"Sir, my guess would be in the range of four to five thousand millrems. We are not going to allow that to happen."

"Thank you for looking out for me." From his window the president saw the massive piles of rubble - which used to be productive refineries employing hundreds of people - glowing white-hot. He saw the cracking towers lying on the pipelines and was surprised that under the intense heat they had not melted. He could see the remains of all four refineries, and in each, there were a series of massive storage tanks that seemed to be feeding the fires. He looked to his right and saw one of the storage tanks explode and the roof, which might have been three hundred feet across, went flying several thousand feet into the air. The president could feel the heat inside the plane.

Over his headset he heard, "Sir, we have to get out of here. The outside temperature is rising rapidly." As the pilot veered off to the right to get away from other possible explosions, another storage tank thirty thousand feet below them blew up and sent a massive shock wave that hit the plane.

General Maxwell used the Gulfstream's powerful twin-engine thrust to gain ten thousand feet of altitude in a matter of seconds. This escape maneuver had saved the plane, but it wasn't until they were heading back to Washington that the general saw the millrems gauge reading: three thousand.

Maxwell told the co-pilot to take over. He walked slowly to the back of the plane to sit again with the president and inform him of this situation.

"General, I understand that the level of radiation went to at least 3,000 millrems and there is every likelihood my actions have signed a death warrant for all of us on the plane. I assure you that all of you will get the best possible care for your bravery. I know that it will be very hard to keep this secret, but I need this kept confidential for a few days till we can figure out a plan to save the nation."

"Sir, we all volunteered for this mission and we understood the risks we were taking, I assure you. I will speak to them and as soon as we land. We will all check into the hospital at Andrews. It is possible with new treatments to counteract the impact of the radiation. I haven't figured out how you will be treated yet, but I'll keep you posted.

"Before we land, I want to speak to the crew and the agents on board."

"No problem"

"General, thank you for your service to America."

"Anytime, sir, anytime."

It is now 6:15 PM and the radioactive tsunami has passed through
League City
and is headed to Houston, Texas

CHAPTER 18

Conference Call with Pipeline Owners and Operators

"General, I just don't see how we can shut them all down."

General Powell took a note from Ted Baker of DHS that a Geological Survey satellite could track the radioactive oil and gas in the pipelines and quietly said "Yess!" He passed the note to the others in the room.

"General Powell, this is Red Collins. I want to ask a question or two if you don't mind."

"Go right ahead, sir, and ask your questions. I'll do my best to give you answers; if I don't know how to respond, I will get them for you as soon as I can."

"Thank you General Powell. First, how do we know if in fact the pipelines are contaminated? And second, how long will our pipelines be shut down?"

"Excellent questions, Mr. Collins. To your first question: we have already seen evidence of elevated radiation levels in the town of La Marque, which is about ten miles west and south of the center of Texas City. I must admit that we thought the oil was flowing north; we didn't consider that it would be going in other directions. We have monitors on the ground that are giving us the millrems count and now we have just found out that the infrared satellite used by the oil industry to find oil deposits will soon be overhead and sending us digital maps as to the flow of all contaminated oil, natural gas and product in real time. Now to your more difficult question, as to how long we will have to shut down the pipelines. I think the Secretary of Energy is more equipped to answer your question."

"Ladies and gentlemen, I'm Michael Findley, Secretary of Energy. The energy is becoming radioactive because it's flowing through pipes in Texas City that have been in contact with radioactive material set off by the use of a high energy explosive. The refineries, all the equipment and the pipelines above ground were covered with radioactive debris from this explosion.

"The pipelines are made of steel. Radioactivity seeps through the pipes and attaches itself to the energy product as this travels up the pipeline. I know this is an over simplification, but it's like going through a car wash. Your car goes in dry; it gets soaped, scrubbed, rinsed off, then dried. Similarly, the energy product comes out of the ground, is pumped into a pipeline, and then it proceeds as compressors keep it moving right through Texas City. When the oil hits the contaminated pipes, the radiation attaches to the fuel and travels with it. The heat in the pipeline liquefies the oil and products like gasoline and jet fuel and makes the attraction process even more effective. We have spent some time thinking about the answer to your question and, at the moment, the best we can say is that there are so many variables we just don't know."

"Mr. Secretary, could you guess?"

"Mr. Collins, any guess anybody would make at this moment in time would be ill-advised."

"Mr. Secretary, I have spoken to one of my chemical engineers and he says that the shutdown will be a function of how long the energy stays in the pipeline. So, isn't it within the realm of possibility that it could take years, if not decades, to clean this up? Could it be that these pipelines will never be able to be used again?"

"Mr. Collins, I don't know that I would disagree with that assessment."

All of a sudden, a voice could be heard over all the connections: "we are bankrupt!"

General Powell spoke up, "Ladies and gentlemen, I understand that many of you have all of your investment capital tied up in these pipelines, but unless we find a way to stop this radioactive energy, millions of American will become sick and die. Now, I have a plan to help shut these death traps down. Do you want to save lives or cry about your losses?"

It is now 6:15 PM and the radioactive tsunami has passed
through League City headed to Houston, Texas

CHAPTER 19

Office of the First Lady

Before leaving for Texas City, President Jordan sat with Karen and asked her to put together a team to begin the outline of the speech he would give to the nation tonight. Her Chief of Staff Maggie Cummings and two White House speechwriters – Bill Wringer and Debra White – joined her in her office.

"Okay people, we have a speech draft to produce. As you know, we're operating under Protocol Four. Only those with a need to know can be given information about what we are about to discuss. Your families are not in the need to know. We don't have a great deal of time to get this done. So, do I have your word about keeping the content of the speech private?"

All say in unison, "Yes, ma'am."

"At noon today, a nuclear device was detonated in the town of Texas City, Texas. The entire population has been wiped out."

Debra broke in: "Ma'am how many are dead?"

"At least fifty-four thousand. We just don't know yet; the fires and the radiation have kept us from getting within five miles of the city. We're using satellites and high altitude aircraft to get us pictures of the fires and the destruction."

Bill spoke up: "Ma'am, was this a terrorist attack?"

"Yes."

"Was it Al-Qaeda?"

"No, we believe that this catastrophe was the work of a new group called the Brotherhood of the Red Nile, based in Syria. To the best of our knowledge, the Syrian government is not a state sponsor."

"So, ma'am, this is a rogue group operating on their own?"

"I don't know how to answer that. We know they had two bombs acquired in the black market, so it took a considerable amount of money to purchase them."

"Excuse me, ma'am, but did you say two bombs?"

"Yes", was the grim reply.

"Did they use both bombs in Texas City?"

"We don't think so, but we're not sure."

Maggie finally jumped in. "We've just lost fifty-five thousand Americans and there could be a second bomb, and we have to find a positive spin on this?"

Karen responded, "Maggie, I said nothing about a positive spin. Our job is to help the president tell the truth and inform the country of the events that have taken place and alert them to the possible danger."

"Is there other danger besides a second nuclear bomb?"

The first lady stood and started to pace. "The area that was attacked has massive numbers of pipelines running right through Texas City in all directions. The oil that's passing through there is being contaminated with radiation from the bomb. Massive amounts of contaminated oil are leaving Texas City and heading in all directions. The area of the greatest concern is the slingshot in Oklahoma; if contaminated oil reaches this point then all American pipelines will be contaminated. The pipeline industry, and Departments of Interior, Energy and Defense are working on a plan to shut down these pipelines before the oil hits the slingshot."

"Any good news to report?" Debra looked down at her hands.

"Well, it looks like the government will close the banks and shut down the capital markets indefinitely."

Maggie jumped in, "How can we tell the American people all that you have told us without causing a panic?"

Karen responded, "If we don't tell them, the panic that would result would be many times greater than if we did. We have a chance to get out in front of the horrendous challenge for America and, if we don't get out in front, there will be anarchy.

"We have to be straightforward with the American people, tell them the facts and let them know we're working on trying to find solutions.

"So I suggest that we start writing down the top points and key messages in bullet statements. After, we'll go back and decide how much detail we want to add. Let's get started."

"Ma'am, I think we need to define the attacker. For now, it wasn't a government-sponsored organization; it was a terrorist organization called the Brotherhood of the Red Nile."

"I agree. Let's move on." Maggie continued, "Indicate what was damaged, how it was damaged and the outcome."

Bill broke in, "Mrs. Jordan, we can't tell the American people that some fifty-four thousand people were annihilated by a nuclear bomb."

Deb chimed in, "I agree with Bill."

Karen responded, "The death toll is already being reported by the media. If the president doesn't tell the American people the truth about what has happened, the first question at a press conference will be, 'Mr. President, is it true that over fifty-four thousand people were killed by a nuclear blast in Texas City? And if so, why did you hide it from the American people? Do you think they can't handle the truth?'" Everyone saw the logic.

"Okay, let's move on to another point. The pipelines are contaminated and Departments of Interior, Energy and Defense are carrying out plans to stop the flow as quickly as they can."

Deb responded, "Then stopping the flow of contaminated oil is a positive, yes?"

Karen agreed, "But we will then have thousands of miles of pipelines contaminated with radioactive energy and no way to get rid of it. We could have millions of gallons of contaminated oil, trillions of cubic feet of natural gas and millions of gallons of gasoline, jet fuel and other refined products stuck in the ground sending radiation up from the ground to hundreds of cities in Texas. If we can't stop the flow it will be all over America and the ground will be contaminated, perhaps for decades."

"So ma'am, we're toast, in a matter of speaking. In fact, we may be burnt toast and none of us will need a night light because we will all glow in the dark."

Karen laughed aloud. It was a sparkling mirth that made the others chortle as well. "For the first time today, Bill, you made me smile and giggle.

I can't tell you how much I needed that relief." The first lady stopped pacing and sat down.

It is now 6:45 PM and the radioactive tsunami is 12 miles from Houston, Texas.

CHAPTER 20

Pipeline Conference Call

Secretary Findley took over the call for a moment from General Powell. "We'll get back to the plan, General Powell, in just a moment. I did want to address the issue of the losses incurred by all of you that have to have your pipelines shut down, perhaps for many years or, worst case, permanently unusable.

"Let me say that the government is studying the possibility of purchasing your right of ways, including your pipelines, under eminent domain. I don't have any details but you need to know that we're concerned about your losses and will try to compensate you. With that, let me turn the call back to General Powell."

"Thank you, Mr. Secretary. Ladies and gentlemen, we need to shut down all the contaminated pipelines and prevent the clean pipelines from becoming contaminated. I know that many of you have indicated that you do not have the personnel to shut down all of your compressors and pumps. Clearly, what we have is a logistical problem. We need men and equipment to quickly start the process of shutting them down. Right now, I have one hundred thousand military personnel. Between all branches, we have over five thousand helicopters with pilots. If we need more, I can get more.

"So here is the question. If I can start deploying men and machines in two hours, where should we start?"

"General Powell, as was said before, we can start the trunk line shutdown in about one hour. It will take a while for the momentum to take hold but I think we can stop the flow in about two hours. While we are shutting down, we have to shut down the other end of the lines by shutting down the wells. By shutting down the wells, we will not put any pressure on the energy in the pipeline. If we time it right, we should be able to start shutting the inline valves in about two and a half hours. By closing these valves, we will isolate the contaminated portion of the pipeline thereby protecting the balance of the pipeline. I think the same will be true with the smaller pipelines."

"So, where do I start with the smaller pipelines?"

"General, this is Bud Kessler. I think we have to do the same thing the trunks are doing. We need to shut down the compressor stations at some point past the contamination area and at the source: the pumps at the wells. As best I can recollect, shutting down the compressor station is a matter of throwing the main power switch. Therefore, we'll have two teams or however many we need at each end of each pipeline and they'll start working towards the middle. As soon as they shut down a compressor station, they'll fly the pipeline looking for the next."

Another voice chimed in, "General, this is Dan Matthews and, like Bud Kessler, I run a line. In many cases, these lines run in parallel down a right of way so the same team could be shutting down several compressor stations at the same time. They have locks on the power boxes so you'll need to bring some strong bolt cutters and a whole bunch of new locks to secure the compressors."

"I have another question. I have military personnel and equipment all over the State of Texas. Where do I start to deploy my men and equipment?"

"General, if I may." A new voice entered the discussion.

"Ladies and gentlemen, let me introduce Secretary of the Interior, William Summons."

"Thank you, General Powell. I might be able help answer that question. The Bureau of Land Management is responsible for plotting the exact location of the beginning and ending of every pipeline in the United States regardless of what it is carrying. We can very quickly break the south and southwest area of Texas into regions.

"General, we don't have to cover the entire state just the regions we have identified. We can give you the information and you can immediately start deploying personnel to Houston, Austin and San Antonio. These three cities will be staging areas, and hundreds of teams can fan out and start shutting down compressor stations and well pumping stations."

"Thank you, Mr. Secretary. Do all of you think this will work?"

"By God, let's at least try, I'm in." The rest of the owners all agreed.

Summons wanted to say a couple of more things.

"People, please, the Secretary wants to make a couple of other points.

"Thank you General. The teams will shut down all pipelines in the contaminated areas. We will use our best efforts to contact the owners but, if we can't find them, they are still going to be shut down. We need status reports every time a pipeline is shut down. The team leader will send us an e-mail and we will update a map that will be sent to all team leaders.

"New assignments will come from the joint task force of the Departments of Interior and Defense. If you have questions, please e-mail them to this secured address. Please write it down and never forget it: SaveAmerica@energy.gov. Now, let's go and STOP THAT DAMN OIL!"

It is now 7:15 PM and the radioactive tsunami is six miles from
Houston, Texas

CHAPTER 21

St. James Hospital

Deputy Fire Chief for Hazardous Materials Jones had just got off the phone with Ted Baker of Homeland Security in Washington, DC. He had called DHS a short while ago and spoke with Mr. Baker about the concern both he and Dr. Smith, of the hospital, had about the elevated millrems level in the ambulance and the level in the hospital. Both the chief and the doctor were trying to figure out the source of the radiation.

Baker told Jones, "We think the radiation is coming from the pipelines buried underground and is seeping its way through the dirt and concrete."

"Chief, has the level changed since we talked?"

"I don't know. Let me get Dr. Smith on the line with us." Jones dialed the hospital emergency room number and asked for Dr. Smith. The person answering the phone said, "Hold on, and let me see if I can find him."

"This is Dr. Smith."

"This is Chief Jones. I have Ted Baker from DHS in DC."

"Good afternoon, Dr. Smith. We believe that the source of the radiation is oil, natural gas and other fuels running through the pipelines in your area. The energy is flowing from pipelines in Texas City. We have told Chief Jones, on a confidential basis, that a weapons-grade nuclear device was detonated in Texas City at noon today and that the radiation is seeping through the pipes and contaminating the oil that is flowing through them to La Marque. We're in the process of trying to stop the flow through Texas City, but right now the most important thing for us is to know is if the level of millrems increased above 400."

"Let me check. Hold on."

"Dr. Smith to EMT."

"EMT to Dr. Smith," the radio crackled to life.

"Can you give me a reading on the millrems on your badges?"

"One moment, Doc. They range from 401 to 410."

"Hold on for a moment." He turned back to his phone. "They report the level is 401 to 410."

"Excellent!" said Chief Jones. "Everything I've read is that the human body can handle up to 550 millrems without damage as long as it's not for a prolonged period of time. Doc, I think you're good to go. Bring those brave pilots in and treat them. I want you to check the radiation level in the hospital every hour and if it goes to five hundred call me right away. I think the ground will shield you and keep the level manageable. Doc, one more question. Do you know if there are any pipelines above the ground in the area near the hospital?"

"Not that I'm aware of. I'll ask around and if I hear of any, I'll let you know."

"Thanks, Doc."

Ted Baker stepped in. "Chief Jones, I wanted to let you know we have a satellite that is using infrared technology to track the flow and the intensity of the contaminated oil. I promise to keep you informed if we see any changes."

"Thank you, Mr. Baker. I really appreciate your help."

Baker would need to report to Williams that a town within ten miles of Texas City had a millrems reading that is relatively safe. He would need to tell the Secretary that the depth of the pipeline is an effective suppressor of the radiation. He thought that General Powell's plan to dispatch teams to shut down the pumps, compressors and closing the valves would be more dangerous because the pipes going into and out of the pumps and compressors did not have the shielding of the earth. Not only would the teams have to act quickly, they would have to be rotated in order to control the amount of their radiation exposure. The critical points would be the lines leading to Texas City and the lines coming out; these would be the most dangerous.

Baker thought, *We have to find a massive quantity of suits to protect the people around the pipes; OSHA can help with solving the problem. I need to talk with Under Secretary Williams.* He put in the call.

"It's Ted Baker. Can Mr. Williams see me right away?" He paused. "Excellent, I'll be right there."

It is now 7:15 PM and the radioactive tsunami is six miles from Houston, Texas

CHAPTER 22

Williams' Office

Williams was sitting at his desk and his wife Ellen, who had left work early at Frank's request to be near him, was sitting on the couch across from him.

"Ellen, I need you to do something for us now."

"What do you need to be done that has to be done right now?" she asked.

"I think the president will tell the American people tonight that he is closing the banks for some unspecified period of time. I don't know how much cash we have on hand at the house, do you?"

"Well I don't know for sure but I would guess about two hundred dollars at the most."

"I don't think that's enough, because buying things will get more difficult, and cash will be essential. Our ATM card will allow us to take up to one thousand a day. So, could you go to the ATM and take out a thousand and come back here?"

"It's after five. Will they let me back into the building?" Ellen stood.

"I'll have Marie check with security just to be sure you can get back in."

"I don't want to leave you," she said as she picked up her purse.

"I understand, but we need money to buy food and gas. I really need you to do this for us."

"Have Marie make the call now to make sure I can get back in once I leave. I won't leave till I know I can get back in to be with you."

"I'll call right now."

Marie called to confirm that security had assured her Mrs. Williams could return to her husband.

Ellen walked over to Frank. "Hold me. I'm afraid."

Frank closed the door to his office, slowly walked to his wife, and gently put his arms around her. He feels her fear. He tried to separate himself from her, but she just pulled him back to her.

"This is very important," he put a hand up to her cheek. "You need to be strong and do this for us."

Ellen finally pulled away from Frank. She looked more self-confident and fixed her blouse where Frank ruffled it. She looked him straight in the eyes and said, "When I get back I'm going to have a purse full of money, and I just might let you unbutton my blouse."

Frank responded with a light pat on her butt. "I'd enjoy that and I know you would too." He gently kissed her on the lips and sent her on her way to get them some cash. He stood in the doorway and watched her walk away, hoping that she would be ok. She stopped twice to look back and smile at him.

Frank spied Ted Baker in the hall on his way to give him an update. Williams continued watching Ellen as Baker slipped into his office.

When Williams came back in, he saw Baker and was abruptly returned to reality: Baker filled him in on the satellite tracking, the radiation level in La Marque, as well as the challenges regarding the pipeline shutdown and how to protect the soldiers, who are shutting down the pumping and compressor stations. Williams said he would call General Powell and the Secretary of Health and Human Services to see if OHSA could assist.

With all the updates out of the way, Baker wanted to talk about another issue. "Sir, I understand that there are discussions about closing the capital and commodity markets as well as the banks and that there is even a possibility the president might declare martial law effective immediately."

"It's a real possibility, Ted. In fact, the AG is strongly recommending it. He feels that the local police forces are not strong enough to handle the chaos that will probably follow the president's announcements. He's concerned that the despair will be greater than the fear that gripped the country on 9-11. The fear on 9-11 dissipated after a few days. I agree with the AG that, this time, the fear persist for some time."

"Sir, I agree with you and understand. Furthermore, we have to be prepared for another attack. I have given you my best assessment of the data, specifically that I think Lake Charles is the most likely target for the second bomb, if there is one.

"Sir, my greatest fear is that we are expending a tremendous amount of resources in dealing with the first bomb. Should there be a second bomb, I'm not sure the people involved with the first bomb can handle a second one. Look at all the cabinet resources we have expended just to deal with the first bomb, and we know there are many issues we have not even begun to address, including money, markets, employment, international relations, just to name a few.

"My point, sir, is I'm not sure our country can stand another bomb."

"Ted, unfortunately we have no choice in the matter. I'm afraid that we will find out if we truly are the home of the brave."

It is now 7:15 PM and the radioactive tsunami is six miles from Houston, Texas

CHAPTER 23

Headed Home

General Thomas strolled into the cabin to sit with the president. "Sir, may I sit?"

"Anytime, General."

"Sir, we're about thirty minutes from Andrews and I have just received some information that I believe will make all of us very happy."

"I could certainly use some good news."

"Mr. President we took this plane because it could go higher and faster than the 747. You recall that in the hangar we all changed into these flight suits?"

"Yes I do, so what's the good news?"

"Sir, these suits are made of the same material that astronauts' EVA suits are made of. These suits are rated four thousand millrems."

"So that means we're not going to die?"

"Well, sir, yes, we will all die someday, but not from the radiation dosage we all received today. Some of us, including you, sir, may have had our thyroid exposed if we didn't have the suit zipped up to the proper height, but thyroid problems can be treated easily."

"General, thanks for the best news for all of us today. If you don't mind, I would still like to talk with the crew when we land."

"Not a problem, sir."

"General, can you get my wife on the line? She's one of the few people who knew of our flight."

"I'll patch her through right away."

"Another thing. Is it possible on board to put those pictures on a DVD? I'd like to take them with me, if possible."

"Yes, sir. You will have them on landing."

The phone rang in the first lady's office and an aide answered.

"I have the President of the United States for the first lady. Is she there?"

"Yes, one moment please."

"This is Karen." The first lady wasn't paying attention, as her mind was working on her husband's address to the Nation.

The voice on the other end was not totally clear: "I love you and I'm on my way home."

She snapped to. "I love you too and I'm thrilled you're safe. When do you think you will be here?"

"I hope to be with you by 8:15 – just enough time for a kiss, a hug, and a squeeze and then I have to meet with the cabinet at 8:30 PM. How is my speech coming along?"

Karen breathed a sigh of relief. "We'll have a strong working draft for you by the time you arrive."

"Excellent. Is it straightforward and truthful?"

She smiled. "It's the best we can do, based on what we know. You'll have to probably make some changes, but hopefully not too many so you can spend some time reworking it for your style."

"You are my rock, dear. Thanks for all your help. I'll see you soon. I love you."

"I love you, Nathan." Karen smiled again, hung up, and turned to her speech-writing team. "Let's get this done for him so he will have one less thing to worry about. Let me read what we have so far."

"My fellow Americans, many messages have been delivered to the American people from this Oval Office – both good and bad news. As president, I have the responsibility to tell you all of it. Abraham Lincoln sat in this very building and sent regular messages to the American people. At the beginning of the Civil War, most tidings were bad, but later, when it appeared that as a nation we were surviving the awful war, his messages were full of hope and promise.

"Likewise, Wilson and Roosevelt spoke of great devastation and in turn great victory for America and Americans. I realize that the hour is late for many of you, but I could not make this address until I had as many facts as we could gather in order to speak openly and honestly to all Americans.

"At approximately noon today, terrorists, using a weapons-grade nuclear device, attacked the City of Texas City, Texas. This nuclear device was a weapon of mass destruction both in terms of immensity of human casualties and wide-scale obliteration of physical infrastructure.

"This is the first attack on America and on American soil in over twenty years. It is also the first nuclear attack on American soil. America has paid a high price. To the best of our knowledge, no resident of Texas City survived the attack. The casualty estimates for this attack are in excess of fifty-five thousand lives. It is hard for me to believe that so many people—innocent women, children and men—were killed in a matter of moments.

"The four refineries in Texas City were the targets and they were destroyed. The town is strewn with debris covered by radioactive material. The pipelines running through the disaster area have contaminated oil, natural gas and other fluids running through them at this moment. The pipeline owners and operators, along with our Departments of Energy, Interior and Defense are diligently working to close down these pipelines to stop the flow of contaminated energy and in turn limit the damage. We are closing several other Texas refineries until we can be assured that no contaminated oil has gotten through.

"A disaster of this magnitude will have significant repercussions in the stock, bond, commodity and futures markets on a global basis; therefore I have ordered all exchanges in the United States to be temporarily closed until we can sort out all the issues this disruption in the flow of energy has caused to our country and our financial system. I realize that some will say that I'm taking away the free markets, but I have to be concerned about all the people, not just the traders. Protecting the remaining infrastructure will be vital as we recover and move on from this horrendous disaster.

"For the foreseeable future, the banks will be closed. I'm working with the Chairman of the Federal Reserve and the Secretary of the Treasury to work out an orderly reopening. We know the free flow of money will be important to the recovery and growth of the economy.

"Lastly, I must think about the safety of all Americans. Sadly, there are elements in our country who will prey on the weak and the poor. Therefore, to protect all Americans I will impose, with the cooperation of the attorney general and state and local law enforcement, martial law with a curfew of 6 PM to 6 AM until further notice. Only those with public health and safety responsibilities will be allowed to move about during the curfew.

"Let me make it clear to all who can hear me. There is no evidence that this attack was supported by any nation state. We believe it to be the act of a small group of terrorists called the Brotherhood of the Red Nile.

"Over her long history, America has faced many adverse times. We have to come out on the other side a stronger nation and people because of it. I believe we are again being tested as to our resolve to be the last, best hope of the world. From time to time I will speak to you about the progress we are making. By working together, we will be a stronger nation. I ask that you pray with me – to God, Allah, or Jehovah – by whatever name you call the Deity, and beseech the blessing on America and her people."

Bill stopped reading. "Open, honest, shows a plan to respond and protect America. What do you think ma'am?"

The first lady smiled. "Bill, Deb, Maggie you did a great job." She says again with great pride, "Great job. I believe he will be pleased."

It is now 7:30 PM and the radioactive tsunami is four miles from Houston, Texas

CHAPTER 24

The First Switch is thrown

Red Collins held a brief board meeting by phone, telling the members, "For the good of the country we have to shut down and we have to do everything we can to help the other owners and operators to shut down, also."

The Department of Energy asked Red if they could install a Skype camera so Red could show them the process. "We already have Skype in our system so give us your number and we'll patch you in so you can see what we're doing."

Red responded, "Our team is waiting on the infrared images from the satellite to pinpoint the compressors and valves to shut down. You can see this is a giant control room; it is awash with lights, gauges, and monitors giving us feedback as to what is going on in the pipeline. To me, it has always looked like a NASA launch command center. As you can see here, each compressor and valve has three switches under its location; the lights are red, green, and yellow.

"This control room is indeed massive, almost impossible to see from end to end. As we pan down the control board, you can see there are ten operator stations. Each station is responsible for about fifteen to twenty feet of control panel. One operator is responsible for watching over and monitoring all the lights and gauges at his station, which covers about two hundred and fifty miles of pipeline.

"I can never remember a time in all my years with the company that I have ever seen any significant numbers of lights that were red." Red panned the tiny camera. "We are logging on to the web site of the

Department of the Interior. You can see they have highlighted our trunk line, showing how extensive the contamination is at the moment. The satellite image shows where we should start and finish in order to stay in front of the contamination.

"If the energy is running at about six miles per hour, that means it's traveling about ten feet per second and, even though the compressor has to push it along at six miles an hour, it has significant momentum on its own. The hills and the valleys will influence the speed at which it will stop, so we should start in the middle and the end closest to the source of the energy to shut down. We will shut the pumps at the wells first and we'll also want to shut down the compressor that is closest to the middle of the section. As soon as we see the speed of the oil start to drop to about one mile per hour on this gauge we will quickly shut the valve closest to the well.

"The motor on top of the valve will start closing it very slowly and when the gate is fully seated in the bottom of the valve it will act as a backstop as the product sloshes around, keeping the contaminated oil from going into the wells. I don't know how the guys with natural gas wells will stop the flow; they will have different challenges. Let's throw the first switch. The light goes to red; the rest is repetition.

"The process starts to happen quickly, shutting down the compressors and pumps in what is estimated to be about two hundred miles of pipeline. On average, you have a compressor station every fifteen to twenty miles, depending on the terrain, so we have about fourteen compressor stations to shut down and probably six valves."

Red decided that he needed to talk to his chief engineer off line so he said that he was going to step outside for a moment. He signaled Fred Roberts to join him. They stepped outside and Red looked Fred in the eye and said, "We have to shut down the whole damn pipeline, don't we?"

"Well, we have nothing coming up from the wells so we have to continue to shut down the compressor stations and close the valves for the entire length of our two thousand five hundred mile pipeline. "We will have two hundred miles of contaminated energy and no way to get rid of it and two thousand three hundred miles of empty pipe once we pump it all out."

Red sighed, "I guess tomorrow we'll become an oil exploration company with two thousand three hundred miles of empty pipe."

"My guess is that it will take three weeks or perhaps more for us to empty the pipeline and then this whole company is out of work and I hope all the lights in the country aren't RED."

It is now 8 PM and the radioactive tsunami has reached
the outskirts of Houston, Texas

CHAPTER 25

Ten Minutes Out From Andrews

The Gulfstream was about ten minutes from landing and the president had on a headset so he could talk to all personnel in the aircraft. "Thank you for being part of this historic journey and for risking your lives so I could see the site where so many Americans tragically died. The images of the destruction and our near miss to become part of that destruction will remain with me for not only the rest of my term or terms as president but for the rest of my life.

"Now I must go back to the White House and prepare for what is probably the most difficult address any American president has ever had to make. Thank you for taking me and bringing me back safely. May God bless you and your families for the rest of your lives; America can never repay you for your courage and your valor."

Within a few minutes of the president's remarks, the plane landed at Andrews and all of them got out of their flight suits and departed the plane, now parked in the hangar. The president was dressed as before and, with one person accompanying him, they sped away not to the Georgetown football field, but directly to the White House. No words were spoken in the car in the short drive because both the president and his driver, William Rummels, knew the almost impossible task facing the president. The black SUV pulled up at the side entrance of the White House, the gate opened and the car pulled up to the same side door through which the president had left just four hours earlier. As he stepped through the door, he realized that he was not the same man. He was unsure of what he had to do and say for the American people.

When he reached the Oval Office, he asked his executive assistant, "Where is my wife working at the moment?"

"Sir, I believe the first lady is in her office."

"Please call her and tell her I'm on my way. I want to meet with her and the team to discuss the speech."

"Right away, Mr. President.

Mary called up. "The president is on his way to the first lady's office. Please notify her."

An aide knocked on the door and advised, "Ma'am, the president is on his way up to see you."

Karen Jordan felt her heart skip a beat and her pulse quickened when she heard he was on the way. In moments, he came through the door. She couldn't help herself, she jumped up, went over and put her arms around Nathan and gave him what seemed to all present a rather passionate kiss. She cried as she kissed him.

The president held her tenderly, pulling her in close. He returned her kiss with more control than his wife did.

The first lady's staffers weren't sure what to do, should they leave and wait to be called back or just sit there while the warm, passionate, and intimate display continued between the most powerful man in the world and his wife.

The president solved their dilemma with a smile. "As much as I would like to go someplace with you and continue this in private, we have a great deal of work to do and not much time to get it done.

"Maggie, I need you to work with the White House Press Secretary to get time on all the networks at 11:30 PM. We need to have everything on cable shut down so that the maximum number of Americans can hear my message. The same goes for radio. If there is a ball game, it must be interrupted."

"Mr. President, what do we say when they ask us about the message? Will there be a release to the press before the speech?"

"Your response is that we have a national security crisis that goes beyond 9-11. There will be no handout before the message. We will hand out a transcript afterwards. I want to make this very clear: no exceptions. Those that do not cooperate will be exposed. Understood?"

"Yes, sir."

"Now, I understand that you have a draft of my message to the people. I want to ask your opinion on an item or two that should be included. If we decide not to use what I'm about to tell you then you cannot disclose it to anyone. Am I clear on that?"

"Yes, sir."

"A little over four and a half hours ago, I boarded a Gulfstream jet that took me to Texas City, Texas. I had to see firsthand what the devastation looks like when fifty-four thousand Americans die in a matter of seconds. The plane was able to shoot images of the horror and the destruction.

"My questions are: should I tell the American people in my message that I have been there and witnessed firsthand the loss of life and destruction and, second, should I show them selected images of the carnage?"

Karen, Maggie, Deb and Bill just sat there in their chairs. It was if they were frozen in time.

The president intervened. "We can't sit here all evening in a catatonic state. We have to make a decision. So, people, give me your best advice."

Karen was the first to answer. "If you give America the message at 11:30 PM then most children will be in bed. The images, however, will be the story for days on end and children will see them eventually. It seems to me that we need to select images that convey the destruction but not show images of bodies being burned."

Maggie added, "Mr. President, I think there is something heroic about the president risking his life to witness the place where tens of thousands of Americans died. I think it should be in the message but somewhat understated."

Deb chimed in, "Mr. President, I would take the other side and suggest that some in Congress and the news media might suggest that this was heroic but perhaps ill-advised. What would happen to the country if something had befallen you during the flight?"

Karen turned to Bill and asked for his thoughts. "Well, ma'am, both issues are important but it seems to me that in our draft we have left a lot of issues on the table. While many Americans will be appalled about the trip, some might just say – and excuse me, Mr. President – 'what a damn fool we have as president of these United States?"

"Thank all of you for your insightful thoughts and ideas. Let me see what you've written so I can review it and see if and how I can work in your thoughts and concerns. Right now, I have the entire cabinet waiting for me in the War Room. Once that's done, I'll look over your draft."

It is now 8:45 PM and the radioactive tsunami is beginning to slow to 5.5mph headed to downtown Houston, Texas

CHAPTER 26

The Attorney General's Conference Room

Attorney General Drew Clinton had called a meeting for 6:30 PM in his conference room to prepare for the 8:30 PM cabinet meeting with the president and full cabinet. Clinton had made the recommendation to the president and the cabinet that the president, in his message to the people, declare martial law and set a curfew from dusk to dawn. The AG had been thinking that it is easy to declare both but very difficult to enforce them on a national basis.

The last time martial law was declared nationally was by President Franklin Roosevelt, just after the bomb attack on the fleet in Pearl Harbor. The country had one hundred and thirty-two million people in 1940, and today there are over three hundred and forty-two million people. With two and a half times as many people, it's going to be very difficult to enforce.

As he called the meeting to order, he reminded all in attendance that, under Protocol Four, "You must not discuss this meeting at all, other than on a need-to-know basis with personnel having the appropriate security clearance. Nothing can be said until the president and full cabinet have approved a course of action. Are we clear?"

All nodded in agreement. Represented at the meeting were Homeland Security, the Pentagon, the United States Marshals Service, the National Association of Chiefs of Police and the National Association of Police Unions. Clinton thanked them for coming.

"Gentlemen, the United States was attacked at 12 PM central time in the city of Texas City, Texas. To the best of our knowledge, this was an attack by a new terrorist group operating out of the Middle East called the Brotherhood of the Red Nile. We believe they used a nuclear device purchased on the black market to attack the oil refineries in Texas City. Thousands of Americans were killed and the pipelines running through and around the city were contaminated. The Departments of the Interior and Energy are currently working with the pipeline companies to shut down the flow of oil, natural gas and refined product like gasoline and jet fuel that run through Texas City. We have determined that the flows go in many different directions. We have about seventy-two hours before the flow reaches a section of pipeline in Oklahoma called the 'slingshot'. It is from there that the contaminated oil and gas will be sent to every section of the United States.

"The president has a recommendation to close the capital markets and the banks indefinitely. When Al-Qaeda attacked New York, the capital markets were closed for about six days. The last time that banks were closed was in the Depression, and then it was for fourteen days. I do not know how long the country will be disrupted. The longer it goes unchecked, the more violent I believe it will get. I'm open to ideas, suggestions, and comments."

Ed Murphy of the National Association of Police Unions suggested, "Sir, I don't think we have enough police officers to enforce martial law on a national basis. Based on Hurricane Katrina, there will be a significant increase in crime, especially theft. If people can't get money to buy food, they will steal whatever they can to get food for themselves and their families. The local markets, and then the super markets, will all be stripped of their stock, and when that is gone – if we are still in trouble – people will turn on each other. We can't stop the looting in the stores but we will give top priority to preserving order in the neighborhoods."

William Merchant, head of the U.S. Marshals Service, added, "If we don't have food for the inmates in all the prisons, I would expect to see riots in the prison populations across America. If guards can't get gas for their cars, then they can't get to work to keep the prisons secure. We could be looking at anarchy on a national basis. The only way to keep the lid on is to turn over security to local police and the military."

"I don't know how much of the military we can deploy in addition to the police. While we do have MPs and SPs, I'm sure we don't have enough to help patrol the entire nation."

"General, the military can work with local law enforcement to patrol the streets at night under the curfew. I think their presence will go a long way toward keeping order," AG Clinton pointed out.

"If I'm going to deploy troops, we'll have to move quickly. It will take some time to get them transported. Almost half of the total population of the United States is counted in the top twenty metropolitan areas in the country. As part of our simulations for a national security event, we created a list of those top twenty zones and identified military bases in the vicinity of each one. As soon as the president speaks, we will dispatch up to a full battalion to the center of each city, depending on its size, where the Chief of Police will take control of their placement and any requests for more troops. Once we have the top twenty secure then we can move down to the next twenty and so on till we have at least seventy-five percent of the country under control."

AG Clinton said to the room, "I will want three to four reserve units set aside with equipment that can be deployed to a hot spot on very short notice and I want a detachment of U.S. Marshals stationed with these reserve forces so they can school the troops on how they should perform if called up."

"We can do that and have them located within three hours of any one of the top twenty areas."

"So, on the 'to do' list is for Homeland Security to get to Department of Defense the most current list of the top forty metropolitan areas. General Cutter will liaise with the units closest to each area and let the Chief anchor the locations so he can contact the local police chiefs. The general will also get in contact with Ed Smith of the U.S. Marshals Service to assign teams to the reserve force's location. I have to go to a cabinet meeting shortly, at which I will report our progress. Are there any issues I have missed?"

"Sir, if I may ask, how long do you think we will be deployed?"

"General, I wish I knew the answer to your question. There are issues out of our control that will have an impact on how long the forces will be on duty. I never thought in my lifetime that I would ever hear the words; 'America is under martial law'.

It is now 8:45 PM and the radioactive tsunami is beginning to slow
to 5.5 mph headed to the middle of Houston, Texas

CHAPTER 27

The Secretary of State and the Chairwoman of SEC

In the Secretary of State's conference room were Secretary of State Michelle Borders and the Chairwoman of the SEC, Mary Margret Kelly. On the phone was the Chairman of the NYSE, William Bryant; The American Stock Exchange, Thomas Ruff; the Chairwoman of the Chicago Mercantile Exchange, Pamela Cave Smith; and, Terrance Crown, Chairman of NYMEX.

"Thank you for attending on such short notice. Chairwoman Kelly and I have to discuss some very important issues with you and we don't have a great deal of time. At 12 noon central time today terrorists from an organization called the Brotherhood of the Red Nile attacked America." Borders saw the expressions on their faces as she imparted the full details of the disastrous attack. Apart from her voice, the room was silent.

"The cabinet has supported a recommendation to the president by the attorney general to close the capital markets initially for at least a week. This meeting is taking place concurrently with meetings of cabinet secretaries, their staff and key resources. A full cabinet meeting is scheduled for 8:30 PM with the president.

"We have little time to come up with a plan to notify our partners and try to minimize the impact on the global capital markets. I realize that other markets might try to stay open but we are the largest trading markets in the world and, if we shut down, we need to try to convince the other institutions to follow our direction."

SEC Chairwoman Kelly added, "I realize this will be a devastating disruption to the capital markets, but during the Great Depression all the banks were closed with a bank holiday. I propose that we declare one and get our trading partners to declare a capital markets holiday."

"Madam Chairwoman, this is Bill Bryant, do you have any idea how long the market holiday might take?"

"Bill, I wish I could offer some realistic expectations. The critical issue, as I understand it is the flow of the contaminated oil and gas and other product in the pipeline. Kelly explained the implications and saw initial disbelief change to growing comprehension regarding the potential magnitude of the contamination.

Thomas Ruff of the CME group asked, "Are we talking about the potential contamination of the entire United States?"

"Yes, sir, sadly, I am."

"Madam Secretary, how do you propose to notify the governments about our decision to close the capital markets in the U.S.?"

"In my conversations with the president I have proposed that I call the major players just before the president goes on the air tonight. Unfortunately, the markets will be open in some countries while closed in others, including ours.

"We need to complete a top ten list of the most important countries that I need to call. I'm looking for your recommendations right now."

"Madam Secretary, I would start with the biggest markets in the world, with particular attention of the movement of the trading day. Thus, I would start with, not in any order of importance, but following the trading day: The European Union, the United Kingdom, India, China, Japan, and Australia.

"I would be hard pressed to come up with four more. I understand that there are many other markets around the world, but these six probably have a significant impact the rest. With the big markets closed the smaller markets will have no place to trade and will follow the lead of the top six."

"Madam Secretary, I think each of us would gladly help by calling our counterparts in the six countries after you have made your calls. Have you thought about how you want to call the heads of state?"

Michelle responded, "I'm not sure what you mean."

"Let's suppose you call the President of the European Commission and he wants to talk about other things. He may well burn up all your time before the president speaks and you don't get to the other five."

"What do you suggest?"

"Madam Secretary, why not have one of your undersecretaries set up a conference call with you for let's say 11:30 PM. Let them know it's an extremely important call concerning national security throughout the world and let them know that leaders from the five countries plus the EU will be on the call. By doing it that way, you speak to all of them at the same time and nobody will feel jilted, especially when they hear what you have to say."

"Excellent suggestion, and I can tell each one that the president will speak with him or her as soon as possible."

"If I might, madam Chairwoman ..."

"Who is asking, please?"

"I'm sorry, ma'am, this is Ruff from CME. The one big challenge is going to be the price of oil. As you know, most of the oil is traded in the futures markets. If we have the kinds of problems you're talking about, the swings in the prices of oil and perhaps other related commodities could be devastating. I think we should shorten limits and encourage other exchanges to also shorten their limits on commodity contracts so as to limit some of the losses and at the same time limit the speculative profits on the up side."

Kelly nodded. "How do you other exchange heads feel about limits on the price movements when trading resumes?"

The line went quiet for a while and then several exchange heads commented that the sooner they could get back to the free flow of orders with reasonable limits, the better off America would be globally.

"All right, then." Kelly was taking notes. "Given the circumstances, I could support temporary tighter limits and I would support trying to convince the exchanges outside the U.S. to consider the same restrictions. If we get the European Union on our side, I think everyone will follow suit. Anybody disagree?"

Secretary of State Borders took over the call to remind all the participants that, "Protocol Four is in effect, "No one is to discuss any of this until I get the go ahead from the president. If you hear the president speaking on television tonight about this then you know to make your calls. I have to head to a cabinet meeting and I will relay your recommendations. I would like you to stay on the line with Chairwoman Kelly to determine who is going to call whom. Thank you for your time and valuable input."

It is now 8:45 PM and the radioactive tsunami is beginning to slow to 5.5 mph headed to the middle of Houston, Texas

CHAPTER 28

Secretary of the Treasury and Chairman of the Federal Reserve

Porter Smyth of Treasury and Christopher Mitchell, the Chairman of the Federal Reserve, were in Smyth's conference room try and shore up the monetary system in the country. On Smyth's conference phone were the board members of the Federal Reserve System as well as the heads of the twelve regional Federal Reserve Banks across the United States.

Smyth began, "Gentlemen, the president will be having a cabinet meeting in about two hours. It has been recommended and supported by the cabinet that effective sometime tonight all banking institutions in the United States will be closed until further notice."

Shouts could be heard over the speakerphone: "that's outrageous; is he crazy? Does he know what could happen on a global basis? How will people pay their bills, cash their checks and buy food? Does that include ATMs?"

Porter let them rant briefly and then stepped in. "Enough! Now let me tell you why. Our job is, in less than two hours, to determine how we can support the president. You've all heard about the explosions today in Texas."

The phone speaker suddenly went quiet.

"The explosions were caused by a nuclear device. Radioactive oil, natural gas and other types of energy are traveling through the pipelines in all directions. We have about sixty hours to stop and isolate this energy to keep it from going to the oil slingshot in Oklahoma. If it makes it into the slingshot, within a day the entire pipeline network in America will become worthless. Now, you know why the president wants to close the banks; he wants to avoid a 1932-style run on the banks from happening today."

Mitchell spoke up, "If the supply of money stops then, in a simple way, how do average Americans and, in the bigger picture, governments at all levels, including the federal government, pay their bills?"

Porter suggested, "We have over fifty million Americans who get checks from the government. A large proportion of these people need this money to survive. Businesses large and small need money to pay their employees and the government needs tax revenue to run the government. With no money in circulation, we are headed to a depression greater than the Great Depression."

Christopher was thinking aloud, "The first thing is we are thinking in terms of dollars, greenbacks. Porter, do we have any idea how long this might last?"

"To the best of my knowledge a great deal will depend on preventing the oil from moving into the slingshot. Now, I don't want what I'm about to say to be misunderstood. We can live and survive without Texas oil. If we can keep the radioactive energy confined to Texas, we can work around the problem. But, if we can't contain it, we have some very serious challenges." Porter continued, "Let's suppose we can contain it to Texas. If we could, I suspect we would have to ask all the banks to turn off their ATMs and close their doors for some period of time, perhaps a week to ten days. During that time, we would reroute the Fed wire system around the Texas banks. The other banks would operate as usual but no ATM withdrawals from banks in Texas would be permitted in any part of the country."

Mitchell suggested, "We could send in teams of auditors to look at the Texas banks. We need to figure out loan losses and bankruptcies for individuals, businesses, as well as for governments. Once we can size up the problem we can address how we pay to move those people out of Texas. If the pipelines and the land are contaminated then Texas or some significant portion of Texas is worthless."

Porter pointed out, "You have a Federal Reserve bank in Dallas that could be the focal point for the evaluations. Our recommendations to the president, therefore, are to close the banks until we can find out if we can stop the flow of contaminated oil. If we can stop the oil then we will reopen the banks with ATM restrictions to Texas Banks. The Federal

Reserve Bank of Dallas will be the point in assessing the loan losses and the bankruptcies in affected areas of Texas. We will close down the Fed wire to all Texas banks and Texas branches of national banks outside of Texas. We will present to the president the estimated losses and possible financial solutions to deal with the losses." Porter concluded, "Any other issues?"

Mike Finnegan from the New York Fed spoke. "If I may sir, do we know if any foreign government was involved in the attack on America? Was this an Al-Qaeda attack?"

Mitchell turned to Porter and said over the phone, "To the best of our knowledge this was not a state-sponsored attack. We believe the group that attacked was not Al-Qaeda, but a new group called the Brotherhood of the Red Nile."

"The reason I was asking was to know if we should freeze any bank accounts of the responsible government?"

"We believe that the group came from Syria but they had no connection to the Syrian government." Porter again reminded that he and Mitchell had an 8:30 cabinet meeting with the president. "We both thank you for your valuable insight and help. It's likely to be a long night. I suggest you look for the president to speak at 11:30 PM tonight; then you'll know what you're doing tomorrow."

It is now 8:45 PM and the radioactive tsunami is beginning to slow to 5.5 mph headed to the middle of Houston, Texas

CHAPTER 29

Ellen's Terror

Ellen Williams had just undertaken the task of leaving Frank's office at Homeland Security, of finding the ATM down the street and taking out as much money as the machine would allow.

Frank was concerned that they didn't have enough cash on hand to buy food or gas, so he had asked her to go and get them some money. This seemed a simple enough project to Frank, but he failed to see just how unstable Ellen was at the news of the attack. When they talked about the possibility of this happening some time ago, she had panicked. Frank had never seen her behave this way before, but as time passed she seemed fine and to have adjusted to the fear, or so Frank thought. Ellen was very reluctant to leave, but Frank convinced her it was simple enough and was just a short walk, that she would come right back and then they would be together again.

As Ellen walked down the hall she stopped several times and turned back hoping that Frank would call her back, but he didn't. She went down to security and asked one of the guards, "Can you tell me where the closest ATM is?"

"Yes ma'am, just go out the front door and turn to your left. It's four blocks down; you can't miss it. It's a Bank of America branch. The ATM is just inside the door."

"Thank you."

"You're welcome."

"By the way, I'm Mrs. Frank Williams. He is the Under Secretary for Terrorist Activity."

"Yes ma'am, I remember you from before."

"Will you be here when I get back?"

"I'll be here to 10 PM, and then another shift will take over. Just be sure to wear your pass and swipe it over the scanner and the door will unlock.

"Thank you."

Ellen walked towards the heavy front door and struggled to push open the fifteen-foot-high glass-and-bronze doors. *Why do they have to make these doors so large and heavy?* she wondered. She finally got the door open and the damp cold night air hit her in the face. It was much colder now than when she had arrived at Frank's office. She didn't think she was going that far or be gone that long, so she didn't bring a jacket. She crossed her arms across her chest trying to keep warm.

She started down the street heading towards the Bank of America branch and noticed that there didn't seem to be anybody on the street. She quickened her pace. About a block from Frank's office, she stopped because she thought she heard footsteps. As she started out again, she heard the footsteps, so quickened her pace, glancing at one of the dark store windows to check if somebody was following her. At first, she couldn't see anybody in the window, but just as she started walking again, she was sure she saw a reflected image of somebody in a dark trench coat.

She first thought it was not a coincidence that whoever this was stopped to look in the windows just when she had. The streetlight was burnt out, so it was dark when she reached the second block. At least now she no longer heard the footsteps. She was relieved and thought, *He must have turned off to a side street.* It was still cool, but the adrenaline rush from the fear helped warm her a bit. She increased her speed and then again heard footsteps behind her. Was this someone else or the same person from before? Whoever it was, she wasn't waiting around to find out; she picked up the pace and, just as she did, she spotted a car coming up the street from behind with its lights on low beam and heading right for her.

She was sure they were terrorists coming to capture her and use her for ransom. The car was quite a ways behind her and she knew she couldn't go back. She had to make it to the bank. Ellen was still a block away and saw the car was picking up speed. She bolted and ran for the bank. She was

THE BROTHERHOOD OF THE RED NILE

wearing the wrong shoes for running, but she had no choice. When she picked up the pace, she could see the car also accelerated. She made it to the lobby and used her bankcard to open the door to the ATM center. She hurried inside, and the door locked behind her. The booth was bright and she knew, short of breaking the heavy glass, that at least for now she was safe. She withdrew the maximum of one thousand dollars, put it and the card in her purse and watched the black car slowly go by.

Searching in her purse, she realized her cell phone was back in her office. There was no phone in the ATM booth, so she decided to stay and wait for somebody else to come by.

After a while, nobody came, but she didn't see the black car, either. In fact, she couldn't see anybody on the street. *If I leave the ATM center and walk quickly alongside the buildings and in the shadows, it will be hard to see me.* She waited just a little while longer and then left quickly, crossing the street and keeping close to the buildings. One block gone, then the second, and then the third, and finally she would be at Frank's building. She was just one block from his building when she saw the black car coming towards her again.

She started running to the building. She thought she was safe but couldn't open the door. *Oh God, it's the wrong building! Frank's building is still a block away!* The car was coming closer and, as she finally reached the building, she swiped her card, unlocked the door and rushed inside, desperately looking for the security guard. He was gone and, as he had said, another agent was there. She ran to him and told him what had happened. She pointed to the black car that was pulling away; she was trembling as she spoke, "See? It's that one; that's the car that was following me."

The guard quietly asked, "Ma'am, what black car?"

It is now 8:45 PM and the radioactive tsunami is beginning to slow to 5.5 mph headed to the middle of Houston, TX

CHAPTER 30

Brotherhood of the Red Nile

The Texas City Brotherhood team arrived at the designated hotel, the Comfort Suites Extended Stay in Houston. They stopped on their way to Houston to get a significant amount of food and water for both teams. It was their hope that, if both of the bombs were successful, they might have to stay in Houston for several weeks while America adjusts to its new situation. They would need to devise a plan to get out of the United States, but they couldn't do that until America reacted to its new reality. They had plenty of cash to pay for more food and, for now, the Texas team was just waiting and hoping that their accomplices coming from Louisiana would made it far enough away from the midnight bomb blast to join them safely. It was about 9 PM Louisiana time, so three hours until bomb two would go off.

Sargon had been at the hotel the whole time the teams were traveling to and from their assignments. He had not been passing his time by watching American TV; he had been working on a YouTube video and broadcast network e-mail lists, which were all part of his plan to notify the world that Islam was now in charge. He had found a Wi-Fi café down the street from the hotel, which he would use to upload his video to YouTube and then send his message to all the news outlets and giving them the YouTube video address and explaining why the Brotherhood of the Red Nile set off these first two bombs.

He had spent some time discussing with Adad what the video should say and what images could be downloaded from the Internet to give the communication added impact. Sargon didn't want the message in the video to be full of anger. He wanted it to be as factual as could be. As terrorists, they would have to find a way to frighten America into making the right decisions about its future role when it was no longer a world power

It was Sargon's plan to have the video and e-mail message released within seconds of the time the president began to speak. All the television stations were announcing that the president would be speaking to America at 11:30 tonight on a matter of grave national importance. He had to have the video finished by 11 PM eastern time and uploaded to YouTube by 11:10. It would take some time for YouTube to have the video loaded for broadcast. His e-mail list would be pre-loaded so when he pushed the send button it would flash around the world in seconds.

He knew that it would be impossible to time the release perfectly because the president may not be on time. Sargon decided he would take his smartphone with him and pick up the local radio station on the Internet through his headpiece. He would send his broadcast e-mail as soon as he heard the words "President of the United States".

The leader of the Brotherhood of the Red Nile continued working on the video and took a break to review his draft e-mail one more time. "The two nuclear bombs that exploded in Texas and Louisiana today are the responsibility of the Brotherhood of the Red Nile. We are not part of Al-Qaeda. We are independent of them and we are on a new mission to force America to withdraw from the world stage as the dominant leader, and to help Islam to take a leadership role in governing the world. Go to YouTube and search for Brotherhood of the Red Nile and you will find more information on our small but powerful group."

Sargon was pleased with the draft and believed that the rest of the team would agree. He loaded the list of e-mail addresses and hit 'save.' Now he turned his attention to producing the YouTube video. He wanted no images of any members of the Brotherhood and didn't have enough time to get the photos of the damage in Texas City to load into his video. He wanted the video to convey a message of destruction and fear. It did not have to be totally accurate, but it must convey power and domination over the American government and people.

He started composing the video. Black screen and then this message started to scroll up from the bottom of the screen. "The two nuclear attacks in the United States today in Texas and Louisiana were the responsibility of the Brotherhood of the Red Nile. We are a fundamentalist Islamic organization dedicated to the proposition that Islam should guide the world. We therefore must conquer all non-Islamic nations and convert them to Islam and the Quran. The United States has for many decades taken from all the peoples of the world their riches and made them subservient to the United States. These first two attacks have been focused on America's lifeblood: its oil. Our two bombs have contaminated your oil supply and have made it impossible for you to supply all your people and your economy with enough energy to grow and prosper. You must now choose between your world domination and the survival of your people. We encourage you to choose wisely, for if you make the wrong choice we have more retribution in store for you and your arrogance. Islam is a benevolent religion and once you agree to our terms, Allah will bless you. Ahumduallah, which means, Praise be to God."

Sargon was somewhat concerned that Ishtar and Michael would feel that the message didn't go far enough to strike fear in the hearts and minds of the American people. Nevertheless, they would see what would happen when the second bomb went off in less than three hours. In a matter of days, widespread panic would set in across America.

It is now 9:15 PM and the radioactive tsunami is beginning to slow to 3.5 mph.

CHAPTER 31

Cabinet Meeting in the War Room

Meetings had taken place all over Washington, DC. Each cabinet secretary had conducted meetings with senior staff to discuss the bombing in Texas City, the form of response to be expected from the government, and what the president's talk should include. The meeting was scheduled to start at 8:30 PM, but it was already 8:45 PM and everybody was present except the president. Nathan Jordan had a reputation for always being prompt and, in fact, was usually one of the first to arrive for any meeting. The officials spoke among themselves, speculating why he was late. However, at 8:46, the president walked in with the first lady, which was almost unheard of.

President Jordan knew that some noses were out of joint about this, so he explained that his wife was here because she led the team who had drafted his message to the American people, hopefully to be delivered at 11:30 tonight. "This message is perhaps the most important presidential address since Roosevelt informed America about the bombing of Pearl Harbor. Karen is my confidante and knows everything that has happened from the moment I was notified of the attack. I have always trusted her advice and judgment and I trust her now. There will be no questions or comments on this matter. Let's move on.

"What you are about to see on the monitors around the room is the impact of the bomb that was set off in the heart of Texas City some seven hours ago. These pictures were taken from the plane that took me personally over the site this afternoon." The president heard a rumble of comments.

Finally AG Clinton spoke up, "Sir, you flew to Texas City? You endangered your life and potentially put the leadership of the country in turmoil?"

The president nodded his head to the audio/visual expert in the room and all the monitors came to life with videos and stills of the massive destruction in Texas City. As the horrific images of casualties and fires played on the monitors, someone said, "This must be what Hell is like."

"Mr. Attorney General, fifty-four thousand Americans or more died in a matter of seconds in the first nuclear attack on America. How could I just sit here in DC? How could I face the nation tonight and speak of the destruction without having witnessed it first hand? I realize that I put the crew and myself in serious danger. I asked each one if he understood the potential risk he was taking; a storage tank could have exploded and wiped us out.

"To a man they told me, in so many words, 'Mr. President, I understand why you have to go'. I now hope you also understand why I had to go. We are not here to decide if I made a good choice or a bad choice, but I will tell the American people I went to pay my respects to the innocent victims who died today." He looked around the now silent room. "Let's move on to what we're going to do — as I heard what we repeated in one call today — to stop that damn oil.

"In our meeting of this afternoon, we had a lot of issues on the table. I would like to hear your suggestions for actions we might have to take to deal with this national disaster. I have a lot of catching up to do, so let's start with the Department of Energy."

"Sir, shortly after our last meeting Energy, Interior, and Defense had a conference call with as many of the pipeline companies as we could bring together on short notice. The four major trunk companies have agreed to shut down their pipelines. I'm happy to report that the trunks have reduced the flow of six to seven miles per hour to three and they believe that they will be able to stop the flow through their pipelines in about six hours. General, why don't you take it from here?"

"Sir, the next problem we had to deal with is all the small independent operators. We deployed teams from all branches of the service to fly to the compressor stations and shut them down. We currently have almost seventy-five thousand people and four thousand helicopters shutting down compressors throughout Texas, which is slowing the rate of the oil and gas moving in the pipelines. We have been shutting down compressors and at wellheads. We're turning off pumps to stop the clean energy from flowing into pipelines with contaminated energy. As the energy slows down, we are able to close valves at both ends to isolate the contaminated energy. If I may, sir, I would like to turn the next part over to Interior."

"Sir, I have good news and some very bad news to report. The satellites we use in conjunction with the oil companies to find oil-drilling opportunities, because of their infrared capabilities, can also see the contaminated oil, natural gas and refined products in the ground. When all is said and done, we don't know how many thousands of square miles of land on top of the of pipeline are contaminated but what we can see from space is the growing concentration of land contamination land due to the radioactive energy just sitting in the pipes. The sooner we stop the flow the less soil will become contaminated. Sir, the area from north of Houston all the way to Galveston is contaminated and, based on the images, we think at least twenty miles to the west of Texas City has high levels of radiation. We have no way, nor do we have a place, to move millions of people out of the contaminated area. If we find a place, all the people would have to leave with just the clothes on their backs. They couldn't take anything with them. We don't know the health risks but some scientists are telling us that the potential for deaths due to sustained radioactive contamination could be much greater than the thousands that died in Texas City."

The president held up a hand. "After this meeting, I have another with two Nobel laureates in nuclear science. I intend to bring up the question of evacuation from the contaminated area. I'll let you know what they have to say."

It is now 9:15 PM and the radioactive tsunami is beginning to slow
to 3.5 mph

CHAPTER 32

Frank, Hold Me

Ellen cleared security and rushed to the elevator. The door opened and she jumped in. For a moment, she couldn't remember Frank's floor number. She knew it was on one of the upper levels and pushed 14, 15, and 16. Looking out between the doors she saw somebody clearing security and heading for her elevator. She quickly pushed the 'close' button and the doors shut just before the man reached the door. Just when she felt safe, the doors suddenly opened again, and a man was standing right in front of her. Startled, she quickly stepped to the rear as entered and pressed the button for the 12th floor.

The man turned to her and asked, "Are you okay?"

"I got a little confused," she admitted. "I don't come to my husband's office very often and I wasn't sure what floor to press."

"This whole building is DHS. I work on twelve. What's your husband's name?"

She relaxed a bit when she realized he was with Homeland Security. "My husband is Frank Williams."

"His office is on sixteen. Would you like me to escort you there?"

"I'm fine, thank you. I'll remember his office when I get off."

"I'd be happy to walk with you."

"Thank you for your kindness, but I'm sure I can find my way." The elevator stopped at twelve and the man got off and said, "It was a pleasure to meet you, Mrs. Williams."

"Thank you for your help."

The elevator doors closed, and now she realized that, because she had pushed all the higher buttons, the elevator would stop at every floor on its way to the sixteenth floor. She found herself repeatedly pushing the button for 16, thinking that it would get her to Frank's floor more quickly. The doors finally opened on sixteen and she recognized she was on the right floor. The long hallway would lead her to Frank.

She was about two-thirds of the way down the hall when Frank stepped out of his office, turned and looked down the hallway. Seeing her, he moved quickly to reach her. When they were close Ellen said, "Please hold me right now." As Frank gently put his arms around her, he felt her clutching him in a way she had never done before. Frank had always been sensitive to Ellen's touch or caress, but this time he could feel the trembling not only in her body, but in her soul, as well.

He kept one arm around her and guided her into his office. They went over to the couch and sat. He had one arm around her shoulder and could feel her body relax. He knew she was already starting to feel better. After a few moments, looking to make sure the door was closed, she took his hand in hers and moved it over her heart and kept her hand on top of his. When she did this he felt her whole body gently relax. Frank had the sensation that they were completing an emotional circuit and she now felt safe. They quietly sat there for a while, but when Frank made a move to move from the embrace, she pulled him back to her.

With a little more effort, he pried her grip and asked, "What happened when you went out?" Frank got up, drew up one of the chairs, and turned it so he faced her. He reached out, took both her hands in his, and looked into her eyes, asking, "What happened that frightened you so?"

Ellen took in a deep breath, held it, and exhaled slowly and jaggedly. "Nothing happened, really. I felt somebody was stalking me on foot, then I thought a car was following me. I guess I just panicked. All the things you told me about the bombing and about the thousands of people who were killed … it just overwhelmed me and I lost my nerve. I'm sorry."

"There's nothing for you to be sorry about. After the president gives his address tonight, a lot of people will feel the same way. I was mistakenly insensitive to your reaction at the frightening news, and sent you out on your own. I'm truly sorry I didn't think more about you in my concern for our country."

"Frank, you have to worry about the country. People like you are trying very hard to save this nation, and I'm proud to be your wife. I promise that, if you ask me to do something like this again and I'm afraid, you will hear loud and clear that I don't want to do it. I also realize that this is perhaps the most difficult time in our life, and surely for the Nation. We will be all right, won't we?"

"Ellen, I'm going to do everything I can to protect not only you, but the rest of the country, as well." As Frank looked into her eyes he thought, *I hope that, no matter what happens, we can save as many lives as possible and, given the immensity of the attack, that America can recover.*

"Ellen, I want you to stay here. I have to go to a cabinet meeting with the president. Marie will be here as long as you or I need her. The cafeteria is open all night. Why don't the two of you go have something to eat? But, before you go I want you to come over here."

They walked hand in hand to the closed door. Like before, he pressed her against the door and felt her melt into his body. This time it's different; he wasn't as gentle and neither was she for the fear they both have about what could happen has intensified the passion they feel for each other. Their kiss was hard and passionate, his hand squeezed her breast to the point that she winced and then he let go. She had squeezed him hard but he didn't wince.

They separated, Ellen tucked in her blouse and Frank straightened his pants. They just spent a moment looking into each other's eyes before he opened the door and called for his secretary. "Marie, please accompany my wife to dinner, on the government's tab. I'm off to the White House. Is my car ready?"

"Yes, sir. It's the black sedan downstairs in front of the building."

Ellen was startled upon hearing about the dark vehicle.

It is now 9:15 PM and the radioactive tsunami is beginning to slow
to 3.5 mph

CHAPTER 33

War Room

It was 9:30 and the president had not yet heard from several important cabinet members. Jordan had the scientists to meet with and then he had to work on his Address to the Nation.

"Ladies and gentlemen, I'm not trying to rush you, but I have an address in just about two hours and I need as much information as possible. I suggest we get back to the issues at hand. Make your remarks short and to the point. Let's hear from State."

"Sir, the chairperson of the SEC and the heads of all the exchanges joined me in a conference call to discuss notifications and regulatory interdiction. We have identified the top ten 'must know' leaders of foreign exchanges and we're working on a conference call for approximately 11:25 this evening during which I will read a prepared statement of what you will be saying at approximately 11:30. I will take no questions and I will tell them that President Jordan will be in touch with their respective heads of state within the next twenty-four hours.

"We will send a broadcast message to all our embassies and missions around the world shortly after your address. Those who want to ask questions will be provided the opportunity in a conference call tomorrow."

"What do you expect the responses to be from your ten nations?"

"Sir, I think they all will be very scared, if not outright panicked that, when the markets hear about what is going on in America, the collapse of global markets will wreak havoc with many nations, not to mention tens of thousands of companies globally."

111

"What would you expect to happen to the price of crude oil and natural gas?"

"Sir, it could very well be the largest whipsaw in the history of the market. With the American markets closed, liquidity will dry up quickly. I would expect to see prices spike and then experience a major collapse. We could see crude oil at one hundred dollars today. For those markets that try to open in the morning, I would expect to see crude trading at two to three hundred dollars, perhaps higher. Once the markets get a handle on the extent of the problem in the United States, oil prices could plummet to twenty dollars a barrel. The unknown quantity will be the amount of America's uncontaminated oil. The greater the amount, the higher the price will go. If, on the other hand, the markets believe that the impact is small, and that America will still be a big buyer, the price will probably fall back to today's prices. However, the ride could be deadly."

"How long do you expect our markets to be closed?"

"Mr. President, I wish I knew. I know that the markets were closed for about a week after 9-11 but, with all due respect, as of right now we have not had enough time to assess the real near-term and long-term damage to the energy infrastructure. Until we do, I would not venture a guess as to the time they will be closed, except to say longer than 9-11."

"With that happy thought, let's move to the Treasury and find out about closing the banks."

"Mr. President, I met with the Chairman of the Federal Reserve and the head of the Fed Regional Banks. Our conclusion is that we need to isolate the State of Texas' banking system. No money can go out or into the State without the control of the Dallas Fed. While we understand this will be very difficult on the people and the businesses in Texas, if we don't lock down Texas there could be a run on the banks across the nation. We will allow limited withdrawals from ATMs or teller windows, but we will have to monitor the cash flow requirement of the banks in Texas."

"Thank you for that update. And now, Mr. Attorney General, what about law and order?"

"Mr. President, the only two times martial law was used were just after Pearl Harbor and in the Civil War. Therefore, we don't have a lot of legal precedent for guidance. I have no doubt that, once you make your presentation to the American people, there will be a reaction. I can hope this will be without violence, but the realist in me says that's not likely. We have a complex system of law enforcement in the United States. I met with people from the U.S. Marshals Service, representatives from the leadership of the Association of Chiefs of Police, and the National Association of Police Unions. They all indicated that they do not have the resources to protect our cities under the situation I outlined to them. All agreed that we needed to bring in the military and to start with the big cities, working our way down. The military should report to the highest police authority in each state, and that would usually be the state police. The list of major metropolitan areas and nearby military bases around the country is being updated. We think we can get good coverage. Perhaps a quick show of force will stop people in their tracks and make them think twice when they could be staring down the barrel of a Colt M4 carbine or a foot soldier with a M16A2 rifle.

"If we're going to use the military then you need to give the order now so we can start deploying the troops. It could be too late if we wait until after your presentation, and we may have to use a level of force that could be quite ugly. I repeat, sir, that the decision to mobilize the military has to be made now, so we can start moving the troops. What is your order?"

"Ladies and gentlemen, I agree with the recommendation of AG Clinton. We need to deploy. I shall declare martial law. Any disagreements?" Nobody said a word.

AG Clinton thought to himself, *My God, I have just asked the President of the United States to suspend the Constitution and the Bill of Rights. And he is going to do just that. God help America.*

The president asked the rest of the people in the room if they had any comments that would be of concern to them. The Secretary of the Interior spoke up. "Mr. President. I think it's important to remind you that those people in Texas who live on top of all of those contaminated oil, gas and product pipelines are living with high levels of radiation. We currently have no place to move the oil and, as sad as it is to say, we have no place to move millions of people to escape the radiation. Sir, my greatest fear is that we will have to seal the Texas border and that those people will be destined to die of radiation poisoning and that there will be nothing we can do for them."

It is now 9:43 PM and the radioactive tsunami
is beginning to slow to 2.5 mph

CHAPTER 34

Meet the Experts

The president had told AG Clinton that he would declare martial law concurrently with his message to the Nation. He told General Powell to get
the troops out and have them deployed as quickly as possible. He would
declare a curfew from 6 PM to 6 AM local time until it would be safe to
lift restrictions. He told Treasury Secretary Smyth to close the banks in
Texas and to limit withdrawals and transfers. He told Secretary Borders to
inform the Chairman of the SEC that the capital markets in the United
States would be closed until further notice. He wanted Interior and Energy
to work on closing down the entire pipeline system as soon as possible. He
had one last order to FEMA, to figure out "what can we do for the people
isolated in Texas?"

The president had completed his most difficult cabinet meeting, perhaps
the most difficult of any president. Marie scheduled an eight o'clock
meeting for the president with the two scientists and he was already two
hours late for the meeting. He told all assembled that he wanted to meet
again after he delivered his message, and asked them to stand by patiently.
With that, he concluded his meeting, and the Secretaries who had missions to accomplish got right to their assignments in the War Room itself.
Others used other offices to start on their tasks.

The president hurried down the hallway to the Oval Office and saw
Mary waiting for him. "Mr. President, I have Dr. Perlmutter in your confer-
ence room and Dr. Burrows is standing by at Johns Hopkins. Shall I get Dr.
Borrows on the phone and bring in Dr. Perlmutter?"

"Right away."

She accompanied Perlmutter from the conference room to the Oval Office and introduced him to the president. He was given a seat in a chair across from the president. The president put his phone on speaker and asked, "Dr. Burrows, can you hear me clearly?"

"Yes I can, Mr. President."

"I have in my office someone you know, Dr. Nathan Perlmutter."

"How are you, Nathan?"

"Fine," came the reply.

"Gentlemen, let me apologize for being so late, but I think you'll understand when you hear why." The president spent a few moments explaining what had happened in Texas City, including that a nuclear device had been detonated. "Do either of you have questions? I can try to answer them and, if I cannot I shall get people in here who can."

"I heard on the radio that at least fifty-four thousand are dead. That's a much higher death toll than 9-11."

The president nodded. "Gentlemen, the reason you are here is because I need some help, and you are the most accomplished people in your field. We have all that contaminated energy in the pipelines. The best we can figure is that the average depth of the pipelines in the area is about four to six feet. In one town, about ten to fifteen miles from the blast site, the radiation level is about 400 millrems. My first question is this: if we have no way of safely extracting the contaminated energy from the ground, how long will it be before the radiation will affect the people above the pipelines? My second question: how sick will people get if they remain on the land? My last question is whether we can we do anything to protect the people in the contaminated area?"

Perlmutter was shown the pictures taken from the president's plane. There was silence for several moments.

"Mr. President, given the scale of destruction, this had to be a much more powerful bomb than a suitcase bomb." Perlmutter leaned over to the speaker so Burrows could hear the next question. "Sir, I understand that you have some satellite imaging of the extent of the flow of the contaminated energy. Is it possible for both of us to see the latest image?"

"My image is in real time so I see exactly what is going on. I will have my image broadcast to you, Dr. Burrows. Here we can see it on my monitor." After they both had a few moments to study the contaminated area, Burrows asked, "Sir, what are the latest flow rates?"

"The latest number I saw was slightly under two miles-per-hour and falling, the pipeline operators think they will have the flow stopped by 11:30, about the time of my address."

"Based on that flow rate they should be able to contain the energy to southeast and south central Texas, would you agree Addie?"

"Mr. President, it appears that we can contain it, but we will also have isolated it in the pipelines with nowhere to go. We will have effectively created the largest radioactive site in the world."

The president frowned. "I understand from the Department of the Interior that the average depth of the pipelines is six feet and deeper under rivers and streams. My question is how much protection will the earth afford for the people in the contaminated area?"

"Sir, if you look at this picture on your computer screen you will get some idea of the intensity of the contamination: the brighter the yellow the higher the level of radiation. The further we get from the blast site the cooler the color, in turn the lower level of radiation. Over time, the radiation will lose its intensity and the whole area will cool down and could possibly be inhabited."

"If I may ask, can you be more specific? How long is 'over time?'"

"Well Mr. President, this area in the center of the blast may take decades to decontaminate naturally. I would guess fifty or so years. Would you agree, Addie?"

"Yes, I think fifty years seems reasonable and, as you go out from the center of the site on a radius, you could reduce the restoration time to ten years for every ten miles. Therefore, a point twenty miles out from the center would take thirty years to decontaminate. The problem that concerns me is that the contaminated oil is isolated, so no natural forces can act on that energy to dissipate the radiation. With that being the case, I have no idea how long it would take."

"Let me change the subject and ask both of you: how long can the people continue to stay in the contaminated area before their health is impacted?"

Perlmutter responded to the president's question. "Sir, that depends on how high the radiation level climbs and how long it stays at that level."

"I agree with Nathan, I think people can have a normal life with a level of four hundred to six hundred. A sustained level above six hundred could cause increases in cancer, birth defects and many other illnesses. The sooner we can get those people out of there the better off they will be."

"Dr. Burrows, how much time do I have to move as many as five million people?"

"If you start with the high risk areas – those that have readings above six hundred – those people have about sixty to ninety days. Once you back down to four hundred then you need to move those people in no later than nine months."

"I agree," Perlmutter said.

"If we evacuate five million people, what will they be able to take with them?"

Both men chimed in, "Nothing."

Burrows explained, "You see, Mr. President, every day that goes by all of the things around the people become magnets for radiation. They cannot take any of their belongings with them for, if they do, they will contaminate the new location. In fact, it would be a good idea that all people be decontaminated once they're outside the contaminated area. All the clothes and shoes – everything – will need to be buried deep underground."

"I know I have imposed upon you greatly, but I must ask one more favor. We have yet to discuss what to do with the contaminated energy. I have an address to the Nation at about 11:30 or so. I need you to be available to talk with the cabinet and me about what to do with the contaminated energy. Dr. Burrows, could you make your way to the Baltimore Amtrak station? I shall send a car for you to bring you directly to the White House. If so, please pack a bag for a few days stay."

"Right away, sir. I should be at the station in about half an hour."

The president hung up the phone and turned to Dr. Perlmutter. "We're facing the greatest challenge to America and to the American spirit of this generation. I'm not sure the people are up to it and, between us, I'm not sure I'm up to it. Thank you for coming. I have my assistant arranging accommodations for you." He stood, shook Dr. Perlmutter's hand, escorted him to the door and asked Marie to "take care of the fine doctor."

Jordan turned and, after he closed the door of the most powerful office in the world, he thought, *Do I have the strength and the courage to lead*

America through what might be its darkest hour? Then a horrible thought raced through his mind and, after a brief moment, terror struck his face. *There are two bombs. Where is the second?*

It is now 10:00 PM and the radioactive tsunami is beginning to slow to 2 mph

CHAPTER 35

Karen and Her Writing Team

It was 10 PM, and in an hour and a half Nathan Jordan had a presidential address scheduled, for which he had not yet read the first draft. He needed time to review the text, rework it and make it his own, even though he had no doubt that Karen and her team had done an excellent job. He picked up his phone in the Oval Office and called Maggie.

"Maggie, I want you to call the Press Secretary and tell him that I need more time. Tell him my address will start at midnight. While you have him on the phone, ask him if he has had any inquiries from the press concerning Texas City. Let me know as soon as possible if you hear anything, then come join us in Karen's conference room."

"Right away sir. May I please ask one question?"

"Go right ahead."

"Does the White House press office know what happened in Texas City?"

"Good question, Maggie. The Press Secretary knows. He's been at all the meetings concerning the crisis. However, under Protocol Four, he won't have told more than a few staffers. Call Wilfred Smith directly and have him handle the notification. He can query his staff on any stories concerning Texas City."

"Immediately, sir. I'll get back to you as soon as I'm done."

As the president was walking towards Karen's office, he thought, *Very insightful on her part; she could have followed my initial instruction and this thing could have been leaked before I speak to the nation.*

Nathan arrived at Karen's office and found the door closed. He gently knocked and Deb opened it, surprised to see the president standing in the doorway. After a moment the president smiled and asked, "Can I come in, Deb, or is this a private meeting?" Deb gestured to the president to come in and Karen got up from behind a very messy desk to go over and give her husband a very long kiss and hug. The president finally separated from the first lady and, with a smile on his face, quipped, "What will the children think?"

Karen invited him to sit at her desk, but he took a seat at the table. "So, let's talk about the message." Bill had been working on a rewrite for the last hour and said to the president, "Would you like to hear what we have written?"

"Not yet. I want to hear from all of you what you believe are the most important parts of the message."

Karen spoke up, "We felt the message should be short but cover all the major issues. We all feel that this message has to anticipate the questions the press might ask, and address the concerns of the American people, as well.

"This message will be heard around the world, so it has to be relevant to both the American people and the people of the world."

When Karen wanted to make a point she always called Nathan by his title. It started when he was a freshman congressman. "Mr. President, this will be the biggest news story of our generation and the news media will be very demanding. The fear factor alone, for personal and family safety, of millions of Americans will be so high that the press can be a great help or a significant hindrance. I think if we are going to have a curfew and martial law, we have to have some control over how the press presents this information."

"So Karen, are you suggesting that I impose some form of censorship of the press in addition to the other restrictions placed on the people?"

"Mr. President, there is a great deal we don't know and, with an issue as dangerous and volatile as this, misinformation could fan the fires of anarchy. I think we should have all stories cleared by the Department of Energy for factual accuracy. Granted, the news on this topic may not be as timely as the press would like, but hopefully it will at least be accurate."

Maggie, Deb, and Bill were sitting in their chairs mesmerized by the dialogue between the president and first lady. They had heard curfew, martial law, and now press censorship and they all wondered what had happened to America.

The president looked thoughtful. "I'll take this under advisement. For now, let's move on. What else do you think should be in the message?"

The first lady turned to Maggie, "Mr. President we think you need to give the American people the facts, the five 'w's. Then you should tell the people what you are doing right now: stopping the flow, isolating the contamination to the nation's energy supply, closing some refineries."

Deb spoke up, "Mr. President, you should talk about the disruptions in the stock, bond, and commodities markets. They will be closed or limited for a while until we can assess the true impact on the economy."

Bill jumped in and said; "we must protect the banking system from a run so banking will also be limited for a while. You must tell the American people that we must protect our economy at all costs."

Karen turned and looked at the staff. She is very proud of the openness and candor her staff shares with the president. "Nathan I think you have to talk about the magnitude of the loss and that no nation was involved in this attack. You must reassure the American people that you will use the full force of the government to find the people who perpetrated this act of terrorism against the United States and bring them to justice. Finally you must tell them that you have been to Texas City and have seen the devastation."

Maggie, Deb, and Bill all exclaimed at the same time, "You have already been to Texas City!?"

"Yes."

"What was it like?"

"It is what I imagine Hell would be like, only a thousand times worse."

It is now 10:30 PM and the radioactive tsunami is slowing to 1 mph

THE BROTHERHOOD OF THE RED NILE

CHAPTER 36

Frank Williams' Office

Frank Williams had just gotten off the phone with the president, who stopped to call him just before he went to visit his wife's message writing team.

"Frank, I've been thinking about the intelligence we got from the Israelis about the Brotherhood working on two bombs. I'm no weapons expert, but I flew over Texas City, or what little was left. There was a tremendous amount of destruction, but I can't tell if it was caused by one bomb or two. I had the photos we took sent over to the Pentagon and they tell me they, too, cannot determine if one or two devices were involved. Do we have any information on a possible second target?"

"Sir, we have identified four possible targets and have taken action to do our best to protect them. The potential targets are a power plant in New Jersey, a power substation in Chicago, a refinery town similar to Texas City in Louisiana, and a data storage center in San Antonio. Beyond those we don't have any other ideas."

"Thanks Frank, it makes me very nervous that there could be a second bomb and we don't know where it is."

"I understand, sir. It also scares the heck out of me not knowing."

"If you come up with any other possible targets let me know."

"Yes, sir."

Williams asked his assistant Marie to get a hold of Ted Baker. "Tell him I need to see him right away."

"Yes, sir."

Frank turned and looked at his wife who had fallen asleep on the couch. He asked Marie to find a blanket to cover her. *She looks peaceful and not as scared as she was when she got back from her adventure.* At a knock on the door, Frank got up quietly and walked over to open it. Seeing, Ted, he stepped out of the office and said, "Let's go down the hall to a conference room to talk. My wife's asleep in my office."

They found a vacant room and Williams closed the door behind them. "I just got a call from the president concerning the possible sites for the second bomb. He had photos from Texas City sent to the Pentagon, which responded that they could not tell from the images whether one or two bombs had been used. So he called and asked me if we had any other ideas.

"I know I asked you to look over your notes to figure out where the second bomb might be used. Your intel matched up with that we got from Mossad, but I need you to look at this one more time, just in case we missed something. I need a quick review. The president is scheduled to speak to the country in about an hour to an hour and a half."

"I'll get right on it, sir. I don't think I missed anything, but I'll go over it with a fine toothcomb. I'll get back to you if I find anything."

As Baker headed towards his office, he began retracing his process. Things started with the map and twenty circles. He arrived at his desk, took out a pad of lined paper and started with a pictogram of the map. Next, he added in the meeting site, and then he added the town in Iran where the bomb was upgraded. He added the house in Morristown, and next was Springfield, Texas. As he looked at what he had drawn, he thought the map and the building in Syria were the constants. The terrorists talked about the cities on the map in Syria. At 10:45, Ted picked up his phone and called Megan Brown, the head of Homeland Security's forensics lab. He didn't expect her to be in the lab, but he let it ring, and finally the answering machine picked up. The message said, "To leave a message for Megan Brown, dial extension twenty-four."

He punched in twenty-four, got her voicemail and wrote down an emergency phone number. Baker hung up and quickly dialed the emergency number. After about five rings, Megan answered the phone, "This is Megan Brown."

"Megan, this is Ted Baker. I urgently need your help. I know you've heard about the bombing in Texas City."

"Yes, it was terrible."

"It was but the president has asked us to reexamine all of our material to see if we missed any possible targets. How quickly can you meet me in your lab?"

"Is the office garage open at this time of night?"

"Yes," he confirmed the time on his watch.

"Well, if you don't mind what I look like, I think I can be there in twenty minutes."

"I'll meet you in your lab at ten after eleven."

"I'll do my best."

"Do better than your best. Millions of lives are at stake." Baker hung up the phone and began the process of rethinking the relationship between the map, the circles, and the discussions in Syria. Each of the four members had made their recommendations of the target, but nobody knew until after they arrived in the United States what the targets would be for the two bombs.

Baker pondered, *We were expecting the bombs to come in by ship through Canada, but they didn't arrive via the route we expected. If they didn't come through Canada, then they had to come in through the east coast or the Gulf of Mexico.* The fact that the first bomb went off in Texas, along the Gulf Coast, suggests that both bombs somehow came via the Gulf itself. It would then make sense, then, that the second bomb would be used along the Gulf Coast as well, so his estimate for the City of Lake Charles was, in his mind, still the most logical. *What if I'm wrong? Thousands, maybe millions, may die if I'm mistaken.*

It is now 10:40 PM and the radioactive tsunami has been stopped.

CHAPTER 37

Oval Office

The president had returned to the Oval Office and told Mary, "I'll be in the small conference room working on my remarks."

"Do you need anything?

"Is there water in the fridge?"

"I believe so, let me check."

"That's okay; I'll just get water from the tap."

"If you need anything just call me, sir."

The president walked in and closed the door. It is the first peace he had had all day, and he knew, when he walked out, that door all hell was going to break loose. With all his authority, he could do little to stop what was already in motion. He had the notes from Karen's team. They were excellent, but not his own words. The challenge for him tonight, and it might be the greatest challenge faced any president in the history of the country, was to lead the people. When Abraham Lincoln was president, the black people, both free and slave, called him "Father Abraham" because they saw him as a father figure. When Roosevelt spoke to the people and said, "We have nothing to fear but fear itself," he, too, was cutting a paternal image.

He needed to convey to the American people a sense of calm control. It was necessary to tell them the bad news up front and then calm the panic by explaining the steps required to fix the problems. Citizens needed to know that all would have to make sacrifices but, if everyone worked together, problems would be solved. It will not be easy. As he thought about his remarks he mused, *Should I mention the possibility of the second bomb or even others?* If he didn't tell them, or at least let them know of the possibilities, should a second or more bombs go off, all confidence in him would disappear.

As he pondered this decision, his secure private line rang. On the other end was Secretary of Energy Mike Findley. "Mr. President, I'm very sorry for interrupting your preparations, but I thought you might like to know that the oil is stopped and sealed."

"Thank God for at least some good news. It will help my message greatly. Thank you for calling."

As he returned to his message, he felt better for having something positive to report. He decided to start with the difficult things, even warn them of possible other attacks, and then tell them of the success in stopping the flow of the contaminated oil. He would finish with the controls.

He started reading aloud, testing the sound and style of what he wanted to say. "My fellow Americans, I come to you tonight at this late hour to tell you of a vicious and deadly attack on the United States. This attack, we believe, was carried out by a new terrorist organization called the Brotherhood of the Red Nile. As its name would suggest, this group was formed in the Middle East with the sole intent of destroying America, its values, laws and economy. I believe they want America to withdraw from our leadership position in the world and that the best of America is behind us.

"Make no mistake. They are deeply committed to their cause and, while there has been one attack, there could be more attacks on our country. In this first attack, the entire population of Texas City died and its refining capacity was destroyed. The pipeline network running through that region is contaminated by radiation. This afternoon, I flew to Texas City, or as close as I could, to see the destruction first hand, which is diabolically terrible. However, I am pleased to report that the Departments of Energy, Interior and Defense have helped the pipeline owners and operators successfully shut down the pipeline network and isolate all the contaminated energy.

"We shall have many serious challenges to face in the coming weeks and months to make sure that every American is safe. Most of those challenges are not yet known or fully understood but, as we discover them, we shall solve them. For now, I have signed a temporary order declaring martial law that calls for a curfew of 6 PM to 6 AM until further notice. All banking institutions will be closed, with access to banking activity limited for some period. In order to help stabilize the capital markets, all stock exchanges and commodity markets will be closed until the regulators feel these markets can reopen on an orderly basis.

"Your government is in touch with world leaders to advise them of the actions I am taking tonight. I want to make three final points: first, we are facing the greatest challenge in our history. I believe our history will serve us well to help us overcome this adversity. It will not be easy. We shall have many problems to solve and, undoubtedly, we shall make mistakes. However, by working together we shall be a better nation for this experience. Second, as long as I am your president I shall do everything in my power to protect this country and to make you and America stronger than ever.

"Last, but far from least, I shall devote time every day to discover the identity of the people of the Brotherhood of the Red Nile or any other terrorist organization that wants to destroy America. Let me make my message clear for all who would try to take us down. We will destroy you. You have attacked America and you have killed Americans. Make no mistake: you shall be brought to American justice and you shall die, so help me God.

"Citizens of the United States, may God bless you and your families. May God Bless America."

CHAPTER 38

Megan Brown's Lab

It was 11:15. Megan Brown was walking out of the elevator and saw Ted Baker standing by her door looking at his watch. "I got here as fast as I could."

She unlocked the door, walked in, and turned on the lights with Baker right behind her. She closed the door and turned to Baker who was almost in her face and asked, "What is this all about?"

Baker said, "Williams thinks we, or I, might have missed a possible target and asked me to go over everything one more time to see if I missed something. I thought we could go over it together and see if two heads are better than one.

"We know that there is a relationship between the maps you reviewed, the meeting place in Syria, and the ultimate selection of the bomb sites. All the sites we could identify from the dialogue in Syria are under protection; we need to find if we missed a site."

"Have you looked at both the big map and the smaller maps to see if you have missed something?" Brown asked, "Didn't the small maps match up with the twenty circles on the big map?"

"Well, nineteen of the twenty matched. We have never been able to figure out the relationship of the one site to the other nineteen. We originally thought that map twenty was Springfield, Texas. The circle for map twenty was very large and included Springfield, Houston and Texas City. We thought because of all the activity in Springfield that it was the target. We didn't think about Texas City. One other thing: the map for circle twenty was not an exact match when compared to the relationship of the smaller maps to the nineteen other cities. We confirmed for you that the Chicago, New York and San Antonio maps matched." Baker looked at his watch. It was 11:40 and the president was scheduled to speak to the nation in just twenty minutes.

"So, you have nineteen confirmed, you found the cities that match the circles. What did you do about number twenty?"

Baker explained, "We saw the notes that Mossad sent on the discussion of possible sites. The person identified as Oleg suggested that oil was the blood of America. He also talked about targets in Texas and Louisiana, but did not specify any cities, as did the other three terrorists. So, after Texas City was attacked, we looked in Louisiana and found what you found; that Lake Charles made a reasonable target, it has all the same things that Texas City had: refineries, and a slightly larger population. If they could close down both places, they could have impeded the flow of crucial amounts of energy in the United States. Do you have a map of the Gulf Coast?"

"Yes, let me find it." While she looked for it, Baker looked at his watch yet again. It's 11:45. Megan brought back the map and laid it on the light table in the middle of the large room. They both traced their fingers over the map and found Texas City. They followed the shoreline and found Lake Charles. Baker moved his finger further along the coast and stopped and asked, "Megan what is that?" she started to tell him but he yells, "This is the second target!

"I have to call Williams to tell the president where the second target is." He dials Williams' office and Marie answers, "Is he in?"

"I'm sorry Mr. Baker, but he's on his way to the White House."

"Can you patch me in to him?"

"I'll try, sir." Baker looked at his watch. It's 11:55. Williams came on the line.

"Tell the president that the second bomb is at..."

CHAPTER 39

The Brotherhood

Sargon and the rest of the team had everything in place. As soon as they heard the announcement for the President of the United States, they know two things would happen. First, the second bomb would go off and second, their YouTube video would go live and the e-mail would be broadcast around the world. Sargon was sitting in the Internet café just down the street from their hotel with his eyes trained on the TV screen.

In the next moments, they would do what no nation in the world had accomplished: bring down the arrogant Americans off their high horse of imperialism. He had waited a long time for this to happen. Sargon had sacrificed much; he had given up the opportunity for wealth and position to achieve a goal. When the events of the day were over, he and his 'Think Tank' team would have killed America's spirit. When it is possible, they would return to their homeland and, unless they themselves said something, nobody would know it was the seven of them who brought down America. He thought, *Nobody would believe us, anyway, if we told them.*

Back in the hotel room, the six remaining Brothers are anxiously awaiting the president's message. They decided not to use the cell phone detonator, but a simple clock timer instead. Adad had some concerns with the cell phone working in such a remote area, so the timer was a last minute substitute.

Oleg asked Ishtar, "What time did you set the timer for?"

He responded, "Midnight, as we agreed, to coincide with the president's message."

Oleg quickly picked up his cell phone and dialed Sargon, who picked up and said in a somewhat angry voice, "Why are you calling me?"

"Well, as was said in the American space program, Houston we have a problem," Oleg replied. "Do not send the YouTube link or the e-mail."

"Why not? Ishtar set the timer to 12 AM"

Ishtar confirmed, "Yes, that is correct."

"No, it is not." asserted Oleg. "The president will be speaking at 12 AM Eastern Standard time and Texas is on Central Standard Time, so when it's 12 AM in DC, it's 11PM in Houston. We have one more hour to wait," Oleg explained.

"Can't we detonate the bomb with the cell phone?" Sargon asked.

"No, we disconnected the cell phone process because we weren't sure of the signal strength."

Sargon sighed, "I don't think it makes any difference in the outcome. It will be delayed one hour unless we can find a way to delay the president. We need to think about this for a moment."

Oleg spoke, "All of our cell phones are international phones and if we were to call the White House it would appear that the call was coming from the Middle East. The phone number that would appear on the caller ID would be a foreign country."

"If the time is correct we're just about ten minutes from the president's message." Sargon was processing his thoughts quickly. "We need to call the White House and tell them we are the Brotherhood of the Red Nile and we planted the bomb in Texas City. We'll tell them we have other bombs that we can detonate and we want to speak with the president.

"Nobody in the public knows the name of our organization, so when the president hears the name it will stop him in his tracks. He will have to take the call." Sargon asked, "Whose phone should we use?"

Adad responded, "I think we should use Cyrus'; his number will show Iran."

Sargon spoke softly into the phone and said, "What if we do nothing?"

Adad shrugged and said, "The bomb goes off one hour later, not as dramatic but it doesn't change the outcome does it?"

Mordecai responded, "The bomb is not less effective."

Oleg agreed and Sargon answered, "Our goal was to explode the second bomb in conjunction with the president's speech so we could demonstrate to the American people our power over the press and the president."

Michael, who had been quiet through the entire discussion, jumped in and commented, "I know I'm the youngest, but if we call the White House and identified ourselves as the Brotherhood and say we want to talk with the president, what are we going to tell him that will make him wait till 1 AM to deliver his message?"

Sargon responded, "If we make the call now, and assuming that we get through, what can we possibly say to delay his speech for one hour?"

Adad suggested, "We have the American leadership rattled. If we call, we just may distract him from making the speech till 1 AM."

Oleg said, "Let's go for it. He looks for the White House phone number and sends a text message including the number to Sargon. It is 11:55 when Sargon calls the White House.

"This is the White House. How may I direct your call?"

"I am the leader of the Brotherhood of the Red Nile and I want to speak with the president."

The operator responded, "The president is about to speak to the American people. He can't be interrupted."

"Then tell the president we have another bomb and more Americans will die than died in Texas City if he doesn't talk with us now."

"Please hold." The operator called the Oval Office and got Mary. She told Mary about the message and Mary quickly ran into the Oval Office where they are just about to tell the president to proceed. Mary yelled, "Wait, Mr. President! Someone from the Brotherhood of the Red Nile is on the phone. He says if you don't talk with him now millions more Americans will die with the next bomb."

Jordan ordered, "Shut down the cameras, clear the room." Midnight passes and no message from the president. "Get Mark Simmons from DHS in here quickly and send the call to this office."

Mary pushed the button for the operator and said, "After you transfer the call to me I want you to call the chairman of the Joint Chiefs of Staff, the attorney general and the national security advisor. Tell them to come to the Oval Office ASAP. Now give me the call."

Mary looked at her watch. It's 12:07. "This is Mary Washington the president's assistant. He will take your call now." Mary transferred the call. Nathan Jordan takes a deep breath and picks up the phone.

"This is Nathan Jordan. With whom am I speaking?"

Sargon answers, "This is the Brotherhood of the Red Nile. We are responsible for the destruction in Texas City today."

Mary had called in the chief of White House security. He was in her office trying to get a caller ID from her phone. Because of the security in the White House, caller ID didn't work so he had to go back to the old way of tracing a call. He was on the phone with Verizon, which attempted to trace the call. It was now 12:10.

Jordan asked Sargon, "Why did you kill so many people today?"

"We killed them because your people need to experience the kind of death to which we have been subjected for generations at the hands of America and American interests." It was 12:15 and Sargon knew he had to get off the phone quickly. "We have more bombs and we plan to use them." With that final comment, he hung up. Then he waited to see if the president was going to broadcast.

The president also hung up and saw that the room had filled with cabinet members and other advisors. He turned to them and said, "I have just spoken with the voice of death."

At 12:16, he told Mary to bring the communications people back into the office and asked, "How soon before we can broadcast?" They responded, "The earliest is 1 AM."

"Then make it happen by 1. I will meet with the cabinet while we're waiting." With steel in his voice he said, "I know exactly what I'm going to say."

CHAPTER 40

Another Mistake

The delay in the president's message was not communicated to the State Department, or to the SEC so at just before 12 AM the Secretary called the ten most important countries and sent the broadcast e-mail to all the U.S. embassies and consulates around the world. She was on the phone and didn't see the TV set in her office or else she would have noticed that the president wasn't talking with America. By 12:30 her phone was ringing off the wall with ambassadors from all over the world calling asking what had happened in Texas. Michelle Borders called the Oval Office just before 1 AM to find out what was going on. Mary Washington picked up the phone and Borders in an angry voice said; "I need to talk with the president right away." "I'm sorry, Madam Secretary. He is about to address the American people. I'll have him call you as soon as he can, or perhaps you might want to make your way here to see him personally."

"I'm on my way."

Sargon was in the Internet café with his finger on the "send" button waiting for the words to come across the speaker in the café: "The president…" Sargon hit the "send" button. The bomb at Port Fourchon, Louisiana also went off precisely at 12 AM Central Standard time. The radio crackles. "We interrupt the president: there is a report of a second nuclear bomb exploding in—"

The radio goes dead. After a moment, the radio speaker comes back on and a voice, speaking over the president's, says, "A bomb went off in Port Fourchon, Louisiana. That is all we have … Wait! We're getting a news flash from AP reporting that the bombing in Texas City, Texas, and now in Port Fourchon, Louisiana, is claimed to be the work of a terrorist group known as the Brotherhood of the Red Nile. We return you to the president."

"... Last, but far from least, I will devote time every day to discover the identity of the people of the Brotherhood of the Red Nile or any other terrorist organization that wants to destroy America. Let me make my message clear for all who would try to take us down, we will destroy you. You have attacked America and you have already killed Americans. Make no mistake. You shall be brought to American justice and you shall die, so help me God. To U.S. Citizens, God bless you and your families and God Bless America."

With a satisfied smile on his face, Sargon slowly closed his laptop and left the café. He headed back to his fellow Brotherhood members very pleased with what they had accomplished. He saw that all the lights were on in his neighborhood and was sure hundreds of millions of American had heard the president's speech and his own message. Both would be recorded for posterity. He felt very proud as he climbed the steps to the suite. He gently knocked on the door, it opened, and he was welcomed with open arms, great smiles, and a bottle of champagne.

Back at the White House, the president had just finished his message and received a report of the second bombing, the e-mail, and the YouTube video from the Brotherhood.

"Mary, call a full cabinet meeting in thirty minutes. I want everybody present."

"Yes, sir."

Karen walked into the Oval Office and went over to Nathan. She had closed the door behind her, took him in her arms, and told him, "There was nothing we could have done to prevent this. We need you to lead us. The American people need you, the world needs you, and I need you to lead us out of this darkness and despair."

They walked over and sat on one of the couches and just held each other's hands until it was time for him to go; nothing more was said. They just sat and they both knew their lives – along with those of all Americans – had been changed forever. Nathan Jordan, the forty-sixth president of the United States stood, kissed his wife one more time, and walked toward the door. As he walked down the hallway to the War Room, he asked himself,

Can I truly lead this country out of this darkness and into the light? God, be my constant companion as I face the difficult decisions ahead.

The messages from the Secretary of State and the Brotherhood had been released all over the world. The stock, bond, commodity and currency markets were in total chaos. The price of Brent North Sea crude almost doubled, from $118 per barrel to $230; there was no market for West Texas Crude because the markets weren't sure there is a West Texas oil business any more. With the report of the second bomb going off in Port Fourchon, the price of Brent skyrocketed to $325 a barrel. At the same time oil was exploding in price, gold has moved $500 to $2,300 a troy ounce.

Meanwhile, in his private office just off Red Square, Russian multi-billionaire Viktor Antipova, the uncle of Oleg, was staring at his computer screen and watching the value of his long oil contracts increase tenfold. Based on the most recent price movement he had already made over a billion dollars. He asks himself, *Should I sell the positions and take the profit or watch and see what happens? If I sell half of my positions, I can take my money out and run with the profits. We don't know the full impact. For now, I'm going to let it all ride.*

Viktor was the moneyman behind the Brotherhood of the Red Nile. Under the former Soviet Union, he had been in charge of security for all non-missile-based nuclear weapons. He was the one that not only supplied the obsolete bombs but also paid to have them rebuilt. The profits he was making in his oil trade would no doubt make him one of the richest men in the world.

Day one of the rebirth of America

CHAPTER 41

War Room

The president had just finished his message to America and hoped he has helped the American people understand what had happened. He was now hearing about the second bomb in a place called Port Fourchon, Louisiana. He had never heard of the place and, for that matter, he had never heard of Texas City until twelve hours ago.

He met Simmons, head of Homeland Security as he was walking to the War Room.

"Mr. President, the Brotherhood has used a second bomb on Port Fourchon."

"Mark, I'm aware of that. Why is this place that nobody has ever heard of so damn important?"

"Sir, as best I can tell at the moment the place that nobody ever heard of processes ninety-five percent of all the oil and natural gas that comes from the Gulf of Mexico."

"Ninety-five percent?"

"Yes, sir, and the entire facility is on fire much like what you saw in Texas City. The one good thing is that during the day there are only about two thousand seven hundred workers on site. Because the bomb went off at midnight there weren't as many people killed as there would have been during regular work hours."

Both of them walked through the door to the War Room where everybody had assembled. The president could tell that Michelle was fuming, so he gave her a chance to vent and then said, "I'm truly sorry about the crossed signals. I shall talk to the leaders later today. Mark informed me that Port Fourchon was the second target. This facility processes ninety-five percent of all the oil and gas coming out of the Gulf of Mexico. At present, we can't get to it to shut down the flow."

"Mr. President," Michael spoke up, "Sir, that facility has over five hundred storage tanks full of crude oil that is being fed into the pipeline heading north. Satellite images show the tanks are exploding, sending radioactive and toxic gases into the atmosphere."

Simmons, from Interior said, "The operating leases for drilling in the Gulf come under the responsibility of the Bureau of Land Management, which is part of my responsibility. I recommend the quickest way to stop the flow to Port Fourchon is to shut down the rigs in the Gulf as quickly as possible. I think we should pull the leaseholders' files and start calling them. However, sir I would need an executive order to do this." The president turned to AG Clinton and said, "We set a curfew, we closed the banks and the markets. How tough can it be to shut down the oil and drilling rigs in the Gulf?"

Clinton looked at the president. "You've already declared a national emergency and under your oath of office are required to protect and defend the Constitution. Clearly, we are under attack from someone outside the United States. They have said so in their YouTube video and their e-mail to the world. Under Protocol Four, this is a matter of National Security. I will have the order ready for you to sign within the hour."

"Mr. Simmons, I would like to excuse you so you and your staff can start making your calls. You have a lot to do, and I want you to get an encrypted e-mail address so that the AG can send the leaseholders a copy of the Executive Order. Any questions?"

"No, sir."

"Now then, I want to tell all of you that in a little while we shall meet with two Nobel laureates who will talk to us about the problems we have in Texas in dealing with all that contaminated oil. But I also want to ask: is there any way to stop the oil flowing out of Port Fourchon?"

Findley responded to the president's question, "Sir, I have not had a chance to look at the pipeline map yet, but initially the problem is different in this respect. In Texas, we shut down the wells along with the pipelines. We shut the wells so no new oil or gas could enter and then we shut down the compressors that move the oil and gas. Here we have over five thousand rigs sending oil into Port Fourchon. Until we can close down a substantial number of rigs, we can't reduce the flow through the port into the tanks. This will be difficult to stop."

"Mike, what if we went up the line, say about ten miles, and shut down the compressors and closed the valves?"

"Sir, I'm not a petroleum engineer, but my guess is that, if we shut down the pipelines after Port Fourchon, the pressure of the oil being pumped out of the Gulf would explode the pipeline. Perhaps millions of barrels of contaminated oil would flow into the countryside and get into the water supply and who knows where else. Before we attempted this, I would seek the opinions of several petroleum engineers."

"Well, as if we haven't had the bejeezus scared out of us enough already, you have found a new way to scare the hell out of me." The president shook his head. "We need to table that idea and get engineers on this right away. Mike, how long do you think it would take to shut down five thousand rigs?"

"Sir, I can only guess and say several weeks."

"Earlier this evening I had a conversation with the two most recent winners of the Nobel Prize in Physics. I showed them the images of the oil in the ground and both told me we have to get those people out of there and to understand that, if we can't figure out a way to get the contaminated oil and gas out of those pipelines, they may never be able to go back.

CHAPTER 42

Congress Wants Answers

It was now about 1:30 in the morning and a meeting was taking place in the office of the Speaker of the House. Attending the meeting was the Speaker, Robert Ward; the Minority Leader in the House, James Radcliff; Majority Leader in the Senate, William Wild; and the Minority leader in the Senate, Francis Pollard.

Ward spoke up, "Gentlemen, the United States has been under attack since noon yesterday and we have had no contact with the administration, at least I have not. Have any of you had any contact from the president or anybody at the White House?

"We heard just about thirty minutes ago all the things the president is doing to maintain law and order and to protect our markets but, am I wrong in thinking that he might have consulted with us before he made all of these decisions? Don't get me wrong, I think he has made the right decisions but I think we should have been consulted."

Wild responded, "Mr. Speaker, I agree that the actions taken by the president tonight may in fact be without precedent, but two nuclear attacks on American soil is also without precedent."

Ward answered, "Without question, Senator Wild, but I do not believe the challenges before the country can be solved by the administration only. We in Congress have a role. We are all elected by the people to represent them and we should have a say in what is going to happen to America."

Radcliff suggested, "Mr. Speaker, while you are of the same party as the president, I do not think this is a partisan issue. I think, as the Leader of the

House, you should contact the president and request a meeting as soon as possible. How do the rest of you feel about asking for a meeting?"

All agreed that this was a nonpartisan issue and that the Speaker was the right person to make the call. Ward responded, "Stay here. I'm going to make the call right now."

It was now 2 AM and everybody was starting to get tired. The president was concerned that decisions made without sleep might not be good decisions. "I think we need to take a break and try and get a few hours' sleep, come back, and begin to tackle some other issues." Just then, the phone rang in the War Room and Findley answered. "Sir, it's Mary Washington for you."

"I'll take it … yes, Mary."

"Mr. President, I have the Speaker of the House on the line."

"Please ask him to wait for just a moment." The president looked at the people preparing to leave. "I have the Speaker on the line and my guess is he's not too happy that we have left Congress out of the decisions we've made."

Clinton spoke up, "Sir, none of the actions you have taken requires the approval or the consent of Congress."

"I understand, Drew, but we have to bring Congress into this process sooner or later, and since we have only been at this for thirteen or so hours, now is as good a time as any."

"Sir, if I might suggest your own words: we all need some rest. It would be better to schedule a meeting for tomorrow morning."

"Excellent suggestion, Drew. Mary put through the Speaker."

"Mr. President, it's late. I won't take a lot of your time. I'm in my office with the leadership of Congress. I'd like to put you on speaker phone if that's okay."

"Go right ahead, Mr. Speaker." The president nodded and everyone sat back down.

All of the leadership wanted to know how he was holding up.

"I'm fine, thank you for asking. It's been a long day for all of us. Mr. Speaker, I must apologize for not bringing in the leadership of Congress into the discussions, but all the resources that had to be put into action were the responsibility of the Executive Branch.

"If we're going to solve America's problems as a result of these attacks and with the possibilities of others, we're going to have to work together. To that end Mr. Speaker, all of us need some rest. I suggest that all of you come to the White House tomorrow morning at ten thirty, and we can all try to figure out what to do to save America. Would that be acceptable for you, Mr. Speaker?"

"Mr. President, please be assured that we in Congress want to do whatever we can to assist you in keeping America safe and rebuilding a better America. We'll see you at ten thirty. Thank you, Mr. President, and good night."

The president stood as the called ended. "Ladies and gentlemen, let me thank you for a tremendous job well done on behalf of the American people. We have just begun the process of rebuilding America. We will have many difficult and what may sometimes seem to be insurmountable challenges ahead of us. In a few hours, we'll be meeting with the leadership of Congress, and they will want to know what they can do to help. They don't yet realize we can't answer that question for ourselves right now, but I promise you this: at some point in time, perhaps not in this administration, maybe not for a long time, America will look for revenge for the death and destruction brought on it today by the Brotherhood of the Red Nile."

Then President Jordan sat in his chair with the Great Seal of the United States of America on it, closed his eyes and thought, *May God have mercy on their souls for the retribution that will someday rain down on them.*

CHAPTER 43

Cut Off the Head of the Snake

Ted Baker and Megan Brown had been going over the Google Earth map of the Port Fourchon area. They knew that what had worked in Texas would not work the same way at Fourchon. Shutting down compressors could not turn off the force of the five thousand plus wells in the Gulf. If they could figure a way to stop the flow of the oil then when the pressure dropped, they could shut the valves and keep the contaminated energy from moving north and east.

They zoomed in on the map and could see in the water the pipelines coming into Port Fourchon. What they didn't know was how far the radiation contamination had moved out into the Gulf. As they zoomed out, the vastness of the Gulf of Mexico was nothing short of daunting. The pipeline snaked its way through the Gulf to a main trunk line into Port Fourchon.

Brown turned to Baker, "Ted, this image makes me think of a giant desert horned viper."

"Why?" he asked.

"It's a venomous snake from the Middle East. The image of Port Fourchon is like the head of the snake and the pipeline is its body. The radioactive pipelines running from the Port are like the poisonous venom spewing out of the snake's mouth. We have to find a way to kill the snake and the fastest way to kill this snake is to cut off its head."

"I agree. If we can find a way to cut off its head then we will stop the poison," Ted nodded. "But Meagan, how do we cut off its head?"

"Your superiors have told you they're open to any ideas and that they have already started contacting the rig operators to shut down the rigs. But, that could take a month."

"True, but it would take about two weeks for the contaminated oil and gas to reach New York and the east coast. It would take a little less time to reach the Midwest. So the shutdown process of closing the rigs will not kill the snake, but may in fact kill millions of Americans."

Megan responded, "We need a big knife to slash off its head. As I see it, we have two knives and both would be effective but dangerous."

"What do you mean?" Ted asked.

"If you take a shovel and kill a snake in your garden, you can cut off its head, but for a while it will bleed out. If we cut off the head by severing the pipelines, the oil and natural gas will stop flowing into the port and the pressure will drop. Then, we could close the downstream valves and prevent the contamination from flowing north. Consequently, however, massive amounts of raw crude oil will be pumped into the Gulf of Mexico, doing untold damage until all the oil wells are shut down. What *are* the best ways to sever the head?"

Ted stepped away from the map. "I've been thinking that we have to explore as many options as we can and then present them to Williams and let him take them to the president."

"Okay, what are the options you see?"

"We don't know yet how far out into the Gulf we have to go to get away from the radiation. Once we know that answer then some of the options could be eliminated.

"Option one is we send in a team of Navy SEALs to set charges to blow out a significant amount of the pipeline, perhaps as much as a mile."

"Why at least a mile?" Megan looked up at him.

"Remember, the oil and gas is going directly from the well under significant pressure, so if we don't take out enough pipeline, the force of the oil coming out of the pipe will force it into the other part of the snake and send it on to Port Fourchon. If we take out enough pipeline, then the pressure will drop in the pipeline leading to the head of the snake. Once the pressure drops, we can look at capping that pipe. If the water is too deep to send down divers, then we'll have to move to option two."

"And what is option two?"

"During the Gulf War, we developed 'bunker buster' bombs that, when dropped from planes, could dive through the sand in the desert and impact the concrete walls of the underground command bunkers and explode, destroying everything inside."

Brown asked, "So what happens if the bombs miss the target? Do we just keep sending in more and more bombs until we've destroyed the pipeline?"

"Pretty much so, yes."

"But, if we have bombs under the sea floor that don't detonate, then when the divers go back to cap the pipeline they would be exposed to live bombs!"

"Yes."

"Please, tell me there is an option three."

"Option three is a submarine using its guided torpedoes to take aim at the pipeline and blow it away."

"That seems to me to be the most viable option. We should give that idea to Secretary Williams to present."

"Not so fast. All three options will flood the Gulf with raw crude oil. We have no way of knowing how much oil will be spilled, but my guess is that it will be millions of gallons. Think back to the last major oil spill in the Gulf. The environmentalists will go nuts. They'll come down in favor of contaminating the Eastern half of America instead of killing fish and aquatic life in the Gulf."

Megan asked, "Do we have to tell them up front? Are we required to get their permission to save American lives?"

Ted replied, "No, I don't think we have to get permission, but I do think there will be outrage when they find out. And they will find out."

Megan added, "If the president wants to try this idea, then we can move skimmers and massive amounts of containment equipment in place to suck up the oil. Remember, the BP spill was a wellhead problem thousands of feet down on the sea floor. My hope is that the point where we sever the pipeline will not be as deep and we can salvage much of the raw oil."

Ted nodded. "I like the sub idea best. We need to see Williams right away. I'll call Marie and see if he has time." He called Williams' office.

"We need to see Mr. Williams right away."

Marie responded, "He's in his office with the door shut. Let me put you on hold and I'll see if I can disturb him." Marie buzzed Frank.

Ellen was sleeping on the couch and moved slightly at the sound. "Sir, I have Ted Baker and Megan Brown on the phone, and they say it's urgent that they talk with you about Port Fourchon."

"Put them through." He picked up his phone. "Ted, what's up?"

"Sir, I know it's late but I think we've come up with a way to stop the flow of oil and natural gas to Port Fourchon. Can you come down to Megan's lab and we'll show you?"

"I'll be right there." Williams was at Brown's office in a matter of moments. Walking in, he saw the two of them huddled over the light table and on the big screen monitor was a satellite map of the Louisiana coastline. "Sir, if you would please come over here we'll show you our recommended course of action."

They laid out their ideas on both the light table and the screen, presenting all three of the recommendations. After explaining the options, they told Williams that they thought using a submarine was the most viable. They acknowledged it would cause some collateral damage to the Gulf, but the tradeoffs are worth it.

"I like it a lot and think the president will, too. I don't know if we have a submarine in the Gulf or how long it would take to get one there, but we can find out fast. I'll have Secretary Simmons call Blanchard Powell and ask him to find out. I want both of you to come to the War Room in the morning and make your pitch to everybody. I'll check with the Secretary tonight and let you know what time to be there. Great job you two. Let's go whack off the head of the snake and save the country. Now try and get some rest."

CHAPTER 44

Brotherhood Meeting in Houston

Sargon had asked all of his team members to settle down because he wanted to talk about their next step. "We have done what we set out to accomplish and we all should be proud of what we have done. The Americans have been able to shut down the flow of contaminated energy from the explosion in Texas City. However, they were not expecting the second bomb at Port Fourchon. It won't be as easy to stop the flow of energy from this site.

"Oleg has told us that energy is the life blood of America; if a patient doesn't have enough blood in his body he can't survive. Doctors will push blood in the body in an attempt to keep the patient alive. I think between the two bombs we have drained enough life blood out of America that this patient will die."

Oleg shook his head, "I don't know how much blood the patient has left in him, but I believe that America is far from dead. If they can find a way to shut down Port Fourchon they can save the country."

Adad added, "If only the Iranians had agreed to sell us two other bombs we could have finished off America tonight."

Sargon turned to Ishtar, "If they start shutting down the rigs in the Gulf, do you have a plan to get us back to the Middle East?"

Ishtar responded, "We can't go southwest to Mexico. Because of the contamination, the roads will most likely be closed. I think we'll have to leave through Canada. However, this story is just beginning. We're just over twelve hours into the problems that America is facing. I believe that many have yet to be discovered. I think it'll be several months before we'll be able to leave the country."

Sargon asked, "How much cash do we have and how long will it last? How will we get more money if we need it? With the president closing the banking system, we must be careful how we spend our money, at least for now. With all the restrictions, food will be in short supply quickly and, I expect, will be very expensive. I suggest that during the day we leave in pairs and go out to see what is happening. We need to listen to people and then, based on that information, look for an opportunity to relocate."

Back in Washington, Ted Baker and Megan Brown were still in her lab, going over what they needed to present in the morning. The adrenaline generated from their idea about cutting off the head of the snake had them high, and they knew that for now it was fruitless to try sleeping. They were comfortable that they had all the data for the meeting as Ted raised a new subject.

"We've decided that the bombs came into the United States from the Gulf. If that is true, then it very likely that the senior members and their leader have a personal stake in the outcome, so they would want to stay around and see what happens. They were together almost every day for over three months. The leader spent a great deal of time with each member before the team as a group. Megan, how far is it from Texas City to Port Fourchon?"

"At average speed and under normal conditions, about seven hours," she replied. "But, if the terrorists were driving back to Texas City they wouldn't be able to get there because of the congestion. They would have to go someplace else."

"So, where did they go?" Ted queried.

"I think they'd want to go somewhere that would give them as many exit options as possible." Megan looked at the map on the monitor. "They could have gone south to Galveston, but that would back them into a corner. My guess is Houston."

"I agree. Interstate 10 runs directly from New Orleans to Houston, and it's far enough north of Texas City that they could get around a lot of the traffic."

"The time delay between the two bombs was twelve hours, Texas City at noon and Port Fourchon at midnight. That would allow them to place the bomb in Texas City and then move on to Port Fourchon to plant that bomb and then head for Houston."

Ted mused, "That would work, but if they had any problems with traffic they might not get to the Port or, for that matter, make it back in time to watch the fireworks."

"True, but if the entire membership arrived here, they could have split into two teams operating from Houston and then each team could set have their bombs and returned."

"Good point. We don't know how long the bombs were at each site before they were detonated. So, they could have set the bombs some time ago and then detonated them on their time schedule."

Megan responded, "They could have used a cell phone or a clock timer. Either one would have done the trick."

"So, they sit in their hotel in Houston, push the button when they want to, and wait for the reactions," Ted speculated. "Then they call the White House to taunt the president that they have another bomb and plan to use it. As soon as they hang up, they wait in Houston for the president to start his message to the people, and then they trigger the second bomb and their YouTube video, and send out their e-mail message to the world media, claiming credit for both bombs."

Megan and Ted were standing and saying nothing, they turned towards each other, put their arms around each other and whispered, "The Brotherhood of the Red Nile is in Houston, and Mordecai is with them. We need to find…"

CHAPTER 45

Early Next Morning

It was 6:30 AM and a gentle knock on the president's bedroom door awoke Nathan and Karen. Less than four hours ago, both had wearily crawled into bed with Nathan saying, "To hell with night clothes. Let's just get undressed and go to bed naked."

Karen smiled, because normally, when Nathan suggested they go to bed naked, there was going to be lovemaking in the very near future. She knew tonight was not going to be one of those nights, for the events of the day had drained both of them. They knew that there were going to be many more days of not enough sleep and even less sex. She saw it as her job to keep Nathan stimulated and, when he was ready for lovemaking, she would be a willing participant. For now, she put herself in charge of making sure he was eating properly and getting some amount of sleep on a regular basis, if even for just a few short hours. The challenges ahead would drain any man. For the benefit of the country, she had to keep him healthy and strong.

"We have to get up. I have a meeting with the leadership of Congress and the cabinet at ten thirty." Nathan stretched and yawned.

"Couldn't we lay here for just a few minutes and you can hold me?"

Nathan propped himself up on one elbow and looked at his naked wife lying on her side. He smiled as Karen looked up at him with a smile of her own and asked, "What?"

He slid down off his elbow to the point that his mouth was right next to the nipple and gently leaned in and suckled. After he let go he told her,

"I love you. I feel the best when I'm close to you. As much as you are very, and I mean very stimulating, I'm not interested in a quickie. I want to make love with you and hope it can be soon."

She cradled his head in one arm, pulled it between her breasts and said, "I, too, am at my best when I'm with you. But, Mr. President, this morning, you can't be late."

Nathan thought, *Will I always have to choose between my country and my wife? Perhaps someday I will no longer have to choose, I can just be with her.*

They got up, had a quick breakfast and kissed each other goodbye. "I'll see you when I see you, hopefully earlier tonight than last night." Karen reached out, placed her right hand over his heart, and said, "Be well."

The president was on his way to the War Room when he ran into Mark who told him, "Mr. President, two of my people have come up with a credible way to stop the flow of oil and gas into Port Fourchon. I have taken the liberty to invite them to make a presentation this morning, if that's all right with you."

"I'll listen to any credible idea, but I think I'll have them make their presentation while the Congressional leadership is in the room. It will give everyone a feel for the magnitude of the problems we're facing, and the Congressmen will see how we are dealing with them."

Mark nodded. "I'll have them wait outside until you ask for them."

As Jordan and Simmons approached the War Room, they saw Megan and Ted sitting in the chairs outside the room. Megan turned to Ted and whispered, "That was the president and the Secretary for Homeland Security!" Each time a cabinet secretary walked by they swallowed harder and harder as they realized to whom they'd be speaking in a matter of moments.

Their heads turned as the Speaker and the rest of the leadership from Congress walked through the doors. Megan said, "How will we ever get through this presentation? The leadership of the free world is in this room and they're waiting to hear from us."

"Megan, you have to focus," Ted reassured her. "We're offering an idea that we think is plausible and could help save the United States and millions of American lives. All we have to do is tell our story and let them react. If they ask questions, we must be sure that they are asking us and not another cabinet member. We'll take our cue from Williams. As the question

THE BROTHERHOOD OF THE RED NILE

is being asked, he will raise his chin up slightly if we are to answer. If he moves his head slightly to the left or right that means we should defer to him. Got it?"

"Got it. I just hope I remember it." Megan fingered her laptop nervously.

Within a few minutes of the door being closed, Williams stepped out and asked them to come into the room. He introduced the two of them and simply said to them. "Please share your idea."

The two of them told the severed head story and what it would take to sever the head and what the impact of the action would be for the environment. Then they talked about how it would stop the flow of contaminated oil and gas. It took less than ten minutes to tell their story and then they asked for questions.

"Do you have any idea the amount of oil that would flow into the Gulf?"

They looked at Williams and got the go ahead. "Well sir, it all depends on how fast we can shut down the rigs. Perhaps the Energy or Interior Departments would be a more reliable source for the specific flow rate. We do know that the more quickly the wells are shut down the sooner the flow will stop."

"What type of sub and torpedoes would you need?"

Ted whispers, "No, don't answer." Williams replied, "Mr. Secretary, for that answer we would have to defer to the Pentagon."

General Powell responded, "Mr. Secretary, we have a few subs in the Gulf and could be in position to fire laser-guided non-nuclear torpedoes within twelve hours."

"Mr. Baker, you talked about capping the broken pipes. How long after the strike could we cap the pipes going into Port Fourchon?"

"Mr. Secretary, it would seem to me that we would need several teams of divers on the surface with the caps and welding equipment on barges. As soon as the impact of the explosions has settled we could be in the water."

"Young man, how do you know so much about demolition?"

"Sir, before I came to Homeland Security I was a special ops leader in Langley. Sir, if I may, while it's important to get the sub in place we have to find out the size of the pipe and whether we locate a cap large enough. We can use a larger one fit, and depending on the size available, we may well have to make a smaller one as a plug. I would think Interior or Energy must have some plans on the pipe sizes. The quicker we can learn that, the faster we can begin to locate a plug or a cap. Once we have the wells shut down, we can perform the same process on the other end of the pipeline."

The president looked at Interior and Energy and saw that both were mouthing to him, "We're on it."

The Secretary of the Environmental Protection Agency asked, "Is there any other way than to dump perhaps millions of gallons of raw crude oil into the Gulf of Mexico? Mr. President, I feel that when the environmentalists hear what we're planning they will be very angry."

"Mr. Secretary, I appreciate your concern about what destruction this move might cause to the environment in the Gulf. I also know that the BP oil spill in 2010 lasted eighty-six days. That's over twelve weeks. We're talking about shutting all the wells and stopping the flow in four weeks, at most.

"If I have to make the decision, and I do, between saving perhaps millions of Americans lives or the health of the Gulf of Mexico, I choose people. General Powell, this is now your task. You're in charge. Take these two people and let them work with your team in cutting off the head of the snake. Make it happen now. Understood?"

"Yes, sir!"

CHAPTER 46

We Think We Know Where

Williams left the War Room with Megan and Ted. They started walking down the hallway when Ted turned to Frank and says, "Sir, we think we've figured out where the Brotherhood is."

"Where?"

"Houston."

"How do you know that?"

They shared with Frank everything they had gathered.

Williams said, "You have me convinced. The problem is that both of you are now on assignment to the Pentagon until we get the head of the snake severed. Who do you suggest I put on the case to follow up on your lead?"

Ted spoke up, "Sir, we have Omid on the ground in Springfield, which is less than an hour away from Houston. You could send him and we could brief him while we're waiting on the Gulf action to take place."

"Excellent idea! I'll run it by the Secretary after the meeting."

Omid was Major Omid Rahimi, a Marine on special assignment from the Pentagon to the Department of Homeland Security. He was highly decorated and served several tours of duty in Iraq and was working in the intelligence section as the assistant J-2 for the Joint Chiefs of Staff.

He had come over to Homeland Security just before the security breach in Springfield, Texas, and had been assigned by the secretary to figure out what was going on with the Brotherhood of the Red Nile. The local sheriff had found a map in the basement of the Ridley House, which turned out to be a possible target map for bombs to be used in the United States.

Unfortunately, the sheriff lost one of his sergeants when a booby-trapped bomb went off and killed him.

"Why don't you reach out to the Major and see what's going on in Springfield and see if he is at a point that he can free himself to work on this assignment."

"Yes, sir."

"I have to get back to the meeting but I'll call you later."

As Ted and Megan were walking down the hall, two distinguished looking men walked past them and sat on the chairs that they had been sitting on.

"I wonder who they are and what they have to add to the meeting." Megan commented. Neither of them recognized the Nobel laureates, who were to address the problem of all the contaminated oil in the pipelines.

After a few minutes, the door opened and out stepped President Jordan to escort Perlmutter and Burrows into the room personally. "I want to introduce two very distinguished scientists. Both recently won the Nobel Prize in Physics: Dr. Nathan Perlmutter of UC Berkley, and Dr. Adam Rice Burrows of Johns Hopkins. I spent some time with them last night discussing our problem and am hopeful they have some ideas about what we can do.

"We have the leadership of Congress with us in the room. Most of what they have heard so far is new information. Perhaps one of you could state the problem and then tell us what we need to do to fix the problem."

Perlmutter asked the technician, "Do you have the satellite link you showed us last night?"

"Yes, sir. I'll call it up."

The first images were of Texas City. Perlmutter points, "As you can see by the time stamp on the lower left, these images were taken just a few minutes ago. While this is true devastation, the solution to the problems in Texas City is relatively simple. The best thing to do for now is to let the fires burn themselves out. This may take an extended period of time because of the amount of energy still remaining in the storage tanks and pipelines that run through what is left of the multiple refineries in Texas City. This is a very hot city for two reasons. The first is the intensity of the fires, and the second is the radiation.

"As difficult as it is to say, once the fires are out we must build a high wall around the perimeter of the city, I'd say ten miles out, and then be ready to keep it secure for at least fifty years."

"Doctor, are you saying we may never be able to go back into Texas City?"

"In a word, yes."

"Do you disagree, Dr. Burrows?"

"No, I do not," he said.

"Mr. President, I suggest you get ready to abandon Texas City and get started building the secure perimeter."

The president asked, "Why the rush?"

"People are naturally curious and will go to Texas City to see the disaster for themselves. They will be inclined take some debris as souvenirs away with them. Those articles will be contaminated with radiation, and the carriers themselves will become contaminated. They will leave the site and take the contamination with them when they return home and will contaminate that place. At all costs, we must keep everything inside the walls and all the people out. After the fires are out and the town has cooled down, we can go in and check the radiation levels. I would think we could do this every five years or so and when the radiation is down to a safe level we could consider repopulating the city."

Robert Ward, the Speaker of the House, asked the president if he could ask the physicists a question.

"Of course you can, go right ahead."

"Dr. Burrows, am I to understand that we should walk away from Texas City, board it up and check back in five years. Is this the best we have to offer?"

"Mr. Speaker, there is nobody left in Texas City. They were vaporized within seconds of the explosion. There is nothing to go back to; it is all melted, fused or vaporized. I hate sounding so harsh, but we have no other safe choice. The bottom line, Mr. Speaker, is that no person or animal can live in Texas City, not now and perhaps never."

CHAPTER 47

Omid's Impossible Mission

Ted took out his cell phone and dialed Omid's number. It rang several times before a groggy voice answered. "Hello, who is this?"

"This is Ted Baker from Homeland Security."

"Yes?" He coughed, "Yes, Ted, what can I do for you?"

"Williams will be talking to the Secretary about a new assignment for you. I won't know for sure until after the conclusion of the meeting he's attending, probably later this morning. Can you put Springfield on hold and take on a new assignment close to where you are?"

Omid sat up in bed rubbing his eyes with one hand while holding the phone with the other. He thought about how to answer Ted. He wanted to finish his job in Springfield. He still hadn't figured out where Michael Ridley and his parents, Mike and Mary, were. The bombs in Texas City and Port Fourchon seemed to make what he was doing somewhat moot.

"I would like to follow this case to some conclusion, but if the Secretary needs me to do something else, well, then, I'm a soldier. I take orders and try to carry them out. Will I be working with you on this?"

"For the moment Megan and I are somewhat like you, we're on assignment to the Pentagon."

"Can you tell me what you're working on?"

"Not over a non-secure line. I can tell you that we've been assigned to chop off the head of a snake. When it's over, I'll be able to tell you and I think we'll work together on this project soon."

"Can you tell me what the project is, or is that top secret?"

158

"It is, Omid. All I can tell you for now is that this could be the most challenging assignment in your life. Megan and I believe we have determined that some persons of interest are just down the road from you.

"We suggested to Williams that you were close and that perhaps you could go there and see what you can find out. The White House communications office was able to trace the cell phone call to a phone that was set up in Iran, but used at a Houston Wi-Fi site to make the call. They're trying to locate the Wi-Fi site and said it would take a few days, but they think they have enough data. The caller stayed on with the president for ten minutes."

Ted asked, "So, are you interested?"

"Should I pack now or wait for an official call?"

"I would pack and be ready when the call comes."

"I'm on it. Thanks for giving me the opportunity."

"We'll help as much as we can."

While Ted was talking with Omid from Langley Virginia, John Seacrest, a special agent with the CIA who assisted in the identification of some of the members in the Brotherhood, was sitting at his desk somewhat despondent because in his mind only pure luck would have stopped the Brotherhood's attack on the United States. He thought, *There were too many ways to get the bombs into America, and we couldn't stop them.* From the very beginning of his involvement with the Brotherhood issue, his concern had been that not enough people were working on the project.

He decided to call Captain Oppenheimer of Mossad, part of Israeli intelligence. The Captain had led the mission to observe what was going on in Syria where the Brotherhood had met, built their bombs and launched their attack. He needed to talk to his old friend. He made the call and the Captain answered on the fourth ring, "Oppenheimer here."

"David, John Seacrest here. How are you?"

"The question, my friend, is how are you?"

"We're working on the results of the bombs and how we can cope with the destruction. Do you know we have a curfew and martial law in force?"

"I heard that. How is it being accepted?"

"It's too early to tell. We're still in the first day. We have reports of a run on food and fuel and ATMs being damaged by people angry that they can't get money out of their banks. With the police and the military patrolling the streets after curfew tonight there won't be enough time to break into the machines.

"David, I've been going over my notes and the transcripts of the observations your team made and for the life of me I can't figure out how they got the bombs out of Syria. We knew that there was a plan to take them in Assad's truck to the port, but your team never saw them arrive and be put on the boat."

David replied, "That is correct. We had people at his business and all the ports. Nothing ever came. Clearly, they took them out another way."

"In looking at the notes. David, you had one of your people who made friends with one of the team members. As I recall, she met with Mordecai several times. She apparently hit it off with him. Did she have anything to report about their conversations?" John inquired.

"Not really. I remember she told me that she opened the door to the barn where her team was meeting and knocked him down. Everyone else had already left."

"Anything else you can tell me?"

"Part of her job was to attach a GPS tracking device to Mordecai. She told me that she in fact did attach it."

"Do you know if it was ever activated?"

"No, I don't know if we ever used it. In our rush, I forgot all about it."

"Who gives the order to turn on the device?"

"My director, Nava Dobias," came David's firm reply.

"Do you know anything about the range of the GPS tracker?"

"No, but I can find out. Do you want me to have it activated?

"Yes, as soon as possible. If we have the ability to find Mordecai, we could find some or all of the Brotherhood of the Red Nile. However, making that decision is way above my pay grade. I have to figure out to whom I deliver this information, so the highest possible authority can make the call. Dave, don't tell anybody about this and I'll get back to you as soon as I can." After he hung up, Seacrest thought, "*We just might get those bastards.*"

He put in a call to Ted Baker to tell him about the inactive GPS.

"This is Ted Baker."

"Ted, this is John Seacrest. Do you have a moment?"

"John, for you I will always make time, what's up?"

"Ted, I think it might be possible to locate Mordecai Hagal."

"Mordecai, the terrorist from the Brotherhood?"

"Yes."

"How?"

"When Mossad sent its team into Syria to observe the Brotherhood, they gave the team in the village miniature GPS tracking units. If they had a chance, they were to attach them to the terrorist if they came into town. The woman in charge of the team in the village was Lt. Hadar Hassen, and she was able to attach one of the GPS units on Mordecai."

"Why wasn't it ever activated?"

"I don't know."

"Is it possible to turn it on now?"

"I spoke with Captain David Oppenheimer, a friend of mine who was in charge of the operation and he said that he feels that somebody higher up needs to make the call."

"Who should make the call?"

"I think Under Secretary Williams needs to make the call to the head of Mossad, Nava Dobias and have him turn it on and tell us the location."

"This is great news! As soon as he returns from the White House, I'll speak with him. Thank you."

"Ted, we don't know if the device will still work so let's hold our excitement till we see if we can get the GPS to work and locate Mordecai."

"I'll let you know what happens."

While Baker was waiting for Williams to return to talk about the GPS, he decided to reach out to Omid Rahimi, who was on his way to Houston. He dialed his cell number. It rang several times before Omid picked up. "Rahimi here."

"Omid, this is Ted Baker, how are you?"

"I'm on the road to Houston. Normally it should take about forty-five minutes but I've been on the road for two hours. I'm going to have to get off the freeway and try to find some gas. Otherwise I'll never make it to Houston. It seemed that when the curfew was lifted at 6 AM, the whole world was out and about, if for no other reason because it was permitted until 6 PM. So why do you think the terrorists are in Houston?"

"Firstly, the proximity to the two bomb sites, and secondly, when they called the president, White House communications triangulated the source of the signal to an Internet café in Houston. I'm still waiting for the exact location, but my guess is that they're in a hotel close to where they released their e-mail and YouTube video. As soon as I get the address of the café, I'll forward it to you. Let me make one thing clear, I'm not looking for a hero. Just try to find out where they are, and get back to us so we can send a capture team to assist you.

"We found out that Mossad had an operative in the village near the meeting site and she placed a GPS on one of the terrorists. We're working with the head of Mossad to turn it on and see if it leads us to Houston, where one, if not all, of the terrorists might be."

"How confident are you that the GPS will find him?"

"Based on what we know of the type that was attached, the signal should be readable almost anywhere in the world."

"So, you don't know if Mossad has ever tested it for signal strength?"

"I can't answer that until we talk to them. Keep on working your way to Houston and let me know your progress."

CHAPTER 48

War Room

The president had brought in the two Nobel laureates to ask a very serious question, "Gentlemen, we have, as best we can tell, at least ten thousand square miles – an area the equivalent in size to the State of Massachusetts – that is the site of contaminated oil and natural gas locked into a pipeline. We estimate that, in that area, we have about four million people. We also know that the current level of radiation ten miles from Texas City is at least 400 millrems. So, gentlemen, is it safe for the people to stay or do they need to be evacuated?"

Perlmutter responded, "Mr. President, the two of us have discussed this issue for most of the night and we have concluded that if the radiation level were to stay at its current 400 millrems reading we believe they could stay for a short while – perhaps six months. It concerns us is that no natural forces that can dissipate the radiation. You have effectively sealed all of the contaminated energy in steel tubes. While it is true, for the most part these are very large tubes, the negative is that, in the largest tubes, you have a very high concentration of contaminated energy.

"We fear that with no natural forces to dissipate the concentration of radiation, it could feed on itself and possibly intensify. Mr. President, you must keep in mind that we have no experience - in fact, nobody has any experience - dealing with such a large volume of contaminated material. So, all we can give you is our best judgment. We think the safest procedure is to immediately evacuate all people within a twenty-mile radius from the center of Texas City and start them on iodine. We also believe we need to set up radiation monitors every half mile from ten miles to twenty miles out. If the radiation level increases outside of these areas then the people in that area should also be given iodine and evacuated. With the four major trunk lines being so large, we could have disbursed hot spots, depending on how deep the trunk line is under ground. One other thing that concerns us is the airborne radiation from the fires at Texas City. We think that the satellite which has tracked the flow in the ground needs to check the radiation from the fires and see where it has been deposited."

Dr. Burrows added, "You see, the people in those fallout areas are at risk. Any shift in the winds could deposit material on drilling rigs and platforms in the Gulf of Mexico. We also think that you need an advisory panel to help you monitor the contamination in Port Fourchon. The issues in Louisiana are dramatically different than those at Texas City and, to be honest, we have not spent any time on the latter situation."

"Thank you for your observations and recommendations. I do have an additional question: what are we to do with the contaminated oil, natural gas, and refined product in the shut down and sealed pipelines?"

Burrows responded, "Mr. President, we have given this a great deal of additional thought. In fact, we have not slept much thinking about both problems. The only solution we have, I'm afraid, is not really a solution. We recommend to you that you convene a panel of scientists from around the world to meet and discuss possible solutions. Perhaps better minds than ours can come up with an answer to this very devastating situation. Until then, our plan for monitoring, iodine administration and evacuation of people at risk in Texas is the best we can come up with for the moment. We both wish we had a magic solution for you but, unfortunately, we have none."

The president thanked the laureates and turned to the assembly. "Ladies and gentlemen, our current challenges are finding enough iodine and choosing a place to relocate perhaps one million people, possibly millions more. Based on the recommendations, these people will have to leave everything behind. When they reach the decontamination point, they will be stripped of all their clothes and sent somewhere to try to re-establish a life. They will go without a job and perhaps very little money to live on until they have the possibility of finding work. Some may have family to go to, but many may find, even though they have family, they will be shunned because of the fear of radiation poisoning. While the scientists are working on how to get the contaminated oil out of the ground, we face the challenge of moving millions of people."

Homeland Secretary Simons spoke up, "Mr. President, I have a thought. You talked about all the challenges we have in front of us and I agree they are many, but they also may present some significant opportunities."

The president smiled wanly. "Is that like 'every cloud has a silver lining,' Mr. Secretary?"

"In a way, Mr. President. You see, this may just present a significant opportunity to galvanize the American people to a new goal. America made a commitment to put a man on the moon and we did. All other nations that went to the moon saw one thing when they arrived and that was the American flag. I think the challenges you have given us in some ways are equal to putting a man on the moon."

The president responded, "Like what?"

"Sir, we have to build houses for all these people. Our housing market has been in the doldrums since the collapse of 2008. By my estimate, we may have to build at least a million homes. We will have to start from scratch and probably build twenty new cities with roads, water and sewer, shopping centers, city governments and much more. They will need schools, hospitals, and government services. We can move people and help them with the money to build new cities. Because we have to work quickly, skilled people from all over the United States will come and help build the new cities.

"We have energy that has been capped either in the ground or in the sea. We need to build new pipelines and to move the good energy around the bad, and find a way to get the energy from the Gulf onshore to our refineries. We could create one of the largest economic booms in the history of America. We currently have over eighteen million foreclosed or abandoned houses in the United States. Granted, some may not be in the best neighborhoods but, if we need one million, let's start there. We can hire people to rehab the houses, and folks can move in and live there without cost until they find a job."

The president felt a positive buzz in the room for the first time in the last twenty-one hours. Everyone was smiling and energized by what Mark had to say. "I think what we have just heard is just the beginning of the things that need to be done to give America a purpose and common goal. Perhaps for years to come, we shall have to focus all of our energy on filling the needs of America first, and that means we must use all of our resources to protect our people first."

The president continued, "When times were difficult Roosevelt had his fireside chats. I think we need to revisit that concept for keeping America informed. We must tell the American people the truth, and I cannot do it alone. I shall need all of the governments – federal, state and local – to cooperate in streamlining the process. We can get started today on 'Rebuilding America.'

"Here is what we need to do now." The president realized everyone in the room was prepared to collaborate for the common good. "I want Health and Human Services to call all the drug companies that are making or can make iodine. We need millions and millions of tablets. Get with the Surgeon General's people and figure out the dosage necessary for everybody of whatever age, and tell the drug companies to go on overtime production. I want the results of those calls today.

"Next, I want Housing and Urban Development to go to all the housing agencies and get lists of foreclosed or abandoned homes. I also want the Treasury to contact the banks, and I want a list of all of the houses they hold. HUD, you will be responsible for building the list. Labor, I want a meeting today with the heads of all the trade unions. If they're not in Washington, I want them on the phone. No, and I mean *no* excuses. I will have Mary schedule an update meeting later today. We have many more problems to solve. Agreed?"

In one voice, everyone assembled spoke clearly. "*Agreed*, Mr. President."

CHAPTER 49

Frank Williams' Office

After a long, detailed and invigorating meeting with the president, Frank Williams returned to his office and found Ellen sitting at his conference table with some bagels, cream cheese and a pot of coffee. Frank walked over, "Where did you get this? I'm starving."

She smiled. "I have my sources. Sit down and eat."

"Have you eaten?"

"Yes, Marie and I went down to the cafeteria and had a hot breakfast. We didn't know how long you'd be gone, but we knew you'd be hungry. Frank, I want to apologize for my behavior last night. I think it would be best for me to go home and get back to work, if the office is open. You need to concentrate on helping the country and I will come in when you think we can spend some time together on your couch."

"Do you think that is a good idea?" Frank quickly grabbed his bagel and accepted a steaming mug of coffee.

"Well, I'd like to be here with you but, if you spend most of your day out of the office, you wouldn't be around to see me. No, I think we'll be better off if I also try to help in whatever way I can. So come over here and give me a hug and a kiss, and I'll be on my way."

Frank put down the bagel, got up from the table, and went over and closed the door. He gently moved her up against it and kissed her gently on the lips. She reached down, grabbed his hand, gently put it on her left breast, and kissed him back, saying, "This one has been neglected, since we aren't cuddling."

Frank was tempted to grab a handful but he could feel the tension in her body, so he just gently caressed her and helped her relax. "Call me when you get home and let me know what your plans are. Marie can tell you if I'm out for a meeting, in which case I'll call you back as soon as I can."

Just before Frank let her go he looked in her eyes and saw a frisson of fear there. He softly said, "I love you more than anyone or anything in the world."

She looked back into his eyes and saw the confidence that was always there. It was what made her secure with Frank. "You give me the courage to be the best I can be, and I love you with every ounce of my being."

Frank let her go, his hand falling to his side. He reached out and opened the door for her to leave. Ellen got her purse, checked for her keys, took her coat off the back of the chair and was quickly out the door. This time, as she walked down the hallway, she only stopped once, blew Frank a kiss, and left smiling.

As Frank returned to his office, he saw Ted Baker sitting on the couch in the reception area, with his head against the wall fast asleep.

Marie smiled. "He worked through the night and I thought I'd let him sleep till you were ready to see him."

Williams walked over and touched his assistant on the shoulder. "I'm ready." Ted opened and blinked his eyes.

"Sorry sir, I must have fallen asleep."

"Not a problem. We're all going to be sleep deprived for a while; come in and tell me what you have."

Ted stood up, tried to straighten his suit and dropped his folder. Williams bent over to help him pick it up and they walked into his office. He chuckled when he saw Baker's eyes lock on the bagels and cream cheese. "Have you had anything to eat, son?"

"No, sir."

"When was the last time you ate?"

"Sir, I think it was sometime yesterday."

"Would you like a bagel or two with some cream cheese?"

"Very much, sir."

"Help yourself. Want some coffee?"

"Please."

Williams poured another mug from the pot on the table. As he turned around, Baker had practically finished the first bagel.

"Slow down, you'll choke. There's cream and sugar here. Help yourself."

"Sorry sir, can we talk while I eat?" Ted added sugar to the steaming brew and took a grateful swallow.

"Of course. Go ahead."

"Sir, I just received a phone call from John Seacrest, our friend at CIA who has been helping us."

"Yes, go on."

"Well sir, it may be possible to locate one of the terrorists and, with some luck, we might find all of them."

Frank held his coffee between his two hands, warming them. "How is that possible?"

"Well sir, when the terrorist Mordecai went into the Syrian town, he was met by a Mossad operative named Hadar Hassen. She planted a GPS tracking device on him."

"So, where is the signal pointing?"

"Mossad hasn't activated it yet. They didn't believe that the bombs posed a threat to Israel, so they never turned it on."

"So, how do we get it activated?"

"The captain in charge of the mission told me that it must be turned on by an order of the director of Mossad, Nava Dobias."

Frank smiled. "So, you want me to call my friend Dobias and tell him I need the GPS turned on." His smile faded abruptly, "We need to see where the bastards are so we can go and arrest them. Sit right there, don't move." He picked up his intercom and ordered Marie, "Get me Dobias *now!*"

"Yes sir." Moments later, Marie responded that she has been told that he was in a meeting and will call back.

"You tell whoever is on the other end of the goddamn phone line that I need to speak to Dobias now, or I shall call the President of the United States and he will call the Prime Minister to tell him that he will personally hold him responsible for the loss of millions of American lives. Got that?"

"Yes, sir." Within a moment, Frank heard his old friend's voice.

"Dobias here. I was devastated to learn of the two attacks. How can I help, my friend?"

"Nava, you recently sent an observation team into Syria and gave Lt. Hassen a GPS tracking device, is that correct?"

"Yes."

"It's our understanding that she attached it to a terrorist named Mordecai, but in all the excitement with the redeployment it was never turned on."

"Frank, I have no way of knowing that, but if you hold I will try and find out."

"You bet I'll hold."

A few moments later Nava was back on the line, "I was unable to locate Lt. Hassen, but I have everybody looking for her and, as soon as I find, her I shall ask her about this and get back to you."

"Excellent."

"Frank, when I find her she will have to give me the serial number so I can activate it, do you want me to turn it on before I call you, or wait?"

"Turn it on the first second you can. Millions of lives are at stake!"

CHAPTER 50

Turn It On

After leaving Williams' office, Baker called Megan at the forensics lab.

"Ted, what's up?"

"We need to go to the Special Ops Room at the Pentagon and meet with General Powell and his team as soon as possible. I have Marie on the phone trying to set a time. That oil is moving out of the snake's head at six miles an hour. It's been almost ten hours since the blast, so the oil has moved close to sixty miles north, which puts it just on the outskirts of New Orleans. We have to stop this in the next few hours to keep the contaminated oil from going further north, east and west. I'm expecting to hear from General Powell shortly, so be ready to go on a moment's notice."

Just as he hung up his phone, he got the call from Powell's office about the meeting. "How soon can you be at the Pentagon?"

"We'll be there within the half hour." He sprinted out of his office and immediately headed for Megan's office. She was coming out the door as he got off the elevator. They rushed back to the elevator and pushed the button for the ground floor. As they exited, Baker saw the car he ordered, and both jumped in. "To the Pentagon, and use the flashers and sirens," Ted ordered.

"With the explosions and the fires, the flow may have slowed a little bit so we may have an outside shot of saving New Orleans. That city hasn't recovered from Katrina. If we don't solve this, I'm afraid the city will be abandoned. I've asked for satellite images of the snake to be sent to General Powell."

"Have you heard if the navy has a sub close by?"

Ted nodded. "I got a message from Williams, while he was in the meeting. The general said they have two subs in the Gulf and that one of them is on the way to our site."

"Were you able to find out if a cap is available to plug the pipe?"

"No, I hope to find out when we get to the meeting."

With lights and sirens, they made it to the Pentagon in fifteen minutes flat. They walked through the door and were met by armed guards who asked for identification and the person they were here to see. At the mention of General Powell, they were moved to the front of the line. They quickly cleared security and were escorted to the Special Ops briefing room.

When they entered, General Powell walked over, greeted them and introduced them to his senior military advisors.

Ted gave a little salute to the assembly of two and three stars. "Sir, we have to act with the utmost urgency. Based on the speed the oil is moving, we have a short window to save New Orleans."

"We're ready. We have the satellite image of the pipeline running into Port Fourchon and we have the USS Bonefish in position."

"Sir, we need an image of the radiation so we can figure out how far out we need to make the first cut in the pipeline." Ted spoke to a technician. "Can you call up the most recent satellite image?"

The image quickly appeared on the monitors. General Powell said, "As you can see, the contamination is mostly on shore because the power of the flow of the oil in the pipeline is going to keep the radiation at bay."

Ted warned, "Once you sever the pipe the flow could reverse itself and start flowing through the broken pipe back out into the Gulf."

"That is true, but we have several diving crews circling the projected separation spot, along with a Sikorsky helicopter waiting on shore to bring us the temporary plug for the pipe. If we blow the pipe far enough from the head of the snake, the flow will be mostly good oil and hopefully we can get it capped before the bad oil reaches the divers."

"General, we have given this some thought and have gone over the maps of the Gulf. It appears that, if we blow the furthest point first, the pressure will drop in the remaining pipeline. Then, when you blow the closest point, there shouldn't be a lot of oil for the divers to deal with."

"We agree. Our people have looked at the topographical maps also, and they think we should blow at least one mile of pipeline and wait a few moments for the pressure to drop and then blow the second section. It appears that this pipeline is close to lying on the sea floor so hitting it directly will not be easy."

Ted asked, "Aren't the torpedoes equipped with laser guidance?"

One of the generals replied, "Yes, but using a laser to hit a battleship or another sub is a heck of a lot easier than hitting an eight foot pipeline."

"Do the torpedoes have cameras in them so you can see the target?"

"Affirmative for nuclear missiles, but not for traditional torpedoes," came the reply.

CHAPTER 51

Oval Office

President Jordan had just finished the most upbeat cabinet meeting since the crisis started. As he slowly opened the door to his office, he viewed the rug with the Great Seal of the United States of America. Nathan remembered how Harry Truman changed the direction of the head of the eagle away from the arrows. *His logic was that we had just come through the Second World War and the Korean War, and it was time for peace.* As Jordan looked at the rug, he wondered if he should change it back to the way it was originally. He decided that, when America had recovered, and if he was still the president, he would change it back.

He had asked Mary to call Karen and her team to join him in the Oval Office to discuss fireside chats. For the few moments alone, while he waited for them to arrive, he sat and enjoyed the brief moment of silence. Mary buzzed Nathan on the intercom to let him know they had assembled in the hall.

"Thanks Mary, please send them in."

The door opened and Karen rushed over to Nathan to give him a kiss and a hug. "I've missed you."

"I've missed you, too. I especially miss holding you, but we have work to do. Perhaps we'll have some time later." He gave her a little pat on the shoulder.

"You are here because I believe the American people should be Informed on a regular basis concerning the progress we're making in overcoming our challenges. I want to communicate the specific measures we have to take for everybody's protection."

Karen's chief of staff spoke. "Sir, perhaps you can take us through some of the topics you feel should be told to the American people. Eventually you can tell us the order in which you want to present them. But first we could discuss the 'how' first."

"What do you mean 'how', Maggie?"

"Mr. President, on the surface most people would think the TV is the best way to communicate, and in most situations that would be true. The problem with TV, however, is that not everybody will be in front of a TV, but just about everybody can have access to a radio or access the signal through their computers and mobile devices."

"So, are you suggesting we go back to Roosevelt's era and his radio chats?"

"No, sir, I'm not. I am saying that, despite progress in public media, presidents have continued to use weekly radio addresses as a way to reach the maximum number of people, and that we should give this serious consideration. Radio is still a very powerful medium, and I think it could be more effective than TV."

Karen spoke up, "Mr. President, I think there is significant merit to what Maggie is suggesting. If we can use the weekly message as a way of updating America, I think more people will hear what you want to say. I also think it's important that you control the news cycle to stay ahead of the press."

Bill jumped in, "Sir, I agree with Maggie and also think the messages should be focused and on point. Tell people the problem and what you are doing about it. If we include too much at one time, this will just confuse and scare people. We need to let America know that their president is on the job, doing everything possible and using all the resources the United States possesses to solve the problems."

Deb responded, "Mr. President, I agree with Maggie and Bill, but you also need to communicate that we are in this challenge together. It's important to make the people aware that some in our country are more affected than others, and that we all must work together."

"I agree with everything you've said, so let's start with issue one." The president removed his suit jacket and undid his shirt cuffs, ready to work.

"To the best of our knowledge, about ten thousand square miles of Texas is sitting on top of contaminated energy in various forms. The scientists tell me that we have to move one million people and perhaps more out of the danger area as quickly as possible. The people being evacuated will have to leave everything behind. Once they clear the contaminated area, they will have to go through a decontamination process. They will literally have to give up the very clothes on their backs. We'll have to find places for them to live and work. These people may never be able to go back to their homes again and, while some people will think they will be freeloading because we are going to help them, it is not their fault, and they need our help."

Karen questioned, "Where are we going to put so many people and how long will it take?"

"Excellent questions, dear. I think we have to tell everybody what the problem is, and that we are going to move the highest risk people first. We don't know for sure how many people reside in the high-risk area, but we're estimating about one hundred thousand. The plans are still being worked out, but the system has to be set up to handle at least ten thousand a week. As we get better and more efficient, we should be able to handle more per week."

Deb suggested, "We're going to take ten weeks to move the people at risk?"

"I hope we can move them faster than that, but keep in mind this has never been done before. Before and after Katrina, it was an evacuation. We're talking radioactive decontamination on top of it all."

"What about children first?"

"I understand your concern about the health of the children, but I do not want to break up families. The dislocation of the whole family will be difficult enough. Right now, I want to focus on the best way for me to talk to the country. I think we have to control the flow of information, and at the same time many people, including Congress, will want to know what is going on, and how are we dealing with all the problems and challenges. By the same token, I do not want to be in their faces, scaring them every time I talk."

Karen responded, "It seems to me that radio works the best. We could use your Saturday address to update the people on what is going on in

America. I would also suggest we give the weekly address a name. I think the program should run no more than twenty minutes and, from time to time, you should have guests to address a particular issue that is important at the moment."

"Mr. President?"

"Yes, Deb."

"Perhaps a name for the show could be 'America Rebuilds: An Update.' This sends a positive message. We are rebuilding, and are also being transparent by keeping the whole country informed. At some point, hopefully, we will no longer need the name and can change it to something else. If you broadcast, say, every Saturday at two o'clock, people will get used to the time slot and will tune in to get a quick update, if only to see if the matter being discussed will affect them. We can also ask all the stations to ensure the program is available online so people can access it 24/7."

Bill cleared his throat to get attention, "Mr. President, what about the media and news conferences? If you're giving updates to everybody on Saturdays, will you need press briefings?"

"There will be other issues that the press will want to report on. I'll need to manage their coverage. If they start asking questions about the rebuilding, I'll refer them to these talks. Understand that I see the Saturday address as an update. The press will have access to papers released and briefings giving the details of what we are doing. The Saturday address has to be one of hope, optimism, and facts for the American people, helping trust that their government is telling them the truth, no matter how bad it is. For some time to come, most of the news will be bad."

CHAPTER 52

Pentagon: What Was the Result?

Megan Brown, Ted Baker and General Powell were sitting at a large round table in the Special Ops room at the Pentagon. The rest of the room was full of generals and full-bird colonels waiting to hear the results from the sub that fired its first torpedo. Captain Josiah Bodkins, commander of the USS Bonefish, was given the order to fire. Acknowledging the command from General Powell, he told his first officer to fire tube one. The switch was thrown and the torpedo took off. The first officer estimated they are eight hundred yards from the targeted pipeline and that it would take just over two minutes for the torpedo to cover the distance to the target.

Everybody in the room looked at his watch. One minute passed. All of them leaned in, waiting to hear the sound of the explosion. Baker also glanced at his watch and thought they are about ten seconds out. He noted that Brown was looking at her phone, since she wasn't wearing a watch. The second hand just hit two minutes, but there was no explosion. He turned to Powell. "What happened?"

"We missed." Powell shifted in his chair. "Captain, how close were we to the target?"

Bodkins responded, "We missed it by two feet. Were ready to fire again."

Powell said, "Captain, fire at will."

"Yes, sir."

The captain gave the command. Baker turned to Brown and asked, "Don't you wear a watch?"

"No, I use my phone. A lot of people do, you know."

But, what happens if you your battery runs down?" he asked.

Brown hadn't thought about the possibility that she might not be able to charge her phone. She thought, *I hope I haven't screwed up my chances to get into special ops because I didn't have a watch. Nobody I know wears a watch.* Startled by the sound of an explosion, she dropped her phone. She hoped it wasn't broken, but discovered another reason to have a watch.

Baker smiled, "I think we have cut the snake in two."

Captain Bodkins ordered his first officer, "Fire two in sequence to make sure we have cut it all the way through."

"Yes sir. Fire tube two" could be heard over the speaker and the room relaxed, feeling confident that the pipeline was cut. They also knew that thousands of barrels of raw crude oil were now spewing out of the broken pipeline. All heard the second explosion and, a couple of minutes later, the third. They were sure the pipeline was severed.

Baker asked General Powell, "How long to reposition the sub for the shot to sever the head?"

"My guess is that it will be an hour." Powell signaled to one of his aides. "Would you like something to drink?"

Megan responded, "I could use a Diet Coke."

"Just black coffee, please."

The aide asked, "Do you want something, sir?'

"No. Nothing right now, thank you."

Everyone stood up to stretch and move around. They knew that the severing of the head of the snake and capping the pipeline was the most dangerous and hazardous part of the mission to come.

Baker took the opportunity of the break to reach Williams. He was hopeful that after the War Room meeting he could talk to him about the most recent developments. The phone rang and Marie answered. She could see 'Baker' on her caller ID. "Mr. Baker – Ted – how goes the snake hunting?"

"We have cut the snake in two and are now moving into position to take off the head. Has the Under Secretary returned?"

"He called a few moments ago and is on his way, but first he's going to stop by his house and see how his wife is doing. He'll be in later. Do you want me to call him?"

"Could you have him call me as soon as possible? This is urgent. I'll be expecting his call. Thank you, Marie."

"You're welcome, Ted. I'll reach out to him as soon as we hang up."

As Baker turned around, he was astounded by what he saw. The big screen monitor on the wall showed an image of the sub moving into position to take the shot that would cut off the head of the snake. He turned to General Powell with his mouth wide open.

The general nodded with satisfaction. "It's from one of our monitoring satellites. Because the sub is in such shallow water and the water is clear, we can make out the sub and see the section of the pipeline to be severed."

"How close can you get?"

"We can zoom in to about five hundred feet above the water but at that level we would lose a great deal of detail. We'll zoom in to about one mile above sea level."

Baker watched as the scene shifted before him. "Will we be able to see the torpedoes launched and the pipeline hit? Before you fire, may I ask a question?"

"Go right ahead. We'll do our best to answer."

"General, does this satellite have the ability to detect radiation?"

"This is the same satellite that was used over Texas to detect the radiation flow through the pipes."

"Before you fire can we look at two things? First, let's see if we're getting any back flow from the snake's head towards where we're considering cutting the pipe. Second, I would like to look past the head to see how far the contaminated energy has spread."

Powell turned to his aide and asked, "Can we do what Mr. Baker wants?"

"Yes sir, but do you want to fire the torpedoes first and then move?"

"I think we have to see how far the contaminated energy has moved back down the pipeline. It seems to me the longer we wait, the greater the risk to our divers of back flow covering them from the head of the snake."

Brown walked up to the monitor and pointed to the sub, "General, I think we need to know how far it is between this point and the closest radiation. By switching to the radiation detection we can watch how fast it's flowing backwards and make a decision about firing and getting the divers in the water."

"Ms. Brown, I agree. As soon as we cut the pipeline the pressure had to start declining; the worst thing that could happen for my men is to be in the water, trying to put on the cap, if the radiation starts pouring out of the pipeline." The general turns to one of the other generals and asks how far it is from the sub to the head of the snake.

A few officers huddled and one turned to Powell, "Sir, we estimate that the sub is six miles from the head of the snake."

Brown interjected, "Sir, is it possible to determine the slope of the pipeline? We know that the pipeline is below sea level."

"Why is that important?"

"If the pipeline is full and there is a substantial change in elevation then when we cut the pipeline the slope will cause the oil in the pipeline to fall faster back to the cut. If we can figure out the slope and we know the distance we can figure out how fast the pipeline will empty."

Powell responded, "Good point, Ms. Brown, but we have already cut the pipeline at about ten miles out. We have eliminated the push from the wells, and gravity is already working against us. We need to blow that pipeline and get the cap and divers in the water now."

Baker said, "I agree. Let's blow the pipeline, then switch to radiation detection and help the divers. I also agree with Ms. Brown that we need figure out how fast the oil is moving, so we can get it capped before it starts spilling radioactive energy into the Gulf."

"Captain Bodkins, are you in position, and can you see your target?"
"Yes sir."

"Then fire at will and keep firing until the pipe is severed."
"Yes, sir."

"Commence firing." The captain's commands were loud and clear on the speakers. "Launch the helicopter with the cap and head to the site. I want the divers in the water as soon as the cap arrives. Let's get that pipe covered."

They saw two explosions on the screen and watched the divers hovering, waiting for the cap to arrive. Baker requested that they switch over the satellite to read radiation and aim it towards the area north of the port towards New Orleans. The image of New Orleans on the screen revealed that the radiation has moved faster than they thought, and it had ...

CHAPTER 53

Frank's Home

Marie had called Frank Williams to tell him that Ted Baker needed to talk with him right away. Frank dialed Ted's cell number but did not get an answer and figured that Ted and Megan are still at the Pentagon working on shutting down the pipeline. He left Ted a message to call him.

As he pulled away from the White House, he made a right turn and headed towards Constitution Avenue. Pulling up to a red light, he wavered over whether to turn right to home and Ellen or go left to the office. The light turned green, but he didn't see it until the driver behind him honked. Frank turned right.

Marie already knew he was planning to go home. As he came around a corner, he saw the park bench where Ted and John Seacrest from CIA had met to review photos of the terrorists. While it was only a few weeks ago, the events of the last thirty-six hours made it seem longer.

As Williams drove home, he recalled his conversation with Ellen about the possibility of an attack and her reaction when it actually happened. He knew that he couldn't stay long at the house. It had only been a few hours since Ellen had left his office. His concern for her compelled him to check in on her quickly. He didn't call ahead, so he hoped it would be a surprise. In a short while, he pulled into the driveway. His brick front, two-car garage, two-story colonial home had just been painted a soft yellow with black shutters. Although they both loved to garden, they hired a professional gardener, who came by one day a week to keep everything neat and clean.

He got out of the car and walked up the stone walkway to the front porch. The porch stretched almost all the way across the front of the house and had an antique swing at the opposite end. He slowly climbed up the three steps and went to the front door, with its brass knocker in the center. Looking at the brightly painted red door, he remembered being told a long time ago that a red front door is a sign of welcome. He took out his key and was ready to put it in the lock when, for no particular reason, he tried the knob. The door opened. It seemed strange to him that Ellen would have left the door unlocked.

Frank slowly opened it and walked into the house. He set down his briefcase and looked into both the dining room and living room. No Ellen. He walked down the center hall towards the back of the house and went into the kitchen and breakfast room. No Ellen. He went around the corner to the family room. Still, no Ellen.

Frank's heart was starting to race. He looked out the family room window and couldn't see her in the yard. He raced back down the hallway past his office door and went up the stairs two at a time. He looked in all the bedrooms and bathrooms and she was nowhere to be found. "*Where could she be?*" He slowly came down the stairs and for a moment sat on the bottom step trying to figure out what to do.

Reaching into his pocket, he pulled out his cell phone and dialed her number. He got her voice message. He told her to call him as soon as possible. He was at the house and wanted to see her. He stood up and turned to walk down the hallway towards his office. Ellen rarely went in. She knew it was his space but, just on the slight chance she might be in there, he opened the door. It was empty.

He decided to check out the basement. Opening the door, he turned on the lights and went down into the basement. He looked all over, calling out her name.

Frank was in a panic when the phone rang. He looked at the caller ID, hoping it was Ellen. Instead, it was Ted Baker. Frank thought, *Should I answer or let it go to voice mail and continue to look for Ellen?* Should he answer and tell Baker that Ellen was missing, or should he call Homeland internal security? The phone continued to ring and finally went to voice mail.

Frank went up the stairs and headed into the kitchen to sit and sort things out. *What should I do?* He decided to go back upstairs to the master bedroom. He wasn't sure what he was looking for, but he began to look around. He walked into her closet and saw some empty hangers, some on the bar and some on the floor, almost as if someone had been in a hurry. He walked down the hallway to one of the spare bedrooms. This room was where they stored their luggage. He opened the door and one bag was missing. *She can't have left me. She loves me too much to leave. Was she so scared that when she got home and was alone that she panicked and packed a bag to get away? She had the one thousand dollars she got from the ATM, but where would she go?*

Frank got up and decided that he needed to check in the garage to see if her car is gone. With his head down, he walked slowly towards the garage door, turned the knob, opened the door to the garage, and...

CHAPTER 54

Pentagon Special Ops

Ted Baker had asked General Powell to move the field of vision of the satellite to the north of Port Fourchon and to continue moving north to New Orleans. As the satellite came over New Orleans, Baker asked the general to stop and zoom in on the bridge that crosses the center of Lake Pontchartrain. Baker could see a faint red color running across the lake and it was parallel to the causeway crossing the middle of the lake. Baker called Megan over to look at the image on the monitor and asked her what she thought. As Megan studied the image, she requested the general to zoom in closer.

The closer they got to the causeway, the sharper the image was of a small amount of radiation in the pipe that ran across the lake.

Baker pointed to it, "There must be some leakage out of the pipeline coming up from Port Fourchon. When the pipeline is capped, we need to shut the valve to the south of New Orleans so that no more radiation can get through."

General Powell briefly considered their next actions. "We have to call this in to Secretary Simons immediately so he can report to the president. The local EPA office needs to go to the bridge and measure the millrems along the length of the bridge. We don't want the lake and, in turn the drinking water, for the City of New Orleans to become contaminated so we need to talk with the Corps of Engineers so they can find a place where we can flush the line and dilute the radiation."

Baker put in another call to Williams and got his voice mail.

General Powell called Baker and Brown back to the table and the big screen. "You can see the helicopters with the divers hovering over the spot where the second break occurred. To your right, the heavy-duty chopper is bringing in the cap for the pipeline. It will hover in place until the divers say they're ready. The helicopter has to lower the cap and help the divers maneuver the cap in the water. Now you can see the barge with the welding equipment pulling into the site. It takes a great deal of coordination with all the stuff that could seriously hurt or kill our divers."

"General Powell, how do the divers weld under water?"

"They'll use arc welders, Ms. Brown. You may have seen them on TV. They have a clamp that holds the welding rod and passes electricity into the rod. They'll attach another clamp to the pipeline so that the electrical circuit is complete when the welding rod touches the area between the two pieces of pipe. Have you ever seen the sparks fly when a welder touches his welding rod to the metal he is trying to weld? Once the cap is loosely attached to the pipe, a cage will be placed on each half of the pipe to be welded. The divers will turn a crank that will force the pipe sections together. In essence, the cap is being pulled into place as far as it can go. The divers will weld a few spots around the cap and then disconnect the cables from the helicopter that brought it. With its part over, it will return to base, thus eliminating one of the possible elements of danger."

Baker asked, "General, how do you know so much about the process?"

Powell responds, "I may be the Chairman of the Joint Chiefs of Staff, but I'm a Navy man all the way and was, a long time ago, a Navy salvage diver."

"If I may ask, what are the risks involved in this operation, General?"

"Ms. Brown, the men in the water are at the greatest amount of risk. The welding is easy."

Megan looked at the general's face and saw his expression change all of a sudden. He had stopped talking. "General, what's wrong?"

"The wind has picked up and the waves have suddenly increased."

"Why is that bad?"

"That cap is hanging from the helicopter by cables and acts like an anchor. When the wind and the waves pick up, their force will move the cap, trying to pull the chopper down. They need to get that cap in place right away."

Megan and Ted stared at the screen and could see that the intensity of the wind and the waves was getting much worse. They watched the helicopter being tossed around. It appeared that the pilot was having trouble holding it steady. In the distance, they could see a large wave heading toward the work area.

"Should we call this off and try again later?" Baker asked.

Megan suggested, "General, the welding barge is very close to the cables from the helicopter holding the cap. Should we call it off?"

General Powell yelled as loud as he could, "Abort the mission!", but it was too late. A massive wave rolled over the work site and ...

CHAPTER 55

Frank Williams' Garage

Frank Williams' wife was nowhere to be found in the house. He had looked everywhere. The last place was the garage. He has walked down the hallway to the door that led to it and was turning the knob when his cell phone rang again. He didn't even look to see who was calling. He turned the knob and saw Ellen's car.

He slowly walked over and saw her inside lying on her side. From where he was standing, he could see her suitcase in the back seat. It did not appear that the car has been running; he couldn't smell any gasoline fumes in the air. Frank could see her chest moving up and down, so she was alive. He reached out and slowly pressed the button to open the car door. As he opened it, Ellen stirred. Frank thought she might be asleep, so he opened the door as wide as possible, slipped in behind the steering wheel, and just sat for a moment.

After a while, he reached over to her, slowly lowered his hand to her head and ran his fingers through her hair. She moved a little and slowly opened her eyes. At first, she looked afraid and then saw that it was Frank.

When he was sure she was awake, he said in a gentle voice, "Hello beautiful. I'm so glad to see you."

Ellen sat up, reached out to grab Frank and pulled him to her.

Frank said, "Are you okay?"

She looked him in the eyes and saw his concern. "I'm sorry, I came home and I tried not to be scared, but then I panicked. I felt that the only way for me to be safe was to get out of Washington. I was convinced that with two bombs going off in some obscure places it was only a matter of time before they would explode one in DC.

"I had the thousand dollars from last night, so I packed a few things and was going to my sister's in Harrisburg. I planned to call you later, tell you where I was, and plead with you to come to me. I had convinced myself that your love for me would make you leave here and join me in safety.

"As I walked through the house on my way to the car, I thought that I might never come back to this house and all the memories we have together here. I walked to the garage, put my suitcase in the back seat and got in behind the wheel. I started to reach to put the key in the ignition and my hand started to shake. Then my whole body was shaking and I was crying. I was yelling in the car, "I can't do this to Frank; I can't do this to myself.

"I cried so hard that I was exhausted and lay down in the car and continued to cry relentlessly. I was overcome with waves of memories of the two of us, and then I had one terrible thought that scared me the most."

In a soft and comforting voice Frank gently asked, "What was that?"

"What would I do if you couldn't come to save me? It was then that I realized that I have to stay here to spend whatever time we have left together. I realized just how much I love you and how important it is to be with you. If I left, I might never have a chance to be held by you again, and, just as importantly, I would lose the opportunity to hold you. I just couldn't leave you no matter how terrified I was. I need you with me for as long as I can have you. I had come to terms with what I had to do and I was so exhausted I went to sleep till you found me."

Frank held her gently and asked, "Do you want to go back into the house or stay in the car?"

"I need to go back inside," she said.

"Are you hungry?"

She gave him a small smile. "I could eat something."

"Let's get out of these cramped quarters and go into the kitchen. I'll fix you something to eat. Anything in particular?"

"I'm not sure what's in the fridge, but how about some toast, tea, bacon and eggs? And, oh yes, how about you?"

CHAPTER 56

Danger at Sea

Everyone in the Pentagon Special Ops Room watched in silent horror as a massive wave crashed into the welding barge, picking it up like a toy boat and tossing it into the air.

The power of the wave threw the barge into the wires holding the pipeline cap from the hovering helicopter. The barge crashed into the wires with such force that it snapped them in two while it broke apart. The initial force of the barge careening into the cables pulled the helicopter down towards the water. All watched as the broken cables snapped like a bullwhip up into the blades of the chopper and sliced off the blades. The pilot lost control and, in a matter of seconds, the Army helicopter crashed into the waves and exploded on contact. The debris from the exploding helicopter crashed into the fuel tanks on the welding barge and they exploded, as well. The power of the fuel tanks exploding destroyed what was left of the barge. Debris from the barge and helicopter fell into the water and the general became concerned about the divers in the water. The divers heard the general's plea and took cover under the pipeline.

Powell asked, "How many men have we lost?"

"We don't know yet, sir. We're sending in SEAL teams to assist with the rescue."

"How many in the chopper?"

"Six, sir."

"And how many on the barge?"

"Sir, all the divers were in the water, so that leaves the crew and the divers' support team."

In a firm voice Powell repeated, "So, how many possible dead?"

"Assuming that all the divers are safe and we find no survivors from the barge or helicopter, twenty, sir."

"Make sure we send another barge and extra tanks for the divers—I want a report from the divers on the status of the cap."

"We're trying to establish contact with them, sir. I'll ask for a head count and a status report on the cap."

Everybody sat back in their chairs aghast at what they had just witnessed. Baker and Brown are stunned at the destruction and deaths occurring in just a few seconds; neither of them had a clue as to what to say to the general. Baker thinks, *I just witnessed the deaths of twenty soldiers in less time than it took fifty-four thousand people to die in Texas City. I can't begin to feel what the president felt when he flew over Texas City.*

"General, how long do you think it will take to get another team in place?"

"Mr. Baker, we can have another team in place in less than thirty minutes. The barge will take longer but I want to hear from the divers about what happened to the cap, and depending on their answer... well, I don't know how long it will take to make another. It doesn't make sense to send a barge and divers if we've lost the cap."

As they stared at the screen, they saw one of the divers come to the surface and signal that all of the divers are okay. The general asked to speak with the diver. "Young man, this is General Powell. How are you and your team?"

"We're fine sir, the debris missed us."

"Excellent. I'm very glad to hear that all of you are unharmed. What about the cap?"

"Well sir, that is very strange. We had the cap just about over the opening in the pipeline, but with all the movement of the helicopter we couldn't get it over all the way. However, when the big wave hit, it literally shoved the cap in place just seconds before the cables broke. It was like the wave was helping us seal the pipe."

"Glad to hear it. We have a new welding barge on its way to you. It should be there in about two hours. You need to get your men out of the water and back to the mainland. We'll bring in another crew to finish the work."

"Sir, I know I speak for all of the divers. We would like to finish what we started. We shall go to shore but we want to finish the job, if that's all right with you, sir."

"Young man, it is. I'll send in the chopper to bring you out and back."

"Thank you, sir."

"Mr. Baker and Ms. Brown, we lost some courageous young men today. They gave their lives for our country and that is the greatest sacrifice any soldier can make. Let's hope it's not wasted."

Baker spoke for both of them, "General, today we saw incredible acts of heroism displayed by our soldiers. I can't tell you how proud we feel and, at the same time, the overwhelming sorrow at the losses. We shall never forget them."

"When the team returns, they'll seal the cap, but will also look for their fallen comrades. When the cap is sealed, I shall let you know."

"Thank you, General; and when the bodies are retrieved, will you let us know?"

"Yes, I shall."

CHAPTER 57

The Brotherhood in Houston

Sargon had been surprised at the quick reaction of the government to shut down the pipelines in Texas. He knew that the second bomb went off in Port Fourchon, but he didn't know – in fact, almost nobody knew – what had happened as a result. The president had said nothing about it and the people – at least those in Houston – seemed to be taking this disaster in stride.

Things were much different on television. He was able to get CNBC on his hotel room TV, and the chaos in the markets on a global basis was more than he had hoped for. It had been less than two days since the two bombs went off. The U.S. markets provided the lion's share of the liquidity for the global markets. While it was true that London was a large market, its total activity was less than one-third of that in United States. With the American markets closed, most of the major investors were not in the markets. With fewer investors, the markets were thinner, meaning less could be bought and sold.

Cyrus, the London School of Business and Finance major, explained to the rest of the Brothers what was going on. "In order to have orderly and fair markets, you need willing buyers and sellers. The larger the number of buyers and sellers you have, the more efficient the market. Efficient markets mean small price changes between the buying and selling prices.

"Look at West Texas Crude oil futures. Before we set off the bomb in Texas City, the price for a barrel of West Texas Crude was ninety-nine dollars. It is now two days later and, because of what we did, nobody knows if there is, or will ever be, West Texas Crude for sale again. Because of the uncertainty of supply, nobody wants to trade Texas oil. The oil market shifts to Brent North Sea oil and oil from OPEC. Here is the problem: the American oil traders are not allowed to trade. With fewer traders willing to buy, the price becomes volatile and the spread widens. In our example, you can see on the screen that Brent is offered at $195.00 and sold at $250.00. I suspect that the longer the Americans are out of the market, that price will go higher and the spread will widen."

While listening to Cyrus' explanation, a thought formed in Sargon's mind. He looked at Adad, Cyrus, and Oleg and said, "The night we set off the second bomb, I sent an e-mail and we loaded a YouTube video and made it available to the world. Within hours of releasing the video, we had over fifty million hits on the video. I haven't checked in the last few hours, but my guess is that it may well be over a hundred million views, if not more. Now for the question. If we sent a new message, could we influence the markets?"

Adad responded, "That would depend on the message and if they believe that it is in fact from the Brotherhood. Cyrus, what do you think?"

"If there was some way that it could be identified as truly coming from us, then it could have an impact."

Oleg questioned, "To what purpose would we send the message? Would we want to make money? What?"

Sargon thought for a moment. "We are all surprised at the calm response of the American leadership. My guess is that they suspect we only had two bombs, but they can't be sure. If they don't know for sure, we could create a panic by saying we have more devices and are planning to use them. We could also say, 'Any country that comes to the aid of the United States will be our next target.'"

"So you are saying we should bluff the world into believing we have more bombs and we that have the ability to use them whenever and wherever we want?"

"Yes," Sargon confirmed.

Adad spoke, "That will only work until some nation, including America, calls our bluff. Once we can't deliver, we are no longer a threat."

Cyrus jumped in, "Each time we speak the markets will jump but each time thereafter the reaction will be less and less volatile, especially if we don't deliver. My guess is that the first two to three threats will have the greatest impact. We need to stretch out the times between threats to allow confidence to rebuild and then knock it down again. If you want to do this to make money, our investment has to be now, not later."

"My uncle is very active in the oil markets and I could talk to him about investing money on our behalf."

Adad responded, "We don't have any money to invest."

Oleg smiled, "My uncle has already made billions off of our bomb. I'm sure he will stake us and we can share the profits he makes."

Mordecai spoke up, "You mean I could make some money out of this attack?"

"I think my uncle can make us more money than any of us can imagine. Some we can add to our pockets and some we can use to expand our efforts."

Cyrus reminded the group that when they left Iran, there were three more bombs. "Perhaps they would be willing to sell them for a price?"

Sargon asked, "How can we communicate with the world and be secure at the same time?"

The twins, Michael and Ishtar, had been silent during the whole conversation and now it was their time to shine. They looked at each other and simultaneously responded with one word "Tweet."

"What is tweet?"

"Twitter is a social network that's growing in popularity because it's cleaner than Facebook. People like it because it's fast and clean. When you hook up with a Twitter friend and send one message, you get access to all of their followers. Let's use an example. I know it will sound extreme but it works. We open a Twitter account. Nobody will know who we are. We now send a tweet to Lady Ga Ga. When we send it to her, it can be seen by all of her followers. Based on the recent data of the Top 100 Twitter users she has in excess of thirty-five million followers. We send one message and, if it is re-tweeted, thirty-five million people may see it. We can link up with any number of the Top 100 twitter users and get our message out to the world."

Sargon was not familiar with Twitter, "How secure is it? Can they find us?"

"No, once we set up an account, if we use Internet cafés to send our messages, they can't be traced."

"So, if we use your suggestion we can create fear, at least for a while. Through that fear, Oleg's uncle could make money for us and we could buy another bomb or two from the Iranians and use it to perpetuate our program on a global basis for years. Is that possible?" Michael responded, "Yes, we can!"

CHAPTER 58

A Day Like None Before

Frank and Ellen had their tea and toast, their bacon and eggs, and each other. They went upstairs to make love and, when they got to the top of the stairs, Frank turned to Ellen. "I read recently that the best way for a mother to calm a crying or sick baby was to have the mother take all the clothes off the baby and off herself, climb into bed and hold the baby to her breast and just lie there skin-to-skin. The baby will calm down and be comforted by the skin-to-skin contact."

Ellen responded with a coy smile on her face, "Are you saying you want me to nurse you? I don't think that is possible."

Frank responded, "No, I know I can't nurse from your breast, but I can sure gently suck on your nipples. Let's get naked, climb into bed together, and see if the skin-to-skin concept really works. I know it will excite us and that's okay if there's nothing more. I would like to make love with you. That goes without saying. Let that happen if it does. On the other hand, if you feel more secure just letting me hold you in my arms so we are touching as much skin as possible and that makes you feel secure, then that's all I want for today."

Ellen says, "I'll race you!"

"You're on!"

Clothes were flying in the air and they landed in unusual places, such as top of the light fixture and in the trashcan. For the first time in many years, neither thought about the anticipatory playing around. In the shortest amount of time they had ever taken, they were both naked and laying in each other's arms under the sheets in their king-size bed. In a few moments, arms and legs were intertwined and they became as one. Frank needed to find a way to make her feel secure. After a while, Ellen separated herself slightly from Frank, and said to Frank, "Want to try for some milk to go with this cookie?"

Frank said, "Absolutely." He felt Ellen relax and purr and knew she is ready for him. He was in no hurry to let go. Their love making this time was different. It was slow and deliberate, with no rush, and when the climax came for both, they are amazed how wonderfully exhilarating it was; it reminded them of the intensity of their lovemaking when they were first married.

Still skin-to-skin, Ellen fell asleep in Frank's arms as he wondered, *Is the fear and terror that Ellen has experienced over the last twenty-four hours the same for millions of Americans? Is Ellen's reaction representative of what America is experiencing? Not everybody has someone to get naked with, lie next to, and feel secure.* He knew that he had to go back to work, but he also knew that he had to find a way for the millions of Ellen's in America to feel safe. *She was so overcome with fear that she wanted to run away, but, in the end, she couldn't, At least not today. Will the day come in the future when the fear will be so great she will run, even though she doesn't know where to go to be safe?* Ellen stirred, and when Frank made a move to get up she pulled him back to her.

"I know you have to go back to work, but can I have you to myself just ten minutes more?" She reached down and said, "Perhaps a little more than ten."

Franks smiled and said, "Ready, willing and, I hope, able. It's been a long time since we made love twice in one hour."

It was more than ten minutes later when they went into the bathroom together. Ellen turned on the shower and turned to Frank, "Want to scrub my back?"

"Can I scrub any other parts?"

"Whatever tickles your fancy." They went into the shower together, washed each other down with lots of soap, and cleaned every nook and cranny of each other's body. When they had finished, they held each other under the warm shower water and then, finally, it was truly over.

Ellen turned off the shower and stepped out to dry herself off. She handed Frank a towel so he could do the same. She had put on a large

THE BROTHERHOOD OF THE RED NILE

terrycloth bathrobe, but when she tied the cord, she left it open at the top so most of her breasts were exposed. She went over to the dressing table and sat down on her pink velvet and brass chair. She flipped the light switch, which illuminated the mirror. After brushing her hair, she started to put on her makeup and then watched as Frank, now almost fully dressed, walked by behind her. He turned and looked into the mirror and saw her breasts exposed. With effort, he looked at her face in the mirror and said, "You better put those things away till later or I'll never get out of here. Do you want me to fix you anything?"

She smiled and returned to her makeup. "No, I'm fine."

"I need to make a call. I'll come back up before I leave."

"I'll look forward to seeing you soon," she said as she opened her robe all the way.

"You're a devil, but I love you."

Frank went down the stairs and headed for his office. It was hard to focus on business given the afternoon he just had, but he knew that many people were depending on him. He pulled out his cell phone and noticed several messages from Ted Baker. He went into his office, closed the door and dialed his number. Baker answered on the third ring.

"Mr. Williams, I'm glad you called. I have updates for you. First, we cut and capped the pipeline into Port Fourchon. Unfortunately, because of rough seas we lost a helicopter and a welding supply barge."

Frank grimaced. "How many men were lost?"

"We don't know for sure, but we think about twelve."

"I would like the names of the lost men as soon as possible so I can get them to the White House. The president will want to call all the families."

"The radioactive oil made its way north of the port and some small amount of radiation made it into the pipeline running through Lake Pontchartrain. General Powell has requested the EPA to send people from their local office to monitor the millrems level and make sure that there is no leakage into the lake that could contaminate the drinking water for New Orleans."

"Regarding the GPS on Mordecai being turned on. Dobias may be concerned about activating it."

Williams' question was abrupt. "What in heaven's name makes you think that, regardless of who called him, he wouldn't turn it on right away to find the terrorists?"

"Sir, I spoke with the commander of the mission in the field, Captain Oppenheimer, who was concerned that Dobias would be reluctant to turn it on. The device might be outside of Israel and it could be construed as spying on another country if it got out that they were tracking people."

"Mr. Baker, I told Mr. Dobias to activate the GPS the minute they have the serial number and to give us the location. If we find it's attached to the terrorist, we will retrieve the device and arrest the damn guy. The GPS will be held as evidence. Check with the general, but I need to see you in thirty minutes at my office. He can have you back when we're done."

"I'll check with him, sir."

Williams hung up and got ready to go, but Ellen knocked on the door and asked, "Can I come in?"

Frank responded, "Are you decent?"

"You be the judge." Frank opened the door and there she was standing buck-naked wearing a pair of black high heels. He looked at her and said, "You're not decent but you are flat out dangerous."

"As much as I would like to stay here and make love to you and with you, I have to go save the world. They stayed as one for a while, then Ellen released him.

Frank took his hands off of Ellen, He saw her white robe on the chair in the hall and handed it to her.

She took her robe and covered herself, thinking, *I have gone as far as I dare. I could use sex to keep him here, but he has to try to save the world. That's what he does and that is why I love him so.* This time she walked over to Frank and said, "I'll keep them warm for you till the next time."

Frank once again took her in his arms, reached inside the robe and fondled her. "My guess is that both of them and both of us are going to be really sore in the morning.

"This has been both the worst and best day of my life. I promise you I will do my best to find the Brotherhood and bring them to justice, making your life safe once again. Someday soon we will go away, live naked on a beach and make love whenever we want, so help me God."

As Frank's car pulled out of the driveway, Ellen was just turning away from the window when she saw what seemed to be the same black car that had followed her the other night. She wondered if it was the same car she had seen the night before. Why was it here now?

CHAPTER 59

Oval Office

President Jordan was speaking with his wife Karen and her staff. The chairman of the Federal Housing Administration, Brandon Miles, and the President of the Government National Mortgage Association, Winifred Mott, joined them. The president had called this meeting to find out how many homes these agencies controlled and where they were situated, so that he could use them to relocate the first one hundred thousand people out of the contaminated area in Texas.

"Between your two agencies, how many livable homes can we get our hands on to provide housing for the evacuated families?"

Brandon said, "As best we can tell, we have at least one million houses between our two agencies. But I must point out, sir, we are unsure of their condition."

The president nodded. "I understand many of the units will need some work. We'll have to find some temporary housing while the existing houses are being renovated. I have another question. Some of the people who will be forced to move will have contents that have to be left behind and people may never have a chance to go back and retrieve their belongings. Those folks will be walking away from an important part of their net worth. We have to be able to give them some credit for the houses and/or businesses that they are walking away from, so they can start over again. Do either of you have any suggestions on how to establish a value for their property, for compensation purposes?"

"The problem, sir, is in many cases the value of the home is less than the outstanding mortgage amount, so in reality the house may be worth nothing. On the other hand, the contents may have some insurance value."

"So, how do we find out the value when we can't go in and do an appraisal?"

"Mr. President, there are several online services that can gives us an estimated market value. Some use the mapping and imaging of Google Earth to locate a home and then search the most recent sales to come up with an estimated value.

"I'm not sure about the mortgage amount. I know this is recorded in the tax assessor's office in the county seat, but I don't know if we can have access to the mortgage information online for the affected area."

"You think it's possible to find a value for all the houses then. What about business locations?"

"Sir, I know of similar services that are used to value commercial property, but I don't believe we can value the cash flow from the operating business on the property."

"Is it possible to locate the owner and then search their tax records to find the value of the business?"

Mott responded to the president's question, "Sir, I don't know the legalities of sharing information on people's tax returns. Besides, not everybody reports all of their income."

"If a taxpayer has been taking money under the table and not paying taxes, then the amount of value the taxpayer will receive will be at our discretion. Do you think that both of your services could handle the volume we are talking about?"

Miles responds, "Sir, I have not talked with our offices, but we have used them across the nation for years. I'll call and ask after the meeting but I feel confident they can do what you're asking."

"I need to be sure, because I want to address this problem in my Saturday message in two days."

"Mr. President, you will have answer for you within the hour. "

"I have one more issue that I will need some guidance on from you. We can't just give these people the house. We have to find a way to allow them to acquire them after some period of adjustment. Some will have equity while others will not. What can we do for the first hundred thousand people and how do we scale it if we have to go to one million or more?"

Ms. Mott responded, "Mr. President, these people will need money for food, clothing, cars, mortgage payments, and living expenses at least until they can find work. I think we can work out a special program through mortgage loans with deferred payments for, say, three to five years, with an option to buy. We will contract for all the improvements necessary to make the house livable. We could set up a draw account that would cover the expenses we talked about, and it would be based on the number of people in the household. The idea is to give them enough to get by while they adjust and recover from being evacuated.

"We want to help, but at the same time we do not want to have them as long-term dependents on the government. Mr. President, I recommend you bring in a team from Health and Human Services to assist you in figuring out the level of support."

"Excellent suggestion! Contact the Secretary's office to work out the details. My office will transmit the executive order."

"Mr. President, we'd be happy to work with them and do whatever we can to help the country."

When the meeting was adjourned the president turned to Karen and her team. "We have two days to prepare for the first message to America. I'm thinking that I need to break the message into two parts. An update on what has happened with the two blasts and then second, and probably the most important, what we are doing to rebuild America and what are the challenges ahead of us. What do you think?"

Karen responded, "Mr. President, I think what you have suggested has merit."

The president smiled, "I hear a 'but' coming …"

Karen smiled back, "But I think you need to think in terms of program structure for the long run. You don't want to keep talking about the blasts each week do you?"

"No, I guess not."

Maggie spoke up, "Sir, I agree with the first lady. This week you can talk about both but going forward, you'll need to focus on the challenges and what the administration and government is doing to help Americans."

Deb added, "Mr. President, as much as possible you need to avoid giving your opponents an opportunity to throw a straw man argument into the public debate. You need to clearly state the problem and then provide the concrete solution. For example, problem: you have to move one hundred thousand people out of Texas, but where do you put them? Solution: place them in existing government-owned houses. The government will contract to repair these existing houses, if needed, to make them livable. This will put Americans to work all over America to help their fellow Americans. If you presented it this way, sir, your opponents would have difficulty undermining your efforts."

"Excellent suggestion, Deb. We'll be doing a lot of strategizing on the approach. Let me move on to one other subject. We have all the pipelines in Texas in the contaminated area shut down and effectively sealed off. If these people are ever to return, we have to find a way to get the contaminated oil and refined product out of the pipelines. Where do we put it? I had two Nobel laureates here in the White House last night and I put the question to them. Their answer was that I need to convene a panel of experts from around the world to work on the problem."

Maggie suggested, "Why not ask the people in your Saturday message for their ideas? Have the suggestions go to the Department of Energy. It will give Americans a chance to help in some way. Any good ideas we receive can be run by the expert panel."

"Maggie, I love the idea: engage Americans in solving America's problems. In fact, as we find ourselves with additional problems we should ask the country for its input in solving them. Washington doesn't always have the best answer."

CHAPTER 60

Williams' Office

At 1:30 PM, Ted Baker was sitting in one of the guest chairs outside Frank Williams' office. Ted could see the elevator from his chair; every time it opened, he hoped it would be Williams, and finally he wasn't disappointed. Williams was now walking briskly towards his office, and Baker noticed the expression on his face. When Williams got closer, he acknowledged Baker and pointed to his office, saying, "Let's go."

Williams offered, "Before we get started do you want something to drink?"

"No, sir."

"So, as I understand it, somebody *forgot* that a tracking device was attached to one of the terrorists we're trying to locate and never told Mossad headquarters to turn it on, is that correct?"

Baker is feeling very uncomfortable that the Under Secretary for Homeland Security is chewing him out for something that was not his responsibility and over which he did not have any control.

"Sir, just a moment. I know this might get me fired but..." he lowered his voice, "Sir, it was not my idea to use the GPS. It was, in fact, the head of Mossad. In addition, even when it was attached I had no ability to turn it on, and I still don't. Even the President can't turn it on. My suggestion to you on the phone about calling Dobias was just that, a suggestion." His voice got a bit louder. "I was not in control of any aspects of this mission. So, if you are angry, then take your anger out on the Israelis, sir."

"Now hold on for a moment. I'm not going to fire you. I am angry because there was a possibility that we could have found those bastards and, in some respects, it wasn't in our hands to do so. I understand the problem that Dobias might have, but we lost fifty-four thousand people. Stay right here for a moment." He picked up the intercom, "Marie, please get me Nava Dobias on the phone right away."

"Yes sir."

"He isn't always in his office and he might have to call me back, we'll see."

"Sir, he's in a meeting with the Prime Minister. He will call you back as soon as he can."

"Thank you Marie."

Williams set down the phone and looked at Ted. "So, we have some time. You indicated that you wanted to speak about the reassignment of our Major Omid Rahimi."

"Yes sir, we think that, given the location of the two bombs, Houston would be the likely place to start looking for the terrorists. As you recall, we have pictures of some of them that we could forward to Omid."

"Sending the pictures to the Major may help a little, but isn't this still going to be a needle in a haystack? The population of Houston is over a million. How could he ever find them?"

"Well, we know that the e-mail that he sent was from a Wi-Fi site; probably an Internet café."

"There have to be thousands of Wi-Fi sites in Houston; how would they ever find which site was used?"

"Sir, I have done a little checking. I'm willing to admit this is not my field. However, there are nine clearing hot spots that most of the Wi-Fi signals go through, including e-mail. We need to go back and check for the Wi-Fi spot that sent the e-mail broadcast at the time of the president's Address to the Nation."

"If we can find the clearing hot spot we can potentially narrow the search area."

"Yes, sir. If the GPS is still attached to Mordecai's jacket and he has it with him, when it's turned on, we can locate where he is and send a surveillance team in and see if more of the Brotherhood are near him."

Marie's call interrupted them. "Mr. Dobias is on line two."

Williams picked up the line. "Nava, thanks for calling back so quickly. Where are you on the GPS tracking?"

"Lt. Hassen was given a dozen devices. All were activated. Eleven appear to be in one place, probably still with Lt. Hassen."

"So, Nava, where is the twelfth tracking device?"

"It looks like it's in …"

CHAPTER 61

Oval Office

The president was talking with the first lady and her staff on the structure and content of his first Saturday message to the people in two days.

"I want to go back to Maggie's suggestion for a moment. I like your idea of asking the American people for their help, letting them offer suggestions and making them part of the possible solution. In future, if we run across a problem and can't seem to come up with a workable solution that we are comfortable with, then maybe the American people can come up with an answer. Each Saturday broadcast will have a segment that will allow America to help. I want to set up an 'American Ingenuity Center' in the White House. We'll need a web site and a way to screen e-mail. We can put the office in the old executive office building, with high school seniors and college freshmen manning the lines and e-mails. I shall want a report daily on what America thinks."

Maggie responded, "Mr. President, I'm glad you like the idea. We have to come up with a way to screen out calls, but we must be aware that what might seem crazy just might work, so the filter has to take out all of the political stuff and focus on ideas, no matter how outlandish."

Karen smiled proudly at Maggie, "I agree with your idea. We'll need resources in many different scientific fields to help us evaluate the pros and cons of suggestions. Let's put out a notice to all of the top research colleges and universities indicating that we're looking for 'presidential Solution Scholars.' They won't get paid, but they will be recognized for their efforts and contributions, and we just might solve some of our problems."

Bill piped up, "I think I should call some of my contacts in the computer industry and see if I can't get them to sponsor this program, donate the computers and software and help train the young people. They can help us figure out how to separate the possible from the impossible. When they have a doubt they can pass it along and let the next level assess the practicality of the suggestion."

Karen suggested, "I think we need to think about this Saturday's program and get it down on paper. What are the subjects, in what order? Have we come up with a name for the program?

The president commented, "I liked Deb's suggestion: 'America Rebuilds.'"

Maggie nodded, "Simple, to the point. I like it, too."

The first lady responded, "It's positive and patriotic and easy to remember. Yes, I'm also in favor."

The president turned to Deb and Bill. "You two are the youngest in the room. Do you think the title will work across most age groups? Do younger Americans have any patriotism? Will they get involved?"

Bill looks at Deb. Neither knew who should start, so Bill said, "Ladies first."

"Mr. President, for the first time in many young people's lives they will have to deal with an attack on America. The last real attack was September 11, 2001. Most of our generation has never experienced an attack on this scale. The massive loss of life in fractions of seconds was greater than all the men and women killed in the entire Vietnam War. I think that all Americans have felt the loss of their fellow citizens. Sir, I personally think the title will resonate with people of all ages."

Bill took a different approach. "Mr. President, maybe I'm not answering your question directly. I, too, like the title. However, perhaps for a different reason. You see, while the title is important, it's really what we are doing and saying that has to resonate with people, regardless of age. Your idea of creating an opportunity for high school and college students to man the call and e-mail center is a great one. The message from you has to be one of everybody pulling together to solve some of the most serious problems our country has ever faced. People want to feel like they are really part of the solution. Brother helping brother and neighbor helping neighbor built this country and made it what it is. With that same approach, it can be again. I think it's important for you to be open and honest with the people in every program. I don't think you need to be a cheerleader, but you must lead us through to the other side. Does that make sense to you, Mr. President?"

The president chuckled. "Maybe you should be making the presentation instead of me!"

Karen, Maggie, and Deb were surprised at the elegance of what Bill has just said and agreed with the president that perhaps someday he will be speaking on the 'America Rebuilds' program.

The president took the lead as they reviewed the program lineup. "We'll open with the report on Texas City and stopping the flow and the isolation of the city with walls and guards to keep people out of a very dangerous area. The fires will just have to burn out. We can't get close enough without risking peoples' lives to put them out. The contaminated oil has been isolated and we'll have more on that in a moment. We have to move about one hundred thousand people out of the danger area and relocate them. If the radiation levels go no higher we may still have to evacuate more people, but we just don't know yet.

"As to Port Fourchon, the oil has stopped flowing into the port and like Texas City, the fires will continue to burn. Port Fourchon lost some twenty-five hundred people working and living in the area. Like Texas City, we will have to isolate the port with walls and guards. The pipeline leading from the wells in the Gulf has been severed and we are shutting the wells as fast as we can. We're working to contain the crude oil flowing into the Gulf and other nations are sending us large skimmer ships to help salvage the oil flowing into the Gulf of Mexico. We hope to have all the wells shut down over the next thirty days or less."

Karen suggested, "This is the time to tell the people that they can help and that we are setting up the 'American Ingenuity Center' to let Americans get involved with thinking about solutions. Lastly, America, here is your first challenge: what do we do with the contaminated oil and product in the pipeline? Let us know."

Bill suggested, "Don't close with what everybody expects – 'God bless America' – but with 'God inspire us to Rebuild America.'"

CHAPTER 62

Mossad – Nava Dobias' Office

"Frank, do you have access to a secure server?" Dobias' voice carried clearly across the ocean.

"Yes, I do."

"Can you send me the IP address for your computer?"

"Why?"

"I'm going to hook you into my computer so you can see where the signal is coming from and then we can talk about what you want to do."

Williams gave Nava the IP address and, in about five minutes, a screen comes up with a map and a homing beacon flashing on the screen. "Nava, where is it?"

"Frank, use your mouse and zoom in to the beacon; tell me what you see."

Williams responded, "It looks like it's in central Syria."

"You're right. So, either the terrorists are still in Syria at their meeting site or the GPS is there and somehow was left behind."

"Nava, we have to verify if the terrorists are still in the meeting room or the GPS device is the only thing there."

Nava responded, "I can have a drone over the site in two hours to see if anybody is there. My guess is that somehow the GPS device became dislodged and fell off the jacket onto the floor. I think it's a good idea to check it out using a drone.

212

"Frank, we were talking here about Mordecai. We think that one of our operatives in Syria is the one who planted the GPS on him and may have talked with him on his cell phone."

"Well, Nava, my guess is that the cell phone will be based in Israel and I don't think we can track him through the cell network."

"I agree, but if you read between the lines of the intelligence report on Hassen and Mordecai, something more intimate was going on between them. I think I want to get her into my office and see what I can find out about their relationship."

"How long till you can get her in?"

"I have no idea where she is. Let me find her location and how long it will take her to get back from the field without compromising her cover. When I have more details I shall call you and we can speak to Lt. Hassen."

"I don't care what time it is, call me." Williams said and hung up.

Frank and Ted were still deep in discussion when Marie called Frank on the intercom to tell him, "Mr. Dobias is on line one."

Frank looked quizzically at Ted as he picked up. "Nava, do you have something for us already?"

"We've located her on assignment in Gaza. She'll be on a plane in a few minutes and I expect to have her here in three hours. I told her that we want to review her assignment in Syria and her observations on a person called Mordecai. Judging by the change of her tone of voice, she's nervous about coming in to talk about her relationship with him. I think we'll have to be careful what we ask and how we ask it."

"I agree. She's your operative so you should ask most of the questions. I'll wait for your next call."

Williams turned to Baker, "While we're waiting, let's talk about Major Rahimi and his assignment. You were saying that we have to isolate which Wi-Fi center processed the e-mail that was sent out when the president was speaking, is that correct?"

"Yes sir, we've been able to identify the quadrant of Houston where the message originated. While it is a large proposition, I recommend we concentrate on the Internet cafés first. We can send all the photos we have to Omid and let him start the grunt work of going to the cafés and see if anybody recognizes the people in the photos."

"Ted, could we get some help for Omid from the FBI and local law enforcement?"

"The FBI may be our best bet because I think local law enforcement is going to be overwhelmed with security concerns. I have a contact at the FBI that I can call for help."

"If you find you aren't getting help let me know and I'll personally call the Director. Ted, are you sure we're not looking for the proverbial needle in a haystack?"

"Sir, I know that it seems like an impossible task, but we have to follow every lead if we're ever going to find the Brotherhood of the Red Nile and avenge the horrific loss of life and destruction in America."

CHAPTER 63

Brotherhood in Houston

Sargon was thinking about the opportunity to make money to fund the Brotherhood, and perhaps make enough money to buy two more super dirty bombs from the Iranians. Investing was not his area of expertise, but that of one of his team members, Cyrus, a graduate of the London School of Business and Finance, could be helpful in understanding how to take advantage of this opportunity. He had asked Oleg to contact his uncle to see how much he would be willing to give them and to have him invest on their behalf.

"Cyrus, what do you think is the best opportunity to make money out of this attack?"

"I have to wonder if it may already be too late to get in. What I mean is that the price of oil has already risen to a point that may not be sustainable. Emotion has a big impact on markets and on what people feel they should to do with their money. The fear of not knowing what could happen causes people to develop a herd mentality. For example, oil prices are going up, so I have to buy oil, because I don't want to miss the opportunity. People buy and, if the price sells off a little, they buy more oil. The price might rally just based on people adding more to their investments. The price falls to a low point that is lower than the last low and people are talked into buying the dips, the falling price. When the price of oil goes up it may not go as high as it did before. When investors feel that oil has lost its momentum, they start selling at any price. Then, not only is the profit gone, but so is all their money. I think it's important to think about what is likely to happen to the demand for oil, because it is this demand that has a longer-term effect on the price of oil. What we have heard is that they have stopped the flow in Texas, so those wells are offline most likely forever, or at least our lifetime. We also know that Port Fourchon is shut down, so no oil or gas is coming from the Gulf of Mexico. Until they shut the wells in the Gulf, all that oil will be flowing into the Gulf.

"The world is sending ships to help recover the oil flowing into the Gulf, so a lot of it will be recovered and taken to other refineries. So, here is the real question: America imports sixty percent of its energy. Will our attack slow down the world's economy so much as to reduce the demand for imported oil? At the same time, will the American government go all out to develop energy resources away from Texas so that they will dramatically reduce the need to import foreign oil? If demand from OPEC declines to the point that America no longer needs imported oil, the price will fall before the declining need actually happens. The markets will get a whiff of decreasing flow out of OPEC and see it as less demand from America. The price of oil will fall in anticipation of the decrease in demand.

"With all of that said, I see two investment opportunities. First, we must find out how much we have to invest and then we must stage it in over time. The first thing I would do is split whatever money we have into two pots. One is to invest in oil itself, the other is to short all the oil exporting countries' major equity indexes."

The rest of the Brothers were now listening intensely to Cyrus' suggestion. They didn't completely understand what he was saying, but he seemed to be making sense.

"If demand falls off, prices will fall. If prices fall, then those national economies which need income from the export of oil to run the country will run into major problems. As income falls, so will the stock market and, consequently, the quality of life in those countries. We make money when oil falls and when the economies of OPEC countries do poorly," Cyrus concluded.

Ishtar asked, "I don't mean to be a spoiler, but could we lose all of our money if we do what you say and you are wrong?"

"Excellent question. You're really asking about the greed factor. How much is too much and on the other hand how much is not enough? You have to use limits to protect some of your capital. Simply put, a limit position controls your loss. You have to pay for that protection, but I agree we need some protection in case I'm wrong."

Just then, Oleg's cell phone rang. His uncle had given an amount to Oleg to share with the Brotherhood. "My uncle will loan us twenty million. We can invest with him or on our own. Of the first twenty million we make, half goes to my uncle. If we make another ten million on our investments then that goes to my uncle to repay the loan. In other words, my uncle will loan us twenty million and he gets his money out first. After we have paid him back we keep one hundred percent of everything we make from then on."

Mordecai asked, "If we invest well and turn the twenty million into a hundred million, your uncle gets the first twenty million and we keep eighty million?"

"Correct."

"If we pay your uncle back his twenty million and that is all we have left we make nothing?"

"Correct."

"What happens if we lose it all?"

"My uncle has agreed to forgive the loan." Ishtar responded, "So in reality we have no risk."

"We took the risk to destroy America and, while we haven't destroyed it, we have crippled it for many years to come." Sargon asked, "All in favor of taking the twenty million and taking the risk that America will fail, signify by saying 'aye'."

The "ayes" have it.

CHAPTER 64

Interview with Lt. Hassen

About 3:30, Nava got a call from his assistant that Lt. Hassen had arrived.

"Please, show her in and ask if she'd like something to drink."

His door opened and in walked Lt. Hadar Hassen. She was not wearing her military uniform. In fact, it would have been difficult, by looking at her, to believe she was a soldier at all, let alone an agent in Mossad, Israel's military intelligence organization. She apologized to Nava for her appearance, indicating that she did not have a uniform with her and didn't feel she could have taken the time to change, based on the urgency of the message.

"You're a very attractive young woman without your uniform, Lt. Hassen." Nava studied her and saw a striking woman dressed in black except for a dark grey jacket that fell to just below her hips. High-heeled black patent leather knee-high boots complemented her look. She was wearing a simple black shirt, almost a T-shirt. However, it appeared as if it had been painted on her body, it was that snug. It wasn't bursting at the seams, but fit every curve she had and, with the scoop front, a good portion of her cleavage was exposed. He could tell she wasn't wearing a bra, but she didn't need one, as her bust was full and firm. No sag there, yet! She was wearing a pair of Capri pants that touched the top of her boots. They were also skintight, showing off her narrow waist and rounded hips. He remembered meeting her, but uniforms hide a lot.

"Thank you, sir."

"Please, sit down." He indicated a chair in front of his desk nearest his phone. "Were you on holiday when we called? Were you with someone?"

"Not really."

"What a disappointment. I'm sure there are many young men who would love to be in your company."

"Thank you sir. How may I help you?"

"You may recall we met at the briefing before you went on your mission to Syria."

"Yes sir, you gave me some tracking devices to put on any members of the Brotherhood of the Red Nile if they came into town so that we could track them."

"You have a good memory. In the final intelligence report on that mission, you indicated that you attached one to a person named Mordecai, is that correct?"

"Yes, sir."

"Excellent! Now, before we go any further I want you to know that I'm going to call the Under Secretary for Homeland Security of the United States, who would like to speak with you. I want you to understand that you are in no trouble. Mr. Williams and I are just trying to see if we can find all the information as possible on members of the Brotherhood of the Red Nile, understood?"

"Yes, sir."

Nava dialed Frank and got Marie on the third ring. "Nava Dobias for Mr. Williams. I have Lt. Hassen with me."

In a moment, Frank Williams was on the phone and introducing himself and Ted Baker to her. "Thank you, Lt. Hassen, for coming in so quickly. Lt. Hassen, in your report you stated that you attached a GPS tracking device on a man named Mordecai. Is that correct?"

"Yes."

"Do you know if the device was ever turned on?"

"No."

"You did report that it had been placed?"

"Yes." Hadar anticipated the next question and fidgeted in her seat. She looked at Nava to see his reaction. Nava smiled at her to encourage her to tell what she knows and not to worry.

"Who was your commander on this mission?"

"I reported to Captain Oppenheimer."

"Do you know if he reported the placement of the GPS to the person in charge of the mission?"

Nava jumped in, "Frank, the Captain reported directly to me and he did not report the placement of the GPS."

"Nava, I'm not trying to place any blame. I'm just trying to gather information to see if we can find the damn terrorists. Let's move on. Lieutenant, do you know what happened to the GPS?"

"As far as I know, he still has it on his jacket where I put it."

"The GPS was turned on and it's still at the meeting site in Syria. Do you have any idea why it is still there?"

"Any answer by me would be pure speculation, but my guess is that he took off the jacket to work on the bomb and it either fell off, or the jacket remained behind when they left. If it had been discovered, I would think they would have destroyed it."

"What can you tell us about the times you met with Mordecai?"

"We met a few times. We had coffee and drinks and dinner."

"Can you tell me how you met Mordecai?"

"It was by chance really. I was having a meeting with my team in an abandoned barn outside of town and was the last to leave. I went out through the front door and knocked him down with the door, purely by accident. When I saw his face, I remembered him from the intelligence photos we got. I apologized for hitting him with the door and we agreed that I would buy him a drink later in the café in the town square."

"Did you meet him at the café?"

"Yes," Hassen said.

"Is that when you attached the GPS to his jacket? How did you do it?"

"It was suggested that I use my assets to distract him while I attached the GPS."

"What assets are you talking about?"

Lt. Hassen smiled. "Some people say I'm attractive and have ample assets, so I placed my right breast against his chest and reached around with my arm and attached the GPS."

Nava jumps in, "I don't mean to embarrass Lt. Hassen, but she has ample distracting assets."

"Did you meet with him any other times?"

"Yes, three times."

"Did you use your assets any of those other times?"

"I did dress in a way to accentuate my assets and keep him interested."

"And did he remain interested?"

"Very."

"Did you have sex with him?"

"No."

"Do you think he wanted to have sex with you?"

"Yes."

"Why do you say that?"

"Because he said that he thought the sex would be fantastic."

"Did you think the same way?"

Nava was sitting across from her and could see her body language. He was looking at her reactions for none of this was in the report.

Hadar paused and then said, "Yes."

Nava looked closely at her when she answered "yes" and noticed that her nipples had puckered through to the surface of the shirt. He concluded, *This woman has feelings for Mordecai.*

"Why didn't you have sex with him?" Nava queried.

"I felt if I could string him along, at some point in time I could use his desire for sex with me to gain information to help my country, but for now, no matter what I wanted, I had to think of the mission."

"Did you assume that you would meet again?"

"Yes."

"Where?"

"America."

CHAPTER 65

Oval Office

President Nathan Jordan had just said goodbye and thanks to Karen and her staff for their great work in preparing the first Saturday talk with America. As he closed his door, he walked over to the JFK desk and realized that, for the first time in several days, he is alone. With all the chaos going on in the United States, it seemed eerie to him that it was so quiet. He knew that would change in a few moments, for he had a meeting with the Chairman of the Federal Reserve and the Secretary of the Treasury. The global capital markets were in shambles.

The rest of the world couldn't fill in for the United States, and with every passing hour the world markets were crumbling. *I've closed the banks and the markets and now people can't buy anything. If I don't do something soon America and perhaps the world may experience a depression never seen before.* His phone rang, interrupting his thoughts. It was Mary informing him his three o'clock meeting participants had arrived and were in the small conference room waiting for him.

"Tell them I'll be there shortly. There's one call I must make."

He was about to leave his office, when out of nowhere Karen walked up to him, looked around and didn't see anybody, so she put her arms around her husband and pressed herself as close as she could to Nathan and gives him a passionate kiss. After their lips parted, she put her mouth next to his ear and said very quietly, "I'm very proud of the man I love. Come up for a special dessert if you have the time."

"Is it my favorite flavor?"

"What flavor is that?" she asked.

"Karen," he replied, with a smile.

Karen quickly slipped away to allow the president to get to his meeting. Watching her walk away, he pondered, *What a woman. In all of this turmoil she still looks for an opportunity to tell me how much she loves me. I have got to try to find some time for a taste of Karen tonight, for both of us.*

The president continued down the hall to his conference room and walked through the door. As the two men started to get up, he said, "Gentlemen, please sit down. We have too much to accomplish to stand on ceremony. Porter, is there anything left of the capital markets?"

"Mr. President, as you know, American firms account for more than half of the trading activity in the commodities markets. These markets need buyers and sellers in order to function. The remaining players are not willing to trade with all the uncertainty. The commodity markets function with two major players, those who want to hedge and those who want to speculate, and the markets need both for the markets to function.

"One of the contracts that attracted the most activity and money was West Texas Crude oil. The reason was that it was the purest oil and the easiest to refine. Nobody knows if there will ever be WTC again. What little trading activity there is going on is in Brent North Sea futures. Since the first bomb exploded, the price of the near commodity contract for North Sea oil has doubled to two hundred and fifty dollars a barrel. When news leaked about Port Fourchon, the price shot up to almost five hundred a barrel. It settled back to about four hundred and fifty just before you walked in for our meeting. The important commodity contracts have seen significant declines in volume. We have to figure a way to get the commodity markets open regardless of the potential loss for traders and their companies."

"Mr. Chairman, any good news in the credit and stock markets?"

"In a word, Mr. President, no. Initially, the dollar fell off the table, but a massive buying rally has boosted the value of Treasuries across the board. Currently, our debt is trading at yield levels that are the best ever. I find it very strange that the world is desperately buying America bonds knowing full well that nobody can tell when and if we will ever pay the interest or the principal when due."

"Perhaps Mr. Chairman, the world, at least for now, knows that the rest of the world may be in much deeper trouble."

"You could very well be right, but what can we do about it?"

The Chairman had a nervous look on his face and suggested, "Mr. President, I might have an idea. I think we shall need an opinion from the attorney general on my suggestion but, on the assumption that he will respond favorably, here is my idea. The destruction and dislocation caused by these two attacks will require our country – and for now let's say our government – to buy massive amounts of commodities for the rebuilding.

"Mr. Smyth suggested that in the past there have been two major participants in the commodity markets – hedgers and speculators. My idea is that we will have one category, at least for some time, and that is buyers who want – and more importantly need – all of the major commodities.

"That buyer is the people of the United States of America. We won't be able to do business with all the firms, but we can rotate through them, giving them some revenue so no one firm will be the sole agent for the government. As we assess our need for timber, we can buy futures on construction lumber. This will put people to work earning money harvesting the commodity and people who will use the commodity. We will start the flow of money again so people and companies will have resources."

"Excellent, go on." The president sat forward in his chair.

"Mr. President, if I might add, we at Treasury have thought about how to get money flowing again and I agree with the Chairman. We have a problem of trillions of dollars belonging to Americans that is currently inaccessible from the banks. We call our project the 'Bailey Project'. Not to bore you with all the details: the concept came from a classic American movie, 'It's a Wonderful Life'. There was a run on the bank and George Bailey asked 'how much do you really need?' The answer was less than all their money.

"Mr. President, I don't believe Americans will need all the trillions on deposit. We have to prevent a run on the bank. We have an extensive ATM network in the country. We can program the maximum withdrawal amount within a given period. For those people who are on Social Security or some assistance program, we can get them a card that can be used in the ATM and they will have similar limits on the amount of money they can take out.

"Employers will have similar cards issued to employees who can draw down their wages. Each transaction will have a percentage withheld – about ten percent – which can be divided between the federal and state governments to pay for some of their budgets.

"It's not perfect, but we will start getting money in circulation and more importantly, be putting money in people's pockets.

"We'll be asking America to think about basic needs, spending less and making important decisions on what to do with their money. Again, we realize it's not perfect. There will be many problems, but we think it would be a great start to building a leaner and more controlled spending country."

"Porter, what are the risks in your proposal?"

"Mr. President, if we are in fact, for some period of time, going to be a nation of dramatically less conspicuous consumption, many businesses based on the principle of conspicuous consumption will fail. That will put more people out of work, but we feel, at least for the moment, that the infrastructure needs of the country will create new jobs and new business for America. We think it can be done."

"I want to commend both of you on your insight and excellent approaches to our problems. I will want both of you to speak to the cabinet about your recommendation at the next meeting. For the first time since this crisis began, I have hope and think we can offer hope to the whole country, as well."

"Mr. President, I'm not trying in any way to dampen your enthusiasm, but there is one piece of information that I need to share with you. I'm not sure if you can do anything with it or not, but I would be remiss if I didn't pass it along."

"Porter, is it bad news? Please don't build me up and then knock me down."

"Sir, this is information we are trying to verify. We can't tell you at this moment whether it's good or bad. For now, it's just information."

"Okay, Porter, bust my balloon."

"Sir, the SEC investigation unit has picked up that a Russian oil billionaire, Viktor Antipova, is holding very large positions in long oil futures contracts."

"How large is large, Porter?"

"Mr. President, we think he may control forty percent of the outstanding long futures contracts."

"How is that possible?" The president rubbed his fingers under his chin.

"Sir, he is the head of a cash-rich oil company in Russia that does business all over the world."

"Mr. Secretary, are you suggesting that he had something to do with the bombing of America?"

CHAPTER 66

Lt. Hassen's Surprise

Lt. Hassen had just told Dobias, Williams and Baker that she expected to meet Mordecai in America. Williams jumped in, "What do you mean America?"

"I told him that I was going America as part of my studies. I told him I wanted to be an architect and that I was going to Texas to learn how to use adobe to build houses. When I finished in Texas I wanted to go to Africa and teach people how to build their own homes."

Baker inquired, "How does this relate?"

"He told me something that I thought was strange, because he said he was also heading to Texas."

Williams wondered, "If you were going to Texas and the two of you wanted to hook up, how would you know where to meet him?"

"I asked him if his cell phone was an international phone, and he said yes. I gave him my cell number to call me and when he called my phone it recorded his cell phone number."

Williams' eyes grew large, "You have his cell phone number?"

"Yes I do," came the reply.

Nava watched her body during this portion of the conversation to see how she was reacting. He noticed that her nipples had relaxed, which was a signal to him that she was more at ease when talk of a possible sexual encounter had moved to the back burner.

Williams spoke slowly, "Let us suppose that in fact Mordecai has an international phone and he wasn't just trying to impress Lt. Hassen. What is the best way to use it? You tell us she is an attractive woman and that Mordecai would be attracted. As I see it, we have two choices. First, you give us the phone number, we try tracing the call and hope for the best. Otherwise, Ms. Hassen makes the call and we try to trace it as she tries to set up a meeting wherever he's located. We have Hadar place another tracking device on him and put him under surveillance to see if any other members of the Brotherhood are with him."

Nava responded, "I don't think I want to put her into that much danger."

Baker quickly suggested, "Isn't that Lt. Hassen's decision?"

"No, it is not her choice. It is mine."

Lt. Hassen broke in. "Don't I have any say in this matter?"

"Lt. Hassen, you work for the Israeli government and report to me. I decide what you can and cannot do with your body when you're under my command."

Williams spoke up, "Nava, there are a lot of unknowns at the moment and some things we can do before or even if we want to use Lt. Hassen."

"Like what?"

"If we get the cell number we can ping the number to see if the device is active or not. If we don't get a ping back, then we know that the phone is not on. We would continue to ping the phone until he turns it on. In the meantime, perhaps we should have – if you agree, Nava – Lt. Hassen come to America. Then, if she has to go to meet him, she can get to him more quickly than coming all the way from Israel. I'm sure you'll agree time is of the essence.

"Lieutenant, do you have your cell phone with you?"

"Yes," she replied.

Williams asked, "Lt. Hassen, did you purchase the phone containing Mordecai's number or was it supplied to you by Mossad?"

"It was supplied by Mossad."

"Nava, under your rules, are the phone and its contents the property of the government, or is there shared ownership?"

"We issued the phone to Lt. Hassen. The bill is paid by my agency, so the phone and its data belong to the government."

"Lt. Hassen, if Director Dobias asks for the phone, is there any reason not to give it to him?" Williams asked.

"None."

"Nava, if Lt. Hassen indicates Mordecai's phone number, could you give the number to me to ping?"

"We'd be happy to ping the number for you and give it to you, as well."

Baker broke in, "Mr. Director, this is Ted Baker, one of Mr. Williams' assistants. If you give us the number and we use our system to ping for Mordecai's phone, wouldn't that ping show a different number? One with which he wouldn't be familiar?"

"I'm not an expert, but what you're saying makes sense. If instead we were to use Lt. Hassen's phone he would recognize the number, since he has already programmed her cell number into his. When he sees that familiar number, he might respond."

"I think you may be right," Dobias said.

"Lt. Hassen, do you recall if Mordecai took your picture with his cell phone so he might match it up with your phone number?" Ted asked.

"It's certainly possible. I can't recall if he did, though."

"Mr. Baker, what is your point?" Dobias asked.

"Sir, if he did take a photo and associated it with her phone number, when he phones her picture will appear on the screen. The image will trigger fond memories and temptation may overcome any orders he may have not to use the phone."

Nava responded, "If he is still attracted to Hassen, using her phone would give us the greatest chance for finding him. "Good thinking. Believe me, if he sees her picture he will respond or find a way to respond."

"Mr. Dobias, could you give us a moment?" Ted looks over at Williams.
"Yes."

The phone went silent and Baker turned to Williams, "Sir, we need that girl here in the States. If we make the call, we can get her to a meeting with Mordecai much faster from here than by trying to get her out of Israel."

"Let's get back on the line and I'll ask." Williams reopened the line. "Nava, I need to ask a favor."

"Let me guess, my friend. You want me to attach Lt. Hassen to your Homeland Security and send her there immediately, am I correct?"

Williams chuckled, "I knew there's a reason you're in charge."

Nava turned to Lt. Hassen. "Would you be willing to go on special assignment to the United States Department of Homeland Security to catch the person who may have built the nuclear bomb that killed so many

Americans and who you were attracted to in Syria? Will the possible feelings you might have for him affect your ability to perform your mission?"

"Sir, while I may have some feelings for the man named Mordecai, my first love is my country and if my country wants me to help then I must."

"That's settled then. We will send Lt. Hassen to Washington as quickly as possible, along with her phone."

"If you're in agreement we'll dispatch a military jet to transport Lt. Hassen to the States. Just tell me which airport to use." There was a pause. Frank could hear them talking but he couldn't tell what they are saying.

"Frank, the Lieutenant has agreed to the temporary assignment. Do you have any idea how long she'll be in America?"

"I can't offer an answer to you, my friend. It could be a month but it may also be years. Is that a problem?"

"I don't think so, but I think we must have an end date. That date can be extended as agreed upon by the government leadership of both countries."

"For now, let's say one year. Is that acceptable?"

Nava and Lt. Hassen agreed and responded to Under Secretary Williams their willingness to help their ally as much as possible.

"Frank, I'm no expert, but in the twelve hours it will take her to prepare to fly to the States we can begin the process to test the phone and ensure it's in working order. This should allow Lt. Hassen time to go home, pack and arrange to be away for a prolonged period. I would suggest she keeps what she is wearing. In fact, I'll use her phone to take her picture and send it to you so you will see what I'm seeing. We'll make sure this will be the photo Mordecai sees when Hassen calls. My bet is that he will drop the phone when he sees this picture."

Frank asked, "Lt. Hassen, do you have any questions before you commit to coming to America?"

"Mr. Williams, there are probably many questions I will need answered, and we can discuss them when I arrive. However, I do have a couple right now. Who I shall report to and what shall I be doing? It seems a long way to go to just wait around to make a phone call."

"We have an officer on special assignment looking for the terrorists in Houston, Texas. I think the best thing for you is to go to Houston and report to Major Rahimi."

"Would we be working in civilian or military uniforms?"

"I suggest you bring your dress uniform, some everyday business clothes, your workout gear and, of course, some sexy stuff too. We can provide military utilities if you go on a base. We'll arrange housing and cover your expenses. I shall want you to check in with Mr. Baker at least once a week; you'll need to file a written report of your activities every two weeks to Mr. Baker. We'll send copies of your reports to Mr. Dobias so he can be updated. Any other questions?"

Ted spoke. "Lt. Hassen, do you really think that Mordecai and the rest of the Brotherhood of the Red Nile are in the United States?"

"I have no idea. I know that they are not at the meeting site and that another one of the members — Mr. Assad — has not been seen at his company for over three weeks. Nobody knows where he is; at least they're not telling anybody if they do know."

"Lt. Hassen, you are the most active lead we have to the possible location of the Brotherhood. We're more than ready to welcome you to America." Williams ended the call and looked at Ted. "I don't think she realizes how critical she is to this operation."

CHAPTER 67

Congress is Impotent

Speaker of the House Robert Ward called for a meeting of the leadership in both Houses of Congress and advised them not to talk to anyone about the meeting beforehand. It was ten o'clock on Friday morning and the Speaker dismissed the staff and locked the door. Attending the meeting was Ward; the Minority leader in the House, James Radcliff; Majority Leader in the Senate, William Wild; and the Minority Leader in the Senate, Francis Pollard.

Ward began, "Gentlemen, the meeting at the White House was both amazing and terrifying at the same time. We have a tough job ahead of us and I think the president will need the help of all of us if there is any chance to turn this around. I have invited the president to talk with us on the phone because we both agreed that the president coming to Congress might stir up questions that none of us needs at this time. I'm waiting for the president to call. We spoke on the phone late yesterday and agreed to talk for now. I think we should ask a few questions and then see where it goes from there."

Just then, the phone rang and the Speaker answered. "Good morning, Mr. President. I'll put you on speaker, so all of us can hear you."

Jordan thanked all of them for assembling on such short notice. "We as a nation are facing very tough times. I hope that by working together we can come up with solutions that are the best for the American people. Since the last time we met, we have isolated the contaminated oil in Texas and have successfully severed the pipeline out in the Gulf of Mexico, the pipeline that goes into the city of Port Fourchon, Louisiana. As you've seen in the news reports, Navy divers have successfully capped the line to prevent any backflow of contaminated energy from flowing into the Gulf. However, oil flowing out of the separated pipeline is still spilling into the Gulf. We're not staying ahead of the flow. We've accepted offers for additional support from several nations that have skimmer ships that can suck up a great quantity of oil. One of the challenges we have with the sheer volume of oil pouring out is where to put it.

"I just finished a meeting with the Chairman of the Fed and the Secretary of the Treasury on how to open some of the markets and to start a limited flow of money so people can buy basic necessities of life."

Speaker Ward asked, "How can we help you, Mr. President?"

"Well Mr. Speaker, I'm not sure I know how to answer that question. We may need Congress to pass a law giving the president broad powers for a limited period of time to deal with this emergency."

The president's party, the Republicans, was in control of the House, but not the Senate. A law giving the administration more unregulated power would not sit well with at least some of the Democratic Senators.

Senate Majority Leader Wild wanted to be supportive, but at the same time was very reluctant to give the White House unregulated power so he asked the president, "What kind of additional powers are you thinking you will need, Mr. President?"

"Senator Wild, I wish I could tell you now, but I can't just yet. I'm not trying to be evasive. I plain just don't know if I will need any additional powers to deal with this emergency. I do know that if I have to come to Congress for laws, I hope Congress, for the good of the people, can act quickly.

"I know that the two fires are polluting the air but I can't do anything because of the radiation. I may ask Congress to suspend, for a time, the air quality standards in the South and the Southeast. I could do this through executive order, but I would much prefer the cooperation of Congress."

Radcliff spoke up. "Mr. President, I've been thinking about the curfew and martial law and wondering how long you think these limitations will have to be in effect?"

"Well Mr. Radcliff, we've only had them in effect for a few days and things seem to be relatively okay at the moment. The people are still in shock, so I think the real test will come in about a week if food and money begin to run out. If people find the stores closed, that the filling stations have no gasoline and that the ATMs are empty, then things might well get more difficult. We're working on plans to get money in circulation and limited access to bank accounts. Mr. Minority Leader, my best guess at the moment is that could take years."

The president could not see the shock on the Congressional leaders' faces when he said 'years.'

"I can clearly see a time in the future where I or a future president may come to Congress and ask for a declaration of war against the Brotherhood and all of those people and countries who gave them support. The loss of life in just seconds was greater than the number of all American soldiers killed during the entire Vietnam War. The perpetrators of this death and destruction cannot go unpunished, regardless how long it takes."

The Speaker responded, "Mr. President, we all understand your anger at the Brotherhood for the death and destruction they have brought on the United States, but don't you think we need all the facts to determine who was involved? We can't destroy a nation because they supported the Brotherhood and their attack against the United States."

"Yes, we can, and it is my earnest hope that we shall. We must send a clear message to those who want to destroy us: we *will* destroy you."

CHAPTER 68

Is It Possible?

John Seacrest, Ted Baker's friend in the CIA counter intelligence unit, had helped to get information on the Brotherhood. He had found a CIA asset on the ground in Syria, whom he sent to the meeting site to take pictures of the members of the Brotherhood of the Red Nile and any bombs they might have. His asset went to the meeting site twice, relaying pictures back to John, who forwarded them on to Baker, who in turn distributed them to Israel's Mossad and the president's national security team. In trying to gain as much information about the members of the Brotherhood as possible, he had also sent copies of the photos to Harold Wellington, his Interpol contact in London.

John was keenly aware of the response from the U.S. government. Still, he couldn't do much at this point without an official request from Baker. Seacrest kept in contact with Baker on a regular basis, but Baker, at least for now, had no specific assignment himself.

It was a bright and sunny afternoon. Seacrest could look out of his office window in Langley, Virginia and see the vibrant green on the maples that surrounded his headquarters. Their brilliant color made his window look like a painting hanging on the wall.

John's phone rang unexpectedly, rousing him from his reverie. It was Wellington. "Harold, how are you? What can I do for you?"

"John, we've come across some intelligence that has not yet been confirmed, but we decided that you need to know, even though at this moment we have no hard evidence for the reliability of the information."

"Sounds ominous." John stared out the window.

"We're hearing rumors that at least one more bomb is in the United States. It appears that it is not controlled by the Brotherhood of the Red Nile, but by some other unknown terrorist organization."

"You are not making my day here. When I pass this on, it will not make other people's day either. What else can you share with me?" John looked at the clock on the wall near his desk.

"Well, that's the problem, all we have is chatter. We can find no credible evidence to corroborate this intel. We'll keep digging and listening, but that's all I have at the moment."

"Thanks for the heads up. Keep in touch. One more question. Where is this chatter coming from?"

"Iran."

Seacrest slowly hung up the phone and turned to look out his window. The brightness is gone, dark clouds have moved in and it's beginning to rain. Seacrest picked up the phone and realized that it is late afternoon on Friday. Perhaps Baker has left for the day. He dials Baker's direct number and Ted answers quickly.

"What's up?"

"We need to meet. I received some important information just moments ago from Harold Wellington of Interpol."

"How long will it take you to get to my office?"

"Thirty minutes if I use the flashers. Traffic is really heavy."

"Use the flashers. I'll call Secretary Williams' office and alert him you'll be here in about half an hour. What should I tell him is the subject matter for the meeting?"

"Let's just say it's something we can't discuss over an unsecured line."

"Okay, I hear you." Baker hung up. Before dialing Williams' office, he cursed very loudly, "Goddammit."

He then called Williams' office and put them on alert. Taking out his copy of the After Action Report from the Ridley house in Springfield, he remembered Williams calling him on the carpet over it and later withdrawing his anger when Baker came right back at him. They found an empty but radioactive bomb holder buried in the back yard of the Ridley house. The forensics lab could not tell how long the case had been buried. As Ted read the report again, he remembered the points about two emergency vehicles pulling up, empty stretchers going into the Ridley house, and what appeared as body bags being taken out shortly after. *At first, I thought perhaps the Ridleys were in the body bags. Then we found out that these vans were not even ours. They were stolen from their station in Texas City, but we were unable to figure out who stole them or what they took out of the house or where they took what was in the body bags. We still have many unanswered questions. If there is a new bomb and it isn't linked to the Brotherhood, are we potentially dealing with another terrorist group?*

Baker spent a few minutes just thinking about the possibilities and didn't realize that over half an hour had passed and John Seacrest was standing in his doorway. Ted broke away from his very negative musings and as he turned his chair, he saw Seacrest.

"John, have you been there long?"

"Just a moment or two. When did you last sleep?"

"I think I was about to just now."

"You won't be of much help to the cause if you don't get some sleep."

"I know, but there's just too much to do and we're not staffed to handle this type of emergency."

"How do you plan for a terrorist attack with nuclear bombs?"

"No amount of planning prepared us for this. Let's go see Secretary Williams."

They walked down the hall towards Frank's office. Ted turned to John and said, "I want to thank you for all the work you did in helping us identify as many members of the Brotherhood as you did. I know you took a great deal of heat, and some of the time you had no support."

"All in a day's work trying to save the nation."

They stopped at Marie's desk and Baker asked. "Is he alone?"

"Yes, he's expecting you. Go right in."

"Mr. Under Secretary, you remember John Seacrest from CIA. You made the call that got him out of the brig so we could get the Brotherhood photos from their meeting place."

"Yes, I remember, and sorry about that brig."

"Not a problem, sir."

"Ted tells me that you have some new information."

"Sir, I just received a call from one of our contacts at Interpol. I trust him. He's been working with me since the first attack. He tells me that they are hearing traffic about more bombs in the United States. He also says that so far they have not been able to validate the credibility of the rumors."

"Has he given you any indication of the number of bombs?"

"No, sir."

"Does he have any ideas as to who is behind the traffic and the rumors?"

"Sir, they think it's possible that the first source is Iran."

"Well, that would seem to have something going for it. Is there a number two source?"

"Sir, they think it's…"

CHAPTER 69

Houston and the Major

Major Omid Rahimi was disappointed that he had been reassigned to Houston from Springfield. He was disappointed because he had left his assignment unfinished and he was the type of person that liked to finish what he started. Several issues remain unanswered in his mind. He hoped to fill in the pieces of the puzzle and locate the Brotherhood of the Red Nile. Now he didn't know if anybody would pick up where he had left off. *On that fateful night, who or what was in the body bags taken from the Ridley home? Who was it that came and took away the bodies, or whatever, in the stolen vans? Was it another terrorist group and not the Brotherhood? Where did they take whatever was in the body bags? Why did they steal the emergency vans from Texas City, so far away? How did they know the day and the time Homeland Security was going to be at the Ridley house?*

Then you had the Ridley family; they were a mystery unto themselves. *The family had lived in Springfield for at least eighteen years and Mike, the father, never had a job? How did he pay his bills? Where did he get the money to pay for the foreign adoption of their son Michael? How could Michael, the son, deposit twenty-five thousand dollars a month in the bank without work? Why did Mike not show up for his free ride at UC Berkley? Last, but not least, what happened to the bomb that must have been in the case discovered buried in the Ridleys' back yard?* The questions just kept on coming, and Omid had no answers, at least nothing concrete. His instincts, however, were telling him something and he didn't like what he was thinking.

Omid thought about all of these unanswered questions while he was driving to Houston. He had come to a conclusion about what happened that night, based on the facts. He was convinced that the only way the emergency vans could have arrived when they did from so far away was that there had to be somebody on the inside telling someone what the plan was and about the timing of the raid on the Ridley house. His instincts told him, *Some terrorist organization, perhaps the Brotherhood, or some other group, had a mole inside Homeland Security and the spy was feeding information on the planned activities, at least for now, to an unknown organization.* He wondered if the mole was in fact somebody on the payroll at Homeland Security or a relative of someone working at Homeland Security. Could it be possible that a terrorist group had infiltrated Homeland Security? On the other hand, did the terrorist organization have enough information on a person in Homeland Security to blackmail him or her into getting the desired information?

As Omid thought more about all the work that was left to do, he began to ask himself what he had accomplished during his time in Springfield. Perhaps Springfield Sheriff Jim Whittles, a retired Marine who had worked closely with Omid, could take over where he had stopped. They had become good friends in the short period of time. Omid thought that Whittles was a capable man and just might find some solutions; he just might resolve some of his unanswered questions. *Perhaps John Bowman, Ridley's neighbor, can help Whittles figure things out.*

As a Marine Major, Omid was used to getting things done. He was quite disappointed when Baker informed him they had a strong indication the Brotherhood was in Houston. Privately, Omid had serious doubts he could find them in such a large city under normal circumstances. Now with the relocation of one hundred thousand people, plus martial law and curfew, getting around the city was going to be very difficult at best. He was concerned that this was a wild goose chase.

Homeland Security told Rahimi it had knowledge of the general area of the city from where the Internet connection was made to send the e-mail and upload the YouTube video. There was no guarantee that, even if the Brotherhood sent its messages from Houston, they would still be there several days later. However, Omid had given and taken orders all of his adult life within the chain of command, and he would follow orders.

He would do his best to accomplish his task and then perhaps go back to Springfield and complete that mission.

As he arrived on the outskirts of Houston, the I-45 traffic was very heavy and moving painfully slow. After a while, his patience was wearing thin and got off the outer belt when he had the opportunity. The exit was 67A and the exit sign indicated Happy Valley. The name struck him as the right place to get off the freeway. As he initially drove through the town, Happy Valley seemed to be a pleasant neighborhood of modest homes, set back from the tree-lined curbs. The houses were well maintained and seemed to be of various configurations. As he looked at these homes, he noted that they weren't all the same, as military housing would be. Some were much larger than others, with well-maintained lawns and precisely trimmed shrubs. As he studied the homes, he concluded that this was not a new section. Given the sizes of the houses and the landscaping, they were built some time ago. Some houses were painted dark green; others were dark blue, and occasionally you could spot what looked like a southern mansion with Greek columns, all painted white. The trees were mostly majestic live oaks, the kind you see in movies about the old south.

Omid hit his brakes in the middle of the street, suddenly realizing that nobody was around. He got out of his car and looked in both directions. He saw no one and heard nothing; no dogs, no lawn mowers and no cars, nothing. He was about to get back in the car when he looked at the house in front of him. The front door appeared to be open. Looking to his right and left he saw front doors open up and down the street. One would think that wide open doors would be inviting the criminal element to loot, but he saw no sign of this activity, either. No broken windows, no debris in the yards; nothing seemed to out of place, just no people.

Houston was not, at least to the best of his knowledge, scheduled for evacuation, at least not yet. He wondered why all the people were gone. He needed gas and so he continued down Main Street. All the stores were closed. Again, no signs of vandalism, nothing lying on the sidewalks or in the streets, no broken windows. Just no one around. It seemed to Omid that everybody had simply disappeared; there was no sign of life in Happy Valley. As he continued through the center of the town, he was the only person around. He came upon a Shell station. The lights were on but he saw no one. He pulled in and stopped at a pump. He unscrewed his gas cap, put the nozzle into the tank opening, and flipped the handle and the pump asked cash or credit. Omid swiped his card and the pump started, gas flowed and he filled his tank.

He went into the service area and snack shop, but again there was nobody around. He got a soda, took a sandwich from the cooler, smelled it and it seemed okay. He figured what his purchases should cost and left the money on the counter, went back to his car, got in and drove down the street heading ... nowhere.

CHAPTER 70

Are There More Bombs?

John Seacrest had just received another phone call from Harold Wellington of Interpol that the intelligence chatter is that America may be facing more than two bombs.

"Do you have any idea where this chatter is coming from?" John asked.

"Based on the source, we think it's coming from Russia."

"Why would Russia be talking about bombs in the United States?"

"John, let me be clear, I said we *think* the traffic is coming from Russia not the Russian government."

"Who in Russia would know if there are more bombs in the United States?"

"While we can't prove it we believe the information is false but designed to scare the commodity market," Harold said.

"So, what you're saying is that somebody in Russia is buying long oil futures and wants to drive the price up."

"The only person we know of who could benefit from a further increase in the price of oil is Viktor Antipova, the uncle of one of the terrorists – Oleg Barbulio. It has been rumored that Antipova's companies have massive position in the futures markets that are long near-term oil contracts and are beginning to short the longer-term futures. If he can move the price of oil higher, he expands the value of the contract and his wealth, in turn."

"How much oil does he control at this point?" John asked.

"With all of his corporations, it's difficult to tell how much he owns but from the data we have collected, perhaps a billion barrels."

"So every time the price of oil goes up one dollar he stands to make one billion dollars more." John whistled. "Then the rumors of more bombs in the U.S. are his way of trying to manipulate the market to make more money."

"Yes, John that could be true. We know that Iran had at least three reconditioned bombs when they sold the ones to the Brotherhood. We have to assume that the one they took in trade is or has already been reconditioned, so this gives them at least three bombs and with the success of their reconditioned bombs in America, my guess is that the price has gone up substantially."

"Didn't I read in one of your reports that an empty bomb case was found at the Ridley home?"

"Yes, that is correct. We assumed that the Brotherhood was responsible for that bomb. We thought that it must have been a dud and they went back to Syria to come up with a working bomb."

"John, what if it wasn't the Brotherhood? What if another group was unaware they had bought a dud on the black market until they tried to use it. What if they're still in America trying to figure out how to get another bomb?"

"Where would they go to get a bomb in the United States? My guess is, now that they've seen the work of the Brotherhood, they don't know how many bombs they have and they will try and connect with them to buy one of their bombs or have them fix their bomb."

"My guess is that when the bomb didn't work, they took it out of the case to see if it can be fixed and now they're on a manhunt trying to find the Brotherhood in the United States."

"Harold, let's assume that for the moment the Brotherhood is somewhere in the United States. How would this other group find them?"

"The Brotherhood may be operating as an independent group. It won't take them long to discover, as you did, that the YouTube video and the broadcast e-mail were sent from Houston. Houston isn't that far from Springfield, so my guess is they're already in Houston and have already sent flyers throughout the Muslim community to help them find the members of the Brotherhood and their location."

"In the next few days, we'll have two assets on the ground in Houston. One of them is Lt. Hassen from Mossad, who actually met one of the terrorists while they were in Syria observing them building the bombs. The other is a Marine on loan to us from Department of Defense, whose family is from Syria. His name is Omid Rahimi. He has with him photographs of all the Brotherhood leadership to assist both of them in their search."

"John, do you have a plan should your people locate the Brotherhood of the Red Nile?"

"Unfortunately, to the best of my knowledge we do not yet have a plan. I have been told that the ground assets are to locate, observe and report the activity of the Brotherhood to Homeland Security."

"You said that one of your assets on the ground actually met one of the terrorists. What did she learn from her contact with them?"

"As best as I can piece together, the reason she is here is because it appears she was something more to the terrorist than a casual contact."

"Are you saying they were intimate?"

"No, they didn't have enough time, but clearly there is something between them."

"Are they planning, once they locate them, for her to just run into her friend on the street so they can rekindle their relationship?"

"Well, Harold, that is pretty much the best we have at the moment." *Should I have told Harold that we know that she has his cell phone number and we are still debating how and if she should use it? The cell phone may be the best lead we have and we have to be very careful how and when we use it. We don't want to send any alarms and scare them off. We have to get to them before the other group, assuming there is one.* "Listen, Harold, I must go. Thanks for all your help and, if you hear anything more about who is spreading the rumors, call me anytime. If there is another group and they have bombs and use them… I'm not sure America can survive more attacks."

CHAPTER 71

The First Fireside Chat

It was Saturday morning and the president's first Fireside Chat was scheduled for two o'clock this afternoon. President Jordan had been working
with his staff, planning the twenty minutes of airtime. He knew that the
two most important issues were to calm the people and to ask for their help.
Jordan was keenly aware of the power of radio and the importance of his
ability to engage the American people. A failure to reach out and connect
with Americans could not only eliminate his chance for re-election, but
also compromise the ability of the country to survive. Jordan knew that
both his and America's biggest problem was millions of barrels of contaminated oil, natural gas and refined product in the pipelines through Texas
and Louisiana. Presently it was just sitting there, sending off radiation and
potentially making millions of people sick.

If the president could find a way to get rid of all this contaminated
energy, he could focus on putting people to work building new pipelines
for moving energy around the contaminated pipelines. Jordan invited two
Nobel laureates in physics to the White House and they had no real suggestions. If he asked the American people to help him find a solution, he
could focus their energy on finding a solution and distract them from the
country's crisis. *If we can find answers, we could put people back to work and get
them thinking being great again as a nation. I need to tell the people we'll be better
off because we shall make ourselves energy independent. If we can control our sources
of energy, we can say, as Dr. Martin Luther King once said, 'Free at last, thank God
I'm free at last.'*

Jordan was starting to get excited about the chat. He entered the Oval Office, where things were in about the same place as the last time he spoke to America about the first bomb, when the second bomb went off. He looked at the Kennedy desk he had brought out of storage when he took over as president. Over the last few days, he had had many thoughts about what Kennedy must have been thinking during the Cuban Missile Crisis. He knew that, like Kennedy, he hadn't had much time to think things out after the two bombs exploded. He must make decisions and make them quickly for the good of the country.

Jordan knew that it might not be possible to come up with a solution to the contaminated energy problem but he had great faith in American ingenuity and he strongly believed that they would come through with a viable solution.

It was now fifteen minutes until broadcast. The president stepped into his small conference room off the Oval Office to relax and focus his attention on those very important twenty minutes, perhaps the most important twenty minutes in his life. He heard a soft knock on the door.

"Who is it?"

"It's Karen. May I come in?"

Jordan just realized that he had not seen his wife for almost twelve hours since he rested on the couch in this conference room. He jumped up, and rushed to the door and swung it wide open. He saw her, reached out and grabbed her by the arm, quickly pulled her into the conference room and closed the door.

"I can't tell you how much I missed you, how much I missed holding you in my arms and squeezing you as close to me as possible."

"Nathan, I have missed all of those things and more, but I just wanted to stop by and wish you good luck."

"You're all the luck I need. Let me hug you and give you a kiss that will inspire me to be the best I can be this afternoon." He took her into his arms and, as he wrapped his arm around her, he gently pulled her close to him. As he brought her closer, he could feel her breasts flatten against his chest and her hips snug against him. They both held firm for a moment and then gently loosened the pressure of their caress. Their lips met in a soft and gentle touch for just a moment and then separated. They looked at each other eye to eye and the message was very clear, even though unspoken. *After all these years, I want you and love you.*

They separated and Karen reached for the doorknob. Just before she turned it she said, "I know you are the best for me and the best for the country. Lead us. I'll be listening."

They were still holding hands as she opened the door and slowly let his hand go to walk out the door.

Jordan had a great rush as Karen left, went into the Oval Office and said to one of the crew, "How long to air?"

"Five minutes, Mr. President."

Jordan went around the Kennedy desk and saw the microphone. He sat in his chair and a crewmember came over and put on the mic. The crew did a sound check and said they were ready to go in five … four … three … two … one.

"My fellow Americans, this is the first in a series of discussions between you and me to inform you about what is going on and, most importantly, to get your help in making America great again. I promise you that, to the best of my ability, I shall tell you the truth about the situation at the time I'm speaking. There may come a time when I have to correct something I have said because I got it wrong the first time. I shall be as open as possible, except in matters that might compromise national security.

The president spent the next twenty minutes bringing Americans up to date on the decisions and actions being implemented to put America back on her feet. He explained the evacuation strategies and plans to ensure Americans would have access to money for food and necessities. He spoke about the need to reduce personal spending and consumerism while the country rebuilt its damaged infrastructure and communities.

"Our country has sustained a devastating amount of damage and my administration is focusing all of our resources to getting America back on its feet and growing again. I know it will be incredibly difficult, but I believe America is the home of the free thinker, the tinkerer, and the entrepreneur. I believe we can find solutions to our problems from you, who are the best and the brightest in the world. Right now, I need the power and sprit of America to come up with a solution to a problem that, if it goes unsolved, will keep this country in peril perhaps for decades.

"After this broadcast, all of you who have computers or Internet access, go to the White House web site **www.whitehouse.gov** and look for a section called Texas oil. We need your best ideas on how to get rid of all this contaminated oil, natural gas and refined product in these pipelines, taking millions of people out of harm's way and putting people back to work. Post your suggestions and leave us a means to get in touch with you to follow up on your suggestion. There are no limitations on the ideas. I shall report your suggestions and the ones we are considering. My time is almost up, but I want to make one more point about your suggestions. Each of you - and I mean each and every one - in this great country has the responsibility, regardless of where or for whom you work, to send in your ideas. I promise you will get a fair chance. I don't care if you work in your garage, in a factory, for a government contractor or if you're a government employee, everybody who has an idea will be heard. If we use your idea and it works, you will be paid at least twenty-five million dollars. I would normally end a message asking 'God to bless America', but let me say God has already blessed America with a nation of people who will survive and eventually thrive again."

After the president signed off, millions of Americans began to talk about the twenty-five million dollar prize and the problem posed by the president. At 900 Commerce Rd., New Orleans, Milo Morrison was also considering the problem. As he pondered all that energy underground, a possible solution began to form in his mind, an answer that, if he was right, could change the direction of the crisis and save America. He needed to test his idea by running some calculations and studying the maps of Texas and Louisiana. If his idea could work, would it help rebuild America? If it was possible, at what cost to the country would he dare suggest it? Or should he just let someone else come up with a different and perhaps a less effective idea than his?

CHAPTER 72

The Brotherhood Listens

In Houston, Sargon and the rest of the Brotherhood had been listening to the president's talk and he saw the concern on their faces. "Is there a solution to America's problems that we have not thought about?"

Oleg spoke up and addressed the issue raised by Sargon. He realized he was responsible for the idea of the attack on oil and he sensed that some members of the Brotherhood might have second thoughts about having chosen his plan. "I listened to what the president was saying. If you read between the lines, what he really said is that the government and all of its resources have no clue about what to do with all the contaminated energy.

"My guess is that they have no answer and it is their desperate hope that somebody out here has an idea with which they can try to solve this very serious problem. It is possible that somebody will come up with an idea but it will not be a quick fix and our objective will still be met. We will disable America for many years, not just a few days or weeks."

Sargon asked him, "If we could find out how they plan to implement a solution, could we interfere with their plans?"

Oleg thought for a moment, "That would depend on what they plan to do. I have to assume that the president will tell the nation what the plan is, so we will have plenty of time to consider our possible counterattack."

Sargon spoke to all of them. "We have to believe that America is employing all its resources to find us. The longer we all stay here, the better the chances that we shall all be captured. I don't think it's safe for all of us to stay in America. I would like to suggest that Michael and Oleg stay behind and the rest of us should return to our homeland.

"Michael is an American citizen and has no reason to leave, but I'm not sure he can go back to Springfield. Oleg, with your experience you could be hired to work on the project, depending on the proposed fix. Having somebody on the inside could be extremely valuable if we're going to sabotage the solution."

Both Michael and Oleg agreed that it made sense for them to stay behind. Ishtar spoke up, "I can work on the arrangement to get the rest of you out of the country and back to Iran and Syria. Mordecai, do you want to return to Israel, stay in the United States or go to some other country?"

Mordecai did not immediately respond to Ishtar's question and then answered, "I need to think about that for a while." While Mordecai was unsure, only Adad spoke up about going back to his home in Syria. Cyrus wasn't sure where he wanted to go and said that he needed to think about it.

Sargon spoke up, "We have to assume that American intelligence knows who each of us is, and where we are from. It seems to me it will be difficult for any of us to go back to our homelands."

Adad spoke up, "They may know who we are but they have no evidence to connect us to the actual bombing. I must go home to be with my wife and children and run my business."

All four of them listened to what Adad said and understood they could never go home if they wanted to live. Going home meant certain death. They might not know when but death was coming.

Many parts of the world were rejoicing at America's misfortune and would be surprised at how long it would take America to recover. Some leaders were not sure what the rebuilt America would look like, but they were sure that America would survive and, when retaliation came, they couldn't foresee how America would react. It might take years or decades, but America would respond. The Brotherhood of the Red Nile knew little about how America would respond, but for the first time since they started their journey, an element of fear began to grow. They were changed forever and knew that from now on they would constantly look over their shoulders. In fact, they were unaware that somebody was indeed already very close.

CHAPTER 73

Could Be a Turning Point

Frank Williams requested Nava Dobias send Lt. Hadar Hassen to America and planned use her to call Mordecai, one of the terrorists, and see if he would answer the phone. Williams and Baker had discussed with Lt. Hassen how they might want to employ her because of the feelings Mordecai had shown for her back in Syria. Williams had sent a plane to get her and, with Dobias' agreement, she was on her way to Washington DC. After a discussion with Williams and Baker, she would head to Houston to meet with Major Omid Rahimi, Homeland Security's asset on the ground.

As they waited for Hassen's arrival, they planned the discussion they would initiate with her in DC and what the plan of action would be when she got to Houston. Williams had decided he wanted Baker to accompany Hassen on the trip and for Baker to represent him in the plan discussion. Williams had also had a discussion with the leadership of the Pentagon, Secret Service, FBI and CIA. All had decided that a team with representatives from all the agencies should go to Houston to plan a joint operation. Williams decided that a meeting with all this firepower had to take place away from Houston to avoid attracting attention. After he reviewed a map of airports in Texas, he chose Draughon-Miller Central Texas Regional Airport. It was large enough to handle all the planes coming in and small enough not to attract a great deal of attention.

Baker was able to pull up a Google Earth image of the airport facility on his computer. This showed an Air National Guard hangar which they could use as a meeting point and which was large enough to fit all the small jets inside the hangar. Williams had Marie notify the other agencies to use small craft and to give them the name and location of the airport. Baker found the airport's web site, called to speak with the airport manager and told him what was about to happen. Meanwhile, Williams was also on the phone to the Pentagon, asking Chairman of the Joint Chiefs General Powell to secure the Air National Guard hangar.

General Powell replied, "Consider it done. When do you want the hangar and for how long?"

Williams responded, "They'll be arriving within the next twenty-four hours and I expect the meetings to take two to three days."

Powell said, "When we send in our team, I'll send a detachment of MPs to provide security."

Williams replied, "Great idea, and thank you for all that you are doing, General."

Now that all of the arrangements had been made, Williams and Baker's attention turned to discussing what should happen at the meeting itself and how they were going to employ Lt. Hassen. "She has Mordecai's cell number, but we have no way of knowing if he brought the phone with him or even If he's in the States."

"Not only that sir. She may only get one chance to connect with him, so what she says will be very important."

"How is it possible that this Mordecai person was so strongly attracted to this woman in three brief meetings without sex being involved?"

"Sir, I have seen her military photo. While they are notoriously terrible photographs, I can still tell she must be gorgeous. It appears that the attraction was so strong at first sight the she mesmerized him. It is intriguing that she was just as smitten with him."

"Wait a minute," Williams held up a hand. "Are you saying there is a mutual attraction? How do we keep control of her with all those hormones flying around? Can we trust her to work for us?"

"The best I can say is that when she gets here we need to talk about this with her and try and assess where her loyalty is. If she convinces she's on our side we can decide what we want to accomplish with her on this mission."

Williams' responded, "Don't we want to capture all the bad guys? Round them up and display them to the world? We want to show the world we caught the enemy and that we are bringing them to justice for killing over fifty-four thousand Americans."

"Sir, I would like nothing more than to capture these bad guys, but I want to get *all* of them, together with those funding the attack.

"If we act too hastily we could blow our chance of getting everybody. We need to make sure we cast the widest possible net to catch all the fish, big and small."

Williams asked, "Do we know when we can expect her to get here?"

"I checked with flight operations before I came in and, if the plane is on time, she should be landing now. I have a car waiting at Andrews and expect her here in thirty to forty-five minutes."

"Should we have a conversation with Major Rahimi before she gets here, so he knows what we want?"

"That is fine. I'll have Marie put a call in to him right away," and passes her the instruction. Then he turns to Baker and says, "With all the players at this meeting, how will we keep control of this operation?"

"Sir, I have been considering this issue myself. Whoever captures these terrorists will be famous. Don't get me wrong sir; I would like it to be us. It will be difficult at best for this program to work. Whoever controls Lt. Hassen controls the outcome and I think she should report to Major Rahimi."

"Excellent idea."

Marie called on the intercom, "Sir, I have Major Rahimi on line one."

"Thank you." Williams picked up the phone, asked Omid how he was doing and inquired whether he had anything to report.

"Sir, are you on a secure line and are you alone?"

CHAPTER 74

What Have I Gotten Into?

Williams had sent a small Gulfstream jet to pick up Lt. Hassen in Ramon airport. He chose this airport because it was off the traffic mainline at the Ben Gurion International airport and had a long enough runway for the Gulfstream to land and take off. In the Gulfstream, it should take about nine hours for her to arrive at Andrews and another forty-five minutes to transfer to Homeland Security. There was a seven-hour time difference, so Hadar would be bone tired when she arrives.

Dobias had sent a car to pick her up and take her directly to the airplane. He advised her to pack for at least two weeks, although she could be in the United States for months. He told her if she needed money to contact him on his secure line. The last thing he told her, "Run away if at any point you think your life is in serious danger. Don't talk to anybody until you are sure you're in the clear. We will come and get you no matter where you are. Is this understood?"

"Yes, sir."

"So, go and help our American friends. I'll look forward to your reports."

In the car on the way to the airport, she was both excited and scared. She wanted to help a devastated America, but at the same time her desire for Mordecai excited her. As the car pulled up beside an unmarked plane at the airport, Hadar looked out into the darkness. She could only see plane's running lights in the darkness and, dimly in the distance, the runway lights. She couldn't see any markings on the aircraft except for a number on the tail. The engine on the opposite side of the plane was running and a non-uniformed guard had her car door blocked so she couldn't get out.

She was starting to get nervous about what was going on and was asked herself, *Is this a mistake?* Her eyes were drawn to the ladder coming out of the plane. As soon as it hit the ground, her car door opened and she was quickly escorted to the plane and up the stairs. The security guard had her bag and walked behind her. As soon as she was in the plane, he tossed in her bag and jumped down from the ladder as it was being raised and the other engine was turned on. Within seconds, the plane was moving and Hadar quickly had to buckle her seatbelt. The plane was immediately at full throttle and sped down the runway. It seemed less than a minute since she got out of the car before they were airborne.

There were almost no lights on inside the cabin and she wondered if she was going to have to fly to America in the dark. However, the interior lights came on after about ten minutes and an attendant in uniform approached her, welcomed her aboard and asked if she would like something to drink.

She politely asked, "What do you have?"

The attendant responded, "Miss, I think we might have anything you might like to drink."

Hadar decided she would have some fun and see if she could name a drink that they will not have on the plane.

"I'll have a large glass of ice cold Yotvata dark chocolate milk."

The attendant responded, "Do you want that with cookies?"

Hadar chuckled, "Are you kidding me? You have that on this plane?"

"No, not really, but I've had it and it's truly wonderful. So what else can I get for you?"

"I'll have a Diet Coke with a slice of lime."

He asked Hadar, "Have you had anything to eat?"

"No, and I would like a sandwich. Do you have turkey on Jewish rye, with real mayo and a kosher dill pickle and some chips?"

"That I can do. I'll get your soda and then I'll bring your snack. It will take us about nine hours to arrive at our destination so you will have a chance to sleep and then you'll have another meal about an hour before we land. I'll be right back with your drink."

Half an hour later, she finished her meal and relaxed in her comfortable seat. She was thinking about falling asleep when a different person walked up to her.

"Lt. Hassen, I am Major Fred Johnston and I work at the Pentagon in the area of terrorism defense. I have been asked to give you this folder as a briefing in advance of your meeting with Under Secretary Williams. All of this information is classified top secret. You can look at it throughout the flight, but the folder must be returned to me before we land. Any questions?"

"Am I allowed to discuss the contents of the folder with you?"

"No ma'am, you may not. Your questions, can be possibly be answered by Secretary Williams or his team. I must warn you that some of the images might be disturbing."

Before she opened the file, she thought about Mordecai and the time she slammed the barn door into him so hard it knocked him to the ground. She remembered those meals they almost had and his several quick departures because he needed to immediately attend something urgent. Most of all she remembered the last two kisses and how they stirred her as no other kiss had in her life. *How is it possible that the man I became so attracted to and he to me was responsible for the largest single mass killing in the history of the United States?* She found herself in conflict, for she was on a plane going to America to trap Mordecai and his other terrorist friends; she was going to be asked to use their feelings as bait to lure him out so all of them could be captured and most likely be put to death. *I know these people killed thousands upon thousands of Americans and may have destroyed America as a world leader. How can I have these feelings for him and at the same time send him to his death?*

She slowly raised her hand and extended her index finger toward the attendant call button. Almost as if in slow motion she finally reached the button, pushed it, and it turned white.

Within seconds, the attendant was at her seat, "Yes, Lieutenant?"

"I would like some Jack Daniels over ice with a splash of water, please."

"Yes ma'am. Would you like some mixed nuts or some pretzels?"

"No, thank you."

Shortly, he arrived with her drink, "Will there be anything more Lieutenant?"

"This is fine, thank you." As she sipped her drink, she pushed the button for the overhead light. It was the first time she used the light since the plane took off. Hadar looked around the plane noticed that she and Major Johnson were the only passengers on the plane.

She took the folder that she had been given to review, and after a long swallow of her drink, she opened it and was horrified by what she saw. She found herself reaching for the airsickness bag.

CHAPTER 75

Congress is Out of the Loop

It was several days since the Congressional leadership had been updated about the administration was doing, and the loyal opposition was fuming about the president's 'Fireside Chat', with no time for them to respond with their side of the story. The reality was they had no other side of the story, but to them that was beside the point. If the president spoke, they felt they should have the right to respond. They had not been informed about the Chat and the first they knew about it was when it was happening in real time.

In the Speaker's private conference room, the leadership of both Houses of Congress met to figure out how they and their members could truly help, but also to get some of the credit. Senate Majority leader William Wild begins the meeting by saying, "This is an outrage. How can the president make decisions that will surely affect the entire nation without consulting Congress?"

The House Minority Leader James Radcliff echoed the comments of Wild but went one step further, "Has the president acted in a way that violates his oath of office and the Constitution?"

The Minority leader from the Senate, Francis Pollard, looked at Wild, "Are you suggesting that the president has committed an impeachable offense?" While the rest of the room had been individually thinking the same thing, and Pollard's comments broke the ice on the topic. The Speaker responded, "How could you be thinking of impeaching a sitting president in this time of unprecedented terrorist attacks?"

Wild retorted, "Look at what power the president has taken on without the consent of Congress. He closed the banks, declared martial law on a national scale, ordered a countrywide dusk to dawn curfew and has closed all the capital markets. He did all of this without consulting Congress. All of these activities should come under various committees in Congress, but to the best of my knowledge, none of the oversight committee chairs was contacted. It seems to me that the president has taken control of the country, much like a despot or dictator.

"Congress passes the laws and the administration is responsible for carrying them out. We were not a participant in any of these decisions at the White House concerning the crises."

The Speaker just listened and wondered, *How can we impeach a sitting president when the country is in chaos and we have no idea what is really happening? I understand where Wild is coming from. He is pissed off that he had no part in dealing with the greatest disaster in the history of the nation. However, to impeach the president after a fireside chat asking for all America to help solve the biggest environmental and economic disaster in the history of the country? That won't sit well with the people at all. At this juncture, we can't say he has violated his oath of office or the Constitution and therefore has to go. I just don't see it. I don't think the public or media will, either.*

"Gentlemen, I think we need a meeting with the president as soon as possible to convince the president he needs our help and all of Congress' support in solving the country's problems. The reality is that many Senators and Congressmen are not in Washington, and with the curfew and martial law, they can't get back here. There are not enough travel hours in the day. If we don't have committee chairs present, how can we hold oversight meetings? By the same token, if neither of the houses has sufficient members present for a quorum, how can we pass anything? It seems to me that until we can get the committee leadership back and enough members in both houses, we can't function."

Wild has been listening to the Speaker and the more he hears the more he realizes how difficult it will be to impeach the president now. He suggests that they have a responsibility to meet with the president and stay updated, but also to collect evidence that could be used in a possible impeachment process.

The Speaker announces, "I will call the president and ask for a meeting with him so that the Congress leadership be kept informed on what is going on to deal with the crisis. In addition, despite our limited resources, we will offer any support we can to the president. The reality, gentlemen, is that we don't have anything to do and may not for quite a while. Perhaps we can see who is in town, make a list of people for the president to let him know who is available to help his teams review the suggestions from the public. When things get back to normal – whatever that normal may look like – we can think about your suggestion, Mr. Wild. But for now, move it to the back burner."

CHAPTER 76

Omid on the Phone

Frank Williams and Ted Baker were in Williams' conference room ready to start a conference call with Major Omid Rahimi who was their man on the ground in Houston. Williams had sent him to Houston from Springfield because intelligence agencies had told Homeland that the e-mail and the YouTube video had been posted from a site in Houston.

The original purpose of this call was to discuss the arrival and deployment of Lt. Hadar Hassen from Israel in an attempt to infiltrate and then capture the leadership of the Brotherhood of the Red Nile. Major Rahimi started the call by asking Williams, "Are you on a secure line and are you alone?"

Williams stopped for a moment and considered, *Do I tell him that Baker is in the room with me? Something must be important for the Major to want to make sure their call is secure and private.* "Yes, I'm on a secure line. The only person in the room besides me is Ted Baker and the door is closed, so the room is sound proof. Why are you so concerned?"

Rahimi is already talking. "Hello, Ted, how are you?"

"I'm fine and yourself?"

"I was somewhat disappointed that I had to leave Springfield, but the trip allowed me to focus on some questions that kept coming up while I was there and that need to be answered."

"What's bothering you about Springfield?"

"Sir, I have a series of open-ended questions and some unanswered questions. If we can figure out the answers it may give us more insight into what happened not only in Springfield, but Texas City and Port Fourchon."

"I don't have any problem with Baker in the room, do you, Major?"

"Sir, I don't think so, but with so many unanswered questions I'm not sure. Ted, I'm not accusing you or the Secretary of anything…"

"Hold on there, Major, do you think that Ted or I are involved in the plot?"

"Sir, I don't think so but, to be truthful, I just don't know for sure."

Williams started to get angry with the Major and his veiled accusations. In a stern voice he barked back, "This better be good, Major Rahimi."

"Sir, if I may use one example that has bugged me since the first time I heard the story…"

"Go ahead, Major."

"Sir, we have ascertained that the two emergency vans were not ours. They were stolen from the Fire and Rescue center in Texas City. We know when they were checked out and when they were returned. Whoever took them had to know that DHS was on its way to the Ridley house. With the driving time from Texas City to Springfield being over one hour with good traffic through Houston, the people who borrowed the vehicles had to know the rallying point before Homeland departed, where they were going and when."

Baker jumps in, "So you think somehow these people, whoever they are, were tipped off before our team departed?"

"Ted, think about it. You don't just get a phone call and then go find these two highly sophisticated vehicles and drive down the highway. You have to know well in advance that you might need this equipment, you locate it and then figure out how to get it."

Williams looked at Ted and then said, in a calmer voice, "So what else is troubling you?"

"What happened to Mike and Mary Ridley? Were they in the body bags on the gurneys loaded into those vans?"

Williams responded, "When I arrived, the neighbors were asking that same question."

"I had lunch at a place called Fred's Tacos just across from the Springfield High School. After school, some of the kids came over to get something to eat and Sheriff Whittles asked them about the Ridley family. One student said that there was talk in town that the Ridleys were in the witness protection program."

The Major continued, "Based on his bank records, Mike Ridley had no job, nor did his wife. So, how did they pay their bills? A Russian oil billionaire owned the house they live in – or perhaps I should say they used to live in. The Russian sent money to the bank to pay the property taxes and has done so every year for the last twenty-two years.

"Then we have Michael. He gets a free ride to Berkley and never shows. We don't know what he is doing to earn twenty-five thousand a month, which he has never spent and yet, his checking account is overdrawn."

"Nobody seems to know why DHS was even sent to the Ridley house in the first place and why was the Under Secretary for Homeland Security in the neighborhood a long way from Washington. There are plenty more questions like this, but here is the big one. It is now clear that the case buried in the back yard of the Ridley house at one time held a Soviet-style dirty bomb. Where is that device? Last, but not least, why were there enough explosives to blow up a city sitting in the basement of the Ridley house, and the people from DHS never saw it?" The Major took a breath and for a moment there was silence on both ends of the phone.

The Major jumped back in. "I forgot one other important item. Only by chance and good fortune was a map discovered in the basement of the Ridley house that just happened to have the two bombed cities circled on the map." Still silence and finally Omid spoke up, "Any thoughts or ideas gentlemen?"

Baker spoke up. "I don't know where to start, but let's start by asking ourselves if we have a spy in Homeland Security, or is there another foreign or domestic agency competing with us?"

"I was thinking domestic," Omid said.

Williams finally, in a very somber voice, revealed, "We got an anonymous tip that a terrorist group was using the Ridley house to recondition the bombs. I happened to be on a routine visit to our Houston office and was told about this when the action was being planned. Therefore, I went to see for myself what was going on. We were planning a raid on the Ridley house for that evening so I had plenty of time to get there. You can verify my attendance in the logbook at the Houston office. Under 'Purpose of Your Visit' it will say 'routine inspection'. Ted, please contact the Houston office immediately and have them e-mail the logbook photo image of my arrival in Houston to you and to the Major."

Baker knew that Williams wanted him to get the logbook page right away, but he thought there were more important issues to discuss. "Is it possible that another government agency or department has been supporting the Ridley family and we are unaware? Who in our government could be trying to kill us?"

CHAPTER 77

Mordecai Couldn't Have Done This

Hadar had composed herself, sealed the airsickness bag and called for the attendant to take it away. "Could I have some Sprite with no ice, please?"

"Of course, just a moment." The attendant returns with the Sprite and she sips it slowly, all the while asking herself, *How could Mordecai have built a bomb to cause so much destruction? He seemed young and almost innocent.* She found herself in the conflict of her life; the time she spent with Mordecai was exhilarating, not like with any other person she had met. How could it be possible that in just three short visits she felt like she found a soul mate, even without sex?

Lt. Hassen was also a soldier, and as a soldier her job it was to protect her people and her country. *If America were unable to cover Israel's back then it would be up to them to defend themselves as best they could. The Brotherhood used two bombs on the United States. Looking at the destruction they brought to American shores, how much of Israel could just one of these bombs destroy? If they bombed Jerusalem, over eight hundred thousand people, not counting tourists, would be killed, including Christians, Jews and Muslims alike. The city could never be inhabited again. Mordecai just couldn't do that.*

She opened the folder, took another look at the destruction of life and property, and thought, *Perhaps he could, but how could he?* She read once that terrorist bombers are detached from their victims. The people who go into stores or movie theaters never see the people that they are about to kill but rather they are on a mission and if the mission is successful they will be rewarded in heaven. The bombers are never around to see the results of their work so they have no compassion for their victims.

Their work is for God first and country second. *Is that how Mordecai thought about his work? What do I really know about him other than the physical chemistry?* Then the question that had been lurking in the back of her mind came rising to the surface like a scuba diver, out of air, rushing to the surface. *Would he kill me? When I get to America and try to find him, will he kill me if he thinks I'm a threat to him? Can I do my job and still save him? I have no idea what they want me to do once I arrive. I have to find out if there's a way to deliver the others and save him. Are you nuts? You sound like some lovesick high school girl. You are a grown woman. You know nothing about him except for what is in his profile in this folder.*

Yes, he is attracted to you, and you used your plentiful assets to attract him, as you were told. Is he more in love with your face or your figure than he is with you the person? What does he really know about you? He thinks you're a graduate student going to America to study adobe house building to show Africans a better way to build their homes. What he knows about me is superficial, and a lie to boot. I am not the person he thinks I am.

The best thing for me to do is to listen to the discussion, not commit to anything, and then, when I know what they want me to do, see if there is a way out for both of us. I have to be careful because there is no way of knowing if in fact the conspirators are even still in America. If I use my phone, what do I say if he answers?

CHAPTER 78

The White House

Within moments after the president signed off from his fireside chat, the Internet hit on the White House web site and almost shut it down. Ed Smith, the director of the site, put a call in to the Oval Office to tell them of the near meltdown. Apparently, the Oval Office had forgotten to tell Ed what it was planning to do in asking the American people for their help to solve the contaminated oil crisis.

In a normal day, the site got about four thousand e-mails. In times of turmoil, either foreign or domestic, that number could spike much higher. Ed told the Oval Office that the servers were receiving ten thousand e-mails per hour with no sign of letting up. He is unclear how long the servers can hold up. In about thirty minutes, Smith got a phone call from Mary Washington.

"Mr. Smith, please hold for the president."

"Mr. Smith, I apologize for not warning you about what I was going to do and for all the trouble I've caused you."

"Mr. President, I listened to your chat and I had no clue that America would respond in such volume."

"I think America wants to help and we have to find a way, Mr. Smith, to take every e-mail and review them."

"Sir, I understand that most departments are understaffed and will be until we can get people back to work. We might be able to use the spare capacity at several different departments, but I don't have the authority to ask. Could you help?"

"Mr. Smith, I shall issue an executive order to all departments to contact you and see how we can manage the crunch until it slows down."

"Sir, how soon before you can get this order out?"

"Within the hour for sure. Expect people to start calling shortly thereafter."

"Sir, if I might ask, have you thought about how to process all of these e-mails?"

"I have. We have special teams of interns and pages from Congress who will start screening them today. If it's okay with you, I will have the intern leader, Robert Jones, contact you to start the collection and review process."

"Thank you sir, and God bless you."

"And you too, Mr. Smith.

"Mr. President?"

"Yes."

"Can you call me Ed, sir?"

"Absolutely, Ed. I'll talk with you soon. Keep us posted on your progress."

"Yes, sir."

Later that day, Robert Jones had a conversation with Ed and they worked out a channeling process so his team could begin to review the massive volume of e-mails. The channeling process would start at 8 AM the next day. They agreed to send the e-mail to a new network via Wi-Fi. Jones had visited with the Chief of Staff and had selected the great hall in the Air and Space Museum in downtown Washington, DC. They closed the museum and set up eight-foot long tables with chairs and an extension power cable running the length of the great hall for the computers. They would start with one hundred people, but the space could easily handle seven hundred.

From the moment of the president's chat Jones and his team had been considering how to break down and separate the submitted ideas. They came up with categories such as process, computers, software, machines, and then they had category called 'other' for anything that didn't fit in the other categories. They agreed, as they processed more ideas, that they might have to re-sort into new categories.

By the next morning, his team of one hundred-plus support people were already plugged in and ready to go. Jones called Smith and told him, "Throw the switch."

Smith pressed the button and data started flowing over the Internet into the server at Air and Space, and by Wi-Fi to every laptop in the work area. Within moments, you could hear the sounds of laughter, and every occasionally an 'OMG'. The team quickly began to settle down and its processing efficiency grew rapidly. Each hour, the main computer printed a report of how many suggestions were reviewed and catalogued. Tens of thousands of messages were processed that first day. Most were well meaning but misguided. One suggested that they build tanker spaceships and send the oil to the sun where it would burn and do no harm.

If a suggestion seemed to have any merit, it was e-mailed to Jones who had a team of scientists connected to the Internet through a webcast where they would review and discuss the viability of a qualified suggestion. At the end of the first day, one hundred thousand e-mails were reviewed; ten made the cut, but the scientific teams did not find a solution. After a ten-hour shift, a new team of seventy-five came in and took over for the exhausted departing team. They would eat, get some sleep, come back in the morning, and hope that today was the day they would find an answer.

After a week the president had nothing to report in his next chat. He could only continue to encourage people to submit their ideas. Milo Morrison, in his New Orleans office, listened to the president's second chat and decided he should send in his idea.

CHAPTER 79

Is There a Mole or Is Something Else Going on Here?

The moment was tense when Major Omid Rahimi laid a series of observations on the table in a phone call with Williams and Baker. Williams at the beginning of the call was a little perturbed, but when Omid got to the reasons why he appeared concerned, the Under Secretary was silent. The only thing he said in response to Omid's questions was "call the Houston office and get the reception log for the day in question."

Baker did not want to leave the call so he told the Under Secretary, "I'll get it later. Let's get back to the mole-or-another-agency issue. Omid, let's consider these separately. I want to start with the possibility of the mole."

"I raised the issue of a mole for one reason and I think a very important reason."

Williams finally spoke up, "Major, what happened to make you think we have a spy?"

"Sir, I didn't say spy. I used the term mole."

"I understand, but for now I don't see a difference between the two.

"A mole is someone who works for you while a spy is someone outside your organization, trying to gain information on what is going on the inside.

"The single issue that has bothered me most is that concerning the two unmarked emergency vehicles from Texas City. As I said before, the driving time was at least four hours, so the vans had to be taken and then driven north from Texas City to Springfield. I spoke with the person in charge of the two vehicles, and based on the time they were signed out

271

and the approximate time of the arrival in Springfield, they had less than thirty minutes wiggle room. So, let's say they arrived in Springfield at the Ridley house at 9:30 PM. Based on the logbooks, they were checked out at about 6:30 PM. The driving time from Houston to Springfield is about three hours. The vehicles had to leave Texas City about the same time you left Houston.

The only way they could have known what time to get the vehicles and leave was that somebody told them the team had already left. They had to know that the vans were in Texas City and they had to know, well in advance, of the decision to raid the Ridley house."

Baker turned to Williams, "Sir, when did you find out there might be a problem in Springfield?" As soon as he asked the question he thought, *Oops! I sound like a DA challenging a witness who he believed was lying to him.* "Sir, that didn't come out the way I meant. I'm sorry."

"I understand what both of you are saying. You believe that Homeland Security must have had the Ridley's under surveillance for some time."

Omid asks the Secretary, "Sir, do you know how long DHS had the Ridley's under observation?"

"All I can tell you is that field offices can start a folder on people and can watch them for a period of time before they report anything to us here in DC."

Baker asked, "Sir, our operation is organized into geographic regions and each region reports to a division chief here in Washington DC. For the life of me, I can't think who the new division chief is for Texas." In fact, Baker knew that the Southwest region had been without a division chief since the last chief's sudden death.

Williams replied, "Matt Blackwell was the division chief and seemed to be in good health at age fifty-two. One morning, his wife found him slumped over his desk in his study. The official cause of death was a heart attack."

Omid chimed in, "So that division has not had a chief in at least nine months."

Baker looked on his laptop and tried to bring up the observation files on his computer. He was trying to figure out how long the Houston office had been watching the Ridley's.

THE BROTHERHOOD OF THE RED NILE

When he typed in the names of Mary and Michael Ridley, nothing comes up. Baker turned to Williams, "How is it possible that the Ridley family is not in our database?"

"If I had to guess without checking, my guess is that their file is blocked."

Omid jumped in, "I have a feeling that we may be getting close to some other agency. What agency has the ability to block files at Homeland Security?"

"To the best of my knowledge, no other agency. Neither CIA, FBI nor Treasury can block one of our files, that I know of."

Omid pressed, "Then, Mr. Under Secretary, who *can* block a file?"

After a long pause he answered, "Again, to the best of my knowledge, only two people can block a file: the Secretary of Homeland Security and the ..."

CHAPTER 80

Hadar's Plan

Hadar had been on the plane for six hours and had not been able to sleep. She was desperately thinking about what she could do to save Mordecai and at the same time figure out how she can help Homeland Security capture the rest of the Brotherhood. *The only connection between Mordecai and me, at least on the surface, is my phone, which has Mordecai's number on it. I'll probably be asked to call the number and they will try to triangulate for a trace if I can keep him on long enough to get a fix on his location. I'm not sure, but assume that Homeland Security doesn't even know if Mordecai is still in the United States. If I make the call and we find out he is not in the U.S. then what do we do? Mordecai expects me to be in Texas studying adobe building.*

The challenge for Hadar was whether to reach out to Mordecai and warn him if he was in the United States, while at the same time protecting his location. The longer the phone call, the greater the likelihood they would be able to track him. At least for now she didn't really care If Mordecai was outside America. One of the challenges is that Mordecai didn't have a regular iPhone, but rather an international smartphone based in Syria. Even Mordecai didn't know how many servers a call would go through to reach each other.

She wondered how she could identify herself to Mordecai yet make it difficult, if not impossible, for DHS to trace his phone and get his location. Hadar was not a telecommunications expert, but her logical mind says the shorter the call time the more difficult it would be for them to triangulate his location. Then it came to her, *I need to send Mordecai a text message. I need to think of a word that he will relate to so he can figure out the message is from me. He will be very cautious about answering the phone. All of them will be very protective of their location. If for some reason Mordecai doesn't have his phone on him and the other Brotherhood members see my face on the phone it will not alarm them.* Just then, the Major came over and asked Hadar, "Have you finished with the folder?"

"Yes, thank you. I can't believe the devastation in Texas City; fifty-four thousand killed instantly."

"It is a very sad time for our country. I hope you can help us find the terrorists responsible for this."

Hadar was very uncomfortable because she knew she needed to show sympathy for the victims, but at the same time, she had feelings for Mordecai. She faced the Major as she returned the folder, looked him in the eye and said, "I'm going to do whatever I can on behalf of my country to help the United States find these people and bring them to justice."

"Thank you for all your help. I hope the terrorists are still in America and that we can capture them."

The Major turned away with his head down, thinking about all the people who are dead. He thought, *I have never understood what we have done to these people to make them hate us so much to seek our extermination. We may find out if we can capture them alive. I hope that Lt. Hassen can help us find them.*

The attendant arrived and said, "Lt. Hassen, we are about two hours from Andrews. Would you like some breakfast?"

"Could I have some buttered toast with strawberry jam and hot green tea? If you have any fresh fruit that would be great, thank you."

He smiled at her. "I think I can arrange that."

Hadar knew she now had little time to come up with a simple text message that would tell Mordecai it was she calling. Then it hit her. *Okay, I come up with the text word. What word? I have to plan the next few steps. What I do if he texts me back? I'm sure DHS is going to want us to meet so they can follow him back to the rest of the Brotherhood. DHS will want to know if all the leaders are there before they go after them. I may have to see Mordecai more than once. He can't know that I am working for the U.S. Government until this is all over.* A question worked its way into her thoughts that caused her a great deal of discomfort. She wanted this dilemma to go away, didn't want to face it. As hard as she tried, however, she couldn't get rid of the ever-growing thought: if she saw Mordecai one more time, what would she want to happen between them? In her memory, she returned to the last time they saw each other, the kiss between them, his statement, "can you imagine the sex", and her response, "I was thinking the same thing."

She had thought many times about what sex might be like between the two of them. However, could she give herself to him if she had the opportunity, knowing that she was lying to him? When she started this mission, she was told to use her assets to achieve her objective. It had been suggested again. This time, if she had the opportunity to have sex with Mordecai, would she? Then a big smile came to her face, for she knew what the one word text message would be: 'buttons'. And, if at all possible, she was going to have sex with Mordecai.

CHAPTER 81

Bait for a Trap

In their conference call, Omid pressed Williams again about who had the right to block DHS access to files. Williams replied: the Secretary of Homeland Security and the President of the United States. Baker and Rahimi were quiet for a moment.

Omid asked, "Anybody else?"

"No."

Baker asked Williams, "Is it possible for an underling acting on behalf of one of the two to block a file?"

"Perhaps if it was lower level file regarding a person of interest, but not high priority."

Omid asked, "Is it possible that a mole or a spy could have access to a lower level file and block it?"

Williams, Baker, and Rahimi agreed by now that there must be a mole or a spy who somehow had access to the plans of Homeland Security, had known about the Ridley family and somehow had blocked the file.

Williams suggested, "It's also possible that another agency head could request the White House to block a file."

Omid queried, "As for a person or persons in a witness protection program?"

Williams nodded, "That's very possible."

Since the attack, Williams and Baker used secure telephones, cell phones and computers, but before that they had been using standard equipment that was supposed to be part of a secure network. Williams suggested that

"The most likely breach was through the e-mails we sent out. Somehow, the interested person was watching our e-mails over traffic data, especially the ones to our Houston office that would have been following the Ridleys."

Omid asked Williams, "Is there a way to find out when a file was started, even if a file is blocked?"

"Every file has a number, a Julian date code."

"Does the file show the date it was blocked or released?"

"I believe so, but I would have to ask."

Baker suggested holding off asking that question for the moment.

"I agree; we don't want to attract any attention." Omid offered, "We could ask for information on several files, including the Ridley file, thus masking our research."

Williams interjected, "Omid, Ted when you ran a check on Mike and Mary Ridley what message, in detail, did you get on them?"

"I can't remember off the top of my head but I can pull it up on my laptop. I'm on the classified side." Baker tapped in some information and shook his head when the new screen came up. "The message read Access Denied. User Not Authorized."

Omid asked, "Can you ask who does have access or, if you can't ask that, can you ask when the file was blocked?"

"I'll try." Baker turned back to his laptop. "The response doesn't say who has access, but informs it was blocked with a Julian date 2444263.5. I hope one of you can translate because I can't."

Omid responded, "I grew up in the Marines with Julian dates, give me a moment, I want to double check, but I think it's around the first of January 1980."

Williams exclaimed, "The file has been blocked thirty-three years!"

Omid said, "We know how long it has been blocked but we don't know by whom."

Williams interrupted, "We know who didn't block it."

Baker asked, "What do you mean we know who didn't block it?"

"If this file has been blocked for thirty-three years it could not have been blocked by the Secretary of Homeland Security because there was no such position in 1980. President Jimmy Carter or a high ranking official in the White House blocked the Ridley file." Williams pondered briefly and then said, "We have to find out if we have a mole or a spy. Suggestions, gentlemen?"

Baker responded, "We have to set a trap and bait it. We have to send out some bogus but credible intel. The mole or spy will take the bait, respond and break cover, thus showing us who is compromising our security and our communications." He smiled. "We're going fishing. Our fish is going to take the bait and we'll let it run before we set the hook."

Williams asked, "What one thing does the infiltrator want to know?" All three are silent for what seems to be a long time. Finally, Williams suggests, "Let's make a list and then narrow it down. Brainstorm alternatives. For example, what is the location of the Brotherhood? Where are the Ridleys?"

Baker chimed in, "What was in the body bags at the Ridley house?"

Omid responded, "I'd like to take a different direction. What is it that the mole wants to keep us from discovering? Who was responsible for planning and executing the removal of the two emergency vans? What group planted all the explosives at the Ridley house?"

Baker raised a question, "How did we miss the bomb and the map in the basement?"

Williams responded, "I wondered why the bomb and the map on the wall were not mentioned in the after action report."

"The only way the DHS response team could have missed the bomb would have been the presence of a mole on the team," Omid suggested, "Is it possible we could be dealing with more than one mole, and that a mole deflected the team away from the basement door because he knew there was a bomb on the other side?"

Williams requested, "Ted, I want to see a list of all the team members that were at the Ridley house that night and their personal files within an hour after we're done here."

"Yes, sir."

"So, gentlemen, let's go back to the original question, and tweak it slightly. What one *person* does our agent know the least about? Once we identify that person, we have our bait …"

CHAPTER 82

You've Got Mail

Mike Miller was listening to the call that his partner Terry Dempsey was having with Milo Morrison about his solution for the problem of what to do with the contaminated energy in Texas. He heard his e-mail message 'you've got mail' and swung his chair around to face his screen. He saw that he had a message from **danP1575@aol.com**. Subject: Solution to Another Problem. Mike clicked on the e-mail and read: *"While I know that President Jordan wanted suggestions about what to do with the contaminated energy, I choose to address what I think will be a more significant challenge for our country, both near term and longer term.*

"We can't tap the oil in Texas and may not be able to for many years to come. If we can't drill our own oil, we will have to import more foreign oil, assuming they will sell it to us. I have attached a plan that has been talked about every time the price of gas reaches four dollars a gallon. With the current conditions, my guess is that we could see gas prices shoot to twelve dollars a gallon and perhaps higher if we do not find a new source of energy to power our economy. The attached proposal is one idea that could help save the world and show the OPEC nations we don't need them anymore. Please have somebody review the attached and get back to me, Sincerely, Mike Demetrio."

Mike was intrigued by the idea and saw Terry was off the phone. He motioned him over.

Terry slid his chair around to read the screen. "He has my attention, but we've been told never to open an attachment without clearing it through Security."

Mike said, "Let's call them and see what they want to do."

Terry dialed the number and entered the security code.

"White House Security. How can I help you, Mr. Miller?"

Mike explained the situation. He was responsible for the first level of vetting ideas, but he didn't want to be responsible for the corruption of the White House computer systems in case a nut-bar had attached a virus to his message.

"What should we do?" he asked.

"Stay put. I'm sending a technician to you right away. Under no circumstances open that attachment. Is that understood, Mr. Miller?"

"Yes, sir."

Moments later, a rather large, square-looking man came in the door with a case that looked like it could carry somebody out in one piece. "I'm looking for Mike Miller."

"I'm Mike Miller. How can I help you?"

"You called Security about a message attachment on an e-mail from an unknown sender on the energy problem, is that correct?"

"Yes. It is."

"May I see the computer?"

"It's right here, sir." Mike motioned him over.

"Have you done a search to see if this e-mail address has ever sent an e-mail to the White House before?"

"No sir, I have not."

"Okay, please close all the programs you're using, save your files and shut down your computer. We need to stop your computer from processing anything more until we clear that attachment. May I use your chair?"

"Of course. Could I see your ID first, please?"

Edward Hackett pulled out his White House Security ID and handed it to Miller for inspection. He opened his case and took out a black box about the size of a cigar box, which had several ports and plugs. He disconnected the computer from the router and attached it to the black box. Then he restarted the computer and stood. "I'll need you to sign in and bring up the e-mail account in question."

Miller sat down and entered his password. When his screen came up, he went into the e-mail account that had been set up to receive suggestions. The message reappeared on the screen along with the attachment. Miller let Hackett sit in his chair, he slowly moved the mouse over towards the file attachment and was just ready to click, when he stopped.

He looked up at Miller, "Have you had any traffic with this person?"

"No."

Hackett quickly sent an e-mail to the address with message: "*Mr. Demetrio, please send us your contact information. We wish to speak with you before we can forward your interesting idea up the channels.*" Hackett pushed Send. "Now we wait and see if he responds. If he gives us his contact information I'll call him and try to assess whether he's for real."

Miller asked, "Would you like something to drink while we wait?"

"Bottled water, if you have some."

"We have a fridge full." Miller went to get the water. On his way back, he heard 'you've got mail'. "Is it from Demetrio?"

Hackett nodded. "Yes. I'm going to call him. Stay tuned. Is there a private office or conference room I can use?"

Baker pointed. "Over there in the corner. I'll make sure you aren't disturbed."

CHAPTER 83

Thirty Minutes to Setting the Trap

Hadar had been having a problem focusing on what she wanted to do to protect Mordecai and, at the same time, help Homeland Security capture the rest of the leadership of the Brotherhood. She finally thought to herself, *Get control or you will lose it all. What do they want? How do they think I can help them? They know I have Mordecai's cell number, but nobody, including me, knows if Mordecai has his phone with him. Even if he does, there is no guarantee that he will or can pick up the phone. They are relying on the sexual energy generated between the two of us in Syria to make him want to reach out and touch me. I wouldn't mind that myself. When I go into the first meeting with Williams, I have to do everything I can to control the meeting and determine what it is they want me to do. I shall meet with Williams and Baker in Washington. The suggestion to use my assets to take control was good advice, so I'll change into something more "controlling" before the meeting.* Hadar rings for the attendant and asks, "Is there a place where I can change?"

"Yes ma'am. There's a changing room in the back. I suggest you do it quickly as we only have about thirty minutes before we begin our descent." As Hadar moved to the changing room, she felt like she had things under control and that, with her brain plus her assets, she could save Mordecai. Little did she know she would soon be in over her head.

Williams, Baker, and Rahimi were still on the phone thinking about Williams' question. "What one person does our agent know the least about?" Baker looks at Williams and together they said, "Lt. Hadar Hassen."

"Why her?" Omid asked.

Williams explained, "She is the unknown quantity. Right now, very few people know about her. There has been no traffic with her name. Therefore, when she arrives at the remote airfield, our spy will see the new traffic and wonder why we're sending one person on a private government jet. They are going to be very curious about her identity.

"Won't we be putting her in harm's way?" Omid asked. "I can only protect her in so many places. She could be very exposed where I can't protect her."

Williams said, "She's Israeli trained Special Ops. She can take of herself just fine."

Baker spoke up, "I agree that we are going to ask her to put herself in harm's way, but I have an idea how we can give her some cover."

Williams said, "Tell me more."

"I haven't vetted this idea, but hear me out. I spent a great deal of time working with Megan Brown of our forensics department. She wants to get into CIA Special Ops and has been training on her own. She goes to the Montgomery Police shooting range several times a week, is qualified and is considered an expert shot on everything from pistols to AK47s.

"We could promise her that if she accepts a special assignment, regardless of the outcome, she will get your endorsement to the Director of CIA Special Ops. Sir, if you and she agree, then we have a backup to cover Lt. Hassen between Omid and Brown."

"Let's get her in here right now and see if she's interested. Two unknowns on that plane will drive our spy off the deep end." Williams chuckled. "Omid, we'll call you back when Lt. Hassen arrives. Ted, get on the phone and get Ms. Brown up here right now."

"I'm on it, sir."

Baker stepped out of the conference room and put a call in to Brown. She picks up after two rings.

"Ms. Brown, this is Ted Baker."

"Why so formal? It's Megan."

"Megan, we need you in Williams' office right now."

"I'm on my way." Megan had no idea why they wanted her to drop everything and go, but when the Under Secretary calls, you don't ask why, you just go. She quickly walked to the elevator and, when it opened, pushed the top button several times. Arriving on the top floor, she could see the long corridor to Williams' office. She walked hurriedly, and her momentum was so strong that she bumped into Williams' door, startling Marie.

Marie asked, "Are you okay?"

"I'm fine, thanks. I was told to come here right away. I understand that Under Secretary Williams and Mr. Baker want to see me."

"Yes they do. Please go right into the conference room."

Megan knocked on the door firmly and a voice said, "Come in." She opened the door and saw Baker and Williams standing waiting for her.

"Please sit down, Ms. Brown," Williams welcomed her. "What we are about discuss is classified top secret. You are not permitted to talk about this with anyone else without the express permission of Mr. Baker or myself. Is that clear?"

"Yes, sir."

Baker told Megan about her possible special assignment to work with Lt. Hassen. He warned, "It could be a very dangerous assignment."

She asked what was going on. "Why does she need a back-up?"

"Very simply, Ms. Brown, you can accompany her where a man cannot. I understand from Mr. Baker that you are an expert shot with several different weapons."

"Yes, sir."

"He also tells me that you would like to join CIA Special Ops."

"Yes, sir!" Megan glanced at Ted, who sent her a small smile back.

"Before we talk any more about that, are you interested in this assignment? In addition to Lt. Hassen, you'll be working with Major Omid Rahimi. He's already on the ground and familiar with the investigation."

"Sir, I have done some work with the Major and I think we could work well together."

"So, Ms. Brown, do you want the assignment?"

Megan paused for a moment out of excitement. When she realized her hesitation was sending the wrong message, she blurted out, "Yes, sir."

"Excellent Ms. Brown. There is one other thing."

"Sir?"

"We told you that this could be a very dangerous assignment. Do you understand that there is a possibility that you could be shot or killed?"

"That thought crossed my mind." Her hands were under the table but she could feel them going cold and clammy. "Sir, I would do whatever I need to do to protect Lt. Hassen. If that means getting shot, even killed, I'm prepared to make that sacrifice."

"Ms. Brown, I promise, and I expect you to hold me to it, that if you still want to go to CIA Special Ops after this mission is over, I shall personally call the director and give you the strongest possible recommendation. You understand that you still will have to pass the qualification test."

"Yes, sir."

"If you're willing we have a deal, then. Agreed?"

"Yes, sir."

"Excellent." Williams continued without pause, "Lt. Hassen is due to land at Andrews in less than thirty minutes. I'll call you when she arrives for our briefing."

Baker and Megan left the room and walked towards the elevator. Suddenly, Megan looked around, saw that nobody was around, took Baker in her arms, and gave him a great big kiss on the mouth. "Ted, thank you so much for this."

Baker, shocked, realized he enjoyed the kiss and said, "You're welcome." *I just hope I haven't sent her into a situation from which she'll never return.*

They separated and smiled at each other, both slightly embarrassed. Brown returned to her office to tell her staff she was being reassigned, while Baker headed back to the conference room to discuss with Williams how to bait and set the trap.

CHAPTER 84

You've Got Real Mail

Edward Hackett came out of the conference room and rejoined Miller. "He sounds legit and may have something important to say. You'll want to give him a call." Miller waited while Hackett removed his black box and reconnected his computer to the White House Intranet.

Hackett said, "You're good to go."

Miller sat at his desk once more, took a deep breath and picked up his phone. "Mr. Demetrio, this is Mike Miller from the White House. I read your e-mail and the attached document. I'm not sure I understand how your suggestion solves the problem of all the contaminated oil in the ground. Can you clarify your idea for me?"

"Mr. Miller, my suggestion is not about how to fix the problem of the contaminated energy in the ground. Rather, while we're finding a solution for that problem, we still need energy to run cars, trucks, equipment and homes. You see, Mr. Miller ..."

"Please, call me Mike."

"Mike, we have an abundance of natural gas in the United States and in most cases everything that needs gasoline or diesel can be converted to use compressed natural gas while we change everything over to natural gas. In just a few years, we could eliminate America's need to import energy. In fact, we could be one of the largest exporters of energy in the world, including Saudi Arabia.

"With my suggestion we can put millions of Americans back to work in well-paid jobs, building and installing the conversion kits for tens of millions of cars, trucks, vans, power plants – anything. We can build fueling stations so that the availability of natural gas is expanded. Natural gas doesn't need to be refined when it comes out of the ground; it's ready to use. It's currently about one-third the price of gasoline or diesel. It's cleaner, more efficient and less polluting than gas or diesel and it's made in America. We know it may be a long time before we can pump crude oil out of the ground in Texas again, yet in the upper Midwest we have enough natural gas to replace all that has been lost in Texas. As we increase the demand for natural gas we can get those people in Texas who are now out of work to help find, develop and distribute natural gas."

"It seems so simple. Why haven't we done this before to enable us to be energy independent? Perhaps we could have prevented the nuclear attacks on America." Miller mused.

"Mike, I don't have a simple answer to that. We just never got our minds around the concept of energy independence. However, it's not too late to try, and I think the challenge in front of us makes natural gas a big part of the solution."

"Sir, I will definitely forward your idea to the scientific evaluation team and feel sure someone will contact you soon," Miller said.

"I'll wait for their call."

The next morning, the president scheduled a meeting of the full cabinet to discuss progress. He had five days before he must talk with the nation about the progress the administration was making on solving the crisis. The president had come up to the family quarters after dinner. An aide greeted him, "Mr. President, are you in for the evening?"

"George, that depends on a lot of things, but I hope so. I need some time with my wife."

"I understand, sir. I'll do my best to keep things quiet."

"Thank you George, where is the first lady?"

"She is in the Yellow Room."

Nathan Jordan walked slowly into the Yellow Room and saw Karen writing at a desk. He walked up behind her and put his hands on her shoulders. She extended one hand to touch his. Jordan bent over to kiss her on her neck. She tilted her head so he could have plenty of neck to kiss. As he put his lips on her neck, slid his left around her, and caressed her breast.

Before she put down the pen she turned her head to say, "I have one more" and, with that permission, Jordan reached around and caressed the other.

Karen said, "I miss that and miss you next to me."

Nathan responded, "I feel the same way. I know this has been hard on you. As much as I would love to make love with you, I have to try and fix the nation."

With a warm smile, she looked Nathan in the eyes, "Have you come to fix me tonight?"

Jordan chuckled, "That depends upon how much fixing you need."

"I'll take whatever fixing time you have. Are you ready for bed, Mr. Fix-it?"

"You go ahead. I'll tell George to hang out the 'do not disturb' sign and I'll be right there."

The president found George, who smiled brightly when the Jordon instructed, "Do not disturb unless there is a national emergency." Nathan turned, walked toward the bedroom and shut the door behind him. "He knows I'm married to the most beautiful woman in the world and I get to make love with her tonight, maybe more than once."

And they did.

The next morning there was a knock at the bedroom door. George reminded the president of the cabinet meeting in two hours. They were both still naked from their lovemaking the night before. The room had a soft yellow color from drawn shades and curtains. They both rolled over to face each other. Nathan threw back the sheet just to look at Karen and her beautiful form. He reached out and gently touched a cheek and says, "I love you so much, I don't know what I'd do without you in my life.

"I want you and your team to sit in on the meeting to assist me in preparation for the Saturday chat. I realize that this is short notice, but I heard from the Secretary of Energy that he may have some important information on a possible solution to the contaminated energy in Texas."

Karen smiled, "I'll make the time, but can you hold me one more time and give me a kiss to get me through till next opportunity?"

"Absolutely!" Nathan said with a smile on his face and pulled Karen close in a warm caress.

CHAPTER 85

Williams' Conference Room

Williams asked Baker, "Are you sure Megan Brown is the best person for the job? Couldn't we have gotten somebody from a SEAL team or Black Ops from CIA?"

"I think that would be an excellent idea. However, right now, I don't know of any women in either agency and I'm not sure if they had women that they would admit that they do, so Megan is a good fit. She has an excellent mind, she's in good physical shape and she is weapons trained."

"All right, let's move on to setting the trap."

"Yes sir, it seems to me that the Houston office may present the best opportunity for a leak or a spy. All the information in Springfield was channeled through the Houston office."

Williams agreed. "What I propose is that we send an encrypted message telling Myron Shute, the person in charge of the Houston office, what our plans are and to use this as bait to see if we can find our spy. I want him to know that our people are coming into his area and that he will be responsible for their security while they're in Houston. He needs to know that we're sending Lt. Hadar Hassen of Mossad Special Ops, who has some level of relationship with one of the terrorists. In addition, we're sending Megan Brown of the DHS Criminal Investigations Department. They will be joined in Houston by our agent on the ground Major Omid Rahimi, USMC, to work on a plan to flush out at least one of the members of the Brotherhood. We will take care to give them the location of the office at 5450 North Sam Houston Parkway East, and they will meet you. I want all three of them to board a plane at Houston Ellington Airport bound for the meeting site at Draughon-Miller Central Texas Regional Airport, where they will be met by the teams from the CIA, FBI and Secret Service in less than twelve hours after their arrival. Is this too much information; will it sound contrived?"

"Sir, in the past the protocol has been that, when we're sending people into an area, we generally inform the person in charge why we're sending them into his or her space. So, based on our own protocol, I believe this is what Mr. Shute would expect from us."

"Ted, we shall have given them a lot of information about which they presently know nothing. They'll be hearing it for the first time."

"Yes sir. This might be the first time the mole is hearing this information. Perhaps in their excitement he or he will reveal themselves to us."

"Just how do you propose to catch them?"

"Sir, I'm going to suggest that the CIA assign John Seacrest to this job. I'll fly down as part of John's team and pose as his assistant. That will keep me out of the spotlight, so I'll be able to observe what's going on and look for unusual behavior. I'll be in contact with you if I need information. I'll use our secure computer and you can respond directly to me."

"Ted, should you be in the room with the two women? Megan knows you but Hassen has never seen you. Wouldn't it be smarter for you not to be in the room when Lt. Hadar arrives?"

Ted rubbed his chin. "Good point. However, Hassen has heard my name several times. If I show up at the meeting site and she recognizes me, or if Omid reacts, it could tip off the mole that something is wrong, so I think we should leave things in place. When Hassen arrives, we'll get Brown up here and Omid on the phone to lay out the plan. But only you and I know the real plan to catch our mole."

"Let me call the CIA and ask if we can get John Seacrest to the meeting. I'll ask for a telecommunications drone to circle the meeting site and record all phone, pager and computer communications to and from the site during the entire meeting. I want coverage continued until the last plane takes off. We'll have all the data sent to our forensics lab on a real time basis. I'll meet with the technicians and tell them what we are looking for in the data and what we need them to do with it. I'll meet with them after we brief Lt. Hassen and Megan Brown as to ..."

"Sir, please call General Powell and tell him we want a SEAL team on standby no more than ten minutes out by air from the hangar, just in case there's trouble. We need to catch both a mole and a terrorist."

CHAPTER 86

CIA to the Rescue

Marie called Williams on the intercom, "Lt. Hassen's plane has just landed at Andrews. Depending on traffic she should be here in about thirty minutes."

Baker said, "Sir, while you're talking to the CIA, I'm going to call John Seacrest and make the arrangements." Baker stepped out of the conference room and went down the hallway to his office to call John's cell phone.

"Seacrest here," John answered the phone in a strong clear voice.

"John, Ted Baker. I don't have a lot of time, so let me be brief. You'll be getting a call from the Director telling you that you're being assigned to a special task force that will meet in Texas to develop a plan to capture one and possibly all of the Brotherhood of the Red Nile.

"You will be joined by teams from the FBI, Secret Service and Homeland Security in a remote site in central Texas."

John's phone rang; it was the Director. "Ted, the Director is on my land line. I'll call you right back."

"Okay, thanks." Ted thought, *I know I can trust John. We've been friends for years, I don't think for one second he could be the mole, but I can't take any chances. I'll tell him what he needs to know and that way we won't tip our hand.*

After a few moments, John called back and confirmed that he had his assignment. "Ted, can you tell me what's going on?"

"We are bringing in an Israeli Special Ops person who met one of the terrorists that we identified from the pictures you had your asset in Syria take for us. She is somehow romantically involved and they have each other's numbers on their cell phones.

"Our plan is to bring to one spot all the resources we think we need to build a plan and see if we can catch one or more of the terrorists. Set up one of your communications drones to hover over the site and transmit to DHS all the phone calls, text messages and computer data sent inside and outside that hangar for the entire time of the meeting."

John asked, "How long do you think these planning meetings will last?"

"My guess is probably three days."

"One drone can't hover that long so we'll have to schedule several to move in and overlap to make sure we have full coverage for the entire meeting."

"That works for me."

John asked, "When do you expect the meetings to start?"

"In about three days. Is that a problem?" Ted looked at his agenda. He needed time to clear it.

"I don't think so, but I'll get right on it and let you know."

"One other thing John. I'll be working with you. Introduce me as your assistant."

"You? My assistant? Do you think people will believe that?"

Ted laughed, "I think we can pull it off."

Meanwhile, at the White House, the president had convened a cabinet meeting in the War Room. When he walked in the entire room stood.

Jordan said, "Please, be seated. I have called this meeting for two reasons. First, to get an update on what is going on in the country, and second, to tell you we have very good solutions to two of our problems with energy. But first, Mr. Attorney General, how safe is the nation?"

Clinton spoke, "Sir, things are relatively quiet. There has been some violence, primarily over food, but that has been taken care of. No widespread looting, but my greatest fear is that the food supply is starting to dwindle and if people are hungry, they will do just about anything to feed themselves and their families."

"Mr. Clinton, how much time do you think we have before things get out of hand?"

"Sir, we have to find a way to get the food moving into the warehouses so they can distribute it. We have a real shortage of gasoline and all fuels for trucks and planes."

The president looked over to Powell, "General, can we deploy military transport to take food stuffs to processing plants and warehouses?"

"Mr. President, we have a significant amount of resources deployed helping maintain the peace."

"General, let me put it to you this way. If we can find a way to feed people, we have less need for law enforcement. So, I don't care where you get them, can the Department of Defense help or not?"

"Yes, sir."

"Thank you, General Powell. For the rest of the departments, I want twenty percent of the workforce helping in food and energy distribution. Any questions? Take all of your regional offices and turn them into command centers that work on plans to get people to work, with food and energy flowing again. People, we can do this. Are we agreed?"

In one strong collective voice they responded, "Yes, sir."

"Now, for somewhat good news on the contaminated energy in Texas. An idea has been brought to our attention that the scientific team thinks will work. This plan will put hundreds of thousands of people and probably more to work and will be a way to help start the flow of income into Texas. It may well bring people from all over America to work. The plan calls for building about three hundred miles of pipeline from deep southeast Texas to the end of the capped trunk pipelines in northern Texas near the city of Paris. We will build twenty-four hours a day, seven days a week. They estimate that the pipeline can be built in just over two years. At that pace, we have to build at least one-half mile of pipeline each day seven days a week, rain or shine.

"We will have to dramatically increase the manufacturing of all the necessary materials, from pipes to valves to fittings, pumps, compressors plus the needs of all the workers and their families. It may well be the biggest construction project in the history of the country and when it's done, we will drain all the contaminated energy into the strategic petroleum reserve in the salt caverns in the Gulf of Mexico. We will drain the oil that's in there now and either use it or sell it so the vacated space will hold the contaminated oil thousands of feet below the Gulf floor. And believe it or not, it gets better than that." As the president tells of his first solution, you can feel the positive energy change in the room.

"The second idea that the team will work on is massive development of our abundant natural gas in the United States. At the same time we're drilling for natural gas, we'll be building conversion kits that will allow existing vehicles to run on both gasoline and natural gas. These natural gas projects will also put hundreds of thousands of people to work in well-paid jobs all over the country. Between these two infrastructure projects, we can get the economy growing again, put people to work and reduce our dependency on foreign oil. Unless I hear any solid objections, I plan to introduce these projects to Americans in my Saturday radio chat. Any objections?"

Thunderous applause greeted President Jordan, along with a standing ovation. As the room gradually quieted down, he continued, "I propose that some of us meet with the Congressional leadership tomorrow to inform them how we plan to save this great country and to elicit their support. I truly believe we can rebuild America and make it stronger. Do you agree?"

Another round of applause broke out. Jordan smiled as he heard, "Yes, sir."

THE BROTHERHOOD OF THE RED NILE

CHAPTER 87

Hadar Has Landed

Hadar wanted to make a strong first impression on Under Secretary Williams and Mr. Baker. She was giving serious thought as to what to wear. She concluded these were not privates who could be swayed by a great body, their hormones were in her control. Even Mordecai was attracted to her because of her body and her looks. She was a naturally striking looking woman. She decided that she had to come across as a confident professional; a combination of brains, body, and strength of purpose was what she wanted to portray.

Her dress uniform was very form fitting. Under the fabric, the true shape of a voluptuous woman was pressing at every seam. She had her dress uniform tailored to fit her body like a glove. She looked like the commercials where the sports team's uniforms are painted on naked bodies and the artwork is so good you have to look several times to see they are painted and not just very tight fitting.

Her left breast pocket held all of her ribbons but the size and shape of her breast made the ribbons lay on top of it instead of in front of it. The jacket not only clung to her upper torso, it gathered around her small waist and hugged the small of her back to where it lay on top of her shapely butt. The skirt was also tailored to follow the contour of her hip and was regulation length. She was concerned while dressing that she had not been to the gym in a few days and wondered if she had put on any weight. She didn't want to look like she was busting at the seams, because that would suggest she was out of shape. She finished dressing, looked at herself in the mirror and was pleased with what she saw. She was ready to perform, but just before she reached for the doorknob, her heart raced and her mind turned to Mordecai and the thought of possibly seeing him again and sharing something more than a kiss.

When Hadar opened the door and stepped out into the main cabin, it was safe to say the attendant wondered if she had just painted on her uniform. She took her seat, buckled up and waited for the plane to land, which took thirty minutes. The plane came to a stop and the stairs were lowered. As she deplaned, a car at the bottom of the stairs was waiting with the door open and motor running. Standing at the door was a man in a dark suit, white shirt and a dark navy tie. As soon as Hadar hit the bottom step, the attendant had her bag ready to be unloaded from the doorway. She walked to the car and the security person held the door while she got in. Hadar noticed as she did that the trunk lid was opened. As she was buckled her seatbelt the security guard put her suitcase in the trunk, shut it, tapped on the trunk lid and the car sped away. The driver was dressed the same way as the security detail, so she had no idea who he was or if he worked for Homeland Security or some other agency. She realized, *I didn't ask for any identification. I'm just assuming that this car is from Homeland Security. I hope I'm right.*

Hadar had never been to the United States. She had seen many pictures of the capital – the White House, the Washington Monument and Lincoln Memorial – but now she was seeing them for real. As they came into the city, history was all around her and she was constantly turning and changing positions to see all the sights. For the first time since she got in the car, the driver spoke up, "Is this your first time in DC, ma'am?"

"Yes! It's exciting to see all the places I've read about and only seen in pictures. It's a beautiful city with such wide streets, and it's so green. All the parks and trees, and it's so clean, not like my home."

"Where are you from, ma'am?"

"I'm from Israel."

"You must be important to come into Andrews in a private jet."

"I'm just here to help your country find the terrorists who set off the bombs."

"Thank you so much for coming. I hope you and we can find those murderers."

THE BROTHERHOOD OF THE RED NILE

"I'll do my best. How much longer before we get to the Homeland Security office?"

"Not too much further. I'm going to put up the privacy window so I can make a phone call and let them know we're on the way." Just then, a window slowly rose behind the driver's seat and closed.

Suddenly, the locks on the rear door were activated. Hadar was locked and sealed in the back seat, which was filling with some kind of gas. She wanted to panic but the effect of the gas was dulling her senses. She was getting too drowsy to react. Just as she was about to lose consciousness she felt the car being slammed into by what seemed like another car, or perhaps two.

All of a sudden the rear door blew open, a hand reached in, grabbed her by the arm and pulled her out into the fresh air. As she was dragged out of the car, she looked at the driver. He wasn't moving. The driver's door seemed to be one of the impact areas. She groggily wondered if he was dead. "Ma'am we have to go right now. We have to get out of here."

Hadar was beginning to come around and asked, "Who are you?"

The voice answered, "Ma'am we're a special security detail of Homeland Security. We were sent by Secretary Williams to pick you up at Andrews, but someone delayed our arrival. We think it was a deliberate attempt to extract you and keep you from getting to headquarters."

Hadar's mind was clearing and this time she asked for ID. The leader showed his ID and it looked real but she was still groggy.

Williams was called and told of the attempted kidnapping of Lt. Hadar. He called Baker right away and told him to report to his office on the double. When Baker arrived, Williams told him of the foiled kidnapping.

Baker asked, "Do we know who was trying to snatch her?"

"The driver was killed in the crash and had no identifying information on him. We're checking his fingerprints and any information on the car. It will take some time to run it all down."

"Where is Lt. Hassen now?"

Williams responded, "On her way to the hospital."

"Why would somebody want to kidnap her?"

Williams answered, "To keep her away from us and from Houston."

CHAPTER 88

Meeting with Congressional Leadership

The meeting with the cabinet adjourned and the president headed to the Oval Office, followed by Attorney General Clinton.

"May I have a word with you, Mr. President?"

"Come with me and we'll stop by Mary's desk and see what's on my schedule."

They walked past armed Marine guards who snapped to attention as the president passed and then stood at ease when he was out of their sight. The president opened the door to his EA's office, "Mary, AG Clinton wants to know if I have time to talk with him now. How's my schedule?"

Washington looked at the AG's face and could tell that this was very important. She looked at her computer screen and replied, "Sir, I can re-schedule your next appointment so you can talk with him now. She saw the 'thank you' in the AG's smile.

In the Oval Office, the president sat in a single chair while the AG sat on a couch across from him.

"Sir, I want to talk with you from a Constitutional perspective about some of the decisions you've made. I need more time for my staff to research these issues but on a preliminary basis we believe some recent decisions may be unconstitutional."

"Give me some examples, Drew."

'Sir, I'm not saying that the decisions you made in consultation with the cabinet were bad decisions, just that they might be illegal. In one fell swoop, you closed the capital markets, closed the banks, set a national curfew and declared martial law nationwide. You did all of that without any Congressional approval. All the areas you moved in have Congressional oversight responsibility. My concern is that you might be leaving yourself open, sometime down the road, for impeachment charges.

"Your new plan is very ambitious and I think it has a great chance of succeeding, but again there are many areas where you are stepping on Congress' toes and bypassing it to get things done. For example, I think both projects have major environmental implications. In addition, we're still dumping millions of barrels of crude into the Gulf of Mexico. You are just months away from starting your re-election campaign and you could be vulnerable to some very serious charges."

The president listened very carefully to Clinton's remarks and took notes on his iPod. "Drew, I want to thank you for your concern. No doubt you're a better constitutional lawyer than I, but let me plead my case. In order for Congress to act, they would have to be in session. I don't believe there are enough Congressmen or Senators in town to reach a quorum. If Congress can't get a quorum, then they can't vote to do anything and, between you and me, I don't necessarily think in these times that is a bad thing. We have reached out to the leadership and apprised them of everything that is going on and, as you heard in the meeting, I plan to hold a meeting tomorrow with the leadership to update them, and they me, on the likelihood of Congress coming back in session.

"As to your concerns about environmental regulations being broken, and the other issues, I think the American people will side with me in trying to save them and the country."

"Sir, we all hope that you can turn the corner and bring America back and, in the difficult times of today, I also feel sure that the people would agree with you. However, if you are successful, over time people might see things differently. Look what happened to President Bush. America was attacked and three thousand Americans died. America responded and when things felt safe again, whether they were or not, the American people turned against the president, led by the opposition. I believe, sir, you are taking too many chances that could be challenged by an opponent for the Presidency."

"Drew, I have only one responsibility and that is to the American people. If they want to throw me out of office for what I'm trying to do to save the country, then so be it."

"Sir, if I could be so bold as to suggest, turn your eye just a little to the coming campaign. I want you to help the American people, but it isn't wrong to help yourself at the same time."

Nathan smiled. "Excellent advice, Drew. Thank you for your concern, your advice, and please continue to watch my back."

"Thank you for the time. I hope my comments were helpful." Clinton stood up and thought, *This man is going 24-7. It's impossible for anybody to watch his back all the time. I guess I'm in store for a lot of sleepless nights ahead, but somebody has to protect the good man from himself.*

Nathan reached out to shake his AG's hand. "Drew, thank you for your concern but I have to do what I think is right for the country."

CHAPTER 89

Williams' Conference Room

"How the hell did they – whoever they are – find out about Lt. Hassen and her arrival time?" Williams was clearly angry. Baker listened patiently to his rant; he waited for a lull.

"I think this changes where we think the mole might be. It may in fact be right here in our office. I've done a quick check of the communications concerning the travel arrangements of Lt. Hassen to Washington and can find no trace of her travel plans being sent to our Houston office. I've spoken to no one about the travel plans except the Logistics Office. Sir, who did you tell about the plan to bring Lt. Hassen to Washington?"

Williams rubbed the back of his neck. "In my briefing with the Secretary, I told him we were bringing her to America but not when or where."

"Anybody else, sir?"

"No one that I can think of. No one."

Ted let his questions stream out in a small flood. "Would the team that was sent from Houston to Springfield be made up of only people from Houston? Would the mission have to have been approved in Homeland Security here in Washington? Would the plan to raid the Ridley house come from Houston, DC or both? The last question is: would the Logistics Office be represented in all the planning for the raid?"

"Ted, let me try and answer all of your questions as best I can. First, Houston would not have had all the resources to conduct the raid and the investigation of the site, so we could very well have sent people from here. But, if we sent agents from other offices around the nation, the Logistics

Office would have made those arrangements. Moreover, they would have routed any special equipment to Houston. There would have been a plan made up in advance so the necessary resources were in place in time for the raid. As to the question, who decided to attempt the raid, the normal procedure is that the Houston office would have made the recommendation to the Secretary who would have had to approve it."

Ted ticked off his fingers one at a time. "The common denominator in all of this is the Logistics Office. Did you use it to set up the meeting in Texas?"

"Yes, I did give them all the requirements. I didn't have the time or the ability to set up all the arrangements in my office. That's why we have a Logistics Office."

"So, we have trusted the Logistics Office to make all the arrangements even before the Ridley raid. We need to look back prior to the Ridley raid to see if we can find any leaks that might have compromised other activities of our department."

Williams responded, "I agree, but we have to find a way to investigate without them suspecting it. We could involve the Office of the Inspector General for Homeland Security. It's always auditing somewhere in our agency. What if it received an anonymous tip of possible kickbacks in the Logistics Office? If we can get the OIG to start an investigation, the mole might suspend his activities when he or she hears about it. The mole will want to know what's going on and potentially expose himself. Then, we can start tracking him to see who he's connected to and expose the ultimate leadership."

"Sir, if we do this we could very well jeopardize the viability of the entire Department of Homeland Security. Are you sure you want to risk it?"

"Ted, DHS is already compromised, so exposing the flaw by our own investigation is the best way to secure the reputation of Homeland. We'll take some heat from Congressional oversight and the media, but that's just the price we have to pay to stop the mole."

Baker responded, "Who do we get to make the tip so that all of us will be surprised by the investigation. What should we say in the tip?"

Williams suggests, "I think the OIG will need to be pointed in a specific direction. So, we'll feed them an initial tip and then some follow-up tips to help them focus."

Baker frowned, "How do we do that without being discovered?"

Williams chuckled, "I didn't work at the CIA and not learn a few tricks covering one's tracks. First, we go to Wal-Mart and spend thirty bucks on a Straight Talk Samsung T528G GSM Prepaid Smartphone. Then we go to Starbucks and use their free Wi-Fi to send an e-mail to the OIG. If we need to send more tips, we'll just buy another phone. These phones won't be traceable because when we're done with one I'll just take out the battery and toss it in the trash. It's impossible to trace. While you're headed to Texas, I'll buy the first phone on my way home and send the e-mail from a Starbucks in Bethesda.

"It will take some time for things to start rolling at the OIG, but a second e-mail from a McDonalds on a new phone may get them moving faster. Ted, you'll have to be very careful in Texas to not only protect our two women but yourself."

"Sir, I've arranged for backup that can get to us very quickly. I will be very careful. Until we can set the trap, we're all in danger."

CHAPTER 90

Hadar Delayed

The team sent to protect Lt. Hassen had taken her from the crash site directly to George Washington University Hospital. It was the closest hospital to the location of the accident. All the hospitals in DC were equipped to handle special cases. GW was the hospital that Ronald Reagan was taken to when he was shot. While the team didn't know what gas was used, an air sample was taken and brought along for testing.

The hospital was alerted that a VIP was being brought in for treatment. The team leader told the hospital that he thought it was some type of knockout gas, but that Lt. Hassen had not been in the car long enough to get a full dose.

The doctor on call said, "We'll put her on oxygen and checked her vitals upon arrival." The car had pulled into the Emergency bay but at the far end, out of the mainstream of traffic. They brought out a gurney but Hadar had protested that she could walk into the emergency room by herself. The head of ER was in charge of her case and simply said, "Ma'am, the procedure is that you will enter into the emergency room on a gurney. That is the rule, period."

Under protest, Hadar was placed on the gurney, wheeled into Emergency and whisked off to an examination room, where she was immediately seated on a chair. A nurse came in to take her vitals. Hadar answered her medical questions but asked, "When can I get out of here?"

The nurse replied, "That will be up to the doctor. He'll be right with you."

Dr. Benjamin Myrtle, head of ER came in and saw Hadar in her uniform. "Oh my! I don't think I've ever seen such a striking person in uniform."

Hadar smiled and asked, "When can I get out of here? I have a job to do."

The doctor looked at her docket. "You've inhaled some form of gas. We don't know what it is at the moment. We need to do some blood work to identify the type of gas and see how to treat it. My guess is that it will take a couple of hours."

William Windom, leader of the Secret Service detail said to Hadar, "I shall call Mr. Williams and let him know about you and your possible release time. So, for now, just sit there and relax. Do you want or need anything while you're waiting? Do you want something to eat or drink?"

"I would like some water if that's possible."

Dr. Myrtle said, "Water is fine. Your nurse will arrange it for you. Your arrival caused quite a distraction. It's not every day a beautiful woman in uniform is brought in."

"I apologize for the distraction, Dr. Myrtle. It's just who I am." Hadar put on her best smile. "I sometimes cause distractions."

"Let's get the nurse back in here and get that blood drawn so we can run the tests and get you out of here to distract the rest of the world." The doctor winked at her and left the room.

Windom took out his cell phone, but before he called Williams, he checked in with the protection team to see if everything was clear. He left two of his men outside Hadar's room. They would check the ID of anyone who went into the room where Lt. Hassen was resting. He had two more men at the doors to the treatment area and two on the dock. There were two cars with two men each circling the blocks around the hospital in opposite directions. This would mean that either team was just half a block away if the team inside needed help. Shortly after they arrived at the hospital, a helicopter was hovering overhead in silent mode as additional security.

When he believed that everything was secure, Windom called Williams to alert him of Lt. Hassen's condition, at least as best he knew, and that her expected departure time from the hospital depended on the test results. He told him of the security arrangements and Williams was satisfied that Lt. Hassen was protected.

"If her stay is to be extended, we might want to consider moving her to Walter Reed Medical Center where we have better control of the surroundings."

"Well sir, she sure is a distraction to the staff at GW. I can imagine how much more of a distraction she will be at Walter Reed."

"What do you mean a distraction?"

"You'll see sir, you'll see."

CHAPTER 91

The First Lady's Press Office

The president called Karen and asked her to bring her speech writing team of Maggie, Bill and Debra to her press office for a meeting with him to start drafting the next 'Chat.' He walked in and greeted the team. "We have a lot to cover and we have to figure out how to take complicated material and make it simple so everyone listening understands what we're planning to do and especially how long it will take to turn things around."

The president told the team about building the three hundred mile pipeline and all the people and equipment that would be needed. He described how work would commence on draining the petroleum reserve and how the money from the sale would fund some of the cost to build the pipeline, equipment and pay people.

Next, the president told them about expanding natural gas resources and converting many cars and trucks to natural gas as a fuel alternative to imported oil. He talked about the millions of jobs both projects would create at a time when America desperately needed jobs. The president spent the next half hour with a map showing the new pipeline route and the areas that needed to be explored, including the Gulf of Mexico. He looked at each of the team members and could tell that he had overwhelmed them with details. His gaze was met with glassy-eyed stares.

Maggie said to the president, "Sir, what do you think would mean the most to the American people?"

The president stopped for a moment, and the expression on his face told all of them he was having a serious problem coming up with an answer. Under his breath, so he thought only Debra heard, Bill said, "We're in trouble."

The president said, "I heard that and I have to agree."

Karen had been listening and taking notes. She spoke up. "What I heard you say was, 'we have a solution to the contaminated energy in the pipelines and to fix it we shall need to hire perhaps hundreds of thousands of Americans. These will be good paying jobs that will feed families and make it possible to buy homes. Not only shall we have to build the pipeline, we'll have to build communities in which people can live and prosper.'"

The president looked at the first lady. "Did I say that?"

Karen smiled, "Yes and even more."

She continued, "We need to address our energy needs and our dependency on oil from other countries, some friendly and others not so much. The second idea is to convert as many current cars, trucks, buses and anything that runs on gasoline to natural gas that we find and develop in our own country. In America, we have over one hundred and twenty-five million cars. If we can convert half a million cars a month and every twelve months add two hundred and fifty thousand more a month, we can make America energy independent in ten years or less. Every hundred forty cubic feet or so of natural gas we burn is one less gallon of imported oil. Natural gas will be at least half as expensive as gas at the pump so we will be saving hundreds of billions of dollars every year and we keep that money here."

The president smiled and said, "Where do I sign up?"

"By and large, Americans are more concerned that we are going to try to recover than the detail of how it's going to be done. They want to believe that America can be great again. You need to give them hope, a purpose and a direction. You also need to be honest and tell them it won't happen overnight or next week, next month not even next year."

Debra spoke up, "Sir, we need two national counters which will be on every TV station, every newspaper and every magazine. They will measure our progress ... the way a Community Chest or United Way campaign has a thermometer that shows the goal at the top and a big bulb at the bottom. The thermometer fills up as money is raised. We can use the same concept to count the miles of pipeline laid and the other can count the number of vehicles that have been converted. In the beginning, it will be slow but as we get more people working, the column will begin to rise."

The president looked at Debra, "What an outstanding idea! Thank you very much."

Nathan turned to Karen, "Madam First Lady, your team has done it again. You should be very proud of them."

Karen grinned. "Thank you, Mr. President."

As the president stood to leave the office, he turns to all of them, "Let's get to work. We have a country to save."

CHAPTER 92

Houston and the Brotherhood

In their hotel room, the Brotherhood members were sitting around discussing what's going on in America. Sargon observed, "I don't understand the lack of reaction by the American people to the devastation we've brought on them. They seem to be taking it in stride. For now, they can't get at their money in the banks, there is a shortage of gas for their vehicles and the food stores have very little on the shelves. So why are they not rioting in the streets?"

Mordecai, as the only American on the team, tries to add perspective for the rest of the Brotherhood. "Right now, everything is locked down. Martial law is being strictly enforced, including the nationwide curfew. People go into their homes at night and don't come out. They don't go to bars or restaurants, fast food places or theaters. For now, America has regressed, which is one of the prices they had to pay. Life in America has been changed by our attacks. I don't know if it has been changed forever, but for now it is different.

"History shows us that America changed during the Second World War. The people made great sacrifices on behalf of the war effort. They saved bacon grease, aluminum foil and many other things to fight the war. Ration books limited the amount and kind of food you could buy at any time. Americans lived under this rationing system for almost five years until the war was over. Even when the war ended, it took several years to change over to what they called a peacetime economy.

"What surprises me so far is that Americans are so willing to give up all they had in a very short period of time. If America has capitulated and abandoned its corpulent spending and borrowing ways, we have won. We have accomplished our goal; we have changed America perhaps for generations. If you believe that, I would like to talk to you about a nice bridge for sale in New York."

Sargon asked Mordecai, "What do you think will really happen?"

"I think America is potentially sitting on another bomb; a bomb not of explosives like the ones we set off, but a bomb that will potentially set regions of the country against other regions. Why should the people of the upper Midwest with all of it natural gas resources have to pay for the damage in the Texas and Louisiana energy infrastructures?

"It is entirely possible that our bombs have potentially blown apart the cohesion of America. The fifty states as we know them may not be able to survive and America could become many smaller independent nations."

Cyrus, with his degree from the London School of Business and Finance, had some ideas to share as a follow-up to Mordecai's thoughts. "I believe every rebellion starts over food and energy. Sometimes you have political issues, but people who want to advance their ideas do so through food. Feed hungry people and you can manipulate them to do your bidding. I believe we are in the early stages of a potential food rebellion. Once the people have raided all the supermarkets and picked them clean and the shelves are empty, they will look for food elsewhere.

"America has a great percentage of its population that gets its food directly or indirectly from the government. My guess is that tens of millions of people will have no food in a very short time. The stores are empty, so they will have no choice but to break curfew and start breaking into people's homes to find food. The police and the military will be called in to prevent the insurrection, but the hungry vastly outnumber law enforcement forces, no matter how many guns or bullets they use against them. The government is seen as no longer serving the needs of the people and is dissolved."

Mordecai jumped in, "Under Cyrus' idea, eventually the central government collapses and can no longer function and provide for the people. It's entirely possible that the fifty states secede and become fifty nations. The American central government is disbanded. What becomes critical for the central government's survival is what does in the next few weeks, not months. We could very well see the collapse of America in the next thirty days."

Oleg's opinion differed from those of Mordecai and Cyrus. "In order to grow the food that you need to feed America, you need energy. Our destruction in Texas and Louisiana along with the American shutdown of the drilling for and pumping of oil in the Gulf of Mexico has limited the production of crude oil in the U.S. Both oil and natural gas are important components in growing food in America.

"America can only grow certain crops in the north, while the south can grow food year round. America can move equipment from the north to the south to plant the necessary crops to start feeding America. The real challenge is how will America feed itself while waiting for the crops to come in?"

Adad wanted to add his thoughts. If America could find a way to feed its people, the government would perhaps survive. People with full stomachs would stay the course. As Adad listened to his fellow Brotherhood members, he thought, *They all have well thought out ideas, but America will feed its people while it waits for the crops to grow in the South.*

"Gentlemen – my brothers – I have listened to all of your suggestions and while they all were interesting, I think you haven't considered how America will feed its people. In a word: protein. Is it the best diet? No. Dietitians will say America can't live on a pure protein diet. But they can, for a while. Add a few fruits and a vegetable occasionally and you can live for many years. There can be all kinds of side effects of a protein-based diet. One is that people will live while they're waiting for the crops to come in the south. Fish, farm raised beef, chicken and pork all exist in great quantities and can be harvested to feed America. This source of protein can be reproduced to increase the supply.

"America will be forced to reexamine its values of what it wants to do and what type of life its people will have going forward. My fellow brothers, if we are only half right, we have succeeded beyond our wildest dreams and America will never again become a force on the international stage. However, we must look at the other side. I must warn you, my brothers, that one man can make a change and influence an entire nation. We saw it with Hitler, and in America they had FDR. He led the nation through the

Great Depression and the Second World War. He took a nation in despair, a nation where its people had no hope, and he gave it hope. It took a long time to recover but America did recover and went on to be bigger and stronger. Does the current American president have the ability to be a force to be reckoned with? Or, will he be like President Jimmy Carter and say, "America's best days are behind it?"

CHAPTER 93

Hadar Testing

The doctor wanted to run some blood tests to see if he can identify the gas to which Hadar had been exposed. Because she was such a strikingly beautiful woman, she had disrupted the entire ER. They placed her in a room to take her out of view. The Secret Service had guards posted outside to secure Lt. Hassen from harm. A nurse wanted to go in to draw blood but the guard wanted to see her identification. The nurse showed the guard her badge. He studied the badge, then the nurse, and let her pass.

Nurse Wyatt stepped inside the room and looked at the patient in a dress uniform. She had no idea how this woman got into it or how she was going to draw blood without the woman at least removing her jacket. "Lt. Hassen, I need to get some blood samples, but you will have to remove your jacket. I confess I don't know how you got into it much less how you get out of it."

Hadar laughed and said, "It's not a problem, just watch." Hadar started with the bottom button and then proceeded up to the last button just above her chest.

The nurse half expected one of the buttons to fly off the jacket and hit her. Wyatt noticed that when all the buttons were undone the gap between both sides of the jacket was small. She had to ask, "Who made your uniform? It can't be standard issue."

Hadar responded, "I had it tailor made. They made a plaster mold of my torso. After the mold set, they took it off my body and dried it in a kiln. When it was hard, they poured resin in the mold. When the resin set, they took away the two pieces of the mold and had an exact replica of my body. In essence, they made a mannequin of me. Next, they cut the fabric and fit it to my body mold. They did the same thing for the blouse, so when I put it on it's like another layer of skin that completely conforms to my body."

"Can you roll up your blouse sleeve above your elbow or will you have to take it off?"

"It will have to come off."

"Do you want me to get you a dressing gown?" Wyatt inquired.

"Are you just going to draw blood?"

"Yes, and it should be quick."

"I don't need a gown."

Nurse Wyatt watched as Hadar unbuttoned her blouse and took it off; the visitor was not wearing a bra, yet her breasts had the same look as they did with the jacket. The breasts were large and fully developed. For a moment, she was struck at the pure beauty of Hadar's form.

"Are you going to take the blood sample or just stand there and stare?"

Wyatt blushed. "I'm sorry. I was so struck by your beauty I forgot what I was supposed to do."

She filled four vials and then told Hadar to get dressed. "I will hand carry these samples to the lab."

Nurse Wyatt left and Hadar got dressed. She decided not to button the jacket in case the doctor wanted to run more tests.

She had now been in the hospital for over two hours and her head was almost clear. As she sat down on the edge of the bed, she wondered who wanted to kidnap her and why. She thought *I'm just a lowly lieutenant in Israeli Special Ops. My only connection to the events in America is that I had a flirtation with one of the terrorists. I have his phone number on my cell phone. Why didn't they just grab the phone from me?* Hadar continued to think about why she was so valuable and realized it wasn't just the cell phone or Mordecai's phone number. Whoever was after her wanted her for the same reason the U.S. government wanted her. They wanted to use her beauty to attract Mordecai. A chill came over her when she considered that the U.S. government wanted her to attract Mordecai and trap as many of the Brotherhood as possible, and that whoever was after her was going to use her body and its possible mutilation to force Mordecai to do their bidding. *I think that would silly. The damage is already done.* But another thought made her shudder. *Is it possible that the bombing is not done? I have to get out of here now!*

CHAPTER 94

Williams' Office

With the attack on Lt. Hassen, the meeting in Texas was delayed. Williams and Baker were waiting for a call from Major Rahimi. Meanwhile, they considered the identity of Hassan's would-be kidnapers.

Baker started, "We now believe that the Logistics Office is the source of the mole, but what do they hope to gain? For now, the only person killed was Sergeant Kelly and that was because he was in the wrong place at the wrong time. It was clear, with the timer on the bomb, that they were more interested in blowing up the Ridley house than they were in killing anybody."

"But, Ted, they have increased the risk they're willing to take in trying to kidnap her in daylight at Andrews. So, for some reason, they have escalated their level of commitment to protect someone or something."

Just then, Williams' intercom buzzed and Marie told him, "Major Rahimi is on line one."

Williams thanked Marie and put Omid on the speakerphone after the security door has been closed. "Major, have you heard that someone tried to kidnap Lt. Hassen?"

"No sir, I've seen nothing. Are you sure?"

"Well, a fake government car and driver picked her up at Andrews and was in the process of taking her somewhere when we intercepted it and rescued Lt. Hadar from a car that was filling with an unknown gas."

"What did the driver say?"

Baker responded, "In rescuing Lt. Hassen, the driver of the car was killed. We could find no identifying papers on him, no driver's license, no wallet, nothing."

Omid asked, "Any fingerprint identification on the dead driver? Was the driver of the security car hurt? It seems strange that the security driver would ram the driver's side of the car to stop it. I would think he would have been trained to clip the front of the car or at least to crush the wheel well to force it to stop."

Baker and Williams looked at each other in surprise. That the death of the driver was not an accident hadn't crossed their minds.

Williams raised the question, "Do we know how the security car found the car carrying Lt. Hadar at the time of the accident?

Baker responded, "No sir, I don't."

"I want the agent in charge and the driver of the crash car in my office within one hour."

"I'll get right on it, sir." Baker left the conference room.

Williams continued the discussion with Major Rahimi. "Major, we believe that the spy or mole is connected to someone in our Logistics Office, which was responsible for arranging the assets necessary for the raid on the Ridley home. The Houston office plus personnel from other departments and offices were deployed by Logistics."

"Sir, as you recall from one of my reports, Mike Ridley had no reportable source of income. Yet he had money in the bank, he was never overdrawn and his credit history was stellar. The bank records that we were tracing to the source of deposits on his accounts seemed to hit a dead end. We traced the money to OB Energy LLP. This is a private company and not incorporated in the United States. The money was wired through a series of banks and then arrived in the Ridley account."

"Major, do you know if money is still being wired to the Ridley account?"

"No sir, but if you hold on, I'll find out."

"I'll hold." Omid put Williams on hold and called Mr. Ford at the bank in Springfield. He got the receptionist and asked for Ford.

The president of the bank answered on the second ring. "Major, how can I help you?"

THE BROTHERHOOD OF THE RED NILE

"Mr. Ford, can you tell me if deposits are still coming in to the Ridley account, and if not, when they stopped?" Ford called up the Ridley account, gathered the information and returned to the Major, who was waiting.

"That's strange," he said.

"What's strange?" Omid asked.

"Major, I'll want somebody to double check this for me."

Omid impatiently said, "Mr. Ford, what did you find? I have the Under Secretary for Homeland Security on the other line waiting for your answer."

Ford told Omid what he had found.

"Thanks. If you find something different when your staff checks, call me right away."

Omid flashed his phone, "Mr. Williams, are you there?"

"I'm here. What did you find out?"

"Sir, Mr. Ford told me that the deposits to Mike Ridley's accounts were very regular. The deposits were always wired on the fifteenth of the month, going back many years."

"What else did you find?"

"Sir, I went back to my notes and the Ridleys disappeared on the night of the tenth. There was no deposit made five days later. That means somebody knew that the Ridleys would not be in Springfield on the fifteenth of the month."

"So you're saying that whoever was sending the money stopped because they knew the Ridleys would be gone and wouldn't need the money."

"Yes, but there is one more thing. On the fifteenth, all the remaining assets in the checking and savings accounts were withdrawn."

CHAPTER 95

The Oval Office

President Jordan received the radio chat script from Karen's office and was revising it in preparation for his next chat with the people tomorrow. As he sat behind his desk, he mused, *I have to make the American people, at least a majority to them, believe that there is hope and that America will be great once again. I know, however, that the recovery from the devastation will set us back significantly, perhaps for several decades. The American people will sacrifice, but this time the sacrifice will be longer than at any time in our nation's history. Tens of millions of people are out of work and, while the two pipelines and the conversion to our natural gas will most likely employ millions, I believe that many more millions will never find work. I question whether America has the resources to provide for the rest of the people who will need help.*

Jordan's intercom rang and Mary said, "Mr. President, the Speaker of the House and other leaders of Congress are here for their meeting."

"Mary, please show them to the conference room and tell them I'll be right there. See if they would like anything to drink."

"Yes, sir."

In about five minutes, Jordan walked into the conference room and greeted each of the leaders. "Thank you for coming. We have a lot to do. Mr. Speaker, thank you for coming. I would like to start by asking you a question. Do you have enough representatives and Senators in Washington DC for a quorum in both houses?"

The Speaker turned to the Majority Leader in the Senate, William Wild, and asked him the same question. The Leader of the Senate said, "No." The Speaker said "no" to the question, as well.

Jordan continued, "I have many things to tell you, but without a quorum, I'm concerned that we currently have no central government. Since the legislative branch is unable to function, then in reality we are left with the executive. We need to find a way we can work together and function for the people.

"I am going to tell you about my chat tomorrow and what I'm going to say to the American people." He told them about both the pipeline and fuel conversion programs and said, "I want to move on these projects as quickly as possible. The problem is that Congress has to approve the expenditures and we do not have enough members for a quorum."

Just then, the phone in the conference room rang and Jordan answered. He listened, and said, "Send him in." All the participants turned to the door as Attorney General Clinton walked in.

"Mr. President and leaders of Congress, I apologize for being late, but I had to handle an urgent issue for the president. Mr. President could you bring me up to speed, please?" This took only a few moments.

"So, we have a problem, namely that one third of the government can't function. Mr. Speaker, do you have any idea when you might have a quorum?"

Speaker Ward responded, "I can't say for sure. I'd like to believe it will happen soon but, frankly, I just don't know."

Clinton spoke up. "Mr. President, we may well have a constitutional crisis on our hands. If one third of the government can't function then the whole government can't function."

Francis Pollard spoke up, "Mr. Attorney General, are there any powers under the Constitution that would allow the president to act and then, when Congress can convene, it could pass or not pass a law to confirm what the president has done?"

"Senator Pollard, my staff has found two powers that I believe will work and meet with your approval so we can move the country forward. The executive branch has problems similar to Congress. We have department heads that are isolated and can't function. They can't run their operations.

"Under the Recess Appointment clause, the president can appoint people to positions that would normally require the approval of the Senate. However, because the Senate cannot attain a quorum, it cannot approve the appointments, and the president can still appoint and not be in violation of the law. Next, the president can issue an executive order to run the government. When Congress is back in session, it can approve or set aside the president's orders. I have checked, and the Supreme Court also does not currently have enough judges present to attain a quorum. So, until the court can get a quorum, it can't process lawsuits that would challenge the president's executive orders."

William Wild, the Majority Leader in the Senate, angrily responded to the proposals of the AG. "I can't believe you're suggesting that we set up a virtual dictatorship whose powers will remain unchecked until Congress can resume and vote on the actions of the president." He thought, *How long will the American people look kindly on the first American dictator?*

Jordan had listened carefully to Clinton and Wild; he turned to the Congressional leaders and said, "Gentlemen, I will take the AG's recommendations under advisement. For the moment, let's move on to another issue. The construction projects will employ millions of Americans but we will have millions who cannot be employed for many reasons. We have to find a way to put these people to work. We have to help the homeless, who have lost everything, to find work. I believe the only way to lift the spirits of the American people is to give jobs to as many as possible. Let them feel productive, as if they are making a difference.

"We need to rebuild America. If we look back at FDR, he gave us a model to deal with the Great Depression in the United States. We have to deal with the unemployment of our young people and the unemployment of fathers and mothers so we can keep families together. To do this, I will need your support. I realize that Congress is not in session and may not be for some time but you, as Congressional leaders, can speak out and support our ideas and plans. Then, when you're back in session, you can consider and pass the right bills that will change my executive orders into the law of the land. Can I count on you to help me help America?"

Wild thought, *The benevolent dictator wants our support. I don't think so!*

CHAPTER 96

Hadar has to Spend the Night

The doctor stopped by Hadar's bed in Emergency and told her that they did not yet have the tests back on the gas she ingested, so he thought she needed to spend the night.

"I can't. I have work to do that could mean life or death; I have to get out of here."

"Who do you report to?" The doctor's tone brooked no argument. "Let me call and talk to them and let's see what can be worked out."

Hadar thought, *How do I answer that question? Do I say Williams or Baker? What will he think when I tell him Homeland Security? Well, I have to get out of here, so let's use the top dog.* Hadar looks around and says quietly to the doctor, "I'm here on special assignment for the Israeli government. I report to Mr. Frank Williams, the Under Secretary of Homeland Security for Terrorist Activity. She hands the doctor a card with a phone number on it.

He dialed it.

"Mr. Williams' office. How may I help you?"

"Yes, my name is Dr. Benjamin Myrtle at George Washington Hospital. I have a Lt. Hadar Hassen in my care. I would like to speak with Mr. Williams if possible."

"Hold one moment, please."

"Hello, doctor. This is Frank Williams. I understand you have Lt. Hassen. How is she?"

"She appears to be fine, but she ingested a gas during an automobile accident and we have not yet determined its nature or its possible effects on her. I'd like to keep her here overnight for observation, but she insists she needs to leave. My concern is for her health if she leaves and has a delayed reaction of some kind requiring medical care.

"I understand. May I please speak with her?" The doctor handed the phone to Hadar.

"Sir, can you get me out of this place? I'm hungry and we have work to do."

"Hold on, lieutenant. How do you really feel? No lies."

"I feel fine. I'm not ready to jump out of a plane, but if I had to I could do it."

"Let me speak to the doctor."

Hadar handed the phone back to the doctor, whose face showed he knew what's coming next. He gave a resigned sigh.

"Doctor Myrtle, one of my senior staffers lives within a few blocks of the hospital. What if she stays with him and he watches for any problems. If something happens, he can get her to the hospital within minutes. Would that work for you so she could be released?"

The doctor's face brightened. "Yes, that works for me under those conditions. I'll release her."

Williams smiled. In the background he heard her say, "Yesss! I'm outta here!"

"Ted Baker will be there shortly to pick her up. If you could have her paperwork ready, that would be helpful."

"I'll arrange it."

"Thank you, doctor. May I speak with Lt. Hassen, please?"

As Doctor Myrtle handed the phone to Hadar, he thought, *I wish I were in Baker's place. I think I could stand to watch her myself.*

Williams told Hadar, "Lt. Hassen, Ted Baker will be there to get you within an hour. Don't speak to anyone and stay close to the security detail at the hospital. We'll get you something to eat as soon as you leave. I'll call you later this evening. Stay safe."

Just as Williams was hanging up with the hospital, Baker was in his doorway. "You're going to have a house guest tonight. I almost wish she were staying with me."

"She?"

THE BROTHERHOOD OF THE RED NILE

"Yes. Go to GW Hospital and pick up Lt. Hadar and take her back to your condo for the night."

"Why me?"

"Because you're the closest to the hospital in case she has a delayed reaction to the gas and has to go back. She tells me she's fine and wants out. Get her something to eat and then later this evening we can have a call with the two of you and Omid about the trap." Williams thought for a second and then asked, "What did you arrange about my interview with the escort leader and the driver of her car?"

"The driver is off the clock and we can't get to him right away. The team leader is on his way."

"Did you say the FBI agent who was the driver is unavailable?"

"Yes, sir."

"If an FBI agent is involved in an incident don't they have to make themselves available 24-7?"

"Yes, sir."

"So where is the driver?"

"My FBI contact says he's not responding to phone calls or pages. They are on their way to his apartment right now. We should know something soon. I shall interview the team leader for you, sir."

"Keep me posted. It's 4:30 now. I'm going home to have dinner with my wife and shall have Marie set up a conference call for 8:30 PM. There is a security team at the hospital. I'll arrange to have them cover your apartment just in case someone tries to snatch our pretty lieutenant again."

Just as Baker was walking towards the conference room door, his phone rang. "Baker here."

The voice on the other end told him they were at the driver's apartment. He was not there and it looked as if he had packed in a hurry and left. Baker told Williams what had happened.

"Get a forensics team to that apartment on the double. We have to find that driver; he may well be part of the plot. I want to see his bank records and credit card transactions and anything that has to do with money. And, I want it tonight, understood?"

"Yes, sir."

As Baker left Williams' office, he thought, *Do we have one mole or are we dealing with a broader network that is operating separately from the Brotherhood?*

CHAPTER 97

Time for Ellen

Williams was half way out of his office door. "Marie, please call Ellen and tell her I'm on my way home."

Marie dialed the Williams home and reached Ellen on the third ring. "Ellen, this is Marie. Frank wanted me to call you and let you know that he's on his way home. How are you feeling?"

"I guess like most people – scared to death. At times, I just feel hopeless. I know that millions of people are suffering; it makes my heart break to think of the millions of Americans affected by this staggering attack on our country. I want to help but I'm afraid to leave my house for fear of coming home and finding all our food is gone. I don't blame the hungry people scouring for food; they have themselves and their families to feed." There was a long sigh. "Marie, I'm sorry for dumping all of this on you. You have your own worries."

"I do and I wish I could share my fears and concerns with someone like Frank. Perhaps he can soon make it better for all of us."

Ellen hung up, and while she was depressed, she was beginning to feel better because Frank was coming home. She knew that he might have to leave on a moment's notice, so every moment they had together was precious. She wondered, *Will we have time to make love? What should I wear? Do I want to wear something that says 'I want you' or just 'hold me?' Oh my God, what am I going to fix for dinner?*

Ellen rushed to the kitchen and opened the refrigerator and the freezer to see what she could fix. She had some homemade pasta sauce and some fettuccine in the pantry. The lettuce didn't look the best but with some tomatoes, onions and a strong dressing it would pass for a salad. A frozen loaf of French bread was wrapped in foil. If she let it thaw, she could warm it in the oven. With the dinner menu decided, she again turned her thoughts to what to wear. She put the frozen bread on the counter, took out the pasta sauce, and then dashed upstairs.

She went into her closet and as she flung open the double doors most of her wardrobe was in front of her. As much as she wanted to make love with Frank, if they started and the phone rang or somebody rang the doorbell she knew that they would have to stop and answer whoever was there and they both would be frustrated they couldn't finish. At that moment, she was actually angry with the terrorists from potentially keeping her from making love with her husband when she wanted to. Quickly her anger turned to shame, for millions of Americans were away from their husbands or wives trying to keep the peace and law and order in this troubled land.

It was mid-summer and warm in DC. She spotted a simple white cotton dress that was almost sheer. The dress fit her body well and had buttons down the front. She thought that when Frank got home she would get an indication of his interest in lovemaking by the way he held her. Once she got an indication of his desire, she could undo the top button. Her breasts were still quite firm for a woman of her age and each button she undid would expose more cleavage. She would serve him his salad in such a way that when she leaned over to put down his salad plate he could look into her dress and see more of her.

If she did not catch him looking in her dress, she would button it when she went into the kitchen to bring in the pasta. She could send signals, but if he wasn't receptive, she would understand that he had a great many things on his mind. She knew he loved all of her; he had told her so many times. He had always told her she was a beautiful and enticing woman. Nevertheless, no matter how stunning she looked, she couldn't overpower the serious problems her husband was dealing with, and she accepted that reality.

Just then, she heard a key go into the lock and her heart leapt and she whispered, almost like a breathless new bride, "Frank is home."

CHAPTER 98

Feed the Hungry

So far, the president was having a difficult meeting with the Congressional leadership; he was telling them in the kindest way possible that the only part of the government that was functional at the moment was the Executive Branch, and he intended to use his Recess Appointment powers and executive orders to attempt to save America. He had told the leaders that when they could get a quorum he would be happy to submit his Recess appointments for the advice and consent of the Senate, even though he was not required to do so under the Constitution.

The president had explained the plans to build the pipelines and develop the natural gas resources of the country. He had noticed that the leadership was getting more and more uncomfortable with his decisions and he wanted to change the negative direction of their thinking.

"Gentlemen, we can spend a lot of time speaking and of course debating the recess appointments and the provisions of the Executive Orders. I want to move this discussion to the real people out in your districts and states who will not have a job in the building projects. First and foremost, we need to find a way to feed the needy. We have to find work for them that will give them a new sense of dignity, pride, and the ability to take care of their families, whether in small towns or great urban metropolises."

The president looked at the Majority Leader in the Senate before continuing. Before the terrorist attack, Jordan had heard rumors that Wild was going to seek the presidential nomination for the Democratic Party and run against him.

"I need to tell the American people in tomorrow's chat what we intend to do right away. I want to ask you, Mr. Speaker and Mr. Wild, to join me on the broadcast."

With one careful move, Wild was now in a difficult position. If he refused, then somebody else would be asked and he would be embarrassed. If he agreed to go on the radio show and support the president, it would make it difficult for him to criticize what the president was doing if he ran against him in the next election.

Wild asked the president, "What is your plan for this very serious problem, and what do you want the Speaker and me to say on the chat?"

Jordan responded, "Senator Wild, most Americans do not know that the government has a strategic stockpile of food, most of it in the form of MREs – meals ready to eat. I propose that the government contract with the producers of MREs to start building their capacity to ten million MREs per day as quickly as possible. We will use the military to distribute them at National Guard and Reservist armories across the country.

I shall issue an executive order for all farmers to plant one hundred percent of their tillable land. There will be no further subsidies for not growing crops. As fresh fruit and other crops are harvested, they will be sent to the producers of MREs first, and any excess crops will be available for sale to people who want to pay for them. Farmers will be asked not only to grow crops but also to raise as many pigs, cows and chickens as possible. I want to expand the number of fish farms to grow more protein. I want people out of work to help the farmers and canners to harvest and process the food. I want to make sure that all Americans have the first right to work so I shall close all borders to immigration and all illegal immigrants will be actively pursued, arrested and returned to their country. All foreign aid will cease and those American dollars will be used to support Americans. We will put America and Americans first. We must feed and employ our people."

As Wild listened to the president he could see how it will inspire millions of Americans. The message was a great one that he would tell the president he wholeheartedly supported. He had no doubt that the Speaker would also wholeheartedly support the president's actions. Therefore, he told the president that he would be happy to be on any program supporting the suggested plans. As the Speaker confirmed his support to the president, Wild thought to himself, *The devil will be in the details. His scheme is so grandiose that he probably can't carry it out. By winter, people will be hungry and angry with the president for his failure. I can support the idea now and, when it fails, I can claim that while the idea was great, the president didn't have the capability to see it through. Election season starts in about four months. Many people will want to listen to me come spring. By then, I'll be the leading Democratic candidate for presidential nomination. When I win the nomination and the Presidency, we shall be rid of our benevolent dictator.*

CHAPTER 99

Hello, Lt. Hassen

Baker was on his way to the hospital to pick up Lt. Hassen, take her to dinner, and then back to his condo for the night. Baker took the Metro into work so he has asked Marie to call Homeland's car pool and reserve a sedan. Baker checked the car for damage and then signed the paper work. The car was a new Chevy retro Camaro. As he leaves the garage, he guns the powerful engine just to hear it roar.

It was already dark when he arrived at Emergency, with a light mist of rain. Baker parked and locked the car and made contact with the agent in charge of security for Lt. Hassen to tell him the change in plans. Williams had ordered the security team to provide protection for the two of them through the night.

The agent in charge asked, "Where are you going to dinner?"

"I don't know yet. I need to find out what she prefers. As soon as I find out I'll pick a place and let you know."

Baker walked into Emergency and asked for Dr. Myrtle. "Please tell him that I'm here to pick up Lt. Hadar Hassen."

The receptionist paged Dr. Myrtle and he arrived at the desk within moments. Baker introduced himself, showed his ID and they both went to find Lt. Hassen. The two security guards remained outside the room.

Baker asked, "Are you decent, Lt. Hassen?"

"Yes, come in."

Baker turned the corner of the curtain and sees Lt. Hadar Hassen up close and personal for the first time.

Hadar looked at Baker and smiled. "Mr. Baker, your mouth is open. Haven't you ever seen an Israeli soldier before?"

Baker pulled himself together and nodded, "But not one like you." At first, he had been looking her over from head to toe to see if she was okay. Then he found himself giving her the once over with a different intention. She was a stunner, unlike any other woman he had ever met. "Is your uniform standard issue?"

"No, I had it custom made for special occasions."

"You mean kidnappings?"

She laughed. "No, I wasn't expecting to be kidnapped on my first visit to America."

"Lieutenant, let me get this out of the way. I know you hear this all the time, but you are one of the most striking women I have ever seen in or out of uniform." He blushed. "Wait, that didn't come out the right way."

"Mr. Baker, don't be embarrassed. I'm used to compliments. You have to understand that I'm serious about what I do, and sometimes my assets can be helpful. Yet, at other times, they work against me. How about we just get out of here and find something to eat. I'm famished."

"What would you like to eat?"

"Chinese sounds good."

"Have you ever had Vietnamese? It's really good, as well."

"No, but I'm up for something new. Let's try it."

"Then I know just the place."

As they leave the room, Baker tells the team leader they are headed to Miss Saigon on M Street.

Walking out of Emergency, Hadar suddenly stops. "Where is my suitcase?"

"Did you have it in the car?"

"Yes, they put it in the trunk when they picked me up."

Baker turned to the team leader. "Did you bring the lieutenant's suitcase to the hospital?"

"No, sir. We didn't know she had anything in the trunk."

"Where did they take the car?"

"To the impound lot."

"Get somebody on this right away. We need her suitcase." After they got in the car, Baker asked, "Was the phone in your suitcase?"

THE BROTHERHOOD OF THE RED NILE

"No, I have it in my purse."

"Have you checked to see if it's still there?"

Hadar patted the handbag. "I have it."

"We're just a short drive to Miss Saigon. I think you'll really like it."

"I hope so. I'm starved."

"After dinner, we'll go to my place and you'll take the guest room."

"What if they can't find my suitcase?"

"Don't worry. I have some things that will be good enough to sleep in. After dinner, we have a conference call with Frank Williams about our mission. Lt. Hassen…"

"Please, call me Hadar."

"Hadar, you must promise me that at any time you don't feel well, you'll tell me immediately. We have to be very concerned about your health. It's your most important asset. Is that understood?"

"Yes, sir."

"Call me Ted."

They arrived at the restaurant and the valet parked the car while the security team parked on the street. One man stayed with the car and the other patrolled on foot. At midnight, another team would replace them at Ted's building.

Ted and Hadar sat across from each other at a table in the back behind a stand up silkscreen with hand-painted red dragons on it. Ted gazed into her eyes and thought, *Her eyes are more beautiful than her body. Well, almost.*

Baker had eaten here often. The owner sent a server over with two menus. As Hadar looked at the menu, Ted could see she was confused. "Would you like me to order for you?"

"That would be nice, thank you."

"Do you have any diet restrictions?"

Hadar smiled, "Do you mean to ask if I eat pork?"

Ted chuckled. "I meant that some people are allergic to gluten or soy."

"I'll eat anything, including pork. And if you don't get me something to eat right now I may have to start chewing on this table."

"Yes, ma'am!" Ted motioned the waiter back. "Bring us six spring rolls right away, please. I'll order the rest when we get some food in this young lady."

"Right away, Mr. Baker." The waiter was gone about three minutes and arrived back with six small spring rolls and peanut sauce. Baker held back till Hadar had gotten some food in her and seemed a little more relaxed.

Hadar took a deep breath, "Those were fabulous. What was in them?"

"Steamed shrimp, some rice and vegetables in a rice paper wrapper. The peanut sauce blends all the flavors. Would you like steak, fish or chicken for your entrée?"

"You pick your favorite."

Ted looked at the menu one more time and told the waiter, "I'd like the broiled beef with cashews over shrimp fried rice."

"Works for me. I'll have the same." Hadar asked the waiter, "Do we get those fortune cookies at the end?"

"Absolutely."

As the waiter walked away, Baker turned to Hadar and said, "I'm sorry for being so blunt, but why is a woman with your looks in the Israeli Special Ops unit? You could be married to a wealthy Israeli and living in luxury." Baker looked thoughtful. "I understand you look fabulous in your uniform, but you didn't join for the uniform."

Hadar smiled. "Back on the subject of my looks again?"

"In fact, I'm trying to understand your decision." Baker ran a hand over his hair. "You probably have had a great many choices. I would like to understand the choice you made in joining the army and then moving to Special Ops."

"Why are my decisions so important to you?" Hadar asked, with some annoyance. "I don't have to justify my decisions to anyone but myself."

"I'm just trying to get a better understanding of who you are. We're going to be working closely and shall probably be around each other most the waking day for the foreseeable future. I just want to understand the person behind the beautiful face and body. I already know you're more than just a …"

"Don't say it again."

"Well, your government would not have trusted you to lead a counter intelligence team in a hostile country on a project as important as when you met Mordecai."

"You see? We don't have to talk about my beautiful body, because it isn't that beautiful." Hadar smiled. "I've had more than a few missions in hostile countries. By the way, your body isn't so bad either."

CHAPTER 100

The Williams' Front Door

When Ellen heard Frank's key go into the lock in the front door, she quickly left their bedroom to welcome him. As he opened the door, he saw a vision in white coming down the broad staircase. The dress Ellen was wearing was very sheer. The light from the window landing backlit her so he could see the curves of her body through the dress while her face was in shadow. As she walked down the stairs and towards him, it was as if she were floating on air.

Frank just stood there and watched the vision approach. At first, he wasn't sure if he was dreaming or if the image in front of him was real. The back lighting prevented him from seeing the vision's face until she was about five feet from him.

"Ellen, it's you. I thought I was dreaming." His eyes wandered all over her body and he knew he had to touch her. At the very moment he wanted to touch her, she took his hand and placed it on her breast. She undid the top button so he could slide his hand inside the dress.

Ellen snuggled in closer to Frank. She stood very still as he put his other arm around her waist and pulled her into him. He pressed his lips on hers and gently kissed her. The longer they kissed, the greater their passions were inflamed. Frank pulled back, put his mouth to her ear and asked, "Should we go upstairs or shall I take you right here?"

"I think upstairs might be more comfortable."

They walked up the stairs hand in hand. When they went into the bedroom, Frank sat on the edge of the bed to undress. Just before he finished, Ellen, still wearing the white dress, walked over in front of him.

She slowly undid her dress and when she undid the last button, she put her arms flush to her side and the dress fell to the floor. Frank reached out and put his arms around her hips. In a matter of seconds, they were in bed together. Neither wondered if the phone would ring or the doorbell would interrupt their intimacy.

When Ellen opened her eyes and looked at the clock, they had been in bed for almost an hour and a half; most of it asleep in each other's arms and it felt good. She slipped out of Frank's arms and went downstairs to fix dinner. She wore an oversize white terrycloth robe that was large, warm and comfortable. She heard Frank upstairs getting dressed. It meant he wasn't spending the night; he was going back to work. Ellen was sad but very thankful for the time they had together.

The pasta water was boiling when Ellen heard Frank coming down the stairs. She added the pasta to the pot and opened the top of her robe just enough to make things interesting. The sauce was warming on the stove. The smell of baking bread was all over the kitchen.

Ellen asked, "Do you want some wine with dinner?"

"I'd better not. I'm going back to the office and I don't want any suspicions that I was out drinking before coming back."

"Let's eat our salads, such as they are, while the pasta is cooking."

They started to eat. Frank looked over and saw that Ellen had her robe open just a little too much. "My dear, you better cover them up before they get both of us in trouble."

"Just seeing if you would notice."

"Every man in the world would want to notice them and you."

They talked about everything except what was really happening in the country. Finally, Ellen said, "Frank, the food in the house is getting low. Do you have any idea where I can get more?"

One of the most difficult challenges the administration was facing had reached the kitchen table of the Under Secretary for Homeland Security. He didn't know what to say to his lovely wife.

CHAPTER 101

Great Food

Hadar was wolfing down her dinner and finally slowed and took a deep breath. "That was fabulous! I've never had anything like it before."

"I'm glad you enjoyed it."

The waiter brought over a pot of green tea and two small teacups which have no handles, the kind that are held between the drinker's hands.

Hadar looks Ted in the eyes and says, "Mr. Baker, tell me who you are and how *you* got into this business?"

Baker tells her his background, including that he is not married, but had been some time ago. "I have worked in the spy game the whole time I have worked for the government. I was recruited right out of college. My last years at CIA I worked for Secretary Williams. When he was offered the position at Homeland he asked me to go with him, and I did."

"Now it's my turn, again. Like I said before, how is it that somebody with a figure and face like yours is not married to a rich guy instead of being in Special Ops?"

"How do you know I wasn't married to a rich guy?"

"Great question. I just assumed."

Hadar smiled. "I blossomed, as they say, at a very young age. I became a real woman at fourteen and by the time I was sixteen, I had the body I have today. My face lost its baby fat about the same time. A matchmaker introduced me to a man twice my age. I was told he was wealthy and it would give my parents and me security if I married him. I saw his house; actually, he had several houses, many beautiful cars and many servants. He told me that I would never want for anything, and I didn't. I asked him on several occasions what he did to gain all of this wealth. He said he was in the import and export business. When I asked what he imported and exported, all he said was 'stuff.'

"He was killed when his car hit a land mine when he was out on a business trip about a year after we were married. We had a prenuptial agreement that gave me a very substantial cash settlement. The rest of his assets, however – the houses, cars, and investments – everything went to his brothers. So, I was a wealthy widow at twenty-one. I decided to find out who killed my husband. I had already done two years of compulsory military service before I was married. I rejoined the army and tried to get assigned to Mossad. I figured it was my best route to killing the people who assassinated my spouse."

"What a story!" Ted finished the last food on his now empty plate. "You have the three B's: Brains, Body and Bounty and you have obviously used all three to your advantage."

"I try, I really try," Hadar said between mouthfuls.

"Have you had enough to eat or shall I have them butcher a steer?"

"I've had plenty," she said, putting down her fork. "But where are the fortune cookies?" Just as she was speaking, the waiter brought over two cookies on a small plate and removed their empty plates.

"Ladies first." Hadar chose the one on her right, cracked it and pulled out her fortune. She read it and laughed, and then she read it out loud to Ted. "Fortune will shine on you tonight; be prepared for the unexpected."

Ted cracked open his and read it to himself but did not read it to Hadar.

"C'mon! I read you mine," Hadar reached out for his.

He held it back and felt the heat rising in his face. "A loving man will find peace in love tonight."

Hadar responds, "Hmm. Perhaps we should make our way to your place and ..." she hesitated slightly, "... call Mr. Williams."

"You're right." Ted recovered his aplomb. "It's 7:30. Let's head back to my place and you can take a shower and change into something more comfortable."

"I could use a long hot shower."

Baker thought, *I think I may need a long cold shower before this evening is over.*

Baker paid the bill and they started out of the restaurant. He gave the claim check to the valet and they waited for the car to be brought up. Baker asked Hadar if she was warm enough. The night was cool and the dampness made it seem chiller still. As the car was parked by the valet, Baker noticed the security team was nowhere in sight. Concerned, he looked around and saw that the security SUV that had parked on the street outside the restaurant when they arrived was gone.

He leaned over to Hadar as he opened the passenger door for her and whispered, "Let's get in the car quickly. Something isn't right. The security team isn't here."

They both got into the car and Baker started driving eastbound on M street. For now, he was just trying to see if he was going to be followed and was less focused on where to go. After a few blocks and turns, he looked in the rearview mirror and saw that someone was following them. He took out his phone and called Williams. Williams looked at the caller ID, saw it was Baker and told Ellen "I need to take this."

"Do you want me to leave?"

"No. Just stay there till I see what's up. We aren't scheduled to talk for another hour.

"Ted, what's the problem?"

"Sir, when we came out of the restaurant, the security team was gone. Nowhere in sight."

"Have you called home base to see if they had been reassigned?"

"Not yet. I was just interested in getting Lt. Hassen out of harm's way. We're definitely being followed."

"Hold on, I'll see what I can find out." Williams put Baker on hold and called central operations for the FBI. "This is Frank Williams, Under Secretary for Homeland Security. I want to speak to the watch commander right away."

Williams was forwarded to Special Agent in charge of domestic security, Larry Maze. "Sir, please tell me the password for today and your mother's maiden name."

Williams responded with the correct information and said, "There is supposed to be a security team of eight men covering my deputy and Lt. Hadar Hassen. They were supposed to be covering them at Miss Saigon in Georgetown, but aren't to be seen."

THE BROTHERHOOD OF THE RED NILE

"Sir, GPS tracking indicates the cars are behind Miss Saigon."

"Can you call any of the people assigned to see what's going on?"

"Sir, I'll call the team leader right now."

Maze called the cell number but got no answer. He hung up, tried it again and on the third ring he reached an agent. "This is FBI domestic security. Who am I speaking with?"

The voice said, "This is Special Agent Patrick Finn."

Maze asked for the password and Finn replied with the correct code. Maze requested his location.

"We're behind Miss Saigon."

"Are all eight of you accounted for? Is there anybody out front?"

"Sir, we have two agents walking around the block."

"Get in your cars and head out and go to Baker's address. I will contact him and tell him to meet you at his apartment."

"Yes, sir. Do you have Baker's address?"

Maze said, "I'll get it for you and call you back in a few moments."

"I'll be waiting, sir."

Maze thought, *Something is not right. The assigned detail would know where the people are that they are guarding, and would have been briefed as to the destination.*

Maze picked up another phone and called DCPT terrorism unit and eventually got Captain Ward on the phone. Before he started the conversation, he conferenced in Williams. "For now, please just listen, sir."

Maze told Ward he believed that at least eight of his men might be down by the Miss Saigon restaurant. "Send a team and medical help right away."

"Yes, sir."

"I'll dispatch another FBI unit to join you as quickly as they can get there."

Maze spoke to Williams, "Do you have Baker's cell number?"

"Yes."

"Give me the number and tell Baker to leave his cell phone on so we can get his GPS location. Tell him to get on the Capital Beltway and head to Andrews. We will have a team at Andrews to protect them. And sir, you might want to consider joining me at Andrews so we can sort this all out."

"I'm on my way." Williams got up from the table and stood behind Ellen's chair, reached around and inside the robe and gave her left breast a firm squeeze. "Keep them warm and I'll get back as soon as I can."

As Williams walked out his front door, he thought, *Who can I trust? Who doesn't want this meeting to take place? We have to find out what happened to Mike and Mary Ridley. They must be the key. Somebody in the government wants them to remain hidden. Why?*

He clicked his phone to bring Baker up. "Ted, we don't know for sure, but we think the security team was compromised. DCPT is sending a team to Miss Saigon. FBI command wants you to head straight to Andrews. No stops. Use your flashers and siren. Just get there as fast as you can."

"Sir, we still have somebody on our tail."

"I'll send an escort. Tell me what the car looks like." Williams noted the details. "Your escort should be there shortly. I'll meet you at Andrews."

Williams called General Powell's private cell number. "General, I have a tail on two very important people. Can you send a Blackhawk to provide cover?"

"On the way, sir. Give me your agent's cell number."

Williams gave him the private number. "It's Ted Baker, General. And he has the one person in the car with him who could lead us straight to the Brotherhood."

CHAPTER 102

Leaders Still Talking

The president had been talking with Congressional leaders about what to do to feed the hungry and finding work for the unemployed. People were surprised at how quickly the economy had collapsed following the two attacks. The president told the leadership, "When you are forced to quickly shut down the flow of energy in an economy that is so dependent on crude oil, the cascading effects are swift and dramatic. All the other terrorist attacks have been against buildings, ships, even the stock market. It appears to us that this attack was designed to make our people and our economy suffer for years ahead.

"It will take close to two years to build the emergency pipeline just to get rid of the contaminated energy. The shock in the stock and bond markets caused us to shut the capital markets after September 11, 2001 but they were up and running again in days. The impact of the loss of energy is so widespread that it may well take years to recover."

The president had just come to the conclusion that the logic in attacking America's energy was not the plan of the typical terrorists but of people more sophisticated than Al-Qaeda. *If the Brotherhood is truly responsible for the attack on American energy, what other attacks are they planning?* For the moment, he had to focus holding the country together and rely on his intelligence forces to figure out what and where the next attack on America might be.

He returned to his conversation with the Congressional leaders about what he wants them to do in the next chat. "Gentlemen, tomorrow the

Speaker can support the distribution of food to those in need, and I'd like the Majority Leader to indicate his support for all the building projects."

Wild listened and thought, *The president has just set the trap for himself that will win me the election.*

Attorney General Clinton had been listening to the conversations about the content of the next day's chat. He leaned over to the president and whispered, "When do we tell the people about Recess appointments and the Executive Orders you plan to use?"

The president nodded and turned to the leadership. "AG Clinton has raised a question concerning the unusual combination of powers that I plan to use to manage the crisis. When do you think we can tell the American people?"

The Speaker responded, "That is a very good question. Congressmen and Senators will quickly start asking, how is the president making all of these decisions without Congress in session to act as a check and balance over the executive branch?"

Majority leader Wild commented, "It will only be a matter of time before the media will be asking 'can the president do these things?' We need an answer that will placate the media and calm the people."

The president responded, "We have agreed that once Congress has a quorum, all Recess appointments will be reviewed by the oversight Senate committees. As to the Executive Orders, if Congress does not agree, then they can file a suit in the courts. It seems to me that it is very important that the American people be told in such a way as to not scare them and let them know that the Government is working to solve their problems."

Clinton spoke up. "Mr. President, I don't think tomorrow is the right time but it should be done within the next week or two. Once you announce the projects, people will wonder how all this is going to be done, and that will be the time for the Congressional leaders to come forward and tell the people that safeguards have been agreed upon by the president and the leaders of Congress to protect the rights of the American people."

The Congressional leaders agreed with Clinton: the Speaker and the Majority Leader of the Senate would speak about Constitutional protection one week from Saturday.

Wild thought, *Whom do I need to reach to stir the pot of dissent?*

CHAPTER 103

The Chase is On

Baker was driving along M Street through Georgetown. The mist has turned to rain. He turns on his wipers and checks his rearview mirror to see if he's still being followed. The rain on the back window refracts the oncoming headlights into diamonds in the rearview mirror. He could see that the car right behind him was a white Chrysler Town and Country minivan. Behind it was a dark sedan. He watched as it passed under a streetlight and could see it was black.

He decided to take the long way to Andrews to give the Blackhawk a chance to get to them. "Hadar, please make sure your seat belt is secure."

"It's fastened tight."

"Do you have any experience with a Glock 9 millimeter?"

"Yes, I'm qualified."

With that, Baker reached inside his jacket and handed Hadar his pistol and two spare clips. "The gun is loaded and the safety is on. If the car behind us starts firing, you're going to return fire."

"I can do that. Do you want me to shoot at the tires or the driver?"

"I would prefer to capture whoever they are alive. But if they're trying to kill us, then disable them any way you can."

Smiling, she looked at Baker and said, "Do you treat all your girls this way on the first date?"

Baker responded, "Only the gorgeous ones."

As they approached Pennsylvania Avenue, Baker waited to the very last second to make a sharp right turn and he saw the black car make the same turn and skid on the wet pavement. The next turn would be left onto H Street and again he waited to the last second to make the turn, only this time he was in the center lane. He quickly accelerated and turned left in front of the car in the left lane. The driver honked his horn and stopped abruptly. The black car swung wide around the stopped car and fell in behind Baker.

Baker had no doubt that the black car was after them. He talked to Williams on the speakerphone and told him, "I'm headed down the 395 and will take 295 onto the Capital Beltway 495 and head to Andrews. There is a long stretch of 495 where the Blackhawk can intercept the black car. We don't want to kill these people, but to capture them alive, sir."

"Keep me posted on your turns and when you are on 495 heading east. The Blackhawk is en route from Andrews, so it will be heading toward you and the black car."

"Turning onto 395 south. I'm going to accelerate and see if I can lose him."

"Ted," Williams says, "be careful. I need both of you alive so we can try and figure out what is going on."

"Agreed, sir. On 395 doing eighty. Black sedan still tailing us." Baker saw congestion ahead by the Pentagon exits and slowed down. He started weaving through the traffic. The black sedan was sticking to him like glue. Ted then accelerated, narrowly missed a car and swerved, barely to missing the center divider. Baker looked in his rearview mirror and saw that the black car driver may not have as much skill as he thought; the light rainfall made the road slippery and he saw the black car nick a car trying to get around it, causing the driver of the car to spin and hit another vehicle. The black car slid into the divider to get around the skidding car; Baker could see sparks where the black car scraped against the concrete median.

The black car swerved back towards the center lane and hit another car, without stopping. It then accelerated and pulled away from all the congestion, trying to keep up with Baker. With the black car coming closer, there was nothing between them. The sedan accelerated but kept a certain distance behind Baker's car.

"Sir, I'm turning onto 295 now and the black car is still on my tail. I'm accelerating to ninety. The black car is keeping up but is maintaining a steady distance. If the car is after us, why doesn't he try and overtake us?"

"Where are you now, Ted?"

"I'm just about to turn onto 495."

"Ted, the Blackhawk is about four miles ahead of you. I have a team of FBI agents trailing well behind the black car and more coming up as you pass each entrance ramp to the 495."

"Sir, what is the plan for the Blackhawk?"

"In about thirty seconds, I want you to turn on your emergency flashers. The Blackhawk has zeroed in on your cell phone signal. When it is ready to fly by you, it will train a fifty caliber on the black car and take it out. You're to continue on to Andrews. A team is waiting for you."

"Sir, do you know if the Blackhawk has a sniper on it?"

Williams switched to another line. "General, is there a sniper on the Blackhawk?" He listened and said, "Ted, the general says yes."

"Is the sniper's weapon powerful enough to take out the engine of the black car?"

"Wait." Williams asked, "General, can he disable the car engine?"

Williams relayed to Ted, "It may take two shots but he says he can."

"Sir, let the sniper take out the car by killing the engine and with luck we can take some people alive."

"Good idea. Slow down to about sixty-five to reduce the chance of a bad wreck."

"Another Great idea sir. I'm slowing down now." Baker slowed down and guessed he has about two minutes to contact with the Blackhawk. He turned to Hadar, "You haven't said a word."

"Well I figured that you were kind of busy and I just took my first breath in a while."

"We have about one minute. I'm going to turn on the flashers."

"Ted, I know you're busy, but does it seem strange to you that the black car never got close to us?"

"Thirty seconds, flashers on." Baker and Hadar could see the Blackhawk's floodlight approaching fast. Then, the Blackhawk hovered and was ten seconds... five ... four... three ... two ... one...

Ted and Hadar saw two flashes of light. In the rearview mirror, Baker saw the engine hood explode into the air. The car spun and came to a stop.

Baker took a deep breath and thought about Hadar's question, 'why didn't they close in on our car?' Suddenly, he pulled the car sharply to the

DAN PERKINS

right, stopped and yelled to Hadar, "Get out of the car *now!* Baker jumped out, ran around the car and grabbed Hadar by the arm as she got out of the car. *"Jump!"*

CHAPTER 104

Williams' Office

"Ted, Ted, are you all right?" Frank waited and tried again to reach Baker. "General, what happened?" General Powell reported that the Blackhawk had taken out the black sedan and was hovering in case the passengers tried to get away. "Your backup teams have arrived and are taking people into custody."

"Can you see Baker and Lt. Hassen?"

"Sir, it appears they left the car and jumped over the guardrail and are lying at the bottom of a hill ..."

The sound of a loud explosion stopped all conversation.

Williams held the phone away from his ear. "General, what the *hell* was that?"

"Sir, the black sedan just exploded. The pilot says that car parts are flying in all directions."

"Were any of the detainees or my people hurt?"

"They appear to be fine. They were on the other side of their cars and were sheltered from the blast."

"How about Baker and Lt. Hassen?"

"Sir, they're up and climbing over the guardrail and are headed to the blast site and your team."

"Tell Baker to check his phone to see if we're still connected."

General Powell relayed the message to the people on the ground and Baker called Williams on another phone. His was smashed in the jump over the guardrail.

"We're fine. A little dirty from the fall, but fine. I'd like a bomb squad to look over my car to see if it's been rigged with a bomb before I head to Andrews. Sir, do you know what happened to the security detail at the restaurant?"

"We have a team on site. We found the security people bound and gagged in their cars behind the restaurant. It appears that some type of knockout gas was used to overpower them. They'll be fine, but need some air to clear their heads. How is Lt. Hassen?"

Ted chuckled. "She wants to know if I treat all my first dates this way. Once the bomb people clear the car, we'll head to Andrews. I'll call you from there."

Ted and Hadar walked over to the guardrail and sat while they waited for the bomb squad.

"Thank you for saving my life."

"Nothing any red blooded American wouldn't do for …"

"Don't you dare say it … a visitor from a foreign country." Hadar held up her hand. Ted fell silent.

She asked, "I do have a question for you. As we were jumping over the guardrail, we fell and rolled down the hill together. How is it that you were on top of me and your hand was in an unusual place and it took a while for you to let go and roll off of me?"

"As we were rolling down the hill, you were beginning to separate from me so I pulled you back into me and held you till we came to rest. I didn't realize that I was …"

"… Taking the opportunity to feel me up?" Hadar finished.

"As we were getting to our feet the explosion went off and so I grabbed you in my arms and took you to the ground trying to cover you from falling fragments."

"Thank you for protecting me, but I was quite capable of rolling down the hill on my own."

"I can't explain the difference in my hands other than to say I thought you were in more danger from the explosion and falling debris."

Hadar reached out to take his hand. "What's that in your hand?"

Ted looked down at his hand. It had something that looked like a small fishhook under his skin and a round object attached to it. "I have no idea."

Hadar looked, "I think I know. It's a miniature GPS tracking device. I used a similar one on Mordecai in Syria. I know you didn't get it off me when you were lying on top of me with your hand on my chest. So you must have picked it up when the bomb went off and you rolled over on me and put your arms round my shoulders and neck."

Baker said, "Stand up and turn around."

"So now you want to study my butt?"

"No, not now. I'll do that later. I want to look at your shoulders." Baker placed his right hand on Hadar's right shoulder and slowly slid it towards her left shoulder, stopped just about the middle of her spine and felt a small tear in the collar.

Baker called out. "Does anybody have a flashlight?" One of the FBI agents came over with a small flashlight and Baker turned Hadar with her back to him. The flashlight highlighted the small tear.

"This is where the GPS was attached. Hadar, who would have had access to your uniform jacket and when?"

She thought for a moment as she turned to face him. "I took off my jacket and shirt so the nurse could draw my blood to identify what type of gas I was exposed to. I was naked from the waist up." She saw Baker's eyes flash and hit him in the shoulder. He winced and she continued, "I turned my back on the nurse, put my shirt back on and then she was holding my jacket helping me on with it. The nurse could have put it on my jacket when my back was turned. She was the only person in the room except for the doctor and I don't remember seeing him touch my uniform."

"Do you remember the nurse's name?"

"I don't remember seeing a name tag. I think she had on a sweater that might have been covering it."

Baker called Williams and told him of the GPS find. "Sir, can you have somebody check with the hospital and get the name of the nurse and get a background check on her?"

Williams replied, "Right away."

Hadar said to Baker, "I've only been in this country seven hours and it looks like there have been two attempts on my life so far. What is it about me that makes people want to kill me?"

"I don't know, but I intend to find out." Baker remembered. "I asked Marie to contact Logistics to get me a car so I could come and pick you up from the hospital. Let's get this hook out of my hand and back into your collar.

He called Williams. "Sir, could you call Megan Brown and ask her to come to Andrews and also have Marie get her a car from Logistics? Sir, I request you to send her with your driver. He's very experienced. I don't want anything to happen to Ms. Brown."

"I'll take care of it, Ted."

Hadar put a hand on his shoulder. "Are you cheating on me already? Who is Ms. Brown?"

CHAPTER 105

The Major is Still Waiting

"Marie, after you get a car for Ms. Brown, call my driver and tell him he is to take her to Andrews to meet with Baker. Then, could you track down Major Rahimi, please? We left him hanging in all the excitement. One last thing: I need to get some basic food for Ellen and me at the house, so please see what you can find. I know that some sections of the country have plenty of food while others will be eating MREs.

"Sorry, Marie. I know I'm being very demanding, but a lot of things are happening very quickly. Would you try and get me some phone time with the attorney general?"

When Marie heard 'AG', she knew that this request must be very important. She had quite a few items to take care of, and decided getting Ms. Brown on her way was the first priority. Once she had that task in motion, she would call the AG office. The rest of her assignments would fall into place.

"Ms. Brown?"

"Yes."

"This is Marie in Mr. Williams' office. I'm arranging transportation for you to go immediately to Andrews for a meeting with Mr. Baker. I'm sending you with Mr. Williams' driver."

"I can drive myself."

"There has been a security issue. Mr. Williams insists that you must be driven by his driver, who is on his way to get the car. I expect him to be in front of the building in about fifteen minutes. Please be ready."

"Yes, Marie."

With that done, the next was a call to the AG's office. She dialed the number and a voice answered, "Office of the Attorney General. May I help you?"

"Yes, I'm calling on behalf of Under Secretary of Homeland Security Frank Williams. He needs to speak with the attorney general concerning a matter of national security. When could he be available to talk by phone?"

"Let me call up his schedule." In a short while the voice asked, "Will Mr. Williams be at the White House tomorrow for the president's fireside chat? Perhaps they could talk in person."

"Will you hold?"

"Of course."

Marie checked with Williams and then got back to the AG's appointments secretary. "Mr. Williams would be happy to meet with Mr. Clinton tomorrow before the president's chat. The president will speak at noon. Would 10:30 work for Mr. Clinton?"

"That sounds fine. What is the subject matter for the meeting?"

"Please tell him it concerns files sealed by a previous president."

"Can you tell me the nature of the contents of the file?"

Marie sighed. "We have no idea what is in the file. It was sealed decades ago, but it might provide some insight into the recent nuclear attacks."

"I'll let him know."

Marie told Williams, "You're all set for 10:30 tomorrow morning with Clinton."

"Good. Now, please get me Major Rahimi if you can."

"Yes, sir."

It has been at least six hours since Williams spoke with Omid. When Marie finally got him on the phone, Williams first apologized and then briefed him on the evening's developments.

"Are Ted and Lt. Hassen okay?"

"A little shaken up, but for someone who was gassed, almost kidnapped, stuck in a hospital for several hours, and caught up in a car chase through Washington that ended in an explosion, all within her first six hours in the country, she seems to be in good spirits. She can handle it.

"Major, I have an assignment for you and I want to share with you some very important information. If we can figure out what is going on, we may well save the country from another nuclear attack."

"Sir, are we expecting another bomb?"

"Omid, I don't know, but some of the pieces of the puzzle are fitting together while others are not. Ted and I have been working on your theory that we have a mole or a spy in the middle of this problem. We thought that it had to be somebody in the Houston office; they were in charge of the raid on the Ridley house. We have since learned that all the coordination for the raid was done out of our Logistics Office. The Office was in charge of arranging the pick-up of Lt. Hassen at Andrews, where she was almost kidnapped.

"Logistics was responsible for arranging the car that Ted was using to pick up Hadar at GW Hospital. I can't tell if the mole is trying to divert our attention or is truly a bad person and wants to kill a great many people."

"Sir, do you think that the mole or spy has a connection to the Brotherhood and is working to keep us away from them?"

"I wish I knew for sure but I don't. Here is your assignment. We need to fill in some holes. Stay in Houston but please call two people for me. Call Sheriff Whittles and ask him figure out who in the town of Springfield might have known the Ridley's best. Perhaps that next door neighbor."

"You mean John Bowman?"

"Yes, that's the one."

"Talk with Bowman about what Mike Ridley did with his time. Was he a gardener, did he play golf or tennis? We need to find out as best we can about Ridley's activities. I especially want to know if he was gone for long periods.

"We know he went overseas to adopt Michael but we need to know if he was around and then just disappeared for some period of time. You will need to see if Bowman can come to Houston, or perhaps the two of you could meet half way and talk.

"One last thing. The meeting in Texas, which has been delayed by these events, will take place In Houston. I'd like you to lead the meeting for me. Ted will be there, but he'll be coming in as assistant to CIA agent John Seacrest. It's important for you, Lt. Hassen and Ms. Brown not to indicate that you know Ted. Is that clear?"

"Yes, sir. When do you expect all of them to fly out?"

"I'm waiting for a report on Lt. Hassen's condition and her ability to fly. I'll know that after they arrive at Andrews tonight.

"I have a meeting with the attorney general tomorrow morning about unsealing the Ridley family security file."

"How long has the file been sealed?"

"As best we can tell, it was sealed just about the time Mike and Mary Ridley arrived in Springfield, when Jimmy Carter was president."

"Do you think President Carter was involved?

CHAPTER 106

My Marine Buddy

Major Omid Rahimi had just finished his conversation with Frank Williams, which had been delayed due to the unforeseen attacks on Lt. Hassan. The call gave him a great deal to think about, much of it potentially very disturbing. He took a deep breath and decided his first call was to his fellow Marine, Sheriff Whittles of Springfield, Texas. Omid had established a great relationship with the sheriff and believed he could trust him if, in their discussion, classified material had to be disclosed. Omid dialed the sheriff's office number and got his receptionist.

"This is Major Rahimi for Sheriff Whittles. Is he available?"

"I'll check for you. Please hold." The receptionist returned and relayed that the sheriff was involved on a case and would call back within thirty minutes.

"That's fine. He has my cell phone contact. Please have him call me on that number."

"I'll give him the message. Anything else?"

"Just tell him it's really important I speak with him today."

"I'll make sure he gets the message, Major."

Omid wondered if he should wait to talk with the sheriff before he tried John Bowman. He concluded he needed to move things along so he dialed Bowman's home number. A man's voice answered the phone. Omid asked, "Is this John Bowman?"

The voice responded, "Yes it is. Who is this?"

"It's Major Omid Rahimi. We met while I was in Springfield."

"Oh yes, I remember. How can I help you, Major?"

"I'm calling because I need your help. Do you have time to talk now or would some other time work better?"

"Now is fine."

"I'm going to ask you some questions and I would prefer you think about your responses overnight. In fact, please discuss your ideas with your wife and then call me when you think you have the best possible answers, okay?"

"We'll do our best. Ask away."

"You may recall our conversation about Mike Ridley's work, or rather his lack of work. Do you recall that discussion?"

"Yes, I do and it still puzzles me how he paid for everything, yet never had a job like other able-bodied men in Springfield."

"Excellent, John! That is the very frame of mind that can help me. So let me ask you, were there periods of time when you didn't see Mike in the neighborhood?"

"What do you mean didn't see him in the neighborhood?"

"Did you ever see a car come and pick him up at the house, and then, several days, notice later a similar car returning him to the house?"

"Major, I'd need to think about that one for a while. I'll ask Sarah and see if she can recall."

"John, ask Sarah the same question about Mary Ridley."

"Do you have any idea what you're looking for?"

"No, I don't know anything. Let me ask you one other question for both of you. Who in Springfield might know at least as much about the Ridley family as you two, if not more?"

"That's a tough one. I'll talk it over with Sarah and get back to you. When do you want me to call back?"

"Is Sarah with you now?"

"No, she's out looking for food. I hope she'll be back in a couple of hours."

"Please discuss these two questions thoroughly. If you come up with any answers kindly write them down. Don't trust your memory. Could you call me back in the morning by 10 AM?"

"Major, I don't know what we'll come up with, but we'll do our best and shall call you by ten in the morning. Should we use this number?"

"Yes. I'll be waiting for your call. Please remember, nothing is too small a detail. Write it all down."

John hung the phone and began to think over Omid's first question about ever seeing a car come and pick up Mike. *I always thought he must be somebody important when a car and driver came and picked him up. But, if Mike was not going to work, where was he going?*

CHAPTER 107

The Other Woman Arrives At Andrews

Frank Williams' driver picked up Megan Brown in front of her Homeland Security building and they sped towards Andrews. Ted and Hadar were just about ready to get into the Camaro when Williams called and reported, "Megan Brown is on her way to Andrews to meet you. I've arranged for the three of you to meet in a secure area. I had planned to meet you there, but there's too much happening here. We can talk about at 10 PM.

Williams heard a voice say, "That other woman is coming to meet us at Andrews?"

"Who is that?"

Ted responded, "Lt. Hassen is giving me some grief."

"Grief about what?"

"Nothing important, sir. She's just playing around with my brain."

"You keep Lt. Hassen happy. Understood?"

"Yes, sir."

"I'm sending a secure phone with Ms. Brown to replace the one destroyed. Do you have the parts from the other phone?"

"Most of them, sir."

"Give the parts to security when you get to Andrews."

"Got it."

They got into the car and headed about five miles down 495 to Andrews. "I need a shower and a change of clothes. Did you ever find my suitcase?"

"I was told it's on its way to Andrews and should already be here waiting for you."

"Will I have time for a hot shower and something to eat before we meet the other lady?"

"You ate just two hours ago and you're hungry again?"

"A girl gets hungry after car chases and jumping over guardrails and rolling down hills."

"Okay, we'll find you something to eat."

"What about that shower?"

"Well, now that you mention it, I also could use one." Ted glanced at her and kept a straight face. "Did I tell you there is a water shortage? We'll have to shower together. I'm really good at washing other people's backs."

Hadar grinned. "I'll just bet you are. You can use a bucket."

Hadar made a fist and launched an attack on Baker's shoulder, but he shifted and she hit the metal frame on the seat, letting out a yelp.

"Wimp! Take your punishment like a man." Baker smiled. "Take your best shot. And use those assets to distract your opponent."

"Will you get your mind off my assets? We have serious work to do."

"Believe me, I'm taking your assets very seriously."

Hadar was just about ready to punch him again but she stopped. *There are two reasons why that is a bad idea. First, my hand still hurts from the last attempt and second, I think this guy likes me. After all, he did save my life twice. Still, no joint shower, at least for tonight. And what about my feelings for Mordecai? Has Baker replaced my thoughts of Mordecai just because he saved my life? It wasn't all that bad to have his hands on me, but when the bomb went off and he covered my body with his… I never had somebody risk his or her life to save mine. Maybe there is something to this Baker guy after all.*

Baker pulled up to the famous Pearl Harbor Gate at Andrews, just off 495, and showed his Homeland Security badge. The guard said, "We've been expecting you, Mr. Baker. Please wait here. We shall have you escorted to your area." The MP left his post and another MP stepped up to Baker's car and asked him to pull over to the parking spot on the left of the guardhouse.

"Miss, can I see your ID?"

Hadar pulled out her Mossad ID and presented it to the MP.

"Thank you, lieutenant. We have your suitcase. I'll get it while you're waiting for your escort."

Hadar saw the suitcase coming and was excited about changing into clean clothes. But as the MP came closer, she noticed that Security had ripped it apart looking for something.

"I'm sorry, lieutenant, but it looks like the contents went through a shredder. When we saw the condition of your clothes, we sent a female MP to the BX to find you some replacements for you. They're here in your new bag."

"What is your name?"

"James, ma'am."

"And your last name?"

"Bright, ma'am."

"Sergeant James Bright, thank you for your kindness. What do I owe for the clothes?"

"Nothing ma'am. It's a little gift. I hope they fit," as James' attention focused on Hadar's chest.

"I'm sure they will, Sergeant."

The escort jeep pulled up to Baker's car and led them through one of the largest air force bases in the world. Following the jeep, they turned right on East Perimeter Rd. and after a long way, at the sign for North Perimeter Rd., they bore left. They eventually turned left onto Arnold Ave then went left again onto G Street, to pull up in front of a large building simply identified as Hangar 2. As the escort jeep stopped at the entrance, the MP got out and motioned to Baker to bring his car up to the hangar. As Baker approached, the hangar's massive door started to rise to the point that Baker's car could easily clear it. Another person, not in a military uniform, waved him in. Baker drove through and the door came down. The security agent walked to the passenger side, opened the door for Hadar and said, "Welcome to Andrews, Lt Hassen."

"Thank you," Hadar replied.

"Mr. Baker, Ms. Brown is in the meeting room expecting you," he informed, and led the way.

"Sir," Hadar asked?

"Yes, ma'am."

"Do you have a ladies' shower and bathroom?"

"Yes, ma'am. It's adjacent to the meeting room and next to your sleeping accommodations."

THE BROTHERHOOD OF THE RED NILE

Hadar smiled at him. "Could you tell me about the water shortage?"

"Ma'am, we have had more rain in the last two months than in twenty years. All the reservoirs are overflowing."

"Thank you."

Baker shrugged his shoulder and chuckled, "Who knew? I guess you can't believe everything you hear."

Hadar made a fist and said, "Nice try. Get ready for my sneak attack."

CHAPTER 108

John and Sarah Compare Notes

John Bowman had been waiting for his wife, Sarah, to return from her food-shopping trip to tell her of his conversation with Major Rahimi two hours ago concerning Mike and Mary Ridley. Meanwhile, he brought out a legal pad and made some notes. Many notes, in fact. It was difficult to place exact dates and times, but he was now focused on the number of times Mike left and got into a car that had arrived to pick him up. He remembered they were very frequent in the first ten to fifteen years John lived next door, but it seemed to John that there had been fewer and fewer departures in recent years.

He remembered Mary taking off on her own about the time they were adopting Michael, but he didn't recall any significant number of times that they both left at the same time. John stopped for a moment and looked at his notes, trying to see if there was a pattern. *It's been so long. It's hard to put things down. I just don't know for sure. I wish Sarah were here. She might be of help in figuring things out.* Just then, John heard the garage door open and knew it was Sarah. He went to the door and opened it to find her loaded down with food.

"Did you hold up a supermarket?"

She handed him a bag. "No. I was driving out in the country and saw this small general store. It was open so I went in and bought as much as he would sell me. I asked him why he had so much excess and he told me many of the local people grow their own food, so this time of the year they don't need much. So, as you can see, I don't have a lot of fresh fruit and vegetables, but I do have a good supply of canned goods and fresh beef and pork.

"I bought enough to last us at least a month if we're careful. In about two weeks I'll call him and see what he has left and decide if I should go out and see him."

John helped Sarah to put everything away. When they were finished, he asked her to sit down. "I received a call from Major Rahimi and he asked for our help. I've been thinking for the last two hours and I need your help, too. Major Rahimi wants to know what we remember of Mike and Mary Ridley's comings and goings for as long as we've known them."

"John, we've been neighbors for over twenty-five years."

"That's true, but for those twenty-five years, I presumed Mike had a job. However, we now know he didn't have a job in the normal sense. We never knew where he went when he left their house. I remember that many times, when I was taking Chandler out for his early morning walk, a black car would pick him up. He'd be carrying a small piece of luggage. A few days later the car would bring him back."

"I remember some of those trips myself. I just assumed that he was going away on business."

"Do you recall Mary going out on her own?"

"The only time I can think of was when she went someplace overseas to adopt Michael. I think she was gone for at least a month."

"How do you know it was at least a month?" John asked.

"I remember how excited they both were. She asked if I would look after the mail while she was gone if Mike wasn't home. I said it was not a problem, so I collected the mail, and when Mike came back I took it over to him. I remember one time he stopped by to see if there was any mail. He said that he was looking for a letter from Mary but I never recall seeing one from overseas."

"Do you remember anything particular about the mail you collected?"

"John, that was such a long time ago. Nothing is coming back. Let me start dinner. Perhaps that will jog my memory. How about some nice pork chops and brown gravy along with some green beans and biscuits?"

"I'm so hungry I can hardly wait." John went into the family room and sat in his favorite chair. He looked over at the bookcase and saw the yearbooks from the time Michael Ridley was in second grade until he graduated from high school. He leaned over, took out the second grade book, and opened it. On the inside cover was the calendar for the year. As he turned the pages, each month of the school year had pictures of the children and, in some cases, pictures of the parents with the children. He thumbed through the pages for each month looking for pictures of Mike, Mary and Michael and notices there were times when Mike was not in any school photos with Michael, although Mary was there. John took the third grade book and again, matching the calendar and the pictures, he saw a pattern developing.

"Sarah, come in here. Hurry!"

"What's the big rush?"

John showed Sarah the second, third, fourth grade books, and noted when Mike was in the pictures and when he was not.

"Is it possible that he was out of town when the pictures were taken?"

"Doing what?" Sarah asked.

"I don't know, but maybe it will help Omid."

"Let's eat. Dinner is ready. We can look at the yearbooks after."

"How about we look at the yearbooks with dinner?"

CHAPTER 109

Yearbooks May Hold the Secret

John and Sarah Bowman were having a working dinner that could well help unlock information that had been sealed for over thirty years. John discovered that his son's school yearbooks had calendars and pictures of Mike and Mary Ridley from second grade through high school. All the books followed the same format. The left hand page had the calendar with the dates that correspond to the pictures on the right hand page.

"Sarah, look at September in the second grade. School started on September 6 and the first activity was the first soccer practice on the 18th. Mike Ridley is in the pictures of the practice. But when we look at the sideline in the first scrimmage on the 24th we can see Mary, but not Mike."

"That doesn't mean Mike wasn't there, he was just not in the picture. He could have been sick or out of camera range."

"I agree, but look at the October page. Mike is in the picture for the harvest hayride, but not in the Halloween party later in the month, while Mary is. Let's look at November and see if we can find Mike in the pictures early in the month but not for the Thanksgiving party.

"Look, Mike is helping put up the Thanksgiving decorations on the classroom bulletin board but he isn't in the pictures when they are passing out frozen turkeys just before Thanksgiving. I think I had better call Omid and tell him what we've found."

"I agree, but do you really think it will help Omid fill in some holes in the Ridleys' life?"

He shrugged his shoulders. "I don't know. This is not my field. But, hopefully it will help."

John called Omid's cell number and got Omid on the third ring.

"Omid, this is John Bowman. We spoke a few hours ago about information on Mike and Mary Ridley." John told him what he has discovered in the yearbooks.

"Are you sure there's a pattern?"

"I realize that we have only looked at a few years but, based on the photos, it appears that Mike is around at the beginning of each month and - pardon the pun - is out of the picture at the end of the month."

"John, put the yearbooks in a box and take them all to Sheriff Whittles' office right now."

"You want all eleven years?"

"Absolutely. Take Sarah with you and tell no one what you have learned. Go tonight and call me when both you and the books are secure."

"Omid, do you really think we have found something helpful?"

"I hope so, John. I'll talk to you soon."

Omid dialed Sheriff Whittles and got his office. He was told, "The sheriff has not checked in with dispatch."

"Will you call the radio room and have them try and get through to him? I'll hold."

"You want me to track down the sheriff?"

In a very stern voice, Omid said, "I need to speak with Sheriff Whittles now. It's a matter of national security."

"Yes, sir. Right away. Please hold."

Rahimi held for a while that to him seemed like forever, but in only a few moments a voice came on the line, "I have Sheriff Whittles for you."

"Omid, my friend. What's the rush?"

"Jim, we're trying to get the file on Mike and Mary Ridley unsealed and we need as much information on them we can get. I just spoke with John and Sarah Bowman and they have discovered what could be important information. They're on their way to your office right now. I need you to secure their information and get it ready to be sent to Homeland Security in Washington."

"Important stuff?"

"I don't know for sure, but if we can't come up with reasons to unseal the Ridley files we may in fact be helping terrorists to attack us again. In addition, Jim, while you're on your way to your office, think seriously about this question: who in Springfield might know Mike, Mary, and perhaps Michael, better than John and Sarah Bowman? Don't answer it now. It is important that you give it some serious thought. If you come up with someone, call me on this number when you get to the office.

"I'm going to call my office in DC to make arrangements for the Bowman material to be picked up and flown to DC overnight."

"Omid, the FedEx shipping office is still open. I could take the Bowman material directly to them and have them ship it first thing in the morning. It will be at the front desk of Homeland Security by 8:30 in the morning."

Omid responded, "Give me a minute to think about this. Are you in your car on your way to your office?"

"Yes."

"Stay on the phone. I just need a minute to think about your suggestion." *Williams and Baker have agreed with me that we must have a mole or a spy in our midst. If I call Williams and he in turn calls the Logistics Office, then we risk that the spy knows we're on to something about Mike Ridley, at least. If, on the other hand, we send it FedEx, the only people who will know about how we're getting this material to DC will be Williams, Sheriff Whittles, and myself. The FedEx people won't not know what is in the boxes.*

"Jim, are you still there?"

"Yes."

"Ship them FedEx, but please take the boxes directly to the store, and tell no one."

"Done. By the way, I thought about your question and I think that Martha Ferrell might be a person you should talk to."

"Why her?"

"Martha was…"

CHAPTER 110

Are They Twins?

Hadar wasn't that dirty, but she had been punished twice and her body was aching. She turned the shower on the highest temperature and stood under it, letting the steaming water fall from the top of her head down to her toes. The room was completely institutional white, with four-inch square tiles on the walls. The floor had one-inch tan tiles and the wall fixtures were chrome plated. The panels separating the showers made stalls of a good size with a door and a teak wood bench just outside to dry off when she was done. She didn't have any shampoo or body wash, just army soap. It smelled like pine and the texture was coarse, as if it had some kind of granules embedded in the bar. She lathered her whole body and then got under the showerhead to rinse off. She found herself looking down at her breasts and watched the water cascading off them like a mountain waterfall.

When her stomach started to growl, food became more important than the shower. She stepped out of the stall, took a towel from a stack nearby and began to dry off briskly. She sat for a moment on the teak bench to dry her legs and feet. She wrapped a fresh towel around her and went over to the new duffel bag of clothes that the female MP had purchased for her. She went through her tattered carry-on bag to see if anything could be salvaged but soon discovered everything had been ruined. Hadar opened the new duffel and found panties, socks, shoes, fatigue pants, belt and two T-shirts, no bra--not that she really needed one--but no jacket. Hadar put on everything but the T-shirt. She had two, one black and one white. She put on the white, but it was very revealing. Hadar thought, *This white shirt will be too distracting, and I'm afraid that the men in the room, especially Baker, will spend more time focused on my chest than the work that needs to be done.* Hadar took off the white and put on the black. Neither was going to hide her assets but at least the black shirt didn't call as much attention to them as the white. She would ask somebody for a fatigue jacket but, for now, she was what she was: a soldier with one heck of a body.

Hadar finished dressing and as she was leaving the ladies' room, Baker was coming out the men's room wearing the same pants and black T-shirt. Ted looked at Hadar, "You look better in black than I do."

"I don't think I agree with that," she smiled. "You look pretty good in a tight-fitting black T-shirt yourself."

Baker smiled back. "Not a chance. By the way, I was available to come in and scrub your back but you never called."

With that comment, Hadar reared back as if she really was going to smack him, but she stopped and said, "Maybe someday I'll need my back scrubbed, and you might get the call."

Baker was so shocked he almost fell down.

"Ted, I need something to eat or I will pass out."

"Let's go to the meeting room. They have a table set up with soup and sandwiches. You know, having a guest like you makes a fellow hungry."

"Hungry for what?"

"Later."

The two of them went into the meeting room and Hadar made a beeline for the food, almost knocking Baker down to get to it. Megan observed, "She must be very hungry."

Baker responded, "She's a big, athletic girl and needs a lot of food."

Megan nodded and winked at him. "Yes, she's a very big girl all right."

All three of them got a plate, something to drink and sit down at the table. After a few minutes, Baker looked at his watch; "Mr. Williams will be calling in about fifteen minutes so we need to finish up."

"I'm going back for another sandwich. Want anything while I'm up?"

"Thanks, I'm good," Ted, replied.

Brown observes, "A growing girl."

About fifteen minutes later, the large screen in front of them lit up. On the left was Frank Williams and on the right was Major Omid Rahimi.

Williams spoke, "Are we ready to go?"

Baker responded, "Yes, sir."

"Lt. Hassen, I trust you are well and have recovered from your first day in America?"

"I'm fine, sir."

"I called you here to discuss two things. First, I have a meeting tomorrow morning with Attorney General Clinton to find out why the Ridley files are sealed."

Hadar turned to Baker with a look on her face that said 'who are the Ridley's?'

Baker mouthed back to her, "I'll tell you later."

Williams continued, "Right now, we need to talk about how we can use the information Lt. Hassen has to capture at least Mordecai, if not all of the Brotherhood."

Hadar spoke up, "Sir, all I have is his cell phone number and, at the moment, I have no idea if he is still in the United States. Nor do I have any way of knowing if any of the other members of the Brotherhood are here with him, either."

Williams responded, "I understand, but we may well only have one shot at them and we have to be very careful about how we approach them. If they're still here – and I believe they are – we don't want to spook them."

Hadar thought, *I just got a knot in my stomach thinking about helping capture Mordecai. I agree with Williams, we have to be very careful. However, what is the best approach?*

Omid broke in, "Just so I have my facts straight. Lt. Hassen, are both you and Mordecai Jewish?"

Clearly surprised at the question, Hadar responded, "Why is that important?"

"It's important because I believe, no matter how much he has helped them attack America, that he might give up the others to protect his life and possibly yours."

Hadar responded to the Major, "Are you saying this because you are a Muslim and you don't trust Jews?"

Baker jumped in, "Enough of that, both of you. It doesn't help anyone."

Williams responded, "Ted, in reality, this could be very helpful. If we are successful in locating the Brotherhood through Hadar, I do believe there will be increased tension in the group. Perhaps there is a way to use that tension to our advantage."

CHAPTER 111

Is Brown the Outsider?

Megan Brown had been watching the interchange and was not sure why she was in the room, much less part of the team. Williams and Omid finished the call. Baker asked that the room be cleared and they not be interrupted. As the conversation between Williams and the rest of the team was taking place, Brown thought, *They don't even know I'm in the room. How can I help if they don't even see me? I had such high hopes that I could prove myself and get an opportunity at CIA Special Ops.*

At that moment, there was a knock at the door. Baker got up with an angry look on his face, getting ready to tell whoever was at the door, 'I said I didn't want to be interrupted.' He opened the door and John Seacrest was standing there. His scowl quickly transformed into a broad smile. "Old friend, please come in. I want you to meet some very important people."

They walked towards the two women. Seacrest couldn't help but notice Hadar, but he was more taken with the sleek look of Megan Brown. Baker introduced, "This is Lt. Hadar Hassen of Mossad and this is Megan Brown of Homeland Security."

Seacrest responded, "How is it that I'm so lucky to be working with two of the most beautiful women in the world?"

Both ladies were a little embarrassed by Seacrest's remark. Ted said, "Enough. We have work to do and not a lot of time. We're scheduled to fly to Texas at 9:40 AM tomorrow. We have work and we need some sleep."

John realized that Ted and Hadar are wearing the same outfits, so he asks, "Are you two supposed to be twins? Because if you are, Ted, Hadar is way better looking than you." With that, the ice was broken and everybody laughed.

"Okay, it's time to get to work. John, I'm going to fly with you. We don't want the rest of the attendees to know I'm from Homeland; I'm just one of your assistants. Megan is the official representative of Homeland and speaks for Williams and the department."

Brown was floored, but didn't show it. Nobody told her that in this assignment she would represent Homeland Security. "I'll do my best."

Baker replied, looking her directly in her eyes and says, "I have no doubt that you are ready, and all of us shall help you."

Baker turned to Hadar, "Undoubtedly you've been thinking about the best way to approach Mordecai. So, what do you think?"

Hadar knew this moment would come eventually and she would have to respond. "As far as Mordecai is concerned, I'm an architectural student who, when we met, and was on my way to Texas to study adobe construction. Then I was going to Africa to help people build better housing. The way I left it with him, he also was heading to America and, if I went to Texas, I would call and see if we could get together.

"I have not tried to reach out to him yet. I don't even know if he's in the United States or if he even has his cell phone."

Baker said, "For the moment, let's assume that he is in America, in Texas, and still has his cell phone. What do you think is the best way to reach out to him and not scare him off?"

"I think I need to send him a text message that lets him know I've been thinking of him and I would like to see him if he's around."

Seacrest asked, "Have you thought about the message?"

"About a million times."

John asked, "What would it say?"

"The first time we met I had on a sweater that was buttoned below my chest. The effect was to emphasize my assets."

Baker chimed in, "I could see how that would work."

John sent him a glare. "Go on please, Lieutenant."

"We were able to overhear the conversation in the work room and Mordecai was heard mumbling the word 'buttons' over and over. The last time we met, we kissed and he said, 'imagine what the sex would be like' and I responded, 'I was thinking the very same thing.'

DAN PERKINS

377

"I think the text message should say, 'Mordecai, in Texas and having trouble with my buttons, Hadar.'"

CHAPTER 112

Meeting with AG Clinton

Williams had arranged to meet with AG Clinton to discuss unsealing the Ridley family file. He felt it is very important to find out what was in the Ridley family's past that caused the sealing of their records during the Carter administration. It is unclear to him if President Carter himself requested the sealing or rather a high-ranking bureaucrat in the White House.

Williams had a meeting with Clinton at 10:30 in advance of the president's Chat with the American people. His car was coming at 9 AM, which would give them plenty of time to reach the White House by 10:30. Williams got home late because of his call with Baker and the Texas team. When he looked at his watch, it was well after midnight and Ellen was already in bed. Frank went quietly as he could up the stairs. He was going to change into his PJs, but decided to walk over to the bed to see what Ellen was wearing if anything.

Frank lifted the corner of the sheet and quickly could tell that she was naked. He went in his bathroom and brushed his teeth and walked quietly back to the bedroom and raised the sheet just enough for him to slip into bed and not wake Ellen, at least not right now. Even while asleep, she could always sense when Frank came to bed, and this night was no different. About half an hour later, Ellen rolled over and put her naked body next to Frank's just as she had done so many times before. She put her right hand on Frank's chest and moved all her curves against his body. Frank took his left hand and caressed Ellen's right breast and they both went to sleep.

The next morning, when Frank wanted to get up, Ellen gently pulled him down against her. Frank's response was to grab more of Ellen and squeeze a little more firmly, not to hurt her, but to let her know he would stay for a while longer, even though he would then have to go. When Frank tried to get up a second time, Ellen slowly let him go. She held him long enough to give him a kiss goodbye and she laid down but left her leg uncovered.

Frank dressed, went downstairs for a cup of coffee and then quietly went out the front door to his waiting car. As he was riding to the White House, he was trying to come up with one compelling reason the Ridley file could be unsealed. He had no real clue what was in the file or if the information would be material to connect the Ridley's to the two nuclear bombings in any way. He would simply plead his case to the highest law enforcement official in the United States.

As Williams cleared security, he walked down that same hallway he had used on the way to tell the president about the Brotherhood. This time he went into the president's library. Clinton was already there. The attorney general offered Williams a cup of coffee and asked the others in the room to leave them alone for a while but to notify him when the president and the Congressional leaders were ready to speak.

When the room had emptied, Clinton turned to Williams and asked, "Frank, how can I help you?"

Frank responded, "We're trying to determine if there is a connection between the events in Springfield, Texas, with the Ridley family and the two bombings."

"What makes you think there might be a connection?"

"The Ridleys' son was involved with the making of one of the two bombs used in the attacks."

"How do you know it was the Ridleys' son?"

"We have photographs of him at the work site. We have transcriptions of his conversations with the other members of the Brotherhood while he was rebuilding the bomb. We also have his fingerprints on the bomb map that was in the basement of the Ridley house just before it was blown up. Mr. Attorney General, I believe we have enough evidence to ask the president to break the seal on the Ridley file."

THE BROTHERHOOD OF THE RED NILE

"We'll have to try and meet with him today after his speech. I think you're making an exceptionally circumstantial case, but this is a serious matter. Unsealing a file may give us more information than we need, at least for this moment in time. As someone once said, 'Once you let the genie out of the bottle, you may never get it back in again.'

"Frank, are you willing to take that risk of not being able to deal with what you will have in your hands if we convince the president to open the file?"

Williams responded, "With all due respect, I don't understand your question."

"You don't know what is in the Ridley file and whether any of it will help you or not. But once you open it, the potential for information to be leaked multiplies greatly."

"Sir, we have no way of knowing if Mike and Mary are still alive. We have every indication that Michael and his brother Ishtar are both alive. If Mike and Mary are dead, then anything in the file that would be incriminating to either of them is worthless. Thus, the risk is that we find nothing related to our case, but perhaps incriminating evidence in other matters. Can you reseal the file to prevent anything from leaking that could adversely affect Michael?"

"So, you are proposing limited access to the file. Say that initially you and I and possibly the president jointly look at the file in the Oval Office. If we don't find anything, then the president tells you to reseal the file. If, on the other hand, we find information that helps us understand Mike and Mary and their possible role in the bombings, then we can take whatever action is necessary. That works for me. Let's propose it to the president after his chat."

CHAPTER 113

The Brotherhood Listens

At one o'clock the entire Brotherhood was gathered around the radio in the hotel room, waiting to hear what the president would say to the people. A voice on the radio announced, "The President of the United States."

Jordan informed the people about the pipeline projects and the conversion project to natural gas. He told them about putting millions of Americans back to work with one goal: total energy independence for America.

He announced the cities where the two winners resided who had made the suggestions, but did not give their names, in order to protect their identities. Next, he turned to the Congressional leaders, who spoke about working with the president and the administration to feed the people, while working within the Constitution to implement the procedures that could get America growing again. The leaders reaffirmed the president's wishes to focus on America first. Jordan announced the suspension of all foreign aid and the securing of all national borders. Jordan told the American people that, for now, and until America is on its feet, all the resources America has would be used solely for America.

The president ended his address by saying; "we are facing the greatest challenge in our history. However, I believe the American people are up to the challenge. As long as we do what is best for America, we can never fail. As you go to your houses of worship this weekend, please pray that America will find the determination to succeed and that we shall come out of this horrifying disaster as better people and a better nation."

Sargon along with the rest of the Brotherhood had listened intently to what the president had said to the American people. He asked his brothers. "What did the people hear and what will be the challenges for America? Is there anything we can do to postpone or delay the recovery?"

Each member had a quick reaction, but told Sargon they wanted to think a little more about the challenges before the American government and that they could reconvene later in the day.

Oleg was the first to answer, "I assume that we shall hear more about the two pipeline projects in the coming days. My guess is that it may well take over two years working around the clock to build the pipeline to the storage area. The natural gas pipeline may come faster because it will be smaller and could be mostly above ground. As to the conversion process to natural gas automobiles, this technology already exists and its application will be a matter of ramping up production of the parts and training people to install them on many different types of vehicles. This conversion might happen more quickly if they use compressed and liquefied natural gas.

"The volume of conversions will accelerate over time. My estimation is that, within twelve months of the building of the first facility, a million vehicles a month could be switched over and, in another twenty-four months, the entire new conversion industry will be adapting and supplying natural gas to about two million vehicles a month. This will take a lot of people, perhaps tens of millions of people, to complete these projects."

Cyrus stepped in and said, "I agree with Oleg. This could be one of the largest building projects in the history of the United States, if not the world. By focusing all of its resources on the American economy, the growth in GDP will explode to nearly double-digit growth for a few quarters, but after that growth will settle down to well above trend line. My guess is that GDP will stay in the four to five percent range for several years. If America can become energy independent, then the rest of the world may find itself in a 1930's-era depression, especially the OPEC nations of the Middle East. Many trading partners will find it difficult to trade with the United States because America may well be the lowest cost producer in the world."

Adad thought about what he has just heard and knew that if the OPEC nations crumbled, so would his businesses in these countries. "My business will be destroyed. My children and my wife will have to learn a much different lifestyle because I shall not have the money to support them in the way I have in the past. I need to go home and take advantage of the high price of oil and sell my business and raise as much cash as I can in American dollars."

Sargon raised his hand to interject. "We have talked about how difficult it will be to go back to our home countries. Perhaps we should take the profits that Oleg's uncle is making for us and stay in America. If Oleg and Cyrus are correct, the greatest opportunity is investing in America."

Mordecai chimed in, "We don't have to live in America to invest in America."

Michael and Ishtar agreed with Mordecai. "If we stay here we shall be hunted down. The damage is done, and the president wants the people to move forward. We can leave here, go to a neutral nation and move our money. We can hire bankers to invest in America on our behalf. Adad, you can bring your family to the new country and, with your profits, you can continue sending your children to school in England. The point is that we can, as the Americans say, have our cake and eat it too. If we find a country that does not have extradition to the United States, even better. We can live a wonderful life."

As Sargon listened to all this positive conversation, he thought, *America will grow at the expense of the rest of the world and, while they may not come after us right away, they will pursue us, and all the money in the banks or lack of an extradition treaty will not stop them. Enjoy your fantasy while you can, my friends.*

CHAPTER 114

I Can't Sleep and I'm Hungry

The four agents stayed up for a while after the call with Williams and Rahimi. Knowing they had to get up early in the morning, Baker advised, "Enough conversation. We need to get to bed."

Hadar jumped in, "Alone."

Baker responded, "Alone." Nevertheless, he walked over to Hadar and stuck out his shoulder and said, "Hit me now for what I'm about to say."

Hadar looked at him and could only imagine what he was going to say, so she hit him with a glancing blow.

Baker winced, looked her in the eyes, and said, "Need any help getting ready for bed? That shirt looks like it must have shrunk through the evening."

She grinned. "You wish, but not tonight, bud." She got ready to punch him again; he stiffened up as she approached. While it looked as If she was going to smack him, she simply planted a kiss on his cheek and said good night.

Baker smiled and thought, *She's beginning to like me.*

Ted told the women, "You will have a guard at your doors all night long. Sleep well."

The sleeping accommodations were right next to each other, and they could hear each other getting ready for bed. Megan left her watch on and saw it was 1 AM. She looked at Hadar, who had changed into the white T-shirt, and that was all. "Is that all you're wearing to bed?"

"If I were home, I wouldn't be wearing the T-shirt."

Megan was a little shocked but decided to try the same white T-shirt. It looked a lot different on her than on Hadar. They both lay down on their cots and tried going to sleep. They could hear each other thrashing in their beds trying to get comfortable. At two thirty, Megan asked Hadar, "Are you asleep?"

"No, and I'm hungry."

"You're constantly eating and yet you don't seem to put on any weight. How do you do that?"

"I don't know. It just happens. I must have a very efficient metabolism."

"Lucky you." Megan wanted to talk to Hadar about her work in Special Ops. "If I perform well in this assignment, Under Secretary Williams has promised to sponsor me at CIA. So, what is it like to be in your line of work?"

"Well, to be honest with you, most of the time we do nothing but train. The most dangerous thing I have done in a long time was to get one of the terrorists to notice me."

"From what I can see, that wasn't very hard to do."

"That's the problem for me, and I will guess it'll be the same for you if you get into Special Ops."

"What is the problem?"

"People look at our bodies and think we don't have a brain. When I was in Syria, I was told to use my assets to get the attention of one of the terrorists and then plant a GPS on him. I moved in close and brushed my chest against his to distract him from what I was doing. I'm not saying I did anything wrong, and I don't want to sound stupid, but I know that I'm more than just a great rack."

"So how have you dealt with the challenge of your assets vs. your brain?"

"I've used my assets to get more and more difficult assignments, and I've been proving to my commanders that I can do more than look great.

"When I first saw you tonight, I knew you were also brains and body. Yours is different from mine, but still you are very attractive and, as a result, distracting to the male leadership and sometime threatening to the female leadership in your government. When you understand that, you can use all of your assets in difficult situations to achieve a goal. You'll become a more powerful person in the process."

Megan spoke casually. "I understand that you have an idea how to reach out to Mordecai using those assets that attracted him to you in Syria. But are you conflicted in that you may have feelings for him that could cause you a lapse in judgment?"

That was the question I was expecting earlier and I expected it from Ted, not her. How do I respond without showing the conflict in me, or should I tell her of my conflict? Hadar took a deep breath. "That question has haunted me from the time of my first phone call with Homeland Security. I reviewed the pictures of the destruction in Texas City and Port Fourchon on the plane coming to America. I was trying to convince myself that Mordecai couldn't be responsible for this massive loss of life and destruction of property."

"Have you resolved your conflict?"

"Not really. You see. I still think of him in the town square as somebody on vacation looking to hook up with me, not as a bomb builder. We never had the time to hook up, but at the time there was something special and so part of me wants to find out if there is really anything there or was it just being in the wrong place at the wrong time."

"Do I hear you correctly? This person is directly responsible for the death of at least sixty thousand Americans and you have to find out if you really love him? That's insane. You couldn't love a mass murderer."

"I'm sure somebody loved Hitler."

CHAPTER 115

Can the Seal be Broken?

The president had finished his 'chat' and the White House switchboard was lit up like a Christmas tree. The White House web site was on the verge of crashing, but all of this traffic was overwhelmingly favorable. The president and all the Congressional leaders were pleased with the positive reaction, with one exception. Wild was not showing it, but he was upset that the initial reaction was so favorable. *I know the messenger of the good news is always received well; as they said about other presidents who delivered good news, the initial ratings go up. However, Americans are impatient and two years before we can complete the southern pipeline it will get old quickly. I'll let the president dig his own hole and then I'll show the American people we need a change to complete the dream and that I'm your guy. Some campaign slogan,* he mused: '*We need a change to complete the dream*'.

The president shook hands with the Congressional leaders and other staff. The first lady was not in the room but met her husband outside the Oval Office to congratulate him on his speech. She especially liked how the Congressional leaders supported what he was trying to do. Karen leaned over and whispered in his ear, "You better keep your eye on Senator Wild. Rumor has it that he wants your job."

"I'm aware of the rumor. That's why he's here today. We have a great deal to do and the beginning of the campaign is just six months away." Jordan looks for his EA.

"Mary, what's next on my agenda?"

"Sir, you have a meeting with Attorney General Clinton and Under Secretary Williams in the small conference room."

"Are they here?"

"Yes, sir."

"Please tell them I'll be right in."

A few moments later, the president walked through the door of his small conference room and Clinton and Williams both stood. "Please gentlemen, sit down. Frank, I understand that you want me to unseal a set of records that were sealed in the Carter Administration?"

"Yes, sir, that is correct."

"Mr. Attorney General, to the best of your knowledge, has a presidential seal of records ever been broken by a subsequent president?"

"Sir, I would need to do more research on this question, but my initial reaction would be 'No.'"

"Mr. Clinton, in your opinion, is there any valid reasons to break a presidential sealing of a record?"

"Mr. President, I can think of a couple but I might be on shaky ground."

"Tell me anyway."

"If there is a possibility that the seal is hiding acts of treason, for one."

"Any others?"

"Sir, the second reason is somewhat broad and open to many interpretations."

"Well, I don't have all day, so give me your other reason."

"Mr. President, if a person was acting as or with terrorists to damage or attempt to bring grave harm to the United States and there was reasonable suspicion that the file was hiding incriminating information, the seal could be broken."

"Frank, are you saying that the Ridleys were terrorists and had some kind of immunity from President Carter?"

"Mr. President, we have a great deal of circumstantial evidence which suggests that at least the father and husband, Mike Ridley, may have been a terrorist or involved in terrorist activity. We're hopeful that the act of unsealing the file will give us insight into what he was doing, or did, so that the U.S. Government sealed in his file. We think it's possible that Mike Ridley was doing something and, I stress, we don't know for sure, that his cooperation with our government got him a deal that sealed his record."

"Mr. Attorney General, what happens if we unseal the record, review it and, should we not find anything, simply reseal file and put it back in the vault?"

"Sir, I don't think it's that simple."

"Why not?"

"When a record is sealed nobody – no court, nobody – can or is supposed to see what is in the file. So if you open it, then the confidentiality of the file may be broken and anybody, if they find out that the seal has been broken, could ask to see the contents."

"Frank, you have every reason to believe that the contents of the file may uncover information that, at the time it was sealed, would not be construed as evidence for either of these possibilities. On the other hand, the attorney general has suggested you believe the file needs to be opened since it may have information that is pertinent to the attacks on America.

"Mr. Attorney General, let me plead ignorance. I have never seen a sealed file. Does it have a physical seal on it and, if so, what kind of seal? Can it be resealed without anybody noticing?"

"Mr. President, depending on the volume under seal, the seal is usually a red tape around the file, with a signature and a date on the tape where it crosses over itself."

"So if we open it and reseal it, would people know had been opened?"

"Yes sir, but…"

"I think I like the 'but' coming."

"I'm not saying that we are asking you to do this, Mr. President, but I believe there is one exception."

"And that is, Mr. Attorney General?"

"If the president himself reseals the file and uses the presidential seal to protect the evidence."

"Frank, you may remember in your first briefing I said I was elected to protect the American people against a terrorist attack. I have not done well, but I shall continue to do everything in my power to prevent any further attacks. I shall leave no stone unturned to protect the American people. So, Mr. Attorney General, get me that file and I shall bust the seal to save America."

CHAPTER 116

I Can't Believe I Said That

Hadar had just told Megan that 'I'm sure somebody loved Hitler.'

In shock, she looked at Megan, as tears well up in her eyes. "I can't believe I said that about the man who was responsible for killing millions of my people. It's probably true that somebody loved him, but why did that come out of my mouth?"

Megan got up from her cot, walked over to Hadar's and sat down beside her. Megan wanted to put her arm around her to comfort her, but didn't want to send the wrong message. *In the span of eight hours this woman has been kidnapped, gassed, crashed into, taken on a high-speed car chase through DC, and had a car explode around her. She needs to be held at least for a while.*

Megan put her arm around Hadar's shoulder and pulled her into her body to comfort her. In a few moments, Hadar straightened up and looked Megan in the eyes. "Thank you for that. I guess all the events of the day came rushing in on me all at the same time. I want to be strong, and I know that I come across as self-confident but, between you and me, I'm scared."

"Me too."

"You too? I'm glad I'm not alone and we're together."

"We have to cover each other's back. If we do, we can get through this challenge safe and sound."

Megan spoke quietly. "Let's spend a little time, before we try to get some sleep, discussing the plan for the meeting starting in a few hours. We know you hold the potential key, but only if he has his cell phone with him, it's turned on, and he is allowed to answer it when you reach out to him."

Hadar agreed. "Sounds like a lot of things could go wrong. So how can we put the odds in our favor?"

"Let's assume that everybody, and I mean everybody else, wants to round up and arrest as many of the members of the Brotherhood as quickly as possible." Megan sat forward. "It's possible that their exuberance could get in the way and we may not get all the key players. If that happens, we will have lost a great opportunity."

"I agree. We have to make sure we dot every 'i' and cross every 't' to get all of them. Megan, how do we do that?"

"I think less is more," she replied.

"What do you mean?" Hadar leaned forward as well.

"When we fly to Texas and meet in that hangar, we make it clear to all present that this is a Homeland Security operation. I'm going to be introduced as Frank Williams' personal representative. I shall do my best to take charge and tell people what we are going to do and what resources we need.

"Hadar, if we are going to capture all of the Brotherhood and their resources, we need to let them be comfortable that we're not on their trail. The more people involved, the greater a chance for a leak. We already know that we have either a spy or a mole in Homeland Security. Ted and Mr. Williams believe that the problem is in the Logistics Office. We need to exploit this awareness and see if we can flush out the spy, while at the same time accomplishing our mission to get all of them 'lock, stock and barrel'."

Megan continued, "It will be critical not to scare Mordecai off with your first contact. I think you should forget about the button message. He needs to think you're concerned about him. I think a text message is the right approach, but the message has to convey concern without giving away where you are. We will address that if we get a response."

"Megan, Mordecai knows that I was headed to Texas, but he is not sure of anything. Keep in mind that if his feelings are as strong as you think they may be, he'll want to find out if I was affected by the bombs."

"So let's get back to the message. Let's assume that Mordecai has the phone and that it is off for the moment. We don't know how long it will be before he turns it on. Then he will see he has a text message, but he can't be sure from whom. If we send the right message, it will eat at him until he

THE BROTHERHOOD OF THE RED NILE

finds an opportunity when he can be alone to open it. This is all the more reason that a small operation is best."

Hadar nodded. "I agree. When we get to the meeting, we can ask Omid to help us find a place to live for a while that is far away from where we think they are so we will have no chance of running into them on the street. If the intelligence suggests they're in Houston, we need to get a map and find a place at least twenty-five miles away."

"Even better, let's ask John if the CIA has a safe house near Houston that we can use," Megan said. "If they don't, then we go back to Omid and see what he can do for us."

"Sounds good. If we're going to keep the team small, who else can or should be on it?"

"I think Major Rahimi for one. It's always good to have a seasoned Marine around. That leaves Baker and Seacrest. Baker has the hots for you and you are encouraging him. Can he be trusted to keep his mind on the challenge and his hands off of you, or is attraction just too powerful?"

Hadar smiled but it quickly faded. "Let me think about Baker for a moment. What about Seacrest?"

"John knows a great deal about the people of the Brotherhood. He's an analyst, whereas Ted is a senior assistant to Frank Williams. I think it will be hard for Williams to give him up for an unknown amount of time."

"I agree. We can use Ted as our liaison to Williams and to the resources of Homeland. I think it's better that I tell both men of our decision first thing in the morning."

"I agree. Ted will be disappointed, but he can come and visit periodically and then I'll find out if there is anything between us." Hadar touched Megan on the arm. "Can we have a little fun with the guys in the morning?"

"What do you have in mind?" Megan looked puzzled.

"Let's go to the BX first thing tomorrow morning and get a couple of snug fitting flight jackets with the full zipper down the front and play with the zipper up and down."

"And what will we have on under the jackets?

"How about nothing?" Hadar grinned.

"No, but I will settle for these white see through T-shirts."

"Do I have to, Megan?"

DAN PERKINS

"Yes." Megan smiled.

"Now, one last thing and it's the most important: what should the text message say?"

"Hadar, how about …"

CHAPTER 117

The Brotherhood is Rethinking their Travel Options

The Brotherhood was assembled in Sargon's room. They had some time to think about what they wanted to do. Sargon turned to Ishtar and asked, "If we wanted to leave the United States, how difficult would it be?"

"As you know, we came in through the back door via the Gulf of Mexico. With all the rigs shut down – at least until they fix that pipeline – that avenue is not in play for us."

Adad asked, "What other options do we have to escape?"

"I would guess that all the borders are under close scrutiny, especially for people who look like the three of you. Michael, Oleg, and I have a better chance of getting out because of the way we look. However, let's suppose that you could get out. Where would you go?"

Cyrus responded, "We had talked about going to a Caribbean island that doesn't have an extradition treaty with the United States and then have our money sent to us there so we could live a great life."

Ishtar continued, "One of the things we didn't count on was the possibility of a number of Americans just leaving with nothing but their bank accounts, so now some of our options for places to go will be closed because of the influx of Americans."

Michael spoke up. "We have a significant amount of cash on hand. Why don't we all just stay here until things cool down? Americans have short memories. With the building projects getting under way soon they will be distracted from getting even."

Sargon asked, "How long do you think we shall have to stay here? Should we consider moving to a different location?"

Ishtar responded, "If we move, we must go out into the open and that may call attention to ourselves. I think we should move, but no more than two at a time. I just don't have an answer to your other question. As I see it, Oleg could go back to Russia, and Michael and I could stay here because we look American. As for the rest of you, my guess is going home is not an option; at least not for many months if not years."

Adad cried out, "Did you say years?"

"Yes."

"Why?"

Ishtar continued. "American intelligence probably has pictures of all of you and maybe even of Michael and me. So they have figured out where you're from and they will, if they don't already, have informants on the ground being offered serious money if you appear. So, to go back home is a death sentence for at least Mordecai, Sargon, Adad and perhaps for Cyrus and Oleg. Serious amounts of money can tempt people to turn in their best friend, even their brother.

"There is another factor that may come into play, and that is the presidential election. Perhaps if America changes its president, and I mean perhaps, the new president would want to focus resources in a different direction. Remember, America had a twenty-five million dollar reward on bin Laden and it took ten years to find him. When they did find him, it was over quickly. The quest for bin Laden diminished over time in the public eye but not in the eyes or brains of the staff in all security agencies. They went after him and his leadership and they will come after us, no matter how long it takes. I think Michael and I need to go out for a few hours and look for a couple of places for us to live. Getting out of here on a regular basis will keep the hotel manager from becoming suspicious as to why nobody leaves the rooms.

"While Michael and I are gone, I would like to know when we get back how much cash we have on hand. If we need more, Oleg, you will need to contact your uncle and figure out how to get cash to us out of our profits. My guess is through the closest Russian Embassy or consulate, but he may have a better idea. Now I'm going to suggest something to think about and we can talk about it upon my return. How to you feel about trying to find a job on the pipeline project? Don't answer yet, just think about it, and we can talk in a few hours. We don't have to come to a conclusion today."

Sargon listened to the conversation, concerned that Ishtar was slowly taking control of the Brotherhood from him. Sargon didn't know, at least for the moment, how he felt about that. He would ponder the matter. Sargon held most of the money in the safe in his bedroom. Nonetheless, when Ishtar asked Sargon for a thousand dollars in fifties and twenties, just in case they found a place, Sargon thought the request strange, since he knew Ishtar had to have half a million in a duffel bag in his room. But he said, "Come with me and I'll get you your money."

The two of them walked down the hallway to Sargon's room. He opened the door and let Ishtar into the room, Ishtar walked in and closed the door after Sargon entered. Sargon opened the safe and took out the money Ishtar wanted. When he stood and turned to give it to Ishtar, Ishtar said to him, "Adad has to go."

"What do you mean go?"

"I mean that Adad is a hazard to our lives. He is the only one with a wife and children. The longer he's in captivity, the greater the danger he poses to all of us. His desire to get back to his wife and children may well create an opportunity for him to turn us in and get immunity. So, he has to go and go quickly."

"Do you mean that he has to leave, and we don't tell him of the new hiding places when we get them?"

"No, he has to die," Ishtar said quietly.

"You mean we kill him? One of us will have to kill Adad? Who has the courage to do this awful thing?"

"Whoever does it, the others must never know. Adad has to go out and never return."

"Which one of us has the courage? I don't." Sargon told Ishtar.

Ishtar responded, "I do."

CHAPTER 118

Almost Time to Go

Hadar and Megan went to the Andrews BX and found the zipper-front flight jackets and other items they needed for their trip, and then returned to change. Megan felt very uncomfortable wearing the see-through T-shirt and no bra under her flight jacket. When she turned and faced Hadar to get her approval Hadar said, "The zipper is not supposed to be up around your neck. Bring it down half way. You will not fall out of the jacket with the T-shirt on."

Megan said to Hadar, "Let me see how it looks on you. Whoa! You're not wearing the T-shirt. We expressly agreed that we would both wear the T-shirt. Your zipper is down too far. You could fall out of the jacket."

"Don't worry, I will not fall out no matter how low the zipper goes down."

"I understand what you're trying to do, but please raise the zipper at least half way. *Please.*"

Hadar laughed, "Okay, just for you, but I want to see you in that jacket without the T-shirt. You will be smoking hot."

"Enough about zippers and T-shirts." Megan was all business. "Let's get to the meeting room and the others."

As the two of them walked into the meeting room, Baker and Seacrest had their backs to them.

"Good morning, gentlemen."

The two men turned around and looked at the two women, especially Megan. "Those jackets look great on you." Ted walked over to Hadar, stuck out his shoulder and said, "Hit me now."

"I want to hear what you have to say first."

"I was just going to ask if you need to lower that zipper so you can take in deep breaths to make sure there was no lung damage."

"Yeah, and I bet you want to hear if my lungs are clear."

"I hadn't thought about that, but now that you mention it, that's not a bad idea."

Smack.

Megan interrupted the two of them and said, "We all need to talk about the meeting at Draughon-Miller later today. I have been thinking it over and if we go in guns blasting to capture the Brotherhood, we may well scare them away. I think we need a smaller team of four people: Hadar and Omid, John Seacrest and myself."

"Wait a minute!" Ted interrupted. "Williams put me in charge of this task force. I need to be in Houston."

Megan replied, "It may take many months to find and capture the Brotherhood. While the rest of us are grunts, you report directly to Williams. Surely he will need you in DC for other matters. You can come periodically for on-site updates and get your shots to the shoulders."

"Funny," Ted said.

"However, we all agree that you are too important to sit in a hotel room staring at…"

"Don't go there," Hadar said to Megan.

"As much as I want to disagree, you're right. I'll stay back. Megan, this puts a great deal of pressure on you; are you ready to handle it?"

Megan looked at Hadar, reached up and slides her zipper to half way and said, "I'm ready."

Hadar high fived her, "You go, girl! You are ready, willing and *very* able."

With that settled they jumped into the car that would take them to their plane and off to central Texas.

"John, we're going to need a safe place to stay when we get there," Megan spoke over the back seat. "Can you check with your operations center to find us a safe house in Houston, perhaps for several months?"

DAN PERKINS

Seacrest looked at Baker for approval. Baker nodded. Brown was aware of the potential spy at Homeland Logistics and Baker was pleased that she avoided using that office for the present.

"Driver, stop the car for a moment," Ted tapped his shoulder. "You'll have to step out. What I'm about to say is on a need to know only basis."

"Sir, your plane …"

"That plane takes off when Ms. Brown says it takes off. Is that understood?"

"Yes, sir."

"Let me be clear to all of you. Frank Williams picked Megan Brown as the leader of the mission. He and I have the upmost confidence in her talent and ability. I'm getting out here. Have a safe flight. Megan, call me when you get airborne and I'll give you the details of your contacts at the meeting site. I expect reports on a frequent basis. Is that understood?"

"Yes, sir, and thank you."

"I'll see you in a couple of weeks."

The driver got back into the car and drove them directly to their plane. They boarded and sat at a special configuration onboard the Gulfstream. There were two seats on each side of the table, sides of which folded in during takeoff and landing. Once they were strapped in, the pilot said over the speaker, "We have about twenty-five minutes till takeoff, Ms. Brown."

Megan held back a smug smile. *What a sound! 'We are twenty-five minutes till takeoff, Ms. Brown.' This is more than I hoped for. A smart Special Ops with a personality that, so far, is fun to be with; a brilliant CIA analyst who knows more about the Brotherhood than anybody in the world; and a Marine Major covering my back. What a great team!*

"Hadar and I have been thinking about her first contact with Mordecai. We think it should be a text message and show concern, compassion and interest in him."

Seacrest asked, "What would the text say?"

"Are you safe? H."

CHAPTER 119

Looking For A New Home

Sargon was shocked by Ishtar's notion that Adad had to die to protect the rest of them. The idea that one of them would turn on the rest had never crossed his mind. They had come through so much together. They knew that they were taking a risk, with a reasonable possibility that they all would eventually be hunted down and killed. But to kill one of their own? How could this happen?

It took Sargon a long time to compose himself and come back to the living room where the rest of the team sat and waited for some direction from him. "Ishtar wants us to get some idea of how much cash we have on hand before he returns. I just counted the money in my portable safe and I have about two hundred thousand."

Before they left Syria, Oleg borrowed money from his uncle in advance of projected oil futures trading profits. The money was split five ways and each was given three hundred thousand, so the total pot was US$1.5 million. Sargon had used his money to pay for everything they needed so far. The other four still had their original three hundred thousand each. In total, they had $1.4 million. What the group didn't know was how much Michael and Ishtar had. Sargon knew that Ishtar had over half a million, but he had no idea how much Michael had with him.

Oleg raised the question. "Will we have to share what we have with Ishtar and Michael?"

"I don't know the answer because I don't know how much money the two of them have between them. I do believe that whatever future profits we make in the oil trading with your uncle will have to include an equal share to the two of them." All agreed that the split among all of them was fair.

Adad asked Sargon, "How long do you think it will be before I can call my wife and children?"

"I have no idea, but if we call anybody there is the possibility of the call being traced," Sargon warned. "I'm not sure that is true of all phones, but international cell phones that use different networks are very difficult to trace. The phone I have is a global cell. I won't say it's untraceable but very close. Adad, when things settle down, I will let you use my phone to call home. If the call is short it makes it even more difficult to trace, so you will have to make it short."

Adad nodded. "I shall ask Ishtar when he returns if there's a way though his connections that I can get a message to my wife that I am alive and safe."

Ishtar and Michael walked the streets to see if they could find a couple of furnished apartments to rent. They noticed that there were not many people on the street and most of the small shops were closed. They spotted an open deli so they walked in to see what they could buy. All the bread and milk were gone, but they saw cold cuts in the case, crackers, blocks of various cheeses, and some soda--strangely, there was no beer. Both of them got small shopping baskets and went through the store, surprised at how much else was still on the shelves.

They took their baskets up to the counter to check out and saw a hand written sign 'cash only, nothing bigger than $20 and change only if they have it.' Ishtar emptied his basket, "We were on the outer belt and got off for gas. We couldn't find any so we ran out. Do you know where we can buy some?"

The owner paused and then offered, "I have a reserve tank. I could sell you a couple of gallons but that's about it. I don't have much."

Michael responded, "A couple of gallons won't get us very far. Do you know of an apartment for rent? We've knocked on a bunch of doors but nobody answers."

"The problem is that a lot of people have already headed north to get away from the trapped contaminated energy in the pipeline under your feet."

At that, Ishtar jumped.

THE BROTHERHOOD OF THE RED NILE

The owner chuckled. "You don't have to worry. The pipeline under you is about three hundred feet below. That radiation can't make it up through all the earth and concrete."

"If that's true, why did so many people leave?"

"If you ask me, I think they were just plain afraid of what was down there and they panicked, packed their cars and left." He pointed, "See that building across the street? Number 101?"

The two men nodded.

"Almost all of it's empty. You could go over there and pick any unit you want and you'll probably find the key in the door or on the kitchen counter. Nobody is going to bother you. Check it out."

"Thanks, I think we will."

Ishtar and Michael walked across the street. The front door was unlocked. Nobody was at the front desk. The lights were on in the lobby and they had a decision to make. What floor should they start on? Ishtar looked at Michael. "If we're on the top floor we may well have a great view of the skyline and we would be very secure."

Michael looked at Ishtar and said, "If the power is out then we have a long walk down but a much harder walk up. I'm not sure our friends can make the climb."

"Good point. How about halfway as a compromise?" Ishtar suggested.

"I can live with that. Should we be all on one floor or two different floors?"

"I'll wait and see till we get to the seventeenth floor. Let's start there and see what we can find. Then we can go to the top and search for food as we work our way down. If the units are next to each other, we could secure three units and store all the food we can collect in the middle unit. We can break a hole in the wall from each side for access to the pantry."

"Great idea! Let's take a ride to seventeen and see what's there."

Ishtar pushed the button for the elevator and, when they had stepped in, he turned to Michael, "We have one other thing to talk about."

CHAPTER 120

Draughon-Miller Airport

Major Omid Rahimi had already arrived at the airfield and was checking on security. Baker had given him the contact information for the Special Ops team that was within five miles of the airfield and had made contact with the team leader, who then cleared Omid. The unit commander was Captain William Rogers and he told Omid he had a team of twelve men and a Blackhawk within three minutes of the airfield.

Ground security was provided by the Texas National Guard, which had been activated to help enforce martial law and the dusk to dawn curfew. That local commander was Major Robert Silversmith, and he informed Omid that he had about three hundred men with two Blackhawks and that they had already swept the hangar and cleared it of non-essential personnel. Silversmith further indicated that he had seventy-five men in the hangar, seventy-five surrounding the building, and one hundred and fifty more that were at the ready. Major Silversmith assured Omid that he would rotate personnel to keep fresh troops on guard twenty-four hours a day.

Omid instructed the Major, "I'm expecting three aircraft. One from Homeland Security will include Homeland Security, CIA and a guest from Israel. A second plane is from the Secret Service, and a third is transporting a team from the FBI and Pentagon Internal Security. The head count will be between twelve and fifteen persons, including myself. We have taken over the meeting room in the hangar. We will gather there and take our meals in the same room. If we have to spend the night, all will sleep on their planes. I have arranged with the airport authority to provide three meals a day for three days. If the session goes any longer, we'll have to locate more food. Major, how are your men being fed?"

"We have our own mess facility and food will be delivered as needed. Our mess facility will be set up about three hundred yards behind the hangar."

As the two majors finished their conversation, the first plane arrived and was directed to shut down its engines before being towed into the hangar. Shortly after the first plane arrived, the second and third also landed. All the visitors deplaned, waited for all the planes to be towed in, and then walked to the meeting room.

"I am Major Omid Rahimi of Homeland Security. On behalf of Under Secretary for Terrorist Activity Frank Williams, I welcome you." Next, Omid introduced Megan Brown as the personal representative of Mr. Williams and the chair of the meeting.

"Thank you, Major. I would like to introduce you all to an important guest, but before I do that I think we should go into the secure meeting room." Megan and Hadar were the only women in the meeting, and Megan became very uncomfortable with the way she and Hadar were dressed. *I shall have to keep Hadar on a short leash and keep the meeting focused on the mission and not Hadar's assets.*

As Megan and Omid walked through the door into the meeting room, she asked, "Are the drones operational?"

"Yes ma'am, as of about twenty minutes ago."

"Excellent. When we get in the room, I'm probably going to make some people very unhappy but I have no choice."

"What are you going to do, ma'am?"

"Just trust me." Megan walked in and asked everybody to kindly sit at the table so she could get the meeting under way. She walked over and closed the door. As she walked back to the table, she said, "Please take out your phones, turn them off and set them in front of you. If you have brought laptops, please close their Internet connections. I'll wait."

One of the attendees stood, "Ms. Brown, I need to be in touch with my office at all times. I can't turn off my phone or computer."

Hadar listened to the revolt and wondered how Megan will handle it. *Will she reach for the zipper or will she take a different approach?*

Megan looked at the men around the table. "Let me be perfectly clear. Each of you, as myself, was selected because your superiors thought you had something to offer. They were told you might be out of contact for several days, but that the discussion was so important we did not want to risk a leak, and they agreed. Therefore, I shall ask you one more time. Either you shut down all outside communication devices or I shall ask Major Rahimi to smash all of them. Any questions?"

Hadar tried to keep from grinning. *You go, girl! Kick some butt! Baker would be proud.*

A few minutes later, all the cell phones, at least the ones that were visible, were in front of their owners, along with their laptops. All were turned off.

"Thank you very much. Let's take a moment, go around the room and have each of you to tell us your name, where you work and, if possible, a little about what you do." Hadar was to Megan's right so she started on her left to ensure that Hadar would be last.

All followed the procedure and Megan realized there were some very smart people in the room. She was a little concerned about her being up to the task intellectually, but she could do nothing about it now.

"You're probably wondering why this young lady is last. She is a very important part of why we're here today. She personally knows one of the members of the Brotherhood of the Red Nile."

Megan heard someone say, "The terrorists who bombed our country?"

"Yes, and she has the phone number of that terrorist on her phone."

"Why doesn't she just pick up the phone and call him and suggest a meeting place? We'll follow her and pick him up."

Megan shook her head. "We want to arrest them all and we want to find the source of their funding." Megan paused until she had everyone's full attention. "This mission — and let me say it one more time just to make sure you all understand — this mission is not to capture one, but to take all of them and the source of their money. Any questions about this?"

While Brown was talking, Omid got a text message from the drone controller. It was picking up a low power voice signal from within the room. Omid responded, 'What do you mean?'

The message came back, 'Somebody in the room has a microphone transmitting device.'

Omid replied, 'Can you identify what position is transmitting?'

'Not yet, but we'll be better able to tell on our next pass in about twenty-two minutes.'

Omid decided, for the moment, not to tell Megan her meeting was bugged.

CHAPTER 121

Break the Seal

The president had told the attorney general that he would be the best person to open the file with Williams present. His only request was that he be told if any information was found in the file that was pertinent to the Brotherhood and the bombings. Clinton and Williams agreed that they would meet the 10:30 the next day, Sunday, in Clinton's office at the Justice Department. If Clinton had difficulty retrieving the file, he would call Williams and reschedule.

Williams decided to go home and spend the rest of the day with Ellen, and hopefully the night. "I need to stop by the office first and, if things are quiet enough, I'll head home. I'll let you know when I'm leaving."

It was a beautiful Saturday afternoon and the weather was gorgeous. Not many people were on the street. Frank decided to walk and called his driver. "I'm walking back to the office. You go ahead, and I'll call you when I'm ready to go home."

Williams enjoyed the twenty-five minute walk. He took the time to clear his mind and simply enjoy his beautiful city of Washington DC. As he approached the Homeland Security Building, he almost dreaded going in for he didn't know what awaited him. But he reminded himself of his promise to Ellen to do everything in his power to protect her and the country. Frank took in one more deep breath of the crisp clean air and pushed his way through the revolving doors.

The security guard greeted him, "Good afternoon, Mr. Williams."

"Good afternoon, Malcolm."

"Will you be in your office for long, Mr. Williams?"

"Just for a while, then home to Mrs. Williams."

"Haven't see much of her, have you, sir?"

"No, not much."

Frank walked over to the elevator and pushed the button for the sixteenth floor. The door closed and, with no stops, quickly arrived at sixteen and the doors opened. An idea came to him just as he was ready to step out of the elevator. He was going to do something he had always wanted to try. Just as he stepped through the door, he pushed all the buttons like a little kid. When the door closed Frank grins, *One more thing off my bucket list.*

All the offices were empty as Williams walked down the hallway. Most of the lights were off, so the length of the hallway was exaggerated and seemed to go on to infinity. As he approached the end of the hallway, he turned the corner that led to his office, he was startled to see Marie. "What are you doing here?"

"I knew you had a meeting at the White House and figured you might come back to do some follow up. It has been your second home the past few weeks. I came in and waited to see if you might need my help. I was going to wait till three o'clock and, if you didn't arrive by then, I would go home."

Frank smiled. "Thank you for being so considerate."

"Oh yes, I almost forgot, a FedEx package arrived today from the sheriff in Springfield, Texas. I put it next to the table in the conference room."

"What's in it?"

"I didn't open it. It's marked 'Private and Confidential – To Be Opened by Addressee Only'."

"The Major is at the meetings at Draughon–Miller. Could you see if you can get him on his cell phone?"

"I'll try right away."

Marie looked up Major Rahimi's cell number and called. She reported back, "Sir, I got the Major's voice mail and left a message for him to call back as soon as possible."

"Thank you, Marie. I'm going to open the package. Feel free to leave. I'll be fine. See you Monday morning."

"I'll just wait a few minutes to see if the Major returns the call."

"That's fine, but not past three o'clock, agreed?"

DAN PERKINS

"Agreed, sir."

Williams lifted the box onto the table and saw that it had been sealed with several layers of tape. Frank wondered if the Ridley file would be sealed with as much tape. He had never seen a sealed file, so he had no idea what to expect. He got the scissors from his desk to cut through the tape. After struggling for a few moments, he finally got the box open. Out popped the packing material. "I hate these foam peanuts," he muttered.

He got through the filler and pulled out a couple of aging school year-books. He sat down and began to leaf through the pages of one of them. There were no markings, no signatures, greetings or predictions; just the book as it was published. Frank took all the books out and then laid them on top of the table from left to right, starting with the oldest and moving to the newest.

The phone rang and Frank looked at his watch. It's 3:30. Marie was gone, so he picked up the phone and answered, "Williams here."

Surprised by the fact that Williams answered the phone himself, Omid was a little startled. "Sorry, sir! I didn't expect you to answer the phone."

"Major, I received a box of school yearbooks from Springfield sent via FedEx. Do you know anything about this?"

"Yes, sir. The yearbooks are from the next-door neighbor of the Ridgley's. Their son went to school with Michael Ridley. Sheriff Whittles sent them on my behalf. These yearbooks cover the period of time that Michael Ridley was in the Springfield school system – from second through twelfth grade."

"Why is that important?"

"Sir, do you have them out?"

"Yes."

"Please pick up the second grade book. Notice how it's laid out?"

"I'm sorry, Major. I don't see what you're talking about."

"Sir, on the first set of pages is a calendar for the time the school was in session. Look at the calendar for the month of September and then look at the photographs of parents and students at some activity."

"Okay, what am I looking at?"

"At the beginning of the month we see pictures with Mike and Mary Ridley in them. However, if you look at the end-of-the-month activities, you only see Mary. Now go to October and you will find pictures of Mike in the beginning of the month but not at the end.

"If you go through the whole second grade yearbook you will see this pattern. The same is true through the higher grades. Now, add to this the fact that Mike Ridley didn't have a job or reportable income other than interest at the bank. Sheriff Whittles gave me the name of the babysitter, but she has not yet returned my calls. I did speak to Bowman and he recalls seeing Ridley being picked up on a Tuesday morning and being returned Thursday night.

"The books confirm a regular pattern of Mike Ridley being gone for several days a month. So, we have a man who is out of town on a regular basis, travels by chauffeured limo, and yet has no reportable source of income. So, Mr. Williams, who does Ridley work for?"

"I have a meeting tomorrow with Clinton. Perhaps the Ridley file will tell us who he is. Major, who do you think?"

"Sir, I have two guesses. He either works for the mob or he works for …"

CHAPTER 122

Adad Must Go

Ishtar and Michael had been exploring the building a floor at a time looking for a place to move into from the hotel. They started at the penthouse and saw nobody in any of the condos, but they had found completely stocked pantries in many of the units. They worked their way to the 17th floor. The 17th floor had six units that wrapped around the floor on three sides with the elevator bank on the fourth wall. The configuration is not what they hoped for but it would work. The three units they wanted were well furnished and would give them more room and better food. The two of them sat down on the couch in unit 17A because Ishtar had told Michael they needed to talk about something very serious. "I told Sargon just before we left that Adad has to go. He is a threat to the rest of us."

"What do you mean, 'go'? Are we going to send him home to Syria?"

"No, what I mean is that he has to die."

"Wait a minute, *die?*"

"Yes, he has to die."

"Why?"

"Michael, he is a threat to all of us. He has a wife and children and those are powerful forces that play on a person's mind the longer they are separated. If the U.S. Government were to locate us I believe they would try and convince Adad to turn us in exchange for his immunity, so he could return to his family."

"I can see what you mean about powerful forces, but isn't there any other way?"

"I have thought about this for some time and I can't come up with any alternative."

"Who will do it, when, and how will we tell the others?" Michael had accepted Ishtar's ultimate solution.

"There is only one person we can trust to do the job and that is me. As to when, I'll want to look around the neighborhood before we go back and find a place to take him that won't be discovered."

"What will you say to the rest of the Brotherhood about his disappearance?"

"We haven't told them the address of the new hideout yet. We must leave quickly and make sure all our rooms are swept clean. When we go out, after I kill him, I'll hit myself in the head so I'll be bleeding and take my time to get back to 101. When I get back, I'll tell the group that he was distraught about his family, picked up a brick and knocked me out. We'll check and see if his money is gone. If it is nowhere to be found, we'll have to assume that he was trying to buy his way out of the United States and we'll have to move right away."

"Do you think the others will be suspicious?"

"They may be, but I have to be as convincing as possible and then we have to move on. Brother, I'll need your support on this. Do I have it?"

Michael considered his answer. *I never signed on for murder. But, sixty thousand people died in the two bomb attacks. I guess I never thought of that as murder. One more to support the Brotherhood is a small price to pay. Will I someday also be disposable?*

"Yes brother, I'm with you."

CHAPTER 123

Unseal the File

It was Sunday at 10:30 AM and Frank was outside Drew Clinton's office waiting to be called in for his meeting. Yesterday, after his call with Omid, he spent a few hours looking at the yearbooks with a great deal of concentration and saw the pattern Bowman had discovered. Late in the afternoon, he headed home to see Ellen and thought that, unless somebody called, they could spend the night together. Frank called ahead and told Ellen that he would be home in about ten minutes.

"We'll drive by the Giant Eagle and see if they're open and what they might have to eat."

Ellen replied, "If you don't find anything, we can make something simple here. See you soon."

Williams knew of a Giant Eagle somewhat out of the way. He asked his driver to take him there and they soon pulled into the parking lot. The lights were on and a few cars were out front. He went into the store. He was expecting the shelves to be vacant but to his surprise, while many had nothing, others were stocked. Frank pulled a cart out of the stack and started shopping. To his surprise, he found pasta sauce, pasta, lots of canned fruit and vegetables, three frozen chickens and box of a dozen frozen beef patties. He loaded his cart with as much as he could, then went over to the produce section and found a few fresh vegetables. He chose the best of the lot and then decided to make one more stop. As he figured, the bread aisle was empty but just around the corner he found plenty of flour and other baking ingredients. Williams didn't see any eggs but he did see butter in

414

solid blocks so he added six to his cart. *I'm done. I have provisioned my home and family for a while.* He approached the checkout and knew that the credit card system wasn't working. He had to pay with cash. *Do I have enough?* He wondered.

He had two hundred dollars in his wallet. He watched all the items being scanned and the bill rising. It stopped at $195.63, *Whew!* He commented to the checkout person, "I was surprised to see that you're open and have food to sell."

"So far, so good. People who have cash can buy until the credit card network is up again. We have to pay cash for the food stuffs we get, so for now, cash is king."

Frank loaded the car and went home. Ellen was ecstatic when she saw all the food.

"How did you get all this food? Did you rob the market?"

"No, I just paid cash. We're going to have to do our best to manage our cash so we can eat." Frank and Ellen had a simple meal and went upstairs, got undressed and went to bed and slept in each other's arms. Ellen thought, *No sex, none needed. It's fine just to hold each other.*

Frank was pulled back to the present when Clinton's assistant called. "Mr. Williams? Mr. Williams! The attorney general will see you now."

"Thank you." Frank went through the door. Drew Clinton stood to welcome him. It was just the two of them in the room.

"Will anybody else be joining us?" Frank asked, as they shook hands.

"No, the president has asked us to open the file and report anything we feel is important to national security directly to him."

"What do you think is the best way to proceed?"

Drew replied, "I think we should open the file, look at the oldest part and work our way forward. Should we both agree, at any time during the review process, that something is significant, we should write it down."

"Before we start, I need to disclose two items to you. First, in a briefing yesterday, one of my senior operatives on the ground told me he is certain that Mike Ridley worked either for the mob or some part of the United States Government. Second, we discovered school yearbooks that show strong photographic evidence of a pattern of Mike Ridley leaving Springfield on a regular basis for years. I'm not sure if this means anything or not but I thought you needed to know."

"Thank you, Mr. Williams. I will keep both pieces of information in mind."

A simple brown envelope was bound in red tape with Top Secret stamped in several places on the tape. The envelope was large and about three inches thick. Clinton slid open his desk drawer and retrieved a pair of scissors. "Let's see if we can figure out why Mike and Mary Ridley are so special."

CHAPTER 124

What Is That I Smell?

Omid stepped outside to return Frank Williams' call. While he was on the phone, a strange smell filled the air and, at the same time, he heard a noise like a small helicopter. He stepped away from the building and saw a crop duster spraying a crop in a nearby field. The smell was strong but seemed to fade as the crop duster flew to the other end of the field. He stepped back into the hangar and noticed a difference in the smells. Those inside smelled better than those outside. Omid looked up at the gable of the hangar and noted a series of exhaust fans that were turned on to blow out jet engine fumes. He was perhaps seventy-five feet from the meeting room and turned to look out the window.

He immediately punched in a phone number, got the leader of the SEAL team, and yelled, "Code Red, with gas!" He stood in front of the window and watched National Guardsmen falling to the ground as the crop dusting helicopter sprayed the troops. In two quick passes, the entire group of soldiers was down. Omid couldn't tell if the men were dead or unconscious. He looked to the right and a Blackhawk exploded past him and was on the smaller helicopter in seconds. Omid could hear the command on the pilot's radio, "Land now or be shot down." Very quickly, both machines were on the ground. The SEALs had on gas masks and with automatic rifles trained on the crop duster the command went out, "Shut it down, *now!*" There were only two men in the crop duster. The pilot shut down the engine and both climbed down to the ground.

Omid saw the second Blackhawk hovering over the roof of the building and slowly turning clockwise to see if other danger was near. He turned back to the Blackhawk on the ground and saw four of the six men on the ground scramble back in as the bird took off to join the aircraft still hovering overhead. Omid couldn't see what was going on but he could hear on his radio, even with the two Blackhawks still hovering. Megan and the rest of the meeting members came out and headed towards Omid. He yelled as loud as he could, "*Get back into the room and take cover!*" Brown herded all the participants back into the meeting room and shut the doors.

Rahimi didn't want to go outside. He had no gas mask and didn't want to chance being out of commission. For a moment or two, he could see the two Blackhawks circling the building, but then something new and surprising appeared. *This is not real; this is not supposed to exist.* What he saw coming was an RAH-66 Comanche Helicopter. This had supposedly been canceled and never built. Yet before his eyes, one came straight for the hangar. The two Blackhawks spotted the RAH-66 and split off to approach it from each side. When the RAH-66 saw both Blackhawks approaching, it made a sharp banking movement and moved away from the hangar in order to live and fight another day. Omid could hear the senior pilot command, "Let's get back. We don't want to be away too long. Who knows what might be coming next."

One Blackhawk landed, picked up two-crew members and two prisoners, and rapidly gained altitude.

"Where are you going?" the Major asked.

"Major Rahimi, we're taking the prisoners back to our base to turn over to Army Intelligence. I'm calling in a medical support team to see what happened to the soldiers on the ground."

"Thanks. See you soon." Omid walked over to the meeting room door and asked for Megan Brown.

"What the hell just happened out there?" Megan had one hand on the door, the other on her hip. Her zipper was almost at the top.

"A crop dusting helicopter sprayed something on the ground troops and knocked them out. Some are coming around but others are still down." He cleared his throat. "Then out of the clear blue sky came something that was never supposed to be there. I have to assume that it was a prototype. It was designed to replace the Blackhawk helicopter gunship."

"Please get to your point, Major. We don't have all day." Megan tapped her foot on the floor.

"The RAH-66 Comanche was to be built by Boeing and Sikorsky. It never was. However, one appeared on the horizon just a few moments ago. The two Blackhawks gave chase and the RAH-66 retreated. I sure would like to know where that baby came from."

"So would I," Megan agreed.

Omid called the drone command center. "Are your eyes open, did you see that RAH-66?"

The command center confirmed that it did see it. "We can follow it but we'd have to break off our coverage of the meeting site."

"How long before a sister drone could arrive?"

"About forty-five minutes," came the response.

"Stay on course. I don't want to take a chance." Only one Blackhawk remained to patrol a wide loop around the base.

Megan pulled the Major into the meeting room and closed the door. "With all the airplanes and their jet fuel in this hangar that RAH-66 would have only had to fire a couple missiles at the center of the hangar to blow us all to smithereens. They didn't need to knock down all the troops. They could have fired their missiles from far enough away that they didn't need to worry about the force on the ground. So, why the show?"

"Perhaps they were trying to distract us while something else was going on. Other than that, I have no clue. Megan, why don't you call Williams? I'll update Baker. I need to find out how that RAH-66 exists. As far as I know, money was not even appropriated to build a prototype."

CHAPTER 125

Who is Mike Ridley?

Drew Clinton and Frank Williams were sitting at Clinton's conference table and had the sealed file for Mike and Mary Ridley in front of them. The president had authorized the opening of the presidentially sealed file for review to discover what connection, if any, Mike Ridley had to the recent nuclear attacks on the United States by the Brotherhood of the Red Nile. Clinton used his scissors to break the seal and ribbon around the large brown envelope. Once the file was out, Clinton checked to make sure the envelope was emptied of all contents and then carefully set it aside. He opened the folder and quickly looked through the pile of documents to find the beginning.

Mike Ridley was born on December 12, 1947 in French Lick, Indiana of Michael and Wilma Ridley. He grew up in French Lick and went to the twelfth grade in Spring Valley High School. Mike was a good athlete and an exceptional student. His father served with distinction in both the Second World War and the Korean War in a Marine Corps construction battalion. When he returned from World War II, he got a job in the county engineering department. He resumed work there after coming back from Korea. Some years later became the chief county engineer. Wilma was a public school teacher until she retired.

Mike was an only child. Because of his grades and strong recommendations from teachers and community leaders, young Mike got a full scholarship to Purdue University to study engineering. He excelled to the point that he was offered another free ride for a master's degree at MIT in the new field of computer science. It was at MIT that he met Mary, who was majoring in foreign relations. She dreamed of being an ambassador one day, as the culture, food and people of the Middle East, whom she hoped to help by putting her education to work on their behalf, captivated her.

Mike entered MIT shortly after JFK was shot and was very upset with the assassination of the charismatic president. He had believed that Kennedy would change the American people, the country and the world for the better. Johnson was sworn in on the plane in Dallas. He pursued Kennedy's policy by continuing to send troops into Southeast Asia. This escalated the Vietnam War, and a group of Americans banded together to protest against America's involvement in the conflict. More and more people started to protest the war and the loss of life. Johnson didn't trust the bureaucratic intelligence community in Washington to find out what he needed to know: what was going on in the minds of the leaders of the anti-war movement.

Johnson called in his Chief of Staff, Marvin Watson, and told him he wanted a new intelligence office. This would be the Logistics Office. Its real purpose was to infiltrate the Anti-war movement, to obtain information for the president about the war protesters' plans so Johnson could anticipate and counter their attacks on him and perhaps the country. Johnson believed the protesters would turn violent and cause riots in many American cities. Watson was assigned to find a few good men for the Logistics Office. Johnson wanted only the best and the brightest America had to offer.

Watson thought, *If the best and the brightest are against us, how shall I find a few good men? However, not everybody on every college campus is against the war, so I'll go to some of the most vocal campuses and see what I can find.* Watson didn't initially have MIT on his list of campuses to visit but reconsidered: *There are some of the best and brightest in the nation,* and headed for the Institute. He asked the FBI's Boston office to find any possible candidates. After about a week, Mike Ridley's name surfaced, and Watson had a Boston agent call on Ridley to gauge his interest in a job with the White House Logistics Office. Ridley, being from the conservative Midwest, tended to side with Johnson on most issues. He didn't see how the protests would help support our men in battle.

Anti-war pressure was getting worse for Johnson when Mike Ridley joined the team and, within a few days of starting his new job, found himself sitting in the Oval Office with the president, Chief of Staff Watson and the four other members of the new Logistics Office.

The president was clear: "We have people in this country today who disagree with the government's policy in Vietnam. We also believe there are anti-war factions who are planning more than just protests. I need you, as a team, to find out what is happening, what they're planning and when. You will report directly to me and you will take your day-to-day orders from Mr. Watson. Is everybody clear?"

Mike spoke up, "Mr. President, you want us to spy on Americans?"

"Young man, what is your name?"

"Ridley, sir. Mike Ridley."

"Well, Mike Ridley, these people are planning more than simple protests. I need to know what they're organizing in order to protect the United States, do you understand? I want *you* to help me protect this great country. So, Mike Ridley, are you working for America or not?"

"America, Mr. President," Mike answered. "First and always."

"Then get out there and get me the information I need."

The Logistics team moved quickly. They went out into the camps and headquarters of the protest movement and were soon providing Watson intelligence on a daily basis.

In the dossier, Clinton saw copies of many of the reports that were filed with Watson. After several years of protest and increasing casualties, the news on the war was so bad that Johnson decided not to run for re-election. Matters slowed down, but eventually the Logistics Office was asked to set up the infamous taping system for Nixon in order to preserve his discussions for posterity, so future scholars could study the great man. Mike saw what was happening with the plumbers and the Watergate break-in, and became disenchanted with his job and what was going on in the country. Nixon finally resigned, Carter defeated Ford, and Mike thought there would be improvements. He believed, or at least hoped, that a breath of fresh air had come to the White House with Carter. He was impressed with Carter's commitment to peace in the Middle East. Mary was also pleased with Carter's initiatives since, over the years, she had developed relationships in these countries with many of the women in leadership roles, such as they were.

Carter sent Mike to meet with the leaders of Israel and Egypt, ostensibly to discuss peace terms, but Mike was really in both countries to explore whether the people themselves wanted this peace. He reported to Carter that the two populations longed for tranquility and an end to the conflict. Mike further informed Carter that in both Israel and Egypt there was growing concern about the weakening support for the Shah of Iran and what might happen to the stability of the region if Shi'a dissidents in Iran overthrew the ruler.

On the plane back to Washington after the historic peace signing, President Carter asked Mike Ridley to make potentially the greatest sacrifice for his country. Carter needed to know what was happening on the ground in Iran and its plans against Israel and the United States. Mike had been doing this job for almost twenty-two years. He and Mary never had children. They couldn't, so his job was very important to him. Yet he did want to have a real life and perhaps someday adopt a child.

After speaking with Mary, he made an appointment with Carter to discuss this mission and what he wanted in exchange for risking his life now more than on any previous assignment in his work for the White House Logistics Office.

"Mr. President, I understand you cannot, by law, order me to go to Iran, and that I have to volunteer. I believe I have served my country well over my career, and yet this is the highest risk mission I have ever been given. If I accept the assignment, I need some guarantees for my wife and myself."

"I understand you'll be risking your life and that you want compensation for your wife, should something happen to you. You'll also want benefits for yourself, of course, if you survive this mission."

Clinton turned to Williams, "This guy was trying to cut a deal with the President of the United States. What guts!" He read on.

"Mr. President, currently I'm a D-1 Level V pay grade, and my current pay is $150,000 per year. If I die in or as a result of this mission, I want my wife to receive a D-2 Level V1 pay of $169,000 a year for as long as she lives, plus a housing and food allowance of $48,000 per year. Both the pension and the allowance are to be adjusted for inflation on a yearly basis. I also wish her to receive fully paid medical benefits, which are also be accorded to me if I survive. She is to be the beneficiary of a fully paid $500,000 life insurance policy on me. I ask one last thing: she - and I, if I survive - is to receive $15,000 per year for travel expenses."

Carter responds, "I think we can do that."

"If I survive, I intend to retire immediately, but shall agree to make myself available for a period of ten years as a consultant to the Logistics Office at the rate of five thousand per day in addition to above benefits."

"Anything else?"

"Mr. President, if I make it back, Mary and I must disappear. Furthermore, if I call and say we think we have been compromised, we will be extracted from wherever we are in twelve to twenty-four hours. Finally, my file has to be sealed so nobody can see it without your express permission. In future years, only the sitting president can open the file, but he or she cannot change the deal. I also need one contact in the Logistics Office for the sole purpose of handling payments or arranging our movement."

President Carter had taken many notes throughout the conversation and said to Ridley, "Mike, I need a couple of days to think this over. I shall not ask you to go until you have an answer."

The records showed that the two had shaken hands before Mike left.

CHAPTER 126

Goodbye to Adad

Ishtar returned to the hotel to pick up Adad and take him, at least Adad thought, to the new hideout.

"Are you packed and ready to go?"

"Yes. Is the new place nicer than this hotel?" Adad asked.

"I'm sure you'll find it very comfortable. Perhaps more to your liking than all the places you've stayed since joining the Brotherhood. It's amazing that Americans would just walk out the door and leave so much behind. I don't know if they think they'll be coming back soon and have no concern that somebody would use or steal their stuff."

"How long will it take us to get to the new place?"

"Well, this is my third trip tonight and it has taken about thirty minutes without having to go around the block to avoid the curfew patrols. If we have to do that, it will add another ten minutes. We have to be prepared to go around the block at least once."

"With the curfew, who would be out and about at night other than the police?"

"I don't know, but Michael and I talked to a Quick Mart guy and he told us to be careful because bandits come out after dark looking to rob people of their cash. I have a gun for protection. Should we come across somebody that looks suspicious I shall not hesitate to kill him."

Adad was startled by the coldness in Ishtar's voice, but as he thought about it, *Better for me to have him on my side.* Adad got his travel bag and the money sack.

Ishtar asked, "Do you want me to carry one of those for you?"

"No, I'm fine. They aren't heavy."

Ishtar walked to the door and opened it slightly to look out across the parking lot to see if anybody was watching. He checked the windows in the neighborhood; almost all were dark. People could be looking out with the lights out, but with the parking lot light out, it would be difficult to identify either of them.

They made a left turn out of the parking lot and headed towards their new location. For the first few blocks, they were quiet. Some streetlights are out. Trash blew up and down the street because the trash containers were overflowing.

Ishtar broke the silence. "What would you do with the oil trading profits?"

"I would save it. When I return to Syria, I suspect that many businesses will be for sale very cheap. I would travel throughout the Middle East and buy as many businesses as I can with the money. I will let the previous owners stay on and run the business. I will travel from business to business and collect the profits for my children to go to better schools. I will build my wife a great mansion with many servants. Life will be good."

Ishtar interrupted, "Adad, our new home is just ahead but, if you look across the street you can see two men looking at the building. These men were not here on my last trip. When we get to the corner, I'll check to see if they're gone. If yes, we shall proceed to the new building, the number is 101. We're on the 17th floor, just in case we get separated. Let's go, but keep the same pace to the corner, talking while walking. As we pass the men, don't look at them and then turn left."

Adad and Ishtar started walking and continued past the building numbered 101, but ignored the lobby. They went to the corner and turned left. When they got to the center of the short block, Ishtar put his hand on Adad's shoulder. "I'm going to sneak back and see if the men are still across the street from our building. You stay here till I come back."

After looking, Ishtar quickly caught back up to Adad and said, "They're still there, so let's continue around the block. They proceeded to the corner and turned left. Around the turn, the street was very dark. There were no lights on in the buildings to shine on the sidewalk and the streetlights were broken. "I think we should take our time and give the men a chance to leave."

Ishtar thought. *The men are gone. I need to find the place I picked out this afternoon and shoot him. The street is much darker now than when I scouted it during the day. I need to find the row house with the steps to a basement apartment. I'm sure it was about half way down the block on this side. The railing is large diameter pipe so I can shoot him and let him fall on the pipe railing.*

"What do you think those men wanted?"

"Cash," Ishtar answered. "With all the banks closed, cash is very important. They mug people to take any cash they have." Now Ishtar can see the spot, about a hundred feet ahead where he planned to eliminate a problem. He reached into his coat pocket and felt the revolver with the silencer. He slowed his pace. Adad didn't notice that Ishtar had put some distance between the two of them. All of a sudden, a cold chill came over Adad. He turned around to see Ishtar standing three feet away. He heard the first shot but not the next two.

Adad's body fell against the railing. Ishtar reached down, grabbed Adad's body by the feet, and pushed it over the railing. It landed on the concrete stoop below with a thud. Ishtar walked down the steps, opened the door to the apartment and dragged Adad's body inside. He tossed the clothing bag and money sack into the vacant apartment and shut the door.

Ishtar walked up the steps, looked in both directions and continued on his walk to the next corner. As he got closer to the entrance of 101, he looked at his appearance in a window and saw no bloodstains. He fixed his clothes and stopped for a moment. What was he going to say to the rest of them? The story he had concocted for Michael and Sargon was that the two men across the street had badly frightened Adad. *I need a believable script.* As he walked towards the new hideout, he elaborated his scenario, *He said to me, 'I have to see my family one more time.' When we turned the corner, it was dark and he just took off running. I tried to stop him, but he was sprinting like a man possessed, I started to go after him but then stopped because I didn't want it to look as if I were trying to rob him. All of a sudden, I heard a scuffle and shots fired. I waited a while and then walked cautiously to where I had heard the noise. I found Adad, but his money sack was gone. He was dead, with three shots to his head. I stashed his body in a basement room, went back the other way and came straight here…That works.* Ishtar let a small smile play on his lips. *And I don't have to hit myself on the head with a brick.*

CHAPTER 127

Let's Talk

The National Guard Infantry men had recovered from the knockout gas attack and for the most part all were back on duty. Nobody was seriously hurt, but they were not interested in repelling another assault. Brown had asked all the visitors to return to the meeting room so they could make progress.

Before going back into the building Omid told Megan that there a radio signal broadcast had been detected from the room and that when the drone made another pass, they would be able to tell if the device was still on.

Megan pondered her next move. *Do I tell the others the drone picked up a signal, or do I wait for the drone to indicate exactly who is transmitting?* She considered and finally decided, *I'll let the drone show us who is not following orders.* Megan called the meeting to order. "I ask you again, please be sure your transmitting devices are off and on the table where I can see them." They were a few grumbles but no argument.

"Thank you. Before the interruption, we were discussing the best approach to acquiring the Brotherhood in its entirety. We don't know if they're still in Texas or, for that matter, if they are even in the United States."

Richard Benchley representing the FBI suggested, "If we can find the location with the use of Lt. Hassen's cell phone, then I suggest we set up a team of about twenty-five men and have them staged near Lt. Hassen's location. She could make the call and we'd launch the team using a transponder to find the signal in Mordecai's cell phone. That would lead us to the Brotherhood. The team would attack the site, using the element of surprise to capture the leadership of the Brotherhood."

Omid responded, "Mr. Benchley, my concern is that we have no idea where they are. What if your transponder indicates they're in Syria? Your team is no good then, is it?"

"No, I guess not, but we do have people all over the world, so we could send a team into Syria."

"Mr. Benchley, how do you suggest we get an FBI team into Syria without all of them being killed?"

Megan listened to the dialogue and wanted to laugh but held it back. *This is so John Wayne.*

John Seacrest, who knew more about the Brotherhood than anybody in the room, or perhaps then the entire government, waited for the discussion to run its course before he spoke.

"We have a good idea that there are at least five members of the Brotherhood and, with the addition of the twins, the count goes to seven. Given that the bombs were hundreds of miles apart at the time of detonation, it is possible that a reduced number of the Brotherhood brought the bombs to America. I personally find it hard to believe that anybody stayed behind. I think they're all in the United States so they could see what happened.

"I think the odds are in favor of them being in Texas. Finding where they are in Texas is more of a challenge, Lt. Hassen and her phone can possibly help us locate at least some of them. However, the Brotherhood is only part of the story. It might seem a great victory if we could capture the five leaders alive and execute them. But then the money man behind them would escape, since we would not be able to trace their funding. We need to get all of them alive and have them lead us to the finances behind the plot.

Brown looked at her watch. It was time for the drone to fly over the hangar. The drone controller at Andrews indicated there was no signal coming from inside the building and gave the all clear. *I wonder if someone just forgot to turn off their device or didn't want to take a chance and get caught.*
"Gentlemen it is almost 6 PM and we have had nothing to eat, I suggest we adjourn, step outside and get some dinner. Feel free to be sociable, but there is to be no discussion of the plan outside of this room. At the far end

of the hangar are bathrooms, showers, and sleeping accommodations. After dinner, we should head to our sleeping quarters and get a good night's sleep. I want to start at 8 AM sharp."

As the participants broke up and headed to dinner, Megan hung back to talk with Hadar. "I noticed you didn't say a word all day. Why?"

"Well, first of all, I'm starving, and when I'm hungry I whine." She gave a small smile. "With this subject matter, I didn't think I could or should whine. Besides, people were talking about me as if I had not been in the room and that freaked me out. Nobody asked me what I would do."

"First, let's get something for you to eat, grab some for a bedtime snack and something to stash away for during the night."

"Sounds great," Hadar said. "By the way, you handled yourself very well today. I'd give you high marks."

"Thank you, but tomorrow is your day and I need you well fed and rested. None of these men, at least for now, have reacted to your ample assets. They are focused on the challenge and we have to be better than them, so let's zipper up."

"Not a chance!" Hadar hooted. "Tomorrow, just watch the power of the female form."

CHAPTER 128

Carter Responds

Williams and Clinton continued to go through Mike Ridley's file, which was over thirty-years-old. Mike Ridley had told President Carter what he wanted for Mary and himself, should he undertake the mission the president had asked of him. Mike had presented a series of conditions the government must agree to in order to provide for his wife. The two investigators remarked that they thought the demands reasonable. However, that Mike Ridley made the demands face to face with the President of the United States made them remarkable. Neither thinks they would be able to make these kinds of demands to President Jordan.

Several days later, they read, Carter had called a meeting with Mike to respond to his requests. Mike was sitting in the anteroom of the Oval Office waiting to be called in and the president was a few moments late. When he walked out of the Oval Office, he extended his hand to Mike, apologized for being late, and invited him in. As Mike walked in he thought, *It started in the office under Lyndon Johnson and now I'm back, trying to protect Mary, and myself, should I survive.*

"Mike, I have spoken with the attorney general about your terms and conditions and he believes that you and I could enter into this agreement. However, he is concerned that you truly understand the risks you are taking, Therefore he suggests I compose a list of duties and responsibilities to which we both shall have to concur before he could support this arrangement. I have, for your review, a list of duties and activities that I can define now. However, I need to make it clear that, depending upon the situation, some or all of those activities could change. You have whatever amount of time you need to make up your mind."

The president handed Ridley the list and Mike scanned it for potential questions. "Mr. President, the only factor missing is the overthrow of the Shah's government. At this moment, I don't know the possibility of it happening but, if it does, what do you want me to do for you and for how long?"

"Mike, there is a remote possibility of this occurring, but we don't know of its probability. What I would suggest is that you go to Iran, set up shop and we shall be in contact on a regular basis. Plan to make adjustments as the situation develops."

"Mr. President, how long will I be assigned to Iran? Will I have anybody with me? Will I have any opportunity to come back and see my wife, or at least meet with her somewhere in Europe?"

"Mike, your term would probably be at least two years. Visits with your wife could be arranged every six months, depending on conditions. You will be sent alone, but you will have contacts to work with in Iran."

"Mr. President, I would like to take your memo home and review it with Mary, so she knows what her rights will be. Then I shall contact your office first thing tomorrow morning with my answer. Is that okay with you, Mr. President?"

"That's fine. I expect your answer in the morning."

"Yes, sir." The two men shook hands and Ridley left with an escort.

Williams turned to Clinton, "Mike Ridley was our man on the ground in the hostage crisis that ended Carter's presidency."

"It sure looks that way."

They went through the copies of Mike's reports. In the beginning, there wasn't a lot to report, except the growing anger with the Shah and his government. One report related of the unrest over the extreme wealth of the Shah and the severe poverty of the common people. Williams shook his head. "Drew, I just can't believe we supported such a despot for so long."

They turned to a report about the taking of the American hostages. Mike had found a rooming house several blocks from the main square of Tehran from where he could safely witness all the chaos.

Later, when Mike heard of the failed rescue attempt, he went back to the square and saw the captured military personnel and the helicopters describing it as 'almost a feeding frenzy.' Mike raised the question, "Who planned this fiasco? It doesn't take a rocket scientist to figure out carrier-based helicopters will not function very long sucking in all that sand." During the hostage situation, Mike's reports were much less frequent. He indicated in one report that he felt he was being watched. He had not seen Mary in a year, as he couldn't leave during the crisis. When the announcement came that Reagan was elected president, and that the hostages are coming home, Mike sent a message to Carter, "Is it my turn?"

Carter didn't respond. With the Inauguration ceremony just two weeks away, he sent Carter another message, "Time to come home?"

Carter responded. "The new president will have to make that call. My guess is that he will want to keep you there for a while until he settles in the office. I will pass on your contact information. Somebody will contact you."

Two years later Mike was ordered home. He had not seen or heard from Mary for three years. When he finally arrived at Andrews, there was no band, no greeters, just Mary. When Mike saw her, he ran to her and they hugged each other for a long, long moment. Arm in arm they walked to Mary's car and drove to their suburban DC home. The report cited the agent assigned to follow Ridley, who believed that within moments of walking in the front door they were in bed and that by morning had made love four times.

The next morning, Mike asked Mary for the contract with President Carter. Mike called the Logistics Office. Almost everybody who had been with him when he left for Iran was gone. The office chief reported that Mike wanted to meet with him as soon as possible.

"What do you want to meet about?"

"My retirement."

THE BROTHERHOOD OF THE RED NILE

CHAPTER 129

Adad is Dead

All but Ishtar and Adad had successfully moved to the new location. Oleg spoke to the brothers, "It seems like a long time since Ishtar left. Shouldn't he and Adad be here by now?"

"Maybe they've been delayed in order to avoid contact with anybody. I'm sure they'll both be here soon," Sargon said, but thought, *I know that Adad is not coming back and I'm sure Ishtar will have a good story about what happened.*

A few moments later, Mordecai heard a knock at the door. Ishtar identified himself and the door was opened. But he was alone. He told the others his story. Shock was evident on all faces, including Michael and Sargon.

"What do we tell his family?" Mordecai continued, "Can we even say anything to his family? How would we reach out to them without exposing the rest of us?"

The expressions on the faces of the members of the Brotherhood showed just how isolated they now felt, and their hopes to survive the attacks were on everybody's mind. Being the youngest, Mordecai thought about his brief but powerful encounter with Hadar and wondered, *Will I ever see her again?*

Sargon spoke up after a while, "We must pray for our fallen brother's soul and for his family. Let us ask that the peace and blessings of Allah be upon him, and protect us until we can get out of this terrible country. I suggest that when we make it to the Caribbean, we find a way to send to Adad's family his share of the trading profits."

All agreed.

Sargon continued, "We must be extremely careful now. Perhaps Adad's death was from muggers after his money but we can't be sure. We should confine our outdoor activities to the daytime and not carry any large sums of money. If we go out and are going any distance, we should take our cell phones and only use them in a dire emergency. We must not go out alone. If we're looking for food in the building, then stay in the building and call for help carrying the food. If we go to another building to search for provisions, we must go in pairs. Understood?"

Everybody responded, "Yes."

THE BROTHERHOOD OF THE RED NILE

CHAPTER 130

Airport Hangar: Hadar is On

The team was ready to meet again. Megan and Hadar had worked out their plan. When Megan had called the meeting to order, she turned it over to Hadar. "Lt. Hassen has some aspects we should consider in our plan to capture the Brotherhood."

Hadar stood up to speak. "I listened intently to the discussion yesterday and there are some facts – or at least what we think should be facts – which we should take into consideration as we plan. We have to establish whether they are even in the United States. If it turns out they are here, then we need to find them and ascertain the number present. As Mr. Seacrest said yesterday, the Brotherhood is only one part of the plot. We need to find out how they have been financed and by whom.

"The greatest risk is jumping too soon, springing a trap, and only capturing a few of the terrorists. So, Mr. FBI, we'll need you, but not just yet. When we're in position you can be the first line of attack." Hadar started playing with her zipper, moving it up and down. Megan could tell her colleague had the attention of the men.

Megan stepped in and inquired, "John, we asked you before takeoff from Andrews to check for a safe house in Houston. Do we have one?"

"Yes, it is a three bedroom and centrally located. It should fill our needs."

Megan also asked John, "If we make contact with the Brotherhood and get a fix on their location, can you move one of your drones into place to watch them?"

"If you want 24/7 surveillance, we'll need three drones. Is that what you want?"

"Affirmative."

"As soon as we get some kind of location I'll release the drones."

Hadar sat down as Megan addressed the group, "We're going to use a four person team initially. If we can't get Mordecai to respond to Hadar's outreach in four months, then we have to determine whether they are not here or if they are simply not responding. The team will consist of Hadar, John Seacrest, Major Rahimi and myself. I'd like to move into that safe house this afternoon. This may well be a waste of time and a boring assignment, so if any of you have work you can take care of remotely, then set it up. Once we get to the safe house we can discuss more in detail. Any questions?"

Omid asked, "Will DC be involved?"

Megan responded, "For now, I'm the point person, but Ted Baker has already informed us that, depending upon his schedule, he may come out. Meanwhile, I'll report to DC as soon as there is a need to communicate. For now, we're treating this as a stakeout, even though we don't know who or where our subjects are. Any other questions?"

"Who will contact us when you need ground support?"

"For now, it will be either myself or Ted Baker." Megan looked around. "If that's it, then let's dismiss the National Guard troops, the Blackhawks and the drones and get our planes out of this hangar."

Two hours later, the 4-member team was in the safe house in central Houston and sitting together in the living room. Megan started the discussion. "Hadar and I have worked out the text message to be sent to Mordecai's cell phone: 'Are you safe? H?' The message is simple and to the point. If he answers, we need to be ready to respond. "So, what should Hadar say if the phone rings and Mordecai is on the other end?"

Omid responded, "She can't ask where he is. She should focus only on his safety. Mordecai may ask if she's okay and where she is at the moment. In our discussions, Hadar told us that she told Mordecai that she was going to Texas, but that he suggested she go to Mexico, so she arranged to go to San Juan Pueblo, New Mexico, where there is an active adobe building school. She can tell him it's been very helpful. As they talk, Hadar can gauge how he's reacting: is his voice shaky because he is nervous about calling her or is he upbeat at the chance to see her again and finish what was started in Syria."

John jumped in, "Let him talk as long as he wants. If you do anything that makes him think you're trying to keep him on the line so the call can be traced, he may hang up. By the way, Hadar I need your phone number."

"Calling me for a date?"

"No, I want to get it programmed with a San Juan Pueblo area code."

Megan responds, "Great idea!"

Hadar asked, "When and how often should I reach out to him with the text message?"

Megan suggested, "Try once a week for the first month. If there's no response, then every other week in the second month. If there is no answer then try every three weeks and in the last month once on the last day of the month. I think any more frequently and we could be over playing our hand. If he wants to hook up with Hadar, he will call if he can. His first response will probably be a text and then, if he believes it's you, he will call. So, what is the key to getting him to call?"

Hadar immediately thought of the last contact, the sexual spark they both felt, and how exciting the sex might be between both of them.

"In a word, sex. The last time we were together we kissed and it was electric for both of us. Mordecai told me, 'If the kiss was so exciting imagine the sex.'

"I understand the sexual tension, but we're trying to find a way in a text message to confirm that you are the real Hadar."

"I can ask him if he has had any repercussions from being hit with the barn door. Only he and I would know about that encounter."

"Excellent!" Megan said, "If this is something only the two of you would know about, he will feel secure."

Omid asked John how long it would take to change the phone.

"I'll make the call today and we could send the first text mid-morning tomorrow."

Hadar whined, "I'm hungry. Do we have anything to eat?"

CHAPTER 131

Clinton's Conference Room

Frank Williams and Drew Clinton had been going over Mike Ridley's file for over three hours and are getting close to the end. Mike meets with the head of the Logistics Office and the two of them review the contract that President Carter signed with Ridley.

"Mike, everything looks in order. You have served your country well and you have offered to continue to serve on a limited basis. Have you thought about where you want to go to retire?"

"Sir, when I was in Iran, I met a man in the oil business who told me he owned a home in a place called Springfield, Texas. He needed somebody to look after it for him and asked if I would like to occupy it until he made up his mind about moving there."

"What's his name?"

"Viktor Antipova. I think he was Russian and was developing oil interests. He told me one day he would be the richest man in Mother Russia."

"And is he?"

"I don't know. All I know is that when I was in a difficult situation in Iran he befriended me and probably saved my life. Therefore, I felt I owed him if I made it out alive. He told me how to reach him and I intend to call him today and see if the offer still stands."

"Once you get settled in Springfield or wherever, let me know and we'll set up the money transfer directly to your bank account."

"Mike, one last thing. We have a commitment to protect you and your wife and family, should you have one. So, when you are established we'll

440

develop an extraction plan to get you out of your home if the need arises. Is there anything else you need answered at the moment?"

"I have a commitment to give you so many days a month of service. But, could I have a few months off before I get back in the saddle?"

"Not a problem. I'll reach out to you in about six months. How does that sound?"

"Great! Mary and I will have some time to get to know each other again and work real hard on trying to make that baby."

The last entry was the extraction of Mike and Mary by the two mobile ERs from Texas City, Texas. The reason for the extraction was that a group of people from Iran that Mike had contact with while he was there had become a terrorist group. They had come to Springfield looking for his help in finding somebody to rebuild the Soviet Union dirty bomb they had acquired on the black market. Mike told them he didn't know anybody, but that he had heard that one of the problems was the bombs leaked and they needed to be stabilized out of the case. Mike got them all the ice he had and a tub and they took the bomb out of the case and put it in the tub of ice and left.

Mike called Logistics and told them of the visit. They said, "We'll send a team to get you and Mary out of Springfield. What about your last project on possible terrorist targets?"

"The map is in the basement. I've set up explosives to destroy the map and all the DNA of Mary and me in the house, so keep your people at bay until tomorrow."

Williams turned to Clinton, "This clears up a great deal for me. I think we can reseal the file and tell the president we feel confident that Mike and Mary Ridley were not involved with the group that bombed America."

CHAPTER 132

The First Text

Seacrest had Hadar's phone ID changed to San Juan Pueblo, New Mexico. He gave Hadar his cell number and told her to call him. Her number showed up with the new area code. "Okay. We know the phone is set up correctly. Are you ready to send the first text message?"

Hadar pulled up Mordecai's cell number and typed in the agreed upon text message: "Are you safe? H." She reviewed the message on the screen and pushed the 'send' button. She got the swoosh message indicating that her text was sent. If Mordecai didn't respond, it would be a week until she could send another text.

After his meeting with the attorney general to review the Ridley file, Williams returned to his office and called for Baker to join him and discuss what to tell the president. When he arrived, Williams asked him to join him in his conference room. Frank took the better part of an hour explaining what he found in Mike and Mary's file, concluding, "They're clean. A great many unanswered questions are now resolved. I think the Logistics Office was defending Mike Ridley as per his agreement with President Carter."

"Do you want me to set up a meeting with the head of Logistics or should we just leave it alone?"

"I think it no longer serves any useful purpose to have a discussion with Logistics concerning Mike and Mary Ridley. We could send a confidential memo to the head and indicate that Mike and Mary are no longer suspects."

It is now one week later and Mordecai has not responded to Hadar's initial text, nor has it bounced back. It's time for Hadar to send Mordecai the same text again. "Are you safe? H."

CHAPTER 133

William Wild for President

The Majority Leader of the Senate was in the Speaker's office talking about a run for the nomination for president and the challenges he would face. The campaign for both the nomination and for the presidency would be much different. With curfews and reduced energy resources, Wild believed that the campaign would have to be waged on radio, TV and through social media. He believed the president realized this and one of the reasons for the Fireside Chat was to get a leg up on his challenger.

The Speaker suggested that Wild petition the Federal Election Commission for an early determination on the rules for the campaign. The longer they waited to issue their rules, the more difficult it would be for Wild to compete, or at least that was what he would say to the Commission. Wild would ask that he and other candidates be given airtime equal to that of the president, starting immediately or that the president would have to cease and desist. Wild knew that even if the Commission were to want stop or restrict the president, the courts would bar this in a heartbeat, because the president always had the right to communicate directly with the American people. In times like these, it was very important that the president have free and open access to them.

Wild knows that the president could talk the talk but he seriously doubted the president had the ability to walk the talk. He believed that the building projects were so massive they were doomed to fail and it was his job to support the idea but also to criticize the execution. Wild thanked the Speaker for his advice and headed back to his office to call his team together to file the request.

It is one week later and still no response from Mordecai.
Hadar sends the third text, "Are you safe? H."

CHAPTER 134

The Brotherhood in Shock

Nobody had budged since Ishtar told the story of Adad's murder. Sargon finally spoke, "We must pray for his soul and for the lives of his wife and children. We should find a way to send the trading profits in the oil futures to his family. The question for now is whether we retrieve the body of our friend and brother, or do we leave it alone?"

Oleg asked, "If we go get it, where would we take it? Without a car, how do we get his body from where it is to someplace else without attracting attention to ourselves?"

Cyrus asked, "Ishtar, is it possible to set the building on fire to burn his body?"

Ishtar responded, "I only saw it at night, but I think all the buildings are what they call brownstone, so they will not burn. If we start a fire, we have to have enough combustibles to get the fire hot enough to consume his body. If the fire doesn't consume his body, then it is possible that he could be identified and in turn tied to us."

"But if we don't do something to the body won't the stench attract attention?"

"The door seemed to shut tight and from what I could see in the dark, none of the windows were broken. The rest of the building appeared abandoned. With so much garbage around, it could be weeks before anyone notices a smell."

Mordecai asked, "Should we tell his wife?"

Sargon, who had been quiet throughout the entire discussion, spoke up. "My friends, it is truly unfortunate that our brother Adad is gone. When the time is right, I shall reach out to his family and tell them of their loss. For now, we need to spend some time planning our next move, which I believe should be out of the country. I want Ishtar to take the lead. Some of us may well have to reach out to our contacts, but we must do so on our secure phones. Michael has suggested that, with his American citizenship, he might be able to get work on the pipeline project. This could provide important intelligence. As much as I shall miss my longtime friend Adad, he and all of us should have understood the risks we were taking in this jihad. We all may perish, but that may well be the price we have to pay to avenge our people, our culture, and our country."

Hadar sends the fourth text: "Are you safe? H."

CHAPTER 135

Williams' Solutions

After his meeting with Baker, Williams called the attorney general to bring him up to date concerning the next steps to take with the Logistics Office. Then he closed his office and looked forward to going home to see Ellen. On his way home, he thought about some of the parts of the puzzle that were not clear in his mind. He now believed that Mike and Mary were in fact on the stretchers that were placed in the vans and they were very much alive. The vans were part of the extraction method designed for the two of them and had been on standby to be activated by a call from Mike to the Logistics Office.

Yet, some unanswered questions still lingered in Frank's mind: *What was the relevance of the map, who built the bomb and why did Homeland miss it? I remember Sheriff Whittles asking about bodies being removed; he was told by Homeland that they were terrorists. They were in fact Mike and Mary Ridley. The map was Mike's last assignment. He had been asked to find cities in the United States that could be targets for a terrorist attack. Mike Ridley set the bomb not just to destroy his current project but also to destroy any evidence of Mary or him ever being in the house. The wires on the doors and windows were fake. The bomb was on a timer and set to go off during the night after Homeland Security had left the scene, when nobody should have been hurt. Mike Ridley built the bomb. The role of the Logistics Office was to protect and defend Mike and Mary. They needed to slow things down; not intentionally hurt anyone. By slowing the process down they gave Mike and Mary enough time to get away! I'm going home and hugging my wife.*

CHAPTER 136

Safe House

Three weeks had passed in the safe house, and there was little to occupy their time. Megan checked in with her lab every day but her staff was doing a great job of not missing her. On the other hand, Hadar had nothing to do between texts. She used the exercise room every day, but after three weeks she was already dreading the next text message because there had been no response. Megan comes in the room "it's time."

Hadar took out her phone, turned it on, accessed the text message application, and sent: "Are you safe? H." She looked at the phone and nothing happened. She set it down. A beep would signal a response to her text message. After she finished, Megan told her, "Ted Baker will be here tonight and will be spending the weekend."

Hadar's mood changed dramatically if for no other reason than she would have somebody to play with. She really enjoyed the banter and the danger when she was with him. She was also hopeful that he might have some new information on the Brotherhood and their possible location.

Hadar was beginning to lose hope that she would ever make contact with Mordecai and the Brotherhood. The waiting was very depressing and she knew that next week was the fourth week and that then the time between messages would be extended. She was not sure they would stick to the plan, if she didn't get a response. They might call it all off and send everybody back to their regular assignments.

This part of the assignment, the waiting, was very boring to Hadar, but she had fallen in love with America. In a very short time, she had come to see the natural beauty of this vast country, much different from Israel. During the down time, she had given thought to a conversation she wanted to have with Baker on his first visit, and now that he was coming, she wanted to talk to him about her idea.

CHAPTER 137

War Room

The president was meeting with his cabinet members and getting a status report on the country's situation. He was also concerned about the elimination of foreign aid and what impact it would have on relations with other countries. Energy started with progress with the contaminated pipeline.

"Mr. President, we have two hundred teams of surveyors in the field laying out the route for the new pipeline. We've asked the pipeline companies to supply engineering teams to create a materials list so we can crank up the steel mills and foundries. The steel mills are already making pipe under contract to my department. The foundries know what size and type of valves will be needed, so we are moving quickly. The engineering team is roughing out the right of way and the Justice Department is working on securing the right of way for the pipeline with the use of eminent domain. The EPA has waived all the regulations that might stop the construction. We are beginning to roll, Mr. President. I expect that we will start laying pipe in less than thirty days.

"Outstanding!" said the president and the rest of the members gave the Secretary a robust round of applause.

"Mr. Secretary, any report on the natural gas pipeline?"

"In fact, Mr. President, some years ago there was a plan to build a pipeline from Canada to Texas to ship crude from the Oil sands deposits in Alberta. A great deal of work had already been done. We're ordering pipe, fittings and compressors right now. The right of way is all ready, as is the route. As soon as we can start delivering pipe, we can start connecting. We have already hired an initial ten thousand workers to start clearing the right of way and we have started contracting with local quarries to start delivering roadbed for the pipeline. Mr. President, I think we can be laying pipe in two weeks. It's not a lot, but it will build rapidly."

The president requested another round of applause for the Department of Energy.

"Mr. Secretary of the Treasury, how about the banks and getting money into the ATM network?" "Sir, I think we are close to being able to open the banks, initially for a short period of time. We are thinking one afternoon a week. We'll have money in the ATM network but we will have to limit withdrawals to prevent a run. The maximum withdrawal will be five hundred dollars per day from all accounts. We would like to gradually open more hours but if we see a run we'll have to shut down again."

"So, in my next Saturday address I can talk about banks and ATMs being open but with significant limitations. If people abuse the limits, I shall have to close them again."

"Excellent idea, Mr. President."

"What about credit cards?"

"Mr. President, this is where we have the greatest risk. Many cards today are both credit and debit cards. The debit cards are tied to a checking account. We can limit withdrawals from checking accounts to five hundred dollars per day when the bank is open, but the ATM network is so broad that the opportunity for these cards to start a run on the bank is significant."

"Mr. Secretary, what if you could only use the debit cards at your bank's ATMs and what if we put a limit on credit cards of five hundred per week? Could we enforce those two items?"

"Mr. President, I don't know. I'll have to check."

"Now, what about the markets?"

"Sir, I think we can take the same banking hours approach we're suggesting and apply it to market hours. We start from two to four on Wednesdays and then slowly expand and watch for abuse. We would suggest the same for the commodity exchanges and the bond markets, including all government securities."

"Excellent! That's great news," the president smiled. "How about it, Mr. Secretary of Agriculture? Can we feed America?"

"Sir, we have crops that need to be harvested and processed. We intend to hire one million men and women to bring in the crops of wheat, corn, soybeans, sugar cane, fruits and vegetables. Our challenge is getting the people to the crops, and feeding and housing them during the harvest. We have spent a great deal of time with the Army trying to figure out how we can transport people to the crops, feed them and their families and have a safe place to sleep, as well as sanitary facilities available to all. We're close but I don't want to make any promises that we may not be able to keep. Sir, I think we need another week to work it out."

"Call me as soon as you want to meet. Feeding the people is very – no, not very – it is the most important thing we have to do for the people."

CHAPTER 138

Baker is in Town

As promised, Ted Baker came in town to check on his special team. When he arrived at the safe house, Megan Brown met him at the security door. She led him into the living room where the rest of the team was assembled. He immediately saw Hadar. She looked like she needed to hit him in the worst way. He nodded in her direction and asked all of them to sit. "So, how has it been living in the safe house?"

All of them except Megan chorused in unison, "*Dreadful!*" Baker was taken aback and then asked, "Ms. Brown do you feel the same way?"

"I don't think I would have been so harsh. It has not been easy or stimulating, but we have a mission and, no matter how boring, we have to do it. Our mission is to make contact with Mordecai if possible and use that contact to capture the Brotherhood of the Red Nile and their source of funding. I wish it were more exciting and perhaps it may well be soon. In any case, we were sent here to do a job and I, for one, no matter how boring, am here to serve my country."

"Well said, Ms. Brown. From time to time all of us have had to handle an assignment such as this, and I have no doubt you will all come through. Now, is anybody hungry?"

Hadar grinned. "I'm starving! I thought you'd never ask."

"So where do you eat around here?"

Omid responded, "Most of the time we eat in. I'm a pretty good cook." They all agreed, but Omid continued, "Sometimes it's nice to eat out. The problem, as you know, is that restaurants only take cash, and we don't have a lot of that coming into the house to be spent on dining, so I'm happy to cook something for us."

Baker responded, "Omid, thank you, but we are going out and the meal is on me. Mr. Williams has friends at the Treasury Department. I have five thousand in cash for you."

Everybody including Megan shouted "*Thank you, thank you!*"

"Where should we go to dinner and do we need a reservation?"

Seacrest responded, "I think Morton's for steaks, and I'll make a reservation."

Ted invited Hadar out on the safe house's balcony and closed the door. "I've missed you."

Hadar smiled up at him. "I have missed you also."

Baker leaned over and turned his shoulder towards Hadar, "Go ahead, hit me." For what?"

He took her into his arms, "If you were a U.S. Government employee I could lose my job for this…" and kissed her. He was surprised that she kissed him back. When their lips separated she whispered, "We need to talk" and slowly separated from him.

"Ted, I don't want you to lose your job, but I've been thinking a lot. As you know, all of us have had a great deal of free time for the last three weeks. I want to come to America and work in Special Ops. Before our relationship can go any further, I want to find out if I can immigrate and work for the U.S. Government."

"Well, I didn't see that coming!" Ted looked at her in frank surprise. "Smash a car into a girl, take her on a car chase, try to blow her up, and then lock her in a room with nothing to do for weeks on end and she still wants to live here. Go figure." He grinned. "I'll speak with Williams in the morning to see what can be done. Maybe I can get a two fur?"

"What is a two fur, and should I hit you now?"

"No, but you can hit me anyway. Megan wanted this assignment because she wants to get into Special Ops at CIA and I'm supporting her for the position. If I support you it's a two fur."

"And speaking of two …" *wham* … Hadar hits his shoulder hard.

"What was that for?" Ted rubbed the spot where her fist landed. "I was going to suggest that the two of us go in and join the others for dinner. I have missed seeing them."

The door opened and the two of them looked at the rest of the team. Ted asked, "Ready to go?"

"Yes! We're all hungry!"

Morton's is a short walk and when they enter, the place is about a third full. Ted remarked, "It's like this in DC. You can get in anywhere with cash. I just don't know how long these places can stay in business with such a low turnout."

As they were shown to their table, Ted noted that they were the largest group in the restaurant. The waiter came over, "We don't have a menu. I will tell you what we have. They listened to the specials and gave their orders. The waiter asked if they want some wine now or with dinner and Ted asked, "What do you prefer?"

They all agreed on wine with the meal. Omid was given the list and selected a couple of bottles.

Ted filled them in on the background of Mike Ridley. Ted thanked Omid for his insight that led to the review of Ridley's file. Then he told them the news the president would give in his talk the next day. They were all excited at the positive things the president would say.

Megan said, "Our country needs a lift and this news will be a big help."

All responded, "Hear, hear!"

The steaks and veggies arrived, and in usual Morton's style, the portions were overflowing. Things were quiet while they all savored their food, and then the chatter resumed.

"What a great meal! I actually feel full for a change." Hadar pushed back from the table. "No offense, Omid."

Everybody agreed with Hadar, who thanked Ted for the wonderful treat.

The evening was comfortable and the sidewalks were bustling with people coming and going. Hadar said, "Looking this street and the activity, you couldn't tell what happened."

Omid remarked, "The hurrying you see is people trying to get home before curfew and we should also hurry." They pick up their pace and arrive at the safe house in plenty of time.

Omid said, "I have a bottle of wine if anybody is interested in a nightcap."

Hadar said, "I'm in. I'm just going to hang up my coat."

CHAPTER 139

Help!

Hadar walked down the hallway to her room, opened the door to turn on the light and spotted her cell phone on the bedside table where she left it before going to dinner. She stopped at the doorway and stared intently at the phone, for she saw something she had never seen so far: a small, slowly flickering light on the side of the phone. She walked over and was about to pick it up when she called for Ted.

"Ted, please come here quickly," she said with unaccustomed concern in her voice. They all came running down the hallway. Megan was the first to arrive. One look at Hadar's face told that she was afraid.

Megan walked over and sat next to Hadar. "You have to open the phone."

Hadar picked up the phone and flipped it open. Displayed on the screen was one new message.

"Go ahead, click on the message."

The screen goes black and then it illuminates three words: No. Help! M

PREVIEW OF BOOK THREE

The Brotherhood of the Red Nile, America Responds, due out in 2014

CHAPTER ONE

What should we do?

The Houston Pathfinder team had just returned from a great dinner at Morton's. For most of their stay, they had been eating in to avoid call attention to themselves. The food had been alright, and Omid is a good cook. However, going out to eat was a real treat, especially since the boss was paying. They walked to the restaurant, just a few blocks from the safe house. When they entered they noticed the restaurant is less than half full. All the tables are setup but the restaurant seems uninviting and cold. When you think of Morton's you see crowded tables, a busy wait staff and a lot of noise. They sat down at their table and the waiter came over, "We do not have a printed menu because of the various shortages; we are doing the best we can with what we can get. I want to make sure you were informed that we are cash only?" Baker responded, "Yes, we were. Please tell us what you can offer." The waiter went through the short list and they all decided to have steak in one form or another. The waiter gave Ted the wine list and he ordered a few bottles of wine. As the courses came they enjoyed the food and each other's company. They finished the meal and all agree it's one of the best in a long time, with no offense to Omid. He replied, "None taken."

They all got up bloated with all the food they have eaten and start slowly walking back to the safe house. Baker motioned to Megan to hang back a little, "When we get back I have $10,000 in cash for food and other supplies let me know when you need more." They took the elevator to the 11th floor. Hadar walked down the long hallway from the front door and the hall lights are out. She felt on the wall and turned on the hallway lights and she continued down the hallway to her room.

Hadar went into her room to hang up her jacket in the closet just across from her bed. Just before she turned on the light her eye is drawn over to her bedside table. She stopped and stared intently at the bedside table; this is the table she left her cell phone on when they went to dinner. As she focused all of her attention beams of light were shooting across the room. For the very first time since she came to America she saw a very dim light on the side of her phone and it is slowly blinking. Someone had either sent Hadar an e-mail or a text message; in the single moment she couldn't figure out who it was. Then like a bolt of lightning striking her brain she thought, *It could have come from Mordecai. What should I do?*

Hadar realized that had she turned on the light she may not have seen the LED light on the phone for hours. She called out in a frightened voice, to Ted Baker the head of the team, "Please come to my room." The whole team heard her cry and they knew something was wrong. They all rushed down the narrow hallway avoiding bumping into each other as they approached Hadar's room to see what the commotion was all about. They crowded into her room and saw her sitting on the edge of her bed holding her cell phone in her lap. No lights have been turned on. As their eyes adjusted to the low level of light, they all saw the flashing light on the phone. Baker told her, "Open it, let's see whom it's from."

Hadar slowly flipped opened the phone and on the screen is a text message. She clicked on the message, **"No, help me M."** They all knew it was a possible response to the many texts that Hadar had been sending, but they had no way of knowing if the person responding to her message was truly Mordecai or just another one of the Brotherhood using Mordecai's phone to learn who had been texting Mordecai.

Baker stepped out of the room and called Williams to tell him about the possible contact from Mordecai. Baker reached Marie at Williams' office and asked for Williams. Marie put the call through and Baker told him they had a response to Hadar's text messages. Williams responded, "Keep me in the loop." Baker suggested that they need to figure out something for Hadar to communicate to Mordecai that only the two of them would know. This would be a way of verifying that the other person is in fact Mordecai.

THE BROTHERHOOD OF THE RED NILE

Williams agreed, "Let me know whatever resources you need."

"Sir, I was thinking about that and it seems to me we have a great untapped resource that we could be using."

"Who is that?"

Baker responded, "The Logistics Office."

"Great Idea, should I call them now and alert them?"

"Sir, let's try and find out if it truly is Mordecai on the other end before we marshal our resources."

"Good point I agree, this could be the break we have been waiting for."

"Yes sir, let's hope it pans out, I'll keep you posted."

Baker went back into the room and suggested that they all move to the living room and talk about their alternatives for a response to Mordecai phone text message regardless if it is Mordecai or not. "We don't know for sure if that is Mordecai answering the text message so we need a way to verify that it is he. Hadar, I need you to think of something that you could text back that you can use to verify it is Mordecai and not one of the other Brotherhood members trying to impersonate Mordecai. It has to be something that only the two of you would most likely know."

Hadar thought about the encounters she had with Mordecai and things that transpired between them that only they would know and yet not tip off the brotherhood. Her mind is racing with ideas, *The barn door, or possibly the times he left before they were done eating, the suggestion of where to go to study adobe building in America, or perhaps the last kiss when he said, 'Can you imagine how great the sex might be,' and she had said she was thinking the same thing.* Megan interjected, "Whatever the question it has to been seen as non-threating. Hadar, think of something that can be a one word answer and something only he would remember." "Do you remember the name of dessert we had in the café, I can't remember what it was called?"

John said, "Wait a minute, Hadar you sent a simple message 'Are you safe? H' Somebody responds, 'No, help me. M' and you want to talk about dessert? Why not simply ask, 'How? H'. Does it really matter whether it is Mordecai or not? Somebody is asking for help; let's follow the lead and see where it takes us."

Omid responded, "We don't know if this is Mordecai or not but we are not going to let you get in harm's way; this could be a trap to get a hostage to try and get out of the country regardless of what it might be. Let's respond to the text message simply and then let's see what happens."

They all agreed. Hadar took a deep breath and pushed the keys, **"How? H"** Then she closed her eyes and hit the send button.

Also available from Dan Perkins on line at Amazon, Barnes & Noble, and Smashwords.com The Brotherhood of the Red Nile, A Terrorist Perspective

TESTIMONIALS

Other books by Dan Perkins
Book one of the Brotherhood Trilogy
The Brotherhood of the Red Nile. A Terrorists Perspective

"I couldn't put the book down! Dan Perkins had me glued to the book with such intense and brilliant descriptions, and it felt so real. He truly captivated my attention and I can't wait for the next book."

"It is a heart pounding, page turning book! It has been a long time since I read such an intriguing, hard-to-put-down book, such as The Brotherhood of the Red Nile. Dan Perkins used such descriptive language that I feel as if I know each character personally. What an intense read that had me on the edge of my seat and wishing there was more to read...I highly recommend this book and eagerly anticipate his next book!"

"What an amazing book from beginning to end. It kind of makes you think what is really going on in the world of terrorist. You can tell Dan Perkins put a lot of time researching the data in the book. This would be a good movie!!!!! Double thumbs up!!!!!"

"I thought the brotherhood was well written & really enjoyed it. Keeps you right in the thick of things right to the end. I read it right between a Lee Childs and a John Sanford and it fit right in!! Dan has a wonderful imagination."

"Dan Perkins has written a novel that will capture your imagination while scaring the wits out of you. It is not a body count story and that is what is so frightening. You are forced to ponder this question: could it happen or more to the point- when will it happen? A very good read."

Go to Dan's web site and see more reviews www.danperkinsatsanibel.com

CPSIA information can be obtained at www.ICGtesting.com
Printed in the USA
LVOW11s1045280914

406234LV00004B/700/P